HANDBOOK OF WAR STUDIES

HANDBOOK OF WAR STUDIES

Edited by
Manus I. Midlarsky

Ann Arbor

THE UNIVERSITY OF MICHIGAN PRESS

First published by the University of Michigan Press 1993
Originally published in cloth by Unwin Hyman, Inc.
Copyright © 1989 by Manus I. Midlarsky
All rights reserved
Published in the United States of America by
The University of Michigan Press
Manufactured in the United States of America

1996   1995   1994   1993   4   3   2   1

Handbook of war studies / edited by Manus I. Midlarsky.
    p.   cm.
    Originally published: Boston: Unwin Hyman, 1989.
    Includes bibliographical references and index.
    ISBN 0-472-08224-8 (pbk. : alk. paper)
    1. War.   2. International relations.   3. World politics.
I. Midlarsky, Manus I.
[U21.2.H35   1993]
355.022—dc20   92–46397
                                                        CIP

A CIP catalogue record for this book is available from the British Library.

Contents

Contributors

Dagobert L. Brito is Peterkin Professor of Political Economy at Rice University. His major research interests include mathematical economic theory and strategy and arms control. Recent publications include "Conflict, War, and Redistribution," (with Michael D. Intriligator), *American Political Science Review*, December 1985; "Stock Extremalities, Pigovian Taxation, and Dynamic Stability," (with Michael D. Intriligator), *Journal of Public Economics*, 1987; and "The Potential Contribution of Psychology to Nuclear War Issues," (with Michael D. Intriligator), *American Psychologist*, April 1988. He is co-editor with Michael D. Intriligator and Adele E. Wick of *Strategies for Managing Nuclear Proliferation* (1983).

Bruce Bueno de Mesquita, Senior Fellow at the Hoover Institution, Stanford University, is the author of *The War Trap, Forecasting Political Events: Hong Kong's Future* (with David Newman and Alvin Rabushka), *Strategy, Risk and Personality in Coalition Politics*, and *India's Political System* (with Richard Park). He has also written articles for several political science journals, including the *American Political Science Review, World Politics*, and others. Bueno de Mesquita, a former Guggenheim Fellow, has been the recipient of the Dag Hammarskjold Memorial Award and the Karl Deutsch Award. Together with David Lalman, he is working on a book applying sequential game theory concepts to the study of international crises.

Nazli Choucri is Professor of Political Science and Associate Director of the Technology and Development Program at the Massachusetts Institute of Technology. She is author of several books, including *Population Dynamics and International Violence* (1974); *Nations in Conflict* (with Robert C. North) (1975); *The International Politics of Energy Interdependence* (1976); *Forecasting in International Relations* (co-edited) (1978); *International Energy Futures* (1981); *Energy and Development in Latin America* (1982); and *Multidisciplinary Perspectives on Population and Conflict* (1984). Her major research interest continues to be international conflict and violence. She is currently heading the AAAS study on the new transnationalism and global security.

Paul F. Diehl received his Ph.D. in Political Science from the University of Michigan in 1983 and is currently Director of Graduate Studies and Associate Professor of Political Science, University of Illinois. He is co-editor of *Through the Straits of Armageddon: Arms Control Issues and Prospects*. His work on arms races, defense burdens and territorial conflict has been published in the *Journal of Conflict Resolution*, *Journal of Peace Research*, *Journal of Politics*, and other journals.

Charles F. Doran is Director of Canadian Studies, Johns Hopkins University, SAIS, Washington, D.C. Educated at Harvard and Johns Hopkins, he taught at Rice University until 1979, establishing its international management program, and was Claude Bissell Professor at the University of Toronto in 1985–86. In addition to power cycle theory and its policy implications, his research encompasses security policy and commercial, environmental, and energy resource issues in international politics. His analyses of these issues in the Canadian-American context are widely sought by government and academia.

Thomas W. Graham has an A.B. in International Relations from Stanford University and a Ph.D. in Political Science from the Massachusetts Institute of Technology. He is the Executive Officer of the Aspen Institute's Strategy and Arms Control Group, a Pre-Doctoral Fellow at the Center for Science and International Affairs, the Kennedy School of Government, Harvard University, and was a Foreign Affairs Officer at the U.S. Arms Control and Disarmament Agency. He has published several articles on American public opinion on national security issues in *Public Opinion Quarterly* and the *Journal of Conflict Resolution* in addition to *American Public Opinion on NATO, Extended Deterrence, and Use of Nuclear Weapons: Future Fission?*

Michael D. Intriligator is Professor of Economics, Professor of Political Science, Director for the Center for International and Strategic Affairs, and Director of the Jacob Marschak Interdisciplinary Colloquium on Mathematics in the Behavioral Sciences at UCLA. His major research interests include mathematical economic theory, econometrics, and strategy and arms control. His books include *Mathematical Optimization and Economic Theory* (1971); *Econometric Models, Techniques, and Applications* (1978); and *Strategy in a Missile War* (1967). He is also co-editor of *Handbook of Mathematical Economics* (1981, 1982, and 1985); *Handbook of Econometrics* (1982, 1983, 1986); *National Security and International Stability* (1983); *Strategies for Managing Nuclear Proliferation* (1983); and *East-West Conflict: Elite Perceptions and Political Options* (1988).

Jacek Kugler is Associate Professor of Political Science, Claremont Graduate School. He is the co-author of *The War Ledger* and *Birth, Death and Taxes*, has co-edited *Exploring the Stability of Deterrence*, and is the author of numerous articles on national security and political development.

Jack S. Levy is Professor of Political Science, Rutgers University. He is the author of *War in the Modern Great Power System, 1495–1975* (1983), and has contributed articles to numerous scholarly journals. Levy's research focuses on the question of the causes of war from several different theoretical and methodological perspectives. His recent articles analyze the preventive motivation for war, domestic politics and war, the conditions for successful deterrence, and related topics. He is currently working on a book-length manuscript on the causes of war.

Manus I. Midlarsky is Moses and Annuta Back Professor of International Peace and Conflict Resolution at Rutgers University. He is the founding Past-President of the Conflict Section of the American Political Sciences Association and a Past-Vice President of the International Studies Association. He is the author of *On War: Political Violence in the International System* (1975); *The Disintegration of Political Systems: War and Revolution in Comparative Perspective* (1986); and *The Onset of World War* (1988). Midlarsky is also the editor of *Inequality and Contemporary Revolutions* (1986) and *The Internationalization of "Communal Strife"* (1992).

George Modelski is Professor of Political Science at the University of Washington. In 1987–88 he pursued research at the Netherlands Institute for Advanced Study in the Humanities and Social Sciences. He is the author of *Long Cycles in World Politics* (1987), editor of *Transnational Corporations and World Order* (1979) and *Exploring Long Cycles* (1987), and co-author of *Seapower in Global Politics 1494–1993* (1988).

Benjamin A. Most was Associate Professor of Political Science at the University of Iowa at the time of his death in November 1986. A recognized expert in the study of war and international conflict, methodology and research design, he also published in the area of comparative public policy, focusing on Latin America. His work was represented in numerous articles and chapters appearing in the leading journals of the field. He is co-author of a forthcoming book on the logic of inquiry and theory in international politics (with Harvey Starr).

Robert C. North is Professor of Political Science Emeritus at Stanford University. He is the author of *Moscow and Chinese Communists* (second edition, 1962); *Chinese Communism* (1963); *The World that Could Be* (1976); *The Foreign Relations of China* (third edition, 1976); and *War, Peace, Survival* (1988). North also co-authored the following books: *Kuomintang and Chinese Communist Elites* (1950); *Soviet Russia and the East* (1957); *Content Analysis* (1963); *M. N. Roy's Mission to China* (1963); *Nations in Conflict* (1975); and *International Crisis: The Outbreak of World War II* (1976).

A. F. K. Organski is Professor of Political Science, The Arts & Research Scientist, Center for Political Studies, Institute for Social Research, University of Michigan. He is the author of *World Politics* and *Stages of Political Development*. Organski also co-authored *Birth, Death and Taxes* and *The War Ledger*, and has contributed widely in the fields of world politics, national security, political demography, and political development.

Bruce Russett is Dean Acheson Professor of International Relations and Political Science at Yale University, where he is also coordinator of the International Security and Arms Control Program. He is editor of the *Journal of Conflict Resolution*, and has served as president of the International Studies Association and the Peace Science Society (International). He has published seventeen books and 130 articles on international relations, and has held visiting appointments at many institutions in the United States and abroad.

J. David Singer (Ph.D., New York University) is Professor of Political Science at the University of Michigan, coordinator of its World Politics program, and Director of the Correlates of War Project. He is author of *Deterrence, Arms Control, and Disarmament* (1962 and 1984) and is currently investigating the role of major power decline in the war-to-war cycle.

Randolph M. Siverson is Professor of Political Science at the University of California, Davis. His publications on various aspects of international conflict include articles in the *Journal of Conflict Resolution, International Studies Quarterly, American Journal of Political Science, American Political Science Review,* and *World Politics*. He is the editor of the journal *International Interactions*.

Harvey Starr is Professor and Chair of the Department of Government, University of South Carolina. He has published widely on international conflict, alliance, and foreign policy analysis, with an emphasis on geopolitics and the diffusion of international conflict. Recent books include *Henry Kissinger: Perceptions of International Politics* (1984), *World Politics: The*

Menu for Choice (third edition, 1989, co-authored with Bruce Russett), and a forthcoming volume on the logic of inquiry and theory in international politics (co-authored with Benjamin A. Most).

William R. Thompson is Professor and Director of Graduate Studies, University of Indiana at Bloomington. Among his publications are *Contending Approaches to World System Analysis*, *Rhythms in Politics and Economics* (with Paul Johnson), *Seapower in Global Politics 1494–1993* (with George Modelski), and *On Global War: Historical Structural Approaches to World Politics*. He is currently engaged in projects on the historical linkages between global war and state making and the political economy of relative decline.

Introduction

The previous several decades have witnessed a growth in empirically based theories of international conflict. To those of us actively doing research and writing in this field, as perhaps to all participants in painstaking and difficult endeavors, the pace of progress seemed all too slow and the fruits of this activity appeared too meager. Yet when one does an accounting from some distance, perhaps in the form of a "progress report," a measurable if not important contribution to our understanding of the origins of war has indeed occurred during this time period. This volume may be seen as one such report on the progress of the scholarly community that is concerned with the scientific study of war and peace.

Before introducing the contents of this volume, it is appropriate that I indicate the areas of scholarly activity that are included as well as the reasons for their inclusion. As is apparent from the Table of Contents, all of the chapters, with but one possible exception, are concerned with scientific, empirically based studies of war. The one exception is the chapter by Michael Intriligator and Dagobert Brito on Richardsonian arms race models. The significance of Richardson's model as a seminal contribution to the study of international conflict and the large number of empirical studies of arms races following that initial effort argued strongly for its inclusion.

Any emphasis on one area of scholarly contribution must inevitably entail a deemphasis of others. This unfortunate delimitation of scope meant that important areas of theoretical and scientific inquiry into the origins of war would be excluded. These include, among others, excellent game theoretical treatments of international conflict such as those of Schelling (1960), Snyder and Diesing (1977), Brams (1985), and Zagare (1987) as well as treatments of deterrence such as those of George and Smoke (1974), Morgan (1977), Mearsheimer (1983), Jervis (1984), and Hardin *et al.* (1985). Excellent treatments that emphasize either the diplomacy of the contemporary period (Craig and George 1983) or strategic doctrine (Snyder 1984) also are not within the central purview of this analysis.

The organization of this volume follows loosely from a fortuitous convergence by Waltz (1959) and Singer (1961) on the question of an appropriately chosen level of analysis for the study of war. Whether consciously or unconsciously, investigators generally focus on one level or another as a necessary demarcation of research boundaries. I will take no position on the utility of one or another of these levels of analysis because, as we shall see, all have a major contribution to make, but in different ways. The various contributions fall into three principal areas that I call (1) structure-based, (2) minimally dyadic, and (3) state-centered research.

The first of these categories is fairly clear in its emphasis. This is the international system writ large, in which the structural features of international life, such as alliances, polarity, and broad-scale power relationships, dominate the analytic landscape. Another way to view such an approach is as an N-adic form of analysis in which virtually all forms of reductionism are eschewed in favor of an analytic treatment of the whole.

Chapters in this part of the volume present theories concerned with the impact of structure on the system. They proceed from the most general structural considerations in their influences on war to the more specific impacts of individual nation-states on their structural environment. J. David Singer's chapter presents some of the history of this approach along with major contributions of the Correlates of War Project at this level of analysis. While there is no single theory of war associated with this project—it has from the start affirmed its intent to remain faithful to the statistical findings emanating from the systematic analyses—some of the more prominent contributions are reviewed carefully. One of these, the distinction between nineteenth and twentieth century alliance behavior in regard to war proneness, has echoes in later chapters.

A theory of global war that has been rooted in the structure of the system from the beginning is that of the long cycle. George Modelski and William Thompson have long been associated with this theory of the periodicity of global war. This chapter carefully compares their findings with those associated with other, similar theories. An interesting aspect of the theory is its relationship with kindred theories in economics (Kondratieff), politics (Gilpin), history (Toynbee), and sociology (Wallerstein). The long cycle may, perhaps, be said to be one theory that overarches the various individual contributions emanating from within disciplinary compartments.

My own contribution follows from the theory of the hierarchical equilibrium as an especially stabilizing system structure, which is examined in more detail elsewhere. Here I draw out one major implication of the theory and test it using historical materials. The ultimate "rootedness" of structural theories in history is manifest. In order to fully understand the long-run instability of multipolar systems as the derived implication from the initial theory, one must delve deeply into historical sources. The question of the superior stability of bipolar or multipolar systems has, of course, been a major theme in the structural approach to the study of international relations.

A cyclical theory, but one dependent more on the power dynamics of the nation-state, is that of Charles Doran. Although his theory finds its point of departure in the nation-state, Doran develops the theory equally (if not more so) within the structural contours of the international system. He not only shows how such cycles are rooted in the dynamics of national power change, but how cyclical processes affect neighboring states and the system at large. Issues of polarity, cyclical systemic behavior, and international equilibrium are treated in this chapter, as are the all-important misperceptions that follow upon points of inflection of the power cycle.

From another perspective, given these analyses, structural theories can be seen as ways of imposing a theoretical order on an imposing and apparently anarchic welter of historical detail. Certainly, Singer, Modelski and Thompson, Doran, and I impose these particular orderings on a time span that is at least a century long (and, in the periodic mode, much longer than that).

As a final theoretical cut using the structural frame of reference, Benjamin Most, Harvey Starr, and Randolph Siverson examine the diffusion of international conflict. Here, the mere presence of conflict in one of the N structural nodes of the system can lead to conflict in another. This chapter details the conditions under which the diffusion of international war is likely to occur and, by implication of course, the conditions under which it is less likely to happen. This contribution also explores the logic of this investigative mode, using especially the concepts of opportunity and willingness as analytic linchpins.

Note that the dependent variable of concern in these chapters varies from the global or systemic war (of Modelski and Thompson and of my own analysis) to the larger category of wars involving major powers involved in the power cycle (as studied by Doran) to any war occurring in the system as it has been influenced by other wars (as analyzed by Most, Starr, and Siverson). As in the earlier chapters, an increasingly explicit reliance on international structure per se in the generation of theory apparently yields a greater restriction on the domain of the dependent variable.

As it has emerged in the contributions to this volume, the second level of analysis emphasizes relationships between nations that minimally require the dyad as a basic unit. This is not to exclude higher level, N-adic relationships, but means only that, in contrast to the preceding structural analyses of the whole, the investigations in Part II could not proceed without two international units, typically nation-states or international coalitions. It is likely that a large number of studies of international warfare have been pitched at this level, for it is here that we find the intersection between the policies of at least two nation-states that potentially could lead to war. And here we also find time-honored (and criticized) theories of the balance of power between two or more countries or international coalitions as well as the more recent expected-utility theory of Bruce Bueno de Mesquita and the power-transition theory of Jacek Kugler and A. F. K. Organski.

In the first of these, Bueno de Mesquita outlines the basic elements of his expected-utility theory of international conflict and applies it to expectations concerning the balance of power or the power transition as progenitors of peace or war. He delineates the circumstances under which one condition or another is associated with international stability and shows how the theory can help us in various political forecasts, such as the choice of a leader, the fall of a coalition, or the shifts in basic policies of a government at war. The theory, therefore, has shown remarkable flexibility, especially in its ability to forecast events. Bueno de Mesquita also shows how the theory satisfies certain criteria that Lakatos set forth to evaluate the extent of contribution of new theories.

Jacek Kugler and A. F. K. Organski also use Lakatos' criteria as a bench mark against which to measure their theoretical contribution. The theory of the power transition is contrasted with that of the balance of power as an alternate conceptualization of the onset of war. Either one major power overtakes another in societal force capabilities and, thus, a power transition occurs, or the two powers remain in a relative state of balance. An important constituent element of the theory—power preponderance—is demonstrated to be associated with peace, or at least the absence of major power wars, while the balance of power is associated with the onset of this type of war. Kugler and Organski formally extend the theory to show the conditions under which nuclear war likely would be waged. They also extend the theory to include the concept of political capacity as a means of shrinking or expanding the original bases of national power.

Until this point, the analyses have dealt with power issues in one form or another. Yet the most outstanding indicator of long-term conflict between two international actors, or at least preparedness for conflict, is probably the arms race. In this area, the field of international relations is fortunate to have mathematical models of extraordinary sophistication, which are reviewed by Michael Intriligator and Dagobert Brito. But first the utility of arms races as predictors of the onset of war is reviewed by Randolph Siverson and Paul Diehl. As these authors discover, the findings are mixed in this regard. Although some studies find a clear connection between arms races and the onset of war, others do not, and the conclusions at this point certainly are not definitive. Yet enough evidence already exists to suggest continued extended research into the impact of arms races on international war experience.

In their analysis of the arms race, Intriligator and Brito proceed in a somewhat different direction. After reviewing several variants of Richardsonian arms race models, they focus on the implications of one of these for nuclear deterrence. They identify regions of stable deterrence in a dyadic arms race and regions of instability that have serious implications not only for the arms race but for arms control and disarmament as well. Because these regions of stability or instability can be entered into or withdrawn from during the buildup or reduction of arms stocks, respectively, these analyses have an immediate relevancy. Although these models generally focus on the dyadic level and, therefore, are somewhat limited in scope, the existence of an already well-developed mathematical base augurs well for successful modifications and extensions of these models in the future.

Our final category reduces the dyad to a single unit as the minimum number and explores the state itself as a source of international conflict potential. As in the preceding section, the minimum is precisely that, and it allows for the impact of the state on its environment, whether the environment is a neighboring state or the international structure. Thus, the chapters in this section take the state as the starting point for their analyses and develop their theories largely within this domain. Also, as before, the level of generality here proceeds incrementally from the more abstract to the more specific sources of international warfare.

Bruce Russett and Thomas Graham explore the impact of public opinion on international conflict. This has been a contentious and somewhat ill-defined issue from the perspective of international relations theory; Russett and Graham clarify and shed light on this theoretical nexus. Their chapter examines this relationship not only from the vantage point of international warfare but, more generally, from the purview of national security policy. Public opinions in authoritarian settings are contrasted with those in democratic contexts, the effects of economic conditions are explored, and the structures of belief systems are examined in this far-ranging review of a literature that is not frequently brought into the causes-of-war bailiwick but, nevertheless, may have far-reaching implications for issues of war and peace, especially in political democracies.

As Jack Levy indicates, controversy is a property of the internal–external conflict literature. A careful review of the systematic literature reveals gaps that could benefit considerably from the introduction of historical perspectives and theories generated in this manner. The short time frame of most systematic, empirical analyses may have unknowingly omitted the effects of long-term internal processes on international conflict. Levy carefully scrutinizes this and other problem areas and offers suggestions for new studies that might help alleviate some of the problems. We also find a call for the more extensive use of historical materials, as we saw earlier in the studies found in Part I.

In addition to generally staking out a theoretical problem area (as in Russett and Graham and in Levy), the next chapter offers a specific, state-centered theory of the origins of international warfare. Perhaps most specific in its theoretical formulation, but with highly general consequences, is the lateral pressure theory of international conflict formulated by Nazli Choucri and Robert C. North. Building upon their earlier analysis of the impact of lateral pressure on conflict behavior prior to World War I, they now apply it to the case of Japan with equally successful results. In their hands, the theory of lateral pressure is an outstanding example of a theory capable of great specificity in its initial formulation that, however, delineates consequences not only for the neighboring international environment but for the system at large. Somewhat unique is Choucri and North's ability to lend quantitative precision to the individual impacts of all of the theory's separate components.

There are several implications that emerge from these comparisons. First, as must be obvious by now, we have not been considering a general theory of war—we have been considering many different theories that have important areas of convergence but also diverge in essential details. The long cycle and the hierarchical equilibrium, for example, are almost exclusively concerned with structural influences on systemic or world wars; the expected-utility theory deals with the utility calculations of decisionmakers and their impact on all wars. The power transition and power cycle focus on dyadic and state-level changes respectively, and emphasize major power wars as the outcome to be explained. There exists, in other words, a richness of theoretical perspectives with some overlap and certain divergences to be built upon in the future.

It is also apparent that we are dealing not only with several different theories of the origin of war but also with conceptualizations of war that cannot be put into a single generic category. Systemic or world wars have been emphasized by structural systemic explanations, as have major power wars by theories of the power transition or power cycle. Although the treatment of war as a generic category has proven useful until now, future research may require the systematic delineation among several categories, each of which may require a separate theoretical treatment. Put another way, the search for a theory of war may shortly give way to the search for *theories* of *wars* as the scientific study of war proceeds inexorably forward. Later, when appropriate theoretical distinctions have been made, it may once again be appropriate to attempt the theoretical syntheses that could (but do not have to) yield parsimonious explanations.

Finally, the chapters in the volume provide various approaches to the study of international conflict. Many of these are almost exclusively theoretically based in their explications of relationships among several positive theories and their respective empirical buttressings. These include Modelski and Thompson, Bueno de Mesquita, Kugler and Organski, Doran, and Choucri and North. Others, such as Singer, Russett, and Graham as well as Levy, are more problem based in their explorations of a particular theoretical problem area that requires attention. Here, no single positive theory is being offered, but a particular theoretical problem is researched, clarified, and attended to with very careful reasoning in regard both to logic and to evidence. Most, Starr, and Siverson as well as Siverson and Diehl also follow this model. Others, such as Intriligator and Brito and, to some extent, Bueno de Mesquita, Kugler and Organski, and my own contribution, mix the two approaches in drawing upon a particular theoretical formulation to examine an outstanding problem area such as the stability of deterrence, polarity, or power parity and preponderance.

Overall, these studies show that there are many ways to investigate the phenomenon of international warfare, ways that are both analytically rigorous and empirically valid. The nature of scientific evidence also varies from the strictly quantitative to the explicit use of history in almost (but not quite) traditional form. If, in addition to providing an educational and review function, the studies in this volume also lead to additional efforts at either analytic synthesis or theoretical innovation with the appropriate use of empirical testing, then they will have served their purpose admirably.

Manus I. Midlarsky

PART I

Structure-Based Theories of War

CHAPTER 1

System Structure, Decision Processes, and the Incidence of International War

J. David Singer

University of Michigan

A quarter of a century ago, three young scholars—in an unexpectedly symbiotic fashion—converged to identify and, perhaps, clarify what has come to be called the "level of analysis problem." In *Man, the State, and War* (1959), Waltz carefully articulated the empirical premises that are more or less inexorably associated with the several levels of analysis/ aggregation and concluded that most of the variance in the incidence of war and other major events could be accounted for by the characteristics of the international system. While Singer (1960, 1961) concurred with that theoretical judgment, he pursued the question a bit further, suggesting that each level—the individual, the national society, and the international system—had a role to play in shaping the behavior of the nations and the fortunes of their citizens. The third of the new and interdisciplinary breed of scholars central to this discussion was Kaplan (1957), who not only concluded that the international system was "subsystem dominant" in the sense that the more significant aspects of international politics were determined by the properties and behaviors of the nations rather than the properties of the system, but also went on to postulate a set of axiomatic rules that seemed to govern that behavior. Among others, those who participated actively in these exchanges were Rosenau (1969), Haas (1953), Russett (1967), Hoffmann (1965), Liska (1956), Rosecrance (1966), and Deutsch and Singer (1964).

Fortunately for the discipline, this spate of interesting and insightful speculation was gradually followed by a decade or so of empirical–operational investigations, which were characterized by the reasonable assertion that if deductive argument buttressed by selective anecdote could lead to such diverse conclusions, it might be time to look at the historical evidence. Much of this work utilized the data sets that were being generated by Singer and Small and their colleagues in the Correlates of War Project (1966a, b, 1970, and 1973), but the findings were far from convergent, reminding us that results arise out of a research design that is, in turn, a consequence of some complex mix that includes the theoretical model, the spatial and temporal domain, the choice of indicators, the data aggregation procedures, and, of course, the choice of data analysis strategies.

Before attempting to summarize and make sense of those empirical investigations into the role of the international system vis-à-vis the incidence of international war, it might be useful to lay out the theoretical question in more precise terms. Thus, this first section will examine and compare two different but convergent arguments as to why the properties of the system might indeed be critical in accounting for the incidence of war in international politics. The metaphor here might be that the properties of the sea affect the behavior of marine life, and those of the community affect the behavior of its residents, but only to some finite extent. Some behavior is largely generated from within animals and people; furthermore, that behavior also helps both to perpetuate and to modify the system itself. In the second section, we address the elusive question of how system properties impinge on the domestic decision process in order to reinforce or modify the behavior of their nations. From there, we go on to examine the more relevant empirical evidence.

THE THEORETICAL CONTEXT

Many scholars in the field of international politics would, with little hesitation, dismiss the effort to identify the impact of system properties on the incidence of war (or on any other set of phenomena). Their reasons would be of two sorts. First, from the policy perspective, they note that even if the attributes of the system do affect international interactions, it would only be of "academic interest" because of the relatively slow pace at which these properties (to be described shortly) change and because of the corollary that they are largely unresponsive to the policy moves of the nations. If there is little we can do to modify the system in the short term, why worry about its effects? At best, the system's structural, material, and cultural properties are similar to geographical and climatological phenomena: they must be reckoned with, but they cannot be controlled.

A second and more substantial argument is of a theoretical sort: the nations are highly autonomous actors and, while systemic conditions may impose some modest constraints, national behavior is primarily a consequence of the domestically determined objectives and capabilities of each society. This is, of course, an extreme version of the "subsystem dominated" assumption.

While recognizing the partial accuracy of both arguments, those of us who consider the issue an important one proceed from the following perspective. First, there is the by now familiar refrain that "it is an empirical question," one to be settled by examining the historical evidence rather than by some premature premise usually resting on a biased recollection of a handful of cases or periods. That is, although system properties, especially those of a structural and material sort, do appear to be resistant to rapid and conscious change, some of them do seem more volatile, especially those reflecting alliance formation and dissolution on the structural side and those reflecting technological breakthrough on the material side. Widely shared perceptions on the cultural side, as implied, do occasionally shift rapidly, often in response to the policies of one or two major powers. While the empirical question has remained largely rhetorical with few efforts to measure either the rate of change or the stimuli effecting such change, one promising exception is now under way: Wallace and Singer are well along in a data-based analysis of the system's structural dimensions from 1816 to the present (1989); while the results so far tend to support the more "glacial" of the orientations, it is too early to generalize.

The second counterargument is partly theoretically derived and partly empirical: the system's properties do—or should—affect national behavior regarding war and peace in a discernible fashion. And that is the purpose of this chapter: to examine both the deductive reasoning and the inductive findings that illuminate systemic impact on the military behavior of the component units.

Definitions

Given the dearth of systematic research as well as the diverse meanings attached to the concepts introduced in the previous section, a brief definitional digression is in order, beginning with the reminder that "systemness" is largely in the eye of the beholder; one can look at or imagine an extraordinarily diverse range of social, biological, or physical entities and assign them to a system. Most (but not all) scientists would agree that systemness requires (1) some degree of comparability among its component entities, (2) a modicum of interdependence among the entities, and, less often, (3) a degree of common fate (Campbell 1958). Once the components and the boundaries of the social system are defined, we can go on to describe it along three sets of attribute dimensions. Ranging in order of tangibility, durability, and observability, these are material, structural, and cultural. The first, *material*, embraces geographical, demographic, and technological features. Even though these cry out for more systematic, data-based attention as determinants of national behavior, little has been done to date. These dimensions will be ignored here.

Next are the *structural* attributes of a system, and these are typically distinguished both on a formal–informal dimension (ranging from legal institutions to loose coalitions, for example) and on a vertical–horizontal dimension. By vertical structure, we mean hierarchy, ranking, status ordering, and so on. Horizontal structure reflects the bonds, links, and associations that allow a system to be examined in terms of the extent to which diplomatic ranking correlates with the number of votes in a formal international organization (vertical), or how clearly bipolar the configuration that emerges out of the nations' alliance bonds is (horizontal). Finally, there are *cultural* attributes, which may also, in turn, be disaggregated into the distribution of perceptions, preferences, and predictions among some or all of the individuals in the system, including those elites who speak and act on behalf of the subsystem groups into which the people are organized. As with the material properties of the international system, these also (1) demand, but have not yet received, much greater research attention and (2) will be largely ignored here.

I cannot leave this brief section without a few general comments on the importance of definitional clarity in the social sciences. Largely because ours are the most recent and least developed of the sciences and, thus, are still heavily influenced by practises in the humanities, we tend to follow an excessively permissive approach. One hears with alarming frequency the following phrase: "I don't care what you call it as long as you define your terms!" This may be pleasantly nondogmatic, but it means that each of us needs to carry around a truckload of dictionaries, one for each scholar's own idiosyncratic vocabulary. The central concept in this chapter and in much of the literature in world politics is "structure," yet the variety of definitions (implicit more often than explicit) is awesome. In addition to the configurations and links and bonds and ranks of the component units in a system as used here, one also finds the word applied to (1) any slowly changing condition, (2) any observed or hypothesized regularity in the behavior of social entities, (3) any observed or hypothesized pattern of statistical associations among any sets of variables, and (4) any regularity, observed or imagined, for which no other word comes to mind! Other examples occur, but space is limited and my point should be clear.

Interaction Opportunities

With some of the terminological ambiguities removed (for the moment only, I fear), let us turn now to the more general theoretical argument. In the process, I will suggest that there is an unsuspected underlying unity in the apparent diversity, if not chaos, of the relevant literature. As I understand it, there would seem to be two approaches to the connection between system structure and war. One is that of interaction opportunities, and the other is structural clarity; both—quite naturally—exercise their effects (if any) on internation conflict through the national security decision process. Let me address them separately at first.

The interaction opportunity theme is analogous to the "invisible hand" notion associated with Adam Smith and his theoretical descendents, and it assumes that the less constrained the actors in an economic system are, the more fully they can pursue their natural self-interests. Further, the greater this freedom is, the greater the prosperity of the system as a whole and its members in general will be. Conversely, any tendencies toward restraint, via oligopoly, monopoly, or government regulation, will inhibit such pursuit, weaken the efforts of the invisible hand, and thus redound to the collective disadvantage. Similarly, as we hypothesized in previous work (Deutsch and Singer 1964; Singer and Small 1968) and as the classical scholars argued earlier (Gulick 1955; Kennan 1951), the members of the international system are more likely to enjoy autonomy and security when they are free to pursue these interests via interaction with many other nations. Constraints in the form of alliance obligations or relatively permanent hostility or friendship based on dynastic or ideological considerations will inhibit the efficacy of those multiple cross-cutting ties that permit the invisible hand to work as a self-regulating mechanism in the service of peace and stability.

In sum, this theoretical focus makes a virtue of sovereignty, assumes a sense of national restraint and rationality, and predicts a moderately harmonious state of affairs as long as the rules of the game are generally followed. The point of the argument, then, is that national security elites must be sufficiently competent to recognize the interests of their own state as well as the interests of the others. They must also be sufficiently free of parochial domestic interests—as well as the unnatural bonds of enduirng alliance and alignment—to pursue the former and, in so doing, preserve the system's basic configuration while adjusting to the inevitable shifts in the capabilities and interests of its most salient members. For peace to prevail, interaction opportunities must be kept to the maximum.

Structural Clarity

Turning from the theme of interaction opportunity to that of structural clarity, we once again find a not-so-elusive connection between a structural property of the system and the role of the national security elites. But here the emphasis is less on the need for high competence and wide latitude among the decisionmakers than on the extent to which their predictive abilities are enhanced by the state of the system. That is, the greater the structural clarity of the system, the more accurately they can predict who will be on whose side, and with what capabilities, in a confrontation.

This clarity is found along both the horizontal and vertical dimensions. The former reflects the strength and variety of ways that the nations are linked together in coalitions based on alliances, diplomatic bonds, shared membership in international organizations, trade, and the like. The stronger and more numerous these links, and the more discrete, distinct, and reinforcing the groupings produced by them, the greater the structural clarity on the horizontal dimension. Similarly, the nations can be ranked according to their industrial capacity, military capabilities, economic dominance, diplomatic importance, and so forth. And the greater the clarity and isomorphism of these several rank orders at a given moment, the more obvious are their overall strengths, the clearer the pecking order, and the more readily they can be evaluated vis-à-vis one another. From these two sets of dimensions, as noted previously, the decisional elites can estimate, in a crunch, (1) who will line up with whom and (2) with what overall capabilities.

Working from the structural clarity model, the literature contains two competing interpretations relevant to the incidence of war (Midlarsky, 1981). In one of these, the assumption is that high clarity will produce greater decisional certainty, and such certainty as to the lineup will reduce the likelihood of a dispute or confrontation escalating to war. As the cliché says, under such conditions the stronger need not, and the weaker dare not, fight; thus, we would expect a strong, negative correlation between structural clarity and the incidence of war. But like so many of the theoretical models in the field of world politics, there is an equally plausible counterargument. In this rival version, the hypothesis is that structural clarity is *positively* associated with war because elites are more likely to initiate war when the outcome is relatively clear and, of course, promising. In this version, ambiguity and uncertainty is what inhibits escalatory behavior, and clarity and confidence encourage it on the side of those who enjoy superiority. As should be clear, this is a corollary of the less complex hypothesis on the relationship between parity and war, and as with that long-standing question, the prediction can go either way.

Returning to the interaction opportunity approach, the convergence between these two models should be clear. As such opportunities increase, two consequences allegedly follow. First, as already noted, when there are fewer constraints on the nations from alliances and other bonds, each can more readily pursue its own apparent interests. This produces in turn, the putatively positive effects of the invisible hand, with war that much less likely. But an important and less obvious implication links the theoretical focus quite nicely with the structural clarity/ambiguity focus: when these opportunities are high it is because of the relative absence of clear coalitions that rest on the inhibiting bonds of alignment via unambiguous political and economic association.

In other words, the two dominant foci in the efforts to explain war on the basis of system structure turn out to converge on the theme of decisional certainty at the national level. Interaction opportunities, thus, stem from low levels of structural clarity that result in lower levels of decisional certainty. While making this cross-system convergence evident is a desirable step toward theoretical integration, it nevertheless still leaves us with the elusive empirical question at the national level of analysis: Are nations in conflict more prone to escalation and war under conditions of high certainty and predictability or when configurations are ambiguous, certainty is low, and predictability is more difficult?

Another perspective on this is dyadic. If structural clarity at the global or regional level provides a relatively solid basis for national security elites to estimate the relative aggregate capabilities of the relevant coalitions and, thus, the likely outcome of war (should it come to that), it follows that similar estimates at the dyadic level should have the same effect. That is, if we focus only on the two central protagonists or blocs in a dispute or confrontation and ignore the existence and configurations (commitments and capabilities) of others, we have essentially the same problem facing those responsible for the war/no war decision: How likely are we to win, and at what cost, if the dispute goes to war? Furthermore, this situation poses the same question for the researcher as the analogous situation at the system level, and that is whether the relationship between the predictability of the outcome and the probability of war is positive or negative.

Of course, the simplifying assumption of symmetry that we have been making so far could be misleading. This is because it posits not only that the elites on each side will (1) see the same objective capability and commitment configurations and (2) evaluate it in the same way, but also that they will respond to it in the same way. Such heroic assumptions ignore the differentiating effects of all of those factors that make predicting international events difficult for both the practitioner and the scholarly observer.

Having laid out some of the key concepts and suggested not only the models that rest on these concepts but also the surprising convergence among these models, the next step is to articulate more fully a model of the decision process by which structural properties of the system exercise their alleged effect upon national behavior. More specifically, and despite a massive speculative literature to the contrary, unless one can illuminate the decisional links between environmental conditions and the behavior of the nations making up the system, any model of systemic effects on the incidence of war must remain less than complete. This proposition would seem to hold even if the statistical associations to date between system structure and war were both consistent and robust—which they certainly are not.

And if further justification is necessary, consider the frequency with which we read or listen to arguments about macroeconomic policy and come away confused. As I see it, the explanation is simple: the writer or speaker has not made the decisional connection clear because he or she has not considered it, assumes it to be self-evident, or finds it too elusive to address. Let us see whether we can do better in international politics than in the allegedly most advanced of the social sciences.

THE DECISIONAL CONNECTION

Let me begin with some crucial assumptions of an empirical sort on the premise that my epistemological assumptions are self-evident while those of an ethical sort can be deferred to the conclusion. The first is what my students often call "Singer's First Law": no individual and no organization ever does anything for one reason alone. And I use *reason* here in both senses of the word: the pull of the future and the push of the past. By the former, I mean preferences for the future, "in order to" reasons; these preferences can be thought of as goals or purposes, but only in the sense that actors are willing to allocate energy and invest resources in their pursuit. This is to distinguish between goals, purposes, and objectives on the one hand and idle dreams and fantasies on the other. Many individuals would like to achieve fame, fortune, and power, but very few invest seriously in the pursuit of such ends. Rather, we typically set more modest goals and then proceed to work toward them; becoming a millionaire, a prime minister, or even a Nobel Prize winner is insufficiently salient for most of us to concentrate our energies toward them. Similarly, those who act on behalf of national or multinational states, political parties, movements, or corporations may well fantasize about global domination and so forth, but rarely in history do we find concerted efforts to realize such dreams. Even granting that Napoleon, Hitler, and Stalin may have been acting on such dreams and were able to mobilize people and resources toward such grandiose ends, one must recognize how small a fraction of the political elites of the last two centuries they represent. Furthermore, individuals and groups must find themselves well along the road to these ends before they begin to pursue them as relevant goals—and that, too, is a relatively rare event.

The Pull of the Future

Returning, then, to the pull of the future, it is hardly radical to note that governments and their national security elements are inevitably coalitions made up of subcoalitions of individuals. Nor is it surprising, despite the appreciable effects of selection and socialization, that these individuals and groups will have different goal priorities. Their preference orderings will be at variance, as will the utilities and disutilities they assign to conceivable outcomes. These differences not only reflect diverse views of national interest and diverse models of political reality, but they lead to differences in those short term goals that are seen as instrumental means to longer term goals (March 1981).

Equally important, of course, are the more provincial of their interests: the personal and the bureaucratic. Only those who believe in fairy tales would accept the scenario of hundreds of functionaries, from minister of defense down to assistant desk officers, working assiduously (or even competently) in the selfless pursuit of some higher societal purpose. A more realistic scenario might be what I call "doing well while appearing to do good," which is nicely reflected in the recent case of those officers who sought and achieved financial gains while selling U.S. arms to Iran and passing some of the profits along to the "Contra" factions in the Nicaraguan insurrection. And as I have argued for some years (Singer 1972) it is easier to attend to doing well for oneself and one's bureau or faction when there is considerable uncertainty as to which policies are most likely to do good for the country. This uncertainty, in turn, rests on that lethal combination of inadequate research by the scholarly community and the policy community's ignorance, indifference, and disdain for rigorous research findings in those instances when they exist and are publicly available.

The Push of the Past

Much of the preceding analysis applies equally to the other set of reasons for pursuing and advocating a given national security policy: the "push of the past." Often understood as a learning model in the rational choice literature, the assumption is that decisional elites select those policies and strategies that seemed to have been successful in the past and then utilize them in the pursuit of their goals and objectives. While not unreasonable, this excessively rational assumption is seriously incomplete; we need to incorporate several other types of "pushes" from the past.

That is, in addition to events from the past that are part of the individual and institutional memories of the foreign policy elites, there are several additional components. First, there are those that are incorrectly or incompletely remembered, those from which "lessons" are erroneously drawn. A nice example of this is found in Ray (1987), where we are reminded that, after World War I, scholars and practitioners tended to believe that the polarization of the Triple Entente versus the Central Powers played a key role in converting the pre-1914 crisis into all-out war; the nations involved in the war, therefore, avoided alliance formation during the 1920s and 1930s. But with the close of World War II, the belief that it was the *lack* of alliances that brought on that disaster was instrumental in stimulating the frenzy of alliance building in the 1950s. By generalizing from a single salient case, elites "learned" the wrong thing. Selective recall may represent the push of the past, but it does so hardly in a constructive sense.

Second, and perhaps more potent, is the extent to which the conditions of today are a result of the conditions, events, and decisions taken years, decades, and centuries earlier. The powerful, ever-present hand of the past is instrumental in shaping the structural, material, and cultural context within which the international politics of the present are conceived and executed. While our understanding of those influences remains pitifully inadequate, they are, nevertheless, at work in every aspect of human activity. We may indeed never "step into the river of history at the same place," but step into it we must.

Rational Choice and Realpolitik

The preceding discussion now permits us to address two issues that are central to any systemic—or other—explanation of international war. One issue is that of rational choice, the other is that of reductionism. Despite suggestions to the contrary (Waltz 1975), they are indeed separable; one need not work from the rational choice model in order to utilize a reductionist approach. Let me explain.

If the preceding interpretation of decision making is a fair statement of the problem, it is clear that the discrepancy between political reality and the rational choice model is profound. The argument cannot be salvaged by distinguishing between collective and individual rationality; the individuals in any organization can indeed be expected to pursue their own parochial goals and priorities in a relatively rational manner, but the collective, runs this line of argument, nevertheless shows rationality in pursuit of the larger entity's goals. The only way that this crutch can work is by falling back on the trivial definition of rationality often used in game theory: we pursue outcomes that we most prefer! While on the question of definition, let me suggest a distinction that would make the concept of rationality more relevant in the social sciences. That is, instead of using the trivial definition noted here or applying the concept to the policy decision or choice that emerges from the process of deciding, rationality should be applied only to the *process* itself. Policies may or may not be successful, prudent, or adaptive, but they should not be evaluated on a rationality dimension; that is reserved for the process alone.

Returning for a moment to the fit between national security decision-making and rational choice in its several incarnations, the preceding discussion should indicate the extent of my skepticism. For a more complete and devastating view, two other sources deserve mention. One is the fascinating article by the Swiss economist Bruno Frey (1983) in which we find a veritable catalog of the assumptions found in the rational choice literature of economics (and other social sciences) set alongside the experimental findings of cognitive and social psychologists. The other, in the context of international politics, is that of Philip Schrodt (1985), a political scientist pursuing the application of "artificial intelligence" to foreign policy decisionmaking. In this refreshingly coherent and explicit discussion, we find not only a treatment of the discrepancies between the assumptions of rational choice models and the empirical evidence, but a rejection of the widely accepted notion that our theoretical assumptions need not be empirically correct as long as they are "useful" in the sense that the models incorporating these assumptions turn out to provide accurate predictions.

Having said all of this, let me now hedge somewhat. If we bear in mind that internation conflict can embrace a rather wide range of behaviors and responses, it follows that much—perhaps most—of that conflict occurs in a routine, low-level, low-intensity mode. In that type of context, the line of argument adduced here would seem to hold in most nations and in most cases. Here, it is not surprising that individual and bureaucratic priorities mingle with poor organization, faulty intelligence, and collective ignorance, giving us a decision process rather close to that suggested previously.

On the other hand, what happens in crisis and confrontation? While the hard evidence may be far from adequate, most of us appreciate that "business as usual" gives way to a rather different mood with a somewhat different set of decision rules. Perhaps the most crucial change is that of priorities: among the world's crisis managers, it is taboo to think of or allude to personal or factional interests. Patriotism is the order of the day and the national interest is the touchstone. Another is that of time frame: with the nation at the brink of disaster or opportunity and the world on the knife-edge of destruction, one does not worry about mealtime or family plans. Too much is riding on our timely judgment.

This, in turn, is a result of one of the better documented generalizations: a rapid contraction of the size of the decision-making apparatus. Senior officials, elected or appointed, step in and take charge of matters ordinarily left to their subordinates, and while they may have inadequate familiarity with the details and history and context of the issue, they also have little patience with the glacial pace and seeming irrelevance they associate with the foreign policy and national security bureaucracy. Among the considerations that now may receive shorter shrift are interagency rivalries, public opinion, or the preferences of other governments, allied or otherwise. In other words, there is less interest in "what will sell" and more in "what will work." These, then, are the rare occasions in which something akin to rational choice might exist (Herek *et al.* 1987).

Having said all of this, however, the distinction should not be drawn too sharply. There are three considerations. First, as suggested, the evidence is more anecdotal and intuitively reasonable than it is reproducible. Second, people who have succeeded and have been socialized in one set of decision processes are unlikely to shed the habits of a lifetime overnight; the vestiges of personal, factional, and national politics will inevitably be present—and there is a tomorrow when they will once more dominate. And third, not only are the cultural norms regarding the decision process partially carried over into crises, but the entire configuration of the crisis situation is largely the result of that decision process.

Reductionism and Realpolitik

The line of reasoning to this point provides strong support for those who are skeptical of the realpolitik perspective; other labels that can be used are "realist" or "balance of power," but the former is ideologically self-serving (whether pro or con), and the latter, as Haas (1953) urged years ago, means all things to all people. By realpolitik, we mean nothing more than the assumption that, on the world scene, national policies are (1) driven primarily by the pursuit of national power and (2) in the hands of competent, rational, patriotic officials. While arguing that such an explanatory model is woefully incomplete and, thus, quite misleading, I do not suggest that these considerations are absent or irrelevant. To the contrary, they are always present in the decision process when internation rivalry and conflict are on the agenda, and they exist even when highly collaborative policies are under consideration. But they are so intertwined with and corrupted by the pursuit of individual and bureaucratic–factional power that they provide a poor basis for prediction and explanation. In a later section we will see that this has not always been so; even up to the close of the nineteenth century, one could make a fair case for the realpolitik model. In response to industrialization, urbanization, and democratization, however, these factors began to decline in their analytic potency. One might say that when officials could no longer say or believe with the old French royalty that "l'etat, c'est, moi," all sorts of other considerations began to intrude into the decision process.

Reductionism and Explanation

Enough has been said about the decisional context and process to indicate their importance in examining the effects of system properties on subsystem interactions. It is now time for a brief summary in the context of a crucial epistemological argument. If the goal of scientific research is to explain the variation in some outcome phenomenon across time, places, or cases, we need to distinguish explanation from both prediction and covariation. While neither of the latter is a "piece of cake," they demand much less of the researcher and his or her theoretical model than does the task of explanation. One source of confusion on this score is the oft-heard assertion that the acid test of a theory is its ability to predict, and this is unfortunate as well as incorrect. Think of all the relatively accurate predictions that can be made without fully understanding or being able to explain the connection between input and output or stimulus and response. On the basis of observed or reported covariation alone, most of us can predict that flipping a switch will (usually) turn on a light, that a bicycle's speed will (up to a point) accelerate the longer it coasts downhill, that it takes more strength to get a heavy load moving than to keep it moving, that a small crowd will attract many passersby, that high winds will spread a forest fire, that a baby will cry if its parents scowl at it, and so forth. In other words, it requires relatively modest knowledge to make fairly accurate predictions, but quite a bit more knowledge is needed to explain why the predicted outcome usually results.

This is where reductionism enters the picture. An adequate explanation is one that tells the story, step by step, of how a given event or condition sets in motion a sequence that regularly culminates in a given outcome. That sequence—despite the impression that many social scientists give—is indeed "touched by human hands." While Marxist as well as market-oriented economists think it is self-evident that some macrophenomenon, such as the spread of automated production, will regularly lead to some other macro-event, such as a fall in worldwide wage levels, it may not be at all self-evident either to the skeptic or to the innocent. Or, to take a more immediate issue in the American economy, the conventional wisdom is that a reduction in the individual tax rate will lead, in short order, to increased savings and investment levels. But in boom periods, this is not exactly what happens. First, most of the beneficiaries of a tax cut may be the less wealthy, but the aggregated monetary "return" is very much in the hands of the wealthy few. And second, the latter have little need or incentive to save; consequently, they invest, not in productivity-enhancing activities, but in speculative ones. Looking at the microlevel links can save us from accepting many a foolish generalization.

Another example is that of operations research, in which some tinkering with a system-level variable, such as an increase in oil prices, culminates in lower life expectancy levels (via more air pollution?), or construction of a highway culminates in lower classroom performance (via higher noise levels?). While observing or predicting such correlations is worthwhile from the perspectives of both science and public welfare, understanding the connection between "cause" and "effect" would be more valuable (and also more difficult).

The point, then, is that a theoretical formulation that ignores, avoids, or obfuscates the human decisions that link stimulus to response will be, at best, incomplete and, at worst, downright wrong. There is, of course, an important counterpoint: reductionism can be carried too far. While the macrolevel social scientist may, as I do, insist on bringing the individual into the model, the psychiatrist might want to disaggregate further down to the ego, superego, and libido. The biochemist might require that we examine the role of brain lipids in individual behavior, and the physical chemist could urge including the cells, neurons, and so on. Ultimately, we might indeed develop a unified and integrated theory of all human behavior (Miller 1976), but for the decades ahead, we can be satisfied with the more limited sort of reductionism advocated here.

We conclude this section, then, by noting that any explanation of war—systemic, dyadic, or national; material, structural, or cultural—must attend to the ways in which the putative explanatory factors impinge upon and are affected by the decision process. And even as we move, however slowly and reluctantly, toward the political equivalent of computer-assisted medical diagnosis (or the more advanced computer-assisted automotive diagnosis), human individuals and groups will be involved in reading and responding to certain stimuli in order to produce certain behavioral events. Without that connecting link, the "causal" association between input and output will remain shrouded in speculation, if not outright superstition.

THE EMPIRICAL EVIDENCE

Having laid out the theoretical context and some of the key assumptions affecting the possible link between system structure and the incidence of war, we turn next to the very salient question: How strong is the empirical evidence in support of one version or another of the general hypothesis? To put it simply, it is not strong at all, but quite mixed at this point in the unfolding of the data-based research sequence.

Looking first at an earlier effort to evaluate the structural clarity argument, we (Singer and Bouxsein 1975) reexamined a number of prior studies that reflect not only a diversity of theoretical concerns, but also rest on far from identical data bases. One indicator of polarity in the major power subsystem, reflecting the extent to which alliances had increased structural clarity, was related to war negatively in the nineteenth century but positively in the twentieth century, while another indicator of system-wide polarity was weakly but positively related for both centuries. But when the same author (Wallace 1973) weighted the alliance configurations by the size of the signatories' armed forces, he found that greater polarity predicted to *lower* levels of war. Perhaps more compelling were the findings of his follow-up test of a curvilinear model: very high and very low levels of weighted polarity were positively associated with war, while moderate levels preceded periods of a clear decline in war over the two centuries, as was hypothesized by Rosecrance in 1966.

Another way to look at polarity and structural clarity is in terms of the direction and rate of change rather than the degree of polarity at each fixed observation interval. Thus, after finding only the weakest association between several indicators of the latter and war, Bueno de Mesquita (1978) discovered that the greater the change in the tightness and clarity of the alliance configuration (in either direction), the more international war was in subsequent years. By using a more complex and discriminating model, however, he also found that declining tightness was strongly and *negatively* related to war.

We then turned to another Correlates of War study in which the indicators of clarity were based not on the horizontal configurations produced by formal alliances (or shared memberships in international organizations or diplomatic groupings, which will be alluded to later), but on the vertical configurations produced by the distribution of material capabilities. Here (Singer *et al.* 1972), the results pointed in yet a different direction, with periods of high clarity—as indicated by a heavy concentration of capabilities in the hands of a very few major powers—predicting higher levels of war in the nineteenth century and lower levels in the twentieth century. Once more, on the assumption that the direction and rate of change might be equally or more relevant, we looked at both the net and the gross change in the concentration of capabilities and found that shifts toward higher concentration had the same "effects" as such a configuration in the static sense: more war in the nineteenth century and less in the twentieth century. And using gross changes, a mere redistribution, we found that less change was associated with more war in the earlier century and less war in the current century.

Given these apparently erratic patterns, we shifted from discrete bivariate analyses to the test of a primitive, multivariate model. Using alliance aggregation, polarity, concentration, and net and gross shifts in concentration (for major powers only), we found additional support for the notion that the indicators of structural clarity are indeed strongly associated with war, but once again the *direction* of that association is far from clear. That is, the coefficients of determination (r^2) were rather strong (.74 and .72) for the two centuries, but in opposite directions.

Drawing on those earlier efforts as well as on the research of the following half-decade, we found little to challenge the original conclusion (Singer 1981, 9). In that review article, I concluded that "regardless of the theoretical interpretation, the empirical investigations led once more to inconsistent results." At about the same time, Thompson *et al.* (1980) published the only other study explicitly using the interaction opportunities concept. This team, which has done some of the best research on the link between long economic cycles and war, attempted to replicate the earliest data-based analysis (Singer and Small 1968). Although they used somewhat different procedures, they also found only the weakest relationship over the 1816–1965 period. As with some earlier work, they did find some interesting—but surprising—cross-temporal differences. Rather than the intercentury break, they uncovered a positive, strong association between interaction opportunities and the onset of war, but only for the period since World War II. Equally inconclusive is a comprehensive examination of the effects of polarity in several forms along with capability distributions, in which a variety of additive and interactional models all failed to account for war and no-war outcomes (Bueno de Mesquita and Lalman 1987).

To further convey the absence of clear evidence, Stiglicz (1981) developed an indicator of structural clarity based on the ratio of balanced to unbalanced triads in the system and found that it is moderately but negatively associated with war in the nineteenth century and strongly positive in its "effect" on war in the twentieth century. Once again, it looks as if we probably have a good idea here, but there are so many diverse ways of measuring it that its scientific usefulness is nil (Bueno de Mesquita and Singer 1973). In this connection, it should be noted that, in addition to the index construction efforts contained in these contributions, there is also a formidable number of excellent articles devoted solely to the problems of defining and measuring a range of potentially useful indicators of system structure, but they cannot be reviewed here.

Dissatisfied with the inconsistency of the previous findings, Stoll and Champion (1985) pursued a different tack and looked to levels of major power satisfaction as a possible explanatory variable. While their indicator relied on the soft judgments of their Correlates of War colleagues, including this variable provided an appreciably better fit between the incidence of war (and disputes) predicted by their model and the amounts actually observed. Briefly stated, by identifying blocs of states in terms of their apparent satisfaction with the international status quo, they came closer than their predecessors in postdicting fluctuations (if not precise magnitudes) in war across both centuries.

A more recent review article (Vasquez 1987), which evaluated the Correlates of War project and, in an imaginative fashion, examined the convergence of other research with ours, discerned a clearer set of results. While he does not invoke such systemic concepts as clarity or interaction opportunities, his interpretation of the data-based research at the national, dyadic, and system levels readily lends itself to such treatment, especially in his summary of the effects of military alliances at all of these levels. Starkly put, Vasquez sees such alliances as not only increasing the frequency of war since 1816, but also increasing their duration, magnitude, and severity.

RECONCILING THE FINDINGS AND THE MODEL

While these intercentury differences and other inconsistencies are not found uniformly in every investigation that embraces part or most of the 1800s and 1900s, they occur with sufficient frequency to be taken seriously. Further, they *may* be interpreted as a disappointing reminder that the search for lawlike regularities is a futile task, as many traditionalists with a predilection for the ideographic view of the world do interpret them. But they may also be taken as a valuable reminder that our theoretical models are inadequately specified, which is a pretentious way of saying that we have overlooked an important variable that, once identified, could help explain these apparent anomalies in our findings.

Committed as I am to the nomothetic view that assumes the existence of empirical regularities and recurrent patterns, my tendency is to ask what factor needs to be introduced into our model. If several structural properties of the international system are negatively associated with armed conflict in one century and positively associated with armed conflict in the next century, something must have occurred to "produce" this reversal of effects. In one of the earlier studies to turn up this cross-century shift, we offered a tentative and partial post hoc explanation, which is presented here in a more complete fashion.

With the nineteenth century drawing to a close, the European landscape had begun to change rather dramatically. As the industrial revolution accelerated, so did the rate of urbanization, and along with this came a rise in labor unions and working class militancy. This, in due course, contributed to the rise of the welfare state and, hence, to greater citizen interest and participation in domestic politics along with public education, higher literacy, and wider newspaper circulation. This social mobilization not only gave the political elites greater access to and control over the nation's demographic and economic resources (via, inter alia, conscription, mass education, and taxation), but it also imposed a relatively unfamiliar burden on them. Both the elites and the counterelites found it necessary to generate popular support for their policies, which required, in turn, the articulation of a more coherent ideological argument. While largely focused on domestic matters, this attention, interest, and awareness gradually extended beyond national boundaries; growing interdependence among the nations and growing appreciation of the reciprocal impact of domestic and foreign policies led inevitably to the rising salience of the latter. Briefly put, foreign policy—long the private domain of a small elite—became more and more politicized.

As a consequence, the arcane complexities and subtleties of diplomatic and military practice were translated increasingly into ideological terms. And while such ideological presentations and justification still contained numerous contradictions, there was a powerful incentive to make them *appear* consistent in both the sense of their internal logic and in terms of compatibility with the more dominant national values. This certainly required some departure from the cynical and Machiavellian decision rules of realpolitik; politicians needed to justify their behavior in increasingly moral terms, even to the point of praising or condemning the domestic policies and putative values of other national governments (Hunt 1987).

It is, of course, easy to imagine the impact of these trends as that epoch gave way to the twentieth century. Cooperating with some governments called forth rather elaborate justifications, as did opposing them, offering or withdrawing diplomatic recognition, taking sides in disputes, entering into alliances or other treaties, and, to some extent, even engaging in commerce or negotiating agreements on immigration, citizenship, licensing, extradition, and copyright. What all of this added up to was the formation of international coalitions that were more responsive to the vagaries of public opinion, interest group pressures, media campaigns, and the whole panoply of domestic politics than they were to the more consistent imperatives of a geopolitical, and strategic kind. To repeat an earlier phrase of mine, alliances and other commitments became less and less "affairs of convenience" and more and more "marriages of passion."

This leads, in turn, to the connection between the structure of the international system and its culture, which provides the context within which national security decisions are made. To continue this line of reasoning, then, in those earlier periods, marked as they were by relatively high levels of tolerance and flexibility among political elites, structural ambiguity worked quite well to keep the peace: deep ideological cleavages, obsession with the struggle between the forces of light and the forces of darkness, beliefs that some domestic political forms are inherently evil and some inherently virtuous—all of these are part of the Manichean culture. And this is the outlook that amplifies the sense of fear in both camps, with the word "both" used advisedly to reflect the pressures on most nations to declare for one coalition or the other. Neutralism is, of course, unacceptable: if you're not *with* us, you're *against* us.

Under these more recent conditions of high cultural clarity, the normal effects of structural ambiguity are unlikely to work. As already suggested, the latter requires—if confrontation and war are to be minimized—the application of middle-run rationality to the foreign policy decision process. And this requires, in turn, a detached calculation of not only our own society's general interests and welfare but, more crucial, the interests, objectives, strategies, and capabilities of the others. Passions of hatred, paranoid fear, and self-righteousness, especially as these passions permeate the society and weaken the potential for rational self-correction from other domestic elites and counterelites, will clearly inhibit our ability to think clearly about foreign and military policies. Under these conditions, which are highly contagious in the anarchic international system, each society's elites will be increasingly prone to exaggerate the ambitions and the capabilities of those in the "enemy camp." Also inhibiting the efficacy of the invisible hand mentioned earlier will be the tendency for weaker allies to exploit their dominant coalition partners and the willingness of the latter to acquiesce. The effect here will be the evolution of a double standard, with tolerance toward allies and cynicism toward rivals that further erodes our capacity to apply pragmatic and consistent criteria to foreign-policy decisions.

In sum, the beneficent results of the invisible hand rest on the ability of foreign policy elites to "read" the system and its other members accurately and dispassionately, a capacity that is enhanced under conditions of cultural and normative detachment but inhibited when the system's culture is marked by deep feeling and broad belief that there are well-defined camps and coalitions that distinguish between the decent folk and their enemies. Just as "conspiracies in restraint of trade" make it difficult for *Homo economus* to pragmatically interact with the multitude of other actors in the marketplace, coalitions in restraint of diplomacy make it difficult for *Homo politicus* to deal pragmatically with the less numerous, but clearly sufficient, aggregation of other actors in the global system.

CONCLUSION

Every scholarly article in the social sciences can and should play a number of educational, policy, and scientific roles. Some will open up and clarify a relatively unfamiliar area of knowledge for the reader, others might alert the policymaker or analyst to some pertinent lessons of history, and still others will perhaps theoretically integrate a large fraction of previous research or point toward the most promising research strategy. While I hope that this one will help to illuminate the relationship between system structure and international war—and sensitize the policy-oriented reader to the fact that certain conflictual strategies may be safer under some circumstances and irresponsibly prone to war under others—the main concern has been the scientific one: bridging the gap between what we think we know and what we need to know next. And despite frequent assertions from those who should know better, this is a far cry from "testing the balance-of-power (or any other) theory"; there *is* no such theory, nor will there be one until much more of the work discussed here has been completed (Zinnes 1967; Siverson and Sullivan 1983).

In the case in hand, this is no easy task. On the one hand, we have more than the usual speculative essays based on the selective recall of historical anecdote or, worse yet, based on folkloristic hunches about how individuals allegedly behave (as in much of the literature on strategic deterrence). But on the other hand, as should be abundantly clear, the reproducible findings of the research to date hardly point in one clear direction. Depending on the variables used, the ways in which they were measured, the spatial–temporal domain covered, and the statistical models that were applied to the data, we obtain appreciably different results (Midlarsky 1986a). The task, therefore, is to both reexamine more fully the empirical investigations to date and to construct a theoretical model that best captures what we think we know about the ways in which the structural properties of the system impinge on those who act for nations in conflict. For the moment, while continuing to work on both of these tasks, my bet is on the ultimate ability of the structural clarity–interaction opportunity model—mediated by the changing culture of international politics—to capture the processes by which system structure leads toward and away from the ever-menacing threat of international war.

CHAPTER 2

Long Cycles and Global War

George Modelski[1]
University of Washington

William R. Thompson
Claremont Graduate School

The long-cycle approach brings a time dimension to the study of world politics; it highlights certain notable recurrences, in particular those linked to leadership, alliances, and global war. It also raises questions about evolutionary trends.

Our approach is not, by itself, a theory of major war, but it does single out for special attention the five global wars of the modern world system: the Wars of Italy and the Indian Ocean (1494–1516), the Spanish–Dutch Wars (1580–1609), the Wars of the Grand Alliance (1688–1713), the Wars of the French Revolution and Napoleon (1792–1815), and World Wars I and II (1914–1945). It subjects these wars to empirical analysis and asks theoretical questions that place them in the broader context of world politics.

The long-cycle approach makes three distinct contributions to the study of war:

1. It devotes special attention to one class of war: the "big war." The standard treatment, on the other hand, regards "war in general" as the basic unit of analysis.

2. With respect to empirical reference, data or events, it draws upon the entire record of the modern world system, starting in 1494. Conventional treatments often begin no earlier than 1816 and use wars since that date as a source of samples of the universe of "wars in general."

3. Its policy concern is specifically focused upon means of preventing/avoiding the next global war that might bring an end to the human race. Conventional treatments speak of preventing war in general terms.

In the present essay we shall seek answers to the following questions:

1. What are long cycles, and how is global war related to them?

2. How does the long-cycle approach compare with other theories that raise the "big war" question?

3. What have we learned about global wars so far?

4. What remains to be learned about global wars?

LONG CYCLES?

The behavior of the global political system is time patterned because, over the span of just about a century, the system passes through four character-istic phases. The four phases form one entire cycle, and over the history of the modern world system, several such cycles of global politics have been completed.[2]

Each phase of the long cycle forms a distinct behavioral pattern.[3] The phase of *Macrodecision* (global war) is marked by profound and severe violence, but it also settles the question of leadership. The *Implementation* (world power) phase sees one nation-state, which acts as a global leader, implement major new programs. In *Agenda setting* (delegitimation), ques-tions are raised about the legitimacy of that leadership, and new problems enter the global agenda. In the phase of *Coalitioning* (deconcentration), leadership reaches a low point; it is an open season for challengers and for new coalitions.

The Table of Periodicities

The four-phase model of the long cycle is basic to this analysis, but is it consistent with the record of global politics of the past 500 years? A tabular representation of long cycles should help us answer these questions and help determine if, in fact, the pattern of events since 1494 conforms to the predictions of the model. As shown in Table 2.1 (see also Modelski 1987a,b) it conforms suprisingly well.

In particular the table shows the central role that the "big war" plays in the long cycle. In the Macrodecision (global war) column of Table 2.1 we find the largest, best-known wars of the modern period. These wars are the major beat of each long cycle, and no one would dispute the status of such major conflagrations as the world wars of the twentieth century or the revolutionary conflicts opening the nineteenth century.

Nor is the list of world powers "generated" by these wars particularly surprising. The majority are household names—except, perhaps, for Portu-gal (but even in that case those who have studied the history of the age of

TABLE 2.1
Periodic Table of the Long Cycle of Global Politics (Learning Mode)

	Phases			
Cycle	Agenda setting (global problems)	Coalitioning (core alliance)	Macrodecision (global war)	Implementation (World Power challenger)[a]
1	1430, discoveries	1460, Burgundian connection	1494, Wars of Italy and the Indian Ocean	1516, *Portugal*, Spain
2	1540, integration	1560, Calvinist international	1580, Dutch–Spanish Wars	1609, *the Netherlands*, France
3	1640, political framework	1660, Anglo-Dutch alliance	1688, Wars of the Grand Alliance	1714, *Britain I*, France
4	1740, Industrial Revolution	1763	1792, Wars of the French Revolution and Napoleon	1815, *Britain II*, Germany
1	1850, Knowledge Revolution	1873, Anglo-American special relationship	1914, World Wars I and II	1945, *United States* (USSR)
2	1973, integration	2000, community of democracy	2030	

SOURCE: Based on Modelski (1987c).
[a] The world power is in italics.

discoveries know that victories in the wars of the Indian Ocean elevated Portugal's naval influence to its peak position precisely during the years 1516–1540.

Nor, finally, is the list of challengers surprising. Spain and France were central to earlier global wars, and Germany to the last one. The USSR is shown in brackets in Table 2.1 because after 1945 it did assume the challenger's position; its role in the next macrodecision remains to be played out.

Table 2.1 is the initial support for the argument that long cycles do exist because, even for those students of world politics who are suspicious of "historical-looking" tables (such as this one, even though it really is not), it shows evidence of time patterning. Table 2.1 not only summarizes quite accurately global political developments over a time span of some five centuries, but it also gives an initial plausibility to, and yields a preliminary qualitative validation of, the idea of rhythm.

Some Major Features of the Long-Cycle Approach

One of the most distinctive aspects of the long-cycle theory is its emphasis on a global political system. Most historical interpretations of world politics are strongly anchored in the regional–territorial affairs of Western Europe; long-cycle theory is focused instead on an intercontinental–transoceanic layer that involves long-range transactions and issues of policy (order, security, stability) that are specific to those transactions. Although it is customary to accept the "globalization" of world politics by the late nineteenth century, long-cycle theory stresses that a global layer began to emerge as early as the end of the fifteenth century. The theory itself pivots on the central observation that the management of this global layer and its problems fluctuates according to the relative efficacy of a system leader, which is referred to as the world power. After emerging from a global-war succession struggle, the world power is in the best position to provide some level of global governance, but as its lead in economic innovation and naval power deteriorates, so too does the quality and quantity of governance. Ultimately, another succession struggle becomes probable.

The emphasis on the global political system influences the unusually strong theoretical bias toward translating global-reach capabilities in terms of sea power. As discussed at greater length in Modelski and Thompson (1988), sea power is critical for a number of reasons. During global wars, the winning world power's navy, and those of its allies, exercise command of the sea. The challenger's fleets are rendered less effective than they might have been. The mobility of the challenger's attacks is restricted. It is the challengers that have to worry most about amphibious invasions and seaborne supplies reaching the enemies' troops in the field. It is also the challengers who are most likely to feel the pinch of a worldwide economic blockade, which is supported, in large part, by a superior naval force. To win a global war, therefore, one must have (among other attributes) superior naval strength.

After the global war has been won, sea power continues to be important. It becomes a principal military instrument in enforcing the new, postwar order, in policing sea lanes, and in deterring potential attacks on the world power and its allies and clients. Even after the development of air power in the twentieth century, naval forces, especially those vessels that merge air and sea power, continue to represent a highly significant component in a nation's ability to project power on an intercontinental scale. In or out of war, sea power is a necessary attribute for an active participation in global politics.

These emphases on the global political system, global powers, and sea power influence how the world power's role is interpreted. In contrast to images of hegemonic preponderance and imperial control, world powers start out preponderant "only" in terms of their naval forces and, often more qualitatively, in terms of the dynamism of their economic system—which is the world system's leading economy for a time. The concentration of these capabilities is certainly empowering, but only within very real limitations. World powers are unable to exercise the same type and degree of command and control often attributed to imperial centers.

There are some overt temporal limitations on the influence of successive world powers as well. Within a generation after the last global war, the relative decline of the world power becomes apparent. Old contenders are emboldened, and new contenders begin to emerge. Global problem management becomes increasingly difficult following the four-phased track (global war, world power, delegitimation, deconcentration) sketched earlier (see Table 2.1). There is a long cycle of leadership in the global political system because there is a tendency for post-global-war orders to be temporary; yet the impulse to create order in the global layer recurs with some regularity.[4]

There are other elements of long-cycle theory worth exploring. One major component, for instance, is the intertwining of long-term, Kondratieff, economic waves with the four phases of the leadership long cycle (Modelski 1981, 1982). But topics such as this one, while important, take us away somewhat from this section's focus on how systemic wars are treated differently by various approaches.

There is also a large and growing field of alternative approaches from which to pick our targets of comparison. The greatest contrast might be gleaned from what are essentially rational decision-making approaches (Blainey 1973; Bueno de Mesquita 1981) that, for all practical purposes, ignore the differences between any two states engaged in war and system wars. We might also look at the empirical tradition of searching for periodicities in war and peace. But the values of these comparisons tend to be limited by the negative contrasts obtained from comparing analysts who single out systemic wars as deserving of explanation with those who do not.[5]

A much richer vein for comparison can be found in the other approaches that (1) identify some type of systemic war as a distinctive category and (2) seek to explain why they recur. Even so, space considerations require a sampling approach. We have selected three alternative and, we think, highly representative approaches: Toynbee's (1954) classical realist interpretation, Gilpin's (1981, 1986) neorealist perspective, and Wallerstein's (1974, 1980, 1984, 1986) neo-Marxist, world-economy conceptualization. By selecting these approaches, others—Doran's power cycle model (Doran and Parsons 1980); Organski's transition model (Organski 1968; Organski and Kugler 1980); Midlarsky's (1986a) hierarchical equilibrium model as well as some of the more hybrid approaches exemplified by Värynen (1983) and Goldstein (1985)—may appear to be slighted. But that is hardly the intention of what is intended to be a purposive sampling scheme.

Toynbee's War and Peace Cycle

Toynbee's perspective on general wars can be reduced to two conflicting tendencies, the balance of power and cyclical self-amortization, that are at work in world politics. In a system of two or more states, he argues, there is a tendency to regulate changes in relative strength through the constant adjustments associated with a balance-of-power process. States that improve their relative positions may attempt to exploit their newfound capability gains, and it is the difficult task of the other major states in the system to discourage disequilibrating expansion efforts through diplomacy (if possible) and coalitional warfare (if necessary). Since the diplomatic approach to maintaining balance of power frequently is inadequate to the task of preventing expansion bids, war becomes the dominant instrument in maintaining a political balance among states.

Nevertheless, all wars are not treated equivalently. As Toynbee (1954, 251) puts it,

> the most emphatic punctuation in a uniform series of events recurring in one
> repetitive cycle after another is the outbreak of a great war in which one Power
> that has forged ahead of all its rivals makes so formidable a bid for world
> dominion that it evokes an opposing coalition of all the other Powers. . . .

Thus, there are wars and then there are general wars. General wars are all-engulfing affairs that become increasingly probable as an equilibrium established in an earlier era "falls farther out of gear with current facts and needs." As the gap between reality and systemic operating principles grows, tension levels rise. Ultimately, one state, a continental power occupying a central position with direct access to the main arenas of combat, is tempted to make a bid for world dominion. The threat is sufficiently great that it forces the other great powers in the system to choose sides in what becomes a basic struggle to maintain or overthrow the balance of power.

There is a catch, however, to Toynbee's general wars. While they may be all engulfing, they turn out to be less than completely decisive. They are decisive in the negative sense that the aggressor's expansionary bid has been defeated. But the effort has been so societally exhausting that there is little or no energy left to create a new framework for international relations that fits the changes that have occurred since the last general war. Issues concerning international order that need attention are merely put aside. A "patched up peace" results instead.

The patched up peace suffices for a few years. Eventually, though, the issues that had gone unresolved after the general war lead to further conflict and a period of renewed warfare. The supplementary wars usually are less destructive and more constructive than the general war. Solutions to the issues that had been left unresolved earlier are developed. A more genuine period of peace prevails, at least for a while, until change throws the framework of international relations out of gear once again.

From Toynbee's perspective, this process has been repeated five times in modern history, as outlined in Table 2.2. Beginning in 1494 with the Valois–Habsburg feud over the control of Europe, the number of great powers in the system gradually expanded from an initial two (Valois France and the Habsburg Empire) in the Overture period to three in the 1550s (with the Spanish–Austrian split within the Habsburg Empire). The Netherlands and Sweden emerged in the first regular cycle only to be replaced by Britain and Prussia in the next repetition. A weakened Spain drops out in the second cycle. A strengthened Russia is coopted. Toward the end of the third cycle, Italy, the United States, and Japan brought the great power total to eight before it was reduced dramatically back to two in the fourth cycle.

TABLE 2.2
Toynbee's War and Peace Cycle in Modern Western History

Phase	Overture (1494–1568)	First regular cycle (1568–1672)	Second regular cycle (1672–1792)	Third regular cycle (1792–1914)	Fourth cycle (1914–)
Premonitory wars			1667–1668		1911–1912
The general war	1494–1525	1568–1609	1672–1713	1792–1815	1914–1918
The breathing space	1525–1536	1609–1618	1713–1733	1815–1848	1918–1939
Supplementary wars	1536–1559	1618–1648	1733–1763	1848–1871	1939–1945
The general peace	1559–1568	1648–1672	1763–1792	1871–1914	

SOURCE: Toynbee (1954, 255).

Gilpin and Hegemonic War

An important assumption underlying Gilpin's approach to explaining hegemonic war is the postulate that states

> will seek to change the international system through territorial, political, and economic expansion until the marginal costs of further change are equal to or greater than the marginal benefits. [Gilpin 1981, 10]

Given an uneven distribution of economic, technological and military capability, those states with relative advantages in these areas are the ones most likely to both perceive, and be confronted with, situations in which the incentives for seeking change and expansion are favorable (that is, benefits exceed costs). Among this favored elite of powerful actors, it is conceivable that one state will achieve so great a relative advantage that it will be in a position to dominate the system in which it operates.

Dominant or hegemonic powers provide systemic order and stability. As the most technologically advanced economic power, the "hegemon" has the most to gain from a smoothly functioning system; as a consequence, they govern their systems by providing rules for economic transactions and by protecting property rights. But they are not able to do so indefinitely. Simplifying what is a much more complex process, dominance entails new and rising costs. As the costs of hegemony escalate, the hegemon's surplus diminishes, as does its ability to underwrite its overhead costs. The ongoing diffusion of economic, technological, and military advantage also works to erode the hegemon's relative position.

At its conception, a sociopolitical system reflects the prevailing distribution of power. Actors in positions of greater relative power are likely to ensure that their own interests are protected and favored by the framework of relations that is established. A system's structure—as evidenced by the allocation of privileges, the division of territory, and the hierarchy of the pecking order—will all reflect the initial distribution of power.

The hegemonic wars, which are listed in Table 2.3, involve contests between declining dominant powers and ascending challengers that determine who will govern the system and how it will be governed. A decisive victory in the war can communicate rather graphically whose relative capabilities are superior. The dominant power's prestige in such cases is enhanced tremendously, and its legitimacy as the systemic governor is established. The more decisive the victory, the more likely it is that the postwar hierarchy will remain unambiguous for some period of time. The hegemon's prestige and legitimacy will also benefit by a clear-cut outcome to the war. A period of postwar peace and stability can also be anticipated if

TABLE 2.3
Gilpin's Modern Hegemonic Wars

Hegemonic war	Duration	Comments
Thirty Years' War	1618–1648	Habsburg bid for imperial hegemony finally defeated
Wars of Louis XIV	1667–1713	French bid for imperial hegemony defeated
French Revolutionary/ Napoleonic Wars	1792–1814	French bid for imperial hegemony defeated; Britain emerges as hegemonic power
World War I	1914–1918	First German challenge defeated
World War II	1939–1945	Second German challenge defeated; United States emerges as hegemonic power

SOURCE: Based on Gilpin's discussion (1981, 200).

a hegemon emerges from the struggle—something that, as Table 2.3 indicates, cannot be taken for granted.

Wallerstein and World Wars

As in the earlier cases of Toynbee and Gilpin, Wallerstein's perspective involves a number of arguments that are or can be regarded for present purposes as somewhat tangential to summarizing his theoretical position on world war. Focusing on the components that seem the most germane, Wallerstein views the period between 1450 and 1600/1650 as one of transition that involved the disintegration of feudalism in Western Europe, the emergence of a politically multicentric, capitalist world economy, and a downgrading of the economic significance of the Mediterranean and a parallel upgrading of Northwestern Europe. Northwestern Europe became more significant because it became the core of the world's economy, or the area in which productivity was most efficient.

Within the core, one state occasionally will seize the lead in agro-industrial productivity. Superiority in this realm tends to lead to dominance in commerce and finance as well. When one core state is simultaneously dominant in all three sectors, it can be said to have achieved hegemony in the world economy. Only three states—the Netherlands in the 1600s, Britain in the 1800s, and the United States in the mid-1900s—have achieved this unique and relatively short-lived status.

The rise and fall of hegemons is believed to be associated with phases of expansion and contraction in the world economy.[6] The capital-accumulation process in periods of expansion ultimately is blocked; supply exceeds demand and a phase of contraction or stagnation sets in. A variety of factors, including new markets, new products, and a restructuring of the interstate system, are needed to overcome the contraction phases.

These periods of expansion and contraction are tied to a four-phase model of hegemonic ascent and decline that is identified in Table 2.4. Hegemonic maturity is the phase of full hegemony, economic expansion, and limited conflict. It is preceded by two phases of hegemonic ascent. Ascending hegemony, another expansion period, is a period of acute conflict between the various contenders for dominance within the core. In the period of hegemonic victory, the next hegemonic power bypasses the declining, formerly dominant state. The final phase, declining hegemony, follows the era of maturity and is characterized by contraction, conflict between the hegemon and would-be successors, and attempts to establish monopolistic zones in the periphery.

Recently, Wallerstein (1984) developed a more explicit role for world wars that, as demonstrated in Table 2.4, overlap with the hegemonic maturity phase in the Dutch case and the hegemonic victory phase in the British and American cases.[7] The three world wars are described as hegemonic succession struggles between a land-based and sea- and/or air-based set of principal contenders. Roughly 30 years long, primarily fought on land, and engaging most of the system's major military powers, world wars serve several functions. First, the succession struggle is decided in favor of the sea- and/or air-based contender. Second, the development of that core power's superior position is facilitated by the economic gains achieved during the war. Finally, the hegemon's position is further consolidated by the restructuring of the interstate system after the war ends.

TABLE 2.4
Wallerstein's World Wars and Hegemonic Phases[a]

Hegemonic phases	Alpha cycle	Beta cycle	Gamma cycle
Ascending hegemony	1575–1590		1897–1913/20
Hegemonic victory	1590–1620	–1815	1913/20–1945
World wars	1618–1648	1792–1815	1914–1945
Hegemonic maturity	1620–1672	1815–1873	1945–1967
Hegemonic state	Netherlands	Britain	United States
Declining hegemony	1672–1700	1873–1897	1967–

SOURCE: Based on information in Research Working Group on Cyclical Rhythms and Secular Trends (1979, 499) and Wallerstein (1984, 37–46).

[a] We have modified the 1979 phase information where it conflicts with more recent information on hegemonic maturity dates found in the 1984 source. The implications of changing Britain's hegemonic tenure from 1850–1873 to 1815–1873, however, are unclear for the ascending and victory phases.

Comparing Four Perspectives on Systemic War

The preceding overview of some of the other ways of interpreting the occurrence of systemic warfare suggests important areas of overlap and divergence. Each perspective has a role for systemic warfare, but each also uses different terminology that signifies genuine differences in meaning. One perspective's general war is not really the same phenomenon as another perspective's hegemonic, world, or global war. All see some type of balance-of-power mechanism at work, but they do not see exactly the same mechanisms. Toynbee's general wars suppress bids for hegemony. Gilpin's hegemonic wars performed this function only between 1648 and 1792. After 1792, two out of three wars installed new hegemons. Wallerstein's world wars always facilitate the emergence of a hegemon. Global wars, by definition, defeat succession bids by continental powers and usher in new periods of world power leadership, periods that are based, in part, on the world power's sea power dominance.

There is near-perfect consensus among the group under review after 1792. One quibble concerns how best to treat the not-so-peaceful, 20-odd-year period between the end of World War I and the onset of World War II. Another is whether or not an ascendant Britain defeated a declining France, or if it was the other way around. Three of the four perspectives agree that the end of the 1600s and the beginning of the 1700s encompassed some type of systemic warfare. Prior to the triangular struggle between the Dutch, the English, and the French, much less agreement prevails. The Thirty Years' War (1618–1648) inaugurates Gilpin and Wallerstein's systemic warfare series. Toynbee viewed this same war as an epilogue to the earlier fighting that ended in 1608–1609. In contrast, long-cycle analysts view this admittedly lengthy and bloody set of wars as a regional war fought primarily over less-than-global issues. Adopting the Thirty Years' War as a point of commencement, of course, also means that the earlier candidates, the Italian/Indian Ocean Wars and the Dutch Independence Wars, must be ignored entirely.

Finally, the four perspectives have four very different visions of what is likely to take place in the future. None is deterministic and none argues that a future systemic war is inevitable. But Toynbee thought that the balance-of-power system had approached the point of total deterioration. The next general war was likely to either destroy the system or lead to a unitary empire, which would then have its own internal war cycle with which to contend. Gilpin, in contrast, thinks a new hegemonic war may be averted as long as the conditions surrounding the current bipolar standoff can be perpetuated. Wallerstein, on the other hand, thinks that such a perpetuation of the status quo is not only improbable, but also undesirable. The relative gains made by Japan, Western Europe, and China will continue and the world system will become more multipolar and more prone to a renewed hegemonic succession struggle. Only the demise or complete breakdown of the capitalist accumulation system may head off the need for another world war.

The long-cycle perspective agrees, in part, with Toynbee that another global war is likely to destroy the system. Unlike Gilpin's optimism, the probability of freezing change and suppressing the continued diffusion of power seems unlikely even if the diffusion process slows to a crawl. Some form of multipolarity in the not-too-distant future does seem probable. With the continuing deconcentration of global-reach capabilities, the likelihood of global war is increased. The way to head it off lies not so much in changing the basic nature of the world's economic system: What needs to be changed is the primitive, trial-by-combat approach to resolving global policy and leadership succession problems.

LONG-CYCLE THEORY AND RESEARCH PUZZLES IN INTERNATIONAL RELATIONS

Evaluating new theoretical frameworks for interpreting world politics can be accomplished by using the framework for suggesting solutions to extant research puzzles. The immediate question is not whether everyone agrees that a puzzle has been resolved for all time. After all, it is only human that there should be considerable resistance to new ways of viewing analytical questions. The more modest question to be entertained at this juncture is whether or not novel and plausible answers can be produced by looking at an empirical problem from a different slant. On this puzzle-solving dimension, we suggest that the long-cycle theory offers an ususually rich framework and that, in particular, considerable progress has been made in clarifying some of the major processes pertaining to the advent and impact of global war.

The Fundamental Cycles of War and Peace Puzzle

Perhaps the most fundamental research problem for which long-cycle theory can claim to offer a solution is the question of whether or not there is indeed such a thing as a war–peace cycle.[8] There have been a number of attempts at resolving this problem during the past 50 years or so (Sorokin 1937; Wright 1942, 1965; Moyal 1949; Richardson 1960a; Denton and

Phillips 1968; Singer and Small 1972; Singer and Cusack 1981; Small and Singer 1982; Levy 1983a; Goldstein 1985), and most of these efforts involved searching for statistical regularities in series of unweighted conflict data. The outcomes range from an absence of any discernible regularities to a variety of perceived cycles ranging in length from 20 to 200 years. The sheer variety in the outcomes, to some extent, can be traced to the different data bases and the different time periods inspected. But a more basic reason for vastly different periodicities and the general lack of empirical progress in this area has been the extreme open endedness of the examinations.

If there were strong reasons to expect a strict periodicity in conflict or warfare per se, inductive modeling approaches might be expected to isolate them. However, the theoretical arguments about cyclicality, for example Toynbee's (1954) argument discussed earlier, frequently are not framed in such a way that we should expect the number of battles, wars, or battle-related fatalities to oscillate in a patterned fashion. On the contrary, the theoretical arguments often talk about recurring types of wars or wars that serve some type of systemic function. They may be said to preserve the balance of power, determine leadership-succession struggles, or reorganize the system to better facilitate renewed economic growth. But they are not simply wars or even the most deadly wars or the only deadly wars. Some type of theoretical weighting operation or differentiation is required to filter some of the chaff and noise that is inevitable in series measuring conflict in general.

Still, it is true that the arguments that do differentiate warfare by role or function do not exactly share a consensus on each of the wars that represent the most significant watersheds in modern systemic history. What is unique to long-cycle analyses, at least so far, is that its candidates for global war status have been empirically validated.

Utilizing a 500-year series on the concentration of naval power (Modelski and Thompson 1988) that is based on an inventory of the capital ships of the navies of the global powers in the modern period, it is possible to employ time-series techniques to assess the extent to which each war that is identified as a global war is associated with a significant postwar reconcentration of global-reach capability. It is also possible to check whether or not the war candidates put forward by other frameworks have a reconcentrating impact as well.

Thompson and Rasler (1988) are able to demonstrate that each global war does lead to a statistically significant increase in the global system's level of capability concentration. Figure 2.1 illustrates this finding by showing the percentage share of warships held by the world power (that is, the global power in the position of leadership). It shows five recurring peaks of sea power concentration that match quite closely the "World Power"

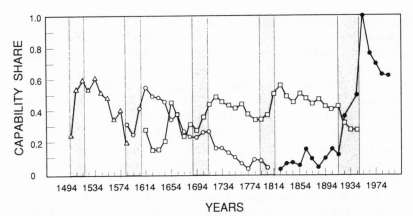

FIGURE 2.1. *Decennial observations of the global system's level of capability concentration as reflected by the percentage share of capital warships held by the world power.* △, *Portugal;* ○, *the Netherlands;* □, *England/Britain;* ●, *United States. Global war periods are shaded.*

column in Table 2.1 and four distinct troughs, which correspond to phases of delegitimation and deconcentration. Other wars that are most frequently put forward as rival candidates—the Thirty Years' War (1618–1648), the Franco-Dutch War (1672–1678), the Wars of Jenkin's Ear and the Austrian Succession (1739–1748), and the Seven Years' War (1755–1763)—failed this reconcentration test. None of these wars was associated with a significant capability concentration at the global level.

Thus, in order to resolve questions pertaining to the possibility of the existence of cycles of war and peace, it is first necessary to specify what types of wars are believed to be recurring. Global wars are wars that determine succession struggles and usher in new leaders of the global political system and new phases of relatively highly concentrated global-reach capabilities. With this assertion in hand, it becomes a straightforward empirical question as to which wars are associated with reconcentration and which are not. The global wars of long-cycle theory have been validated as belonging, uniquely, to the former category.

The Polarity–Stability Puzzle

The crux of the polarity–stability problem has been seen as one pitting the merits and liabilities of bipolar vs. multipolar systems (Deutsch and Singer 1964; Waltz 1964, 1979). Multipolar systems are thought by some to be more complex arenas. The greater the number of great powers, the more difficult it is supposed to be to concentrate on a single adversary. A more diffused distribution of power should also facilitate the emergence of cross-cutting cleavages. The chances of wars becoming so intense that the system erupts into a destabilizing conflict that threatens the existence of the system, therefore, are less in multipolar systems than in bipolar ones.

Bipolar advocates stress the advantages of less complex, more rigid, two-principal-actor systems. Decisionmaker uncertainty should be lower in bipolar systems than in multipolar ones. The main adversary is obvious, and what must be done to adjust to the opposition's gains is not likely to be as unclear as is the case in the murkier multipolar systems. The certainties of bipolarity are also supposed to work toward promoting actor self-restraint. The relative uncertainties of multipolarity, in contrast, lead to more frequent competition and conflict.

These arguments over the number of poles and the consequences of uncertainty overlook several important facets of structural history. By dwelling only on bipolarity and multipolarity, an important third structural alternative, unipolarity, is omitted altogether. In comparison with bi- and multipolarity, the stability advantages as well as the empirical record of unipolarity is quite impressive. Warfare between the global powers is least likely during the unipolar years that, in terms of global-reach capabilities, are more common than is frequently supposed (Thompson 1986).

Introducing the notion of postwar unipolarity also emphasizes another characteristic of polarity structures—they do not persist forever. From a long-cycle perspective, postwar unipolarity has repeatedly given way to bipolarity and multipolarity. Yet these other structural categories are temporary too. It is also instructive to note that both bipolarity and multipolarity have preceded the advent of global war and, in time, the return of a unipolar phase. Multipolarity has, in fact, provided the most common structural environment for global war, but it is structural change and transformation that reflects the true norm. As such, they are also the ultimate sources of systemic destabilization.

The Preponderance–Parity Puzzle

Related to the debates over polarity are the disagreements surrounding the relationship between power concentration and conflict levels. One way to look at the controversy is to again focus on decisionmaker uncertainty. Deconcentration increases the level of uncertainty, but, as observed in the polarity debates, analysts disagree over whether more or less uncertainty encourages an increase in the probability of conflict and war. The major empirical test of this dispute (Singer *et al.* 1972), however, found support for both sides of the argument. Their nineteenth century evidence strongly supported the conclusion that capability concentration and an ongoing war are positively correlated. Yet a weak, negative correlation was found to characterize the same relationship during the twentieth century.

Why should the relationship change signs over time? Do the strong nineteenth century findings contradict the long-cycle argument that instability increases as capability concentration erodes?[9] The answer is that it depends on how one approaches the question. Thompson (1983b) demonstrates that the Singer *et al.* (1972) findings rest upon a set of assumptions pertaining to the actors that were looked at (great powers), the time period investigated (1820–1964), which capabilities were measured (six equally weighted demographic, military, and industrial indicators), and how warfare was measured (nation-months of participation by all states).

A long-cycle perspective leads to a modification of these research design decisions. The time period examined should be pushed back at least 4 years to the end of the Napoleonic Wars. Some marginal great powers, such as Austria and Italy, can be excluded from the power concentration calculation. Naval capabilities are distributed differently than other capability indicators, such as urban population or army size. Since a focus on the nation-months of war participation by all states leads to the conclusion that the Korean War was a more severe war than World War I, it is worth considering a more restricted focus on the duration of global power war participation. Once these analytical changes are introduced, the test outcome changes radically. Regardless of how (or if) the 1816–1964 time period is divided, the relationship between capability concentration and ongoing warfare is consistently negative, which supports the preponderance and long-cycle arguments.

The Transition and Succession Puzzle

Organski (1968) proposed an intriguing model relating the structural conditions for war and peace to the degree of asymmetry in the relative positions of a system's powerful and satisfied actors as opposed to powerful and dissatisfied challengers. Siding with the preponderance camp, Organski argues that war becomes increasingly likely as a challenger's strength begins to approximate the position of the system's dominant power. Even so, challengers miscalculate and tend to attack prematurely, thereby helping to seal their own fate. Organski and Kugler (1980) tested this proposition; they argued, however, that not only was rough equality the most dangerous condition but also that challengers probably won sooner or later. The 1980 study performs an empirical test of these arguments for the post-1860 period and generates findings supportive of the rough equality reinterpretation. Nevertheless, the test is one that is difficult to interpret because of a number of debatable analytical assumptions, including equating the 1870–1871 Franco-German and 1904–1905 Russo-Japanese "transitions" with the transitions related to World Wars I and II and excluding the United States from the analysis until after 1945.

When the transition model is applied to nearly 500 years of fluctuations in the sea power positions of the global powers (Thompson, 1983a), a different picture develops from the outcome reported in Organski and Kugler's analysis. Immediately prior to the outbreak of global war, it is not unusual (but not always the case) for the challenger's position to be on the ascent and the world power's relative position to be in decline. This, however, does not mean that a dissatisfied number two power is likely to attack the fading lead power. With the partial exception of the period immediately prior to 1792, the global war situation tends to be basically triangular in the sense that one rising continental power tends to be confronted by two maritime powers. Since the seventeenth century, one of the two maritime powers is the system's declining world power. The other maritime power is its eventual successor.

Within this context, the challenger's attack may or may not seem premature if one looks only at the declining world power's position. It definitely appears premature, however, when the challenger's position is compared to both of its ultimate maritime opponents. Admittedly, the contest is not determined by naval capabilities alone, but the asymmetry in naval positions does help to explain the decisive outcome in favor of the maritime coalition.

The outcome also suggests that the original transition model over-simplifies what is taking place. Rather than a dissatisfied challenger biding its time until it is ready to supplant the system leader, continental challengers make bids for regional primacy without fully appreciating the likely identity of their ultimate maritime or global opposition. Some regional wars become global wars only after the leading maritime powers realize that the challenger's regional success will create a more competitive base for mounting a genuine global challenge. In this respect, it is a future, two-step threat of transition in the global layer that provokes a structural crisis for the global political system. The maritime powers enter the war ("globalizing" it in the process) in order to ensure that the regional threat does not become a global reality.

The Domestic Impact of War Puzzle

That wars have a variety of impacts on the societies that wage them is not a particularly controversial proposal (see, for example, Stein and Russett 1980). Analysts disagree, however, on which specific wars had what types of impact on which particular set of countries. Was the U.S. involvement in the Indochinese wars of the 1960s and 1970s unusually inflationary for the American and world economies? To what extent did the fledgling American motor vehicle industry benefit from the increase in demand associated with World War I (World War II)? Did German aerial bombing and its consequent effects on social solidarity pave the attitudinal way for the postwar expansion of the British welfare system? How significant were the French Revolutionary and Napoleonic Wars to the advent of the late eighteenth/early nineteenth century Industrial Revolution in Britain? Or, more generally, to what extent do states owe their very existence and institutional forms to preparations for, and participation in, warfare? Is the economic impact of warfare episodic, random, and temporary in nature— not unlike other natural disasters such as floods or storms?

Many of these specific and general questions are unlikely to be resolved completely in the very near future. There is simply too much ground that needs to be covered. But long-cycle theory has made a contribution to this literature by demonstrating the recurring impact of global wars on the global political system's principal actors. The competition among these states for international position, access to various parts of the non-European world, and security from retaliation at home and abroad were major reasons for creating European states in the first place. Effective state organizations became necessary, although not sufficient, prerequisites for doing well in global politics. They also became critical for winning global wars.

Global wars, in turn, have served as a repetitive impulse for expanding the scale of the state's activities in terms of spending, taxes, and public debt (Rasler and Thompson 1983, 1985a, 1989). In part because global wars are now such intensive affairs and because the stakes are so high, the point to be stressed is that global war, in contrast to other types of interstate blood-letting, is the most likely to influence the "state making" of the system's most powerful actors. As a consequence, major power state making tends not to be a matter of linear progression, but a more spasmodic, step–level pattern punctuated by the sequential impacts of global wars.

In addition to domestic political systems, the economies are significantly influenced as well. For instance, global wars tend to facilitate the ascent of the world power's leading economic sectors (Thompson 1988), an important aspect of that state's lead in industrial innovation and dynamic growth.

The overall pace of economic growth, nonetheless, appears to be only temporarily influenced along fairly predictable lines—positively for the winners and negatively for the losers—although global wars have created permanent economic losers from the ranks of both the military losers and winners (Rasler and Thompson 1985b). Global wars also have had dramatic effects on inflationary pressures on economies at both national and world levels. In this fashion, global wars have been demonstrated to be critical components in long-term, *Kondratieff* price fluctuations (Modelski 1981, 1982; Thompson and Zuk 1982).

Not all of these findings are novel. A number of authors have argued that wars are crucial to state making and economic growth. What long-cycle analyses are able to demonstrate empirically is that it is the patterned sequence of global wars, not just wars in general, that is critical in connecting activities than are "external" to the state with the political and economic phenomena that are far too often regarded as purely "internal" in nature.

CONTINUING QUESTIONS

We have now established the distinctiveness of our approach and pointed out the ways in which it may help to solve some of the major puzzles in the study of world politics. In this last section, we turn to other matters that are likely to absorb our attention in the future.

First, we shall raise some questions regarding the study of global wars in general; then, to round out the discussion, we shall take a look at a range of remaining, though far from minor, research problems. We must start, though, with a brief look at the "causes-of-war" puzzle.

Causes-of-War Puzzle?

Traditionally, studying the problem of war centers around the problem of causation. A war is to be explained by its causes, and preventing war amounts to dealing with these causes. Hence, a substantial portion of the literature, as represented classically by Quincy Wright's *Study of War* (1942), deals with causes: political, economic, and so on.

Those seriously considering the idea of oscillations or rhythm in world politics, of pulsations that govern the long-term time structure of this process within which individual choices must be made, attach less importance to the causes-of-war riddle.

If global war is indeed an essential part of the basic pulse of the global political process, then its occurrence is not really surprising. If it is a component of the long cycle, then, in certain defined portions of the cycle, war is to be expected. The precise circumstances of such occurrences need to be clarified; the triggering mechanisms must be understood, and the economic, social, and cultural conditions surrounding it must be investigated. Unequal (that is, differential) growth will be noticed and will be seen to be linked to the rise of the challengers and, hence, to the potential for major confrontation. Generational turnover will need to be considered.

But if global war can be viewed, basically, as a macrodecision (that is, as a quasi-electoral process, a phase in which the global system selects a new management group and a new program of basic policies), then its occurrence is not really surprising. Students of electoral or party politics do not ask "What causes elections?" because it is obviously not their central concern. Recurring elections in a well-functioning political system do not require social-scientific explanations. In some systems, such as the United States, the timing of elections is, in most cases, a routinized part of a fixed political calendar; in other systems, such as the British, the prime minister has some, but not much, leeway in choosing the date of the election. In our argument, global wars are likewise part of the political calendar. If there is merit in regarding global wars as a form of macrodecision, the puzzle over its causes assumes a much reduced, if not a minor, form.

In reality, a reformulation of the question is needed. In a most basic sense, the "cause" of a global war is the absence of an alternative. In that perspective, past global wars have been caused by the lack of a substitute mechanism of global decisionmaking. So far, such a mechanism has not been conceivable, let alone available.

Comparative Study of Global Wars

If we decide to bypass the causes-of-war question as possibly fruitless or resolved by a concept of long cycles, then the substance of our work begins with the comparative study of global wars.

John Stuart Mill formulated the essence of the comparative method in the sciences as consisting in the search for similarities and differences. In the study of our subject we take the population of the five global wars of the modern world system and ask what properties they have in common, how they differ, and why. We search for the similarities and differences among global wars.

Global wars are similar for two reasons, because they differ from all other wars and because they are isomorphic (similar in structure) in some of their essential properties. Global wars differ among themselves because they show a pattern of rising evolutionary complexity.

THE DISTINCTIVENESS OF GLOBAL WARS
Global wars are, in our view, distinctive (that is, different from all other wars) for the following reasons:

1. they are a particularly virulent form of global conflict;
2. they are located in a distinct system: the global system; and
3. they form the macrodecision phase of the behavior of the global political system.

In the first place, global wars are a form of global conflict; in fact, they are its most prominent and protracted form. But they are not its only form. In the years since 1945, for instance, the cold war has constituted a lesser form of global conflict. Global conflicts can be found in all the four phases of the long cycle, but they assume the sharpest character in the phase of global war.

The intensity of conflicts is commonly measured by the number of casualties—or the cost in human life—associated with them. It is now fairly well established that global wars are those that have accounted for the greatest loss of life. One estimate that compares the total battle fatalities of interstate war between 1494 and 1945 with those inflicted in that period by global wars alone reaches the impressive finding that the latter, the five major conflicts that are our special concern, account for close to 80 percent of the total (Modelski and Morgan 1985, 398). In other words, just a few of perhaps a 100 or more wars account for the bulk of the loss of life.

Such estimates are admittedly imprecise, if only because the loss of life in the conflicts of earlier centuries is notoriously difficult to determine (and, possibly, even ultimately unknowable). Certainly more work on this question is called for. What we need, more basically, is a set of data that would depict global conflict for the entire span of modern politics. We need a global conflict series that would tell us about the intensity of conflict at the global level for each year since 1494. To do that we must (1) distinguish, operationally, global from regional and national conflicts and (2) distinguish effectively among global conflicts according to their degree of intensity. Such a series should confirm our suspicion that a "global conflict dimension" will show exceptionally high readings at times of global war and lower readings in the other phases of the long cycle.

We have just alluded to the need for distinguishing global from regional wars, and this brings us to the next criterion of distinctiveness. The study of long cycles does not purport to illuminate directly events at the regional or national levels. In particular, it does not describe European interstate politics as it is conventionally pictured in history texts even though, in the first four cycles, much of the substance of the process centers on Western Europe, a region that constitutes the active zone, the headquarters as it were, of the global system.

But that does not mean that, in relation to this area we cannot distinguish between global and regional politics (in general) and global and regional wars (in particular). For instance, while Portugal's efforts upon the oceans circa 1510 clearly occupy the global level, the protracted Franco-Spanish wars over, and in, Italy are largely, though not exclusively, to be understood as a conflict for regional mastery, a conflict basically of regional significance. The Thirty Years' War (1618–1648), which is so powerfully imprinted upon the consciousness of Central Europe to this day, was, at best, a European regional conflagration; more properly, it might be called a German civil war with strong external interventions. The Iran–Iraq war of the 1980s is a particularly striking instance of a regional war.

Whatever happened in Western Europe at that time, of course, obviously did have some significance for the entire world system, if only by way of example. For the purpose of analysis though, we need to make, and keep, these distinctions, and the distinction between global and regional wars is a very basic one. In part, the capacity to make that distinction is, of course, a function of the state of the world system. One of the processes that the world system undergoes is that of differentiation. From 1494 onward it is possible to talk about an emerging global system not only because of Portuguese activities on the oceans and Spain's efforts across the Atlantic, but also because the distinctiveness of these efforts was, in that year, recognized for the first time in a formal agreement: the treaty of Tordesillas. Over the years, the Portuguese–Spanish global system first consolidated, then came under attack, and, in the end, was largely supplanted by later Dutch and British initiatives. These, in turn, gave the system even greater weight so that, by the twentieth century, global interactions have come to form a substantial part of world organization. The weightier the global system, the clearer the distinction we can draw between the conflicts located within it and those located outside of it.

That is why we make so much fuss about the years around 1500. They mark the onset of a more complex organization of world affairs that was brought about by a process of vertical differentiation and that, in its train, created not only a distinctly global system, but also new forms of organization at the regional, national, and local levels of politics and economics.

While this differentiation started spectacularly some time ago with the age of discoveries, it need not be regarded as having reached completion. The four levels of interaction that we have distinguished are not yet as fully organized and, therefore, not yet as clearly distinct as we might wish them to be for the purposes of a clear analysis (or as clear as they might yet become in the future). But the fourfold structure can be perceived at the moment of birth of the modern epoch. If we are alert and look for it, then our concepts make the search easier and our analysis sharper, and they help us to draw, among other things, the basic distinction between global and regional wars. Global wars decide the constitution of the global system; regional wars concern regional organization.

The Western European setting of long cycles applies only to the first four of them. Since 1945, but in a movement that could be anticipated (and was anticipated by acute observers in the nineteenth century, including Alexis de Tocqueville in the 1830s), the active center of the global system has moved away from Western Europe, to North America. The fifth cycle, in at least some respects, therefore differs from the preceding four and marks a new era of world politics. The character of global conflicts has been affected by that shift as well.

Last, global wars are distinctive because they may be regarded as a form of macrodecision for the global system. We began our account by pointing to the fourfold structure of the long cycle as one of its key characteristics, and we can now use that phase structure as an aid to this argument.

The basic fact about global politics as viewed in the long-cycle perspective is that it reveals features that are not only cyclical but also strongly evolutionary. It is already quite remarkable that global wars have repeated themselves in the modern world in a decidedly regular pattern. What is more, each has been greater and more complex than the preceding one, and the underlying system also has grown: not linearly, but stepwise, in punctuated form, with the global wars acting as the principal form of punctuation.

For an evolving system of that kind, an evolutionary learning model supplies an explanation. It argues that expanding social systems need to pass through a regular sequence of phases, a sequence that is governed by the functional requirements of that system and by the logic of the evolutionary process. Parsonian macrosociology suggests that each of the four functional requirements responds to one phase of that process, and evolutionary theory can be read as suggesting that such a system needs to experience both the generation of variety and the working of mechanisms of selection. Both can be found in the phase structure of the long cycle (Modelski 1987c).

From these perspectives the global-war phase of the long cycle might be interpreted as a phase of "macrodecision," that is, as one during which the system undergoes a collective decision that "selects" from the available candidates for leadership, and from the available programs for the future of the global system. Past global wars have selected such leadership and have embodied programatic choices—hence, their importance.

THE ISOMORPHISMS OF GLOBAL WARS

A preliminary review of the evidence suggests that our five global wars have been significantly isomorphic. In fact, the hypothesis could be advanced (and seriously defended) that they have basically been repeated replays of one basic theme: one grand war fought several times over (Modelski 1984, 1986). Let us examine briefly just one striking instance of that isomorphism: *the winners and losers of the global wars puzzle*.

A most interesting puzzle arises out of a close study of global wars, one that concerns winners and losers. The winning coalitions and the losing side of these great combats have been summarized, in short-hand form, in Table 2.5. On the left-hand side are the global powers who won; on the right, those who lost. Broadly speaking, the winners have been members of the oceanic coalition, and the losers have been continental powers. England (or Britain) has invariably been a member of the team of winners, and the same may also mostly be said about Portugal, the Netherlands, and the United States. In other words, it is not farfetched to suggest that the same side, even the same states, won all the past five global wars, and that the continental challengers inevitably lost, which is indeed food for thought for those who might be thinking about a hypothetical sixth global war.

This is a striking and surprising insight, and it reveals a degree of organization in the global system that goes far beyond the conceptions of anarchy that are currently in vogue. Many students now approach wars as if they were instances in a large-scale process of random choice, as though fate or nature were tossing coins to determine who might lose or win a normally distributed sequence of confrontations. But if this were the case, should not prominent states be expected to share about equally in both the wins and the losses? In marked contrast, the five global wars exhibit a disconcerting degree of similarity in participants, duration, location, and outcome. But these facts should be disconcerting only to those who shy away from the idea of regularity and repetition.

TABLE 2.5
Winners and Losers of Global Wars

Global war	Winning coalition (summary)	Challenger
1	Portugal, England, Burgundy, Spain	France
2	U.P. Netherlands, England, France	Spain
3	England, U.P. Netherlands	France
4	Britain, Russia	France
5	United States, Britain, Russia/USSR	Germany

SOURCE: Modelski (1984, 1986).

How might we explain this regularity, this persistence of oceanic victories? One thought that suggests itself is to maintain that the lead powers of the world system, as the principal global problem solvers, have been privileged in the evolutionary sense and, for that reason, have prevailed. A complementary explanation might be derived from the observation that the world powers have never had a completely free run, even in their own cycle. Their ascendancy, so demonstrably convincing at the end of the global war, soon encounters (usually in one regional context) a challenge, a strong competitor. For example, Britain's role in Europe after 1860 was decisively eclipsed by the rise of Germany; that of the Dutch in the 1600s was eclipsed by the power of France under Richelieu and Louis XIV. In other words an internal fluctuation between world powers and challengers that could serve to attenuate the starkness of the trend toward a persistence of oceanic victories might be built into the long cycle. But the question calls for more analysis, especially because it invites extrapolating the future. It is one of the cardinal puzzles of world politics.

Another interesting example of isomorphism is the question of *Russian* participation in global wars. In at least three of our five global wars, Russia played a distinct, important and yet also structurally similar role. Not only was Russia a member of the winning coalition in all three (see Table 2.5; indirectly so in the wars of Louis XIV), she also (1) suffered initial defeats at the hands of the continental challenger (in the case of the wars of the Grand Alliance, by France's ally Sweden), (2) reached a temporary accommodation with the challenger, (3) experienced extensive invasions of her home territory, (4) underwent dramatic reorganization, and (5) emerged, ultimately, in a greatly enhanced international position—in the last two instances as a key member of the winning side (Juday 1985).

This pattern could be extended even further. At the time of the Spanish–Dutch Wars (1580–1609), Russia experienced a "time of troubles," a period of internal turmoil that brought foreign intervention that was linked to the global war alignments, intervention that even reached Moscow. In response to outside pressure the Romanovs emerged as the new native dynasty (1613) that was to be overthrown three global wars later.

The massive Russian landmass on the borders of Europe makes it likely that she would be involved in every global war that was fought over (and in) Europe when it was the active zone of the world system. But are we entitled to project such a role into the future, now that the Soviet Union herself has emerged as the principal challenger, in a world system whose active zone is no longer parochially European?

THE DIFFERENCES AMONG GLOBAL WARS

So far, we have stressed the similarities among the five global wars, but their differences are striking too. Although it goes without saying that every global war must necessarily be *sui generis* in some respects, we have also noticed the striking fact that, as we look closer, the differences between these events are systematic as well. We observe that each successive global war was larger (for example, in terms of the size of the armies and the participation in coalitions) and more costly in lives and resources. Each was also more complex and more pervasive than the preceding one.

One illustration relates to the size of the battles: the major land and sea battles of the Italian and Indian Ocean Wars involved, at most, 50,000 men; those of Louis XIV exceeded 100,000 men, and both world wars involved over 1,000,000. A parallel progression can be seen in respect to casualties. Another illustration concerns the diplomatic process. In 1500 residential embassies were largely unknown outside Italy, and the procedures of diplomacy were quite rudimentary; in the twentieth century, diplomacy is a most elaborate system, and the settlements produced by it are complex and have greater staying power.

The growth in the size and complexity of wars suggests, as mentioned earlier, an evolutionary process. Like the rest of the system, global wars have been subject to evolution—political, social and cultural. They have grown and expanded at least in step with the rest of the world system. Once again, provocative questions arise if the trends are to be properly appreciated. A deeper understanding of such trends requires a thorough investigation of the evolutionary hypothesis.

The Question of Alternatives to Global War

A principal question facing global-war researchers is that of alternatives. The problem of alternatives is, by itself, not unfamiliar to students of war. William James posed it in a widely noticed essay in the years just before the outbreak of the last global war, but the way he formulated it did not prove to be immediately fruitful. The study of long cycles suggests that the problem of finding a substitute for *all wars* may be too diffuse and wide ranging to be practicable. Instead, we need to focus on a narrower problem, the problem of finding an alternative to the next *global* war; in other words, we must concentrate on just one war.

We have already pointed out that the theory of long cycles does not view another global war as inevitable. No part of it suggests the necessity of another global conflict fought by means of ultimate violence. But it does suggest two other things: (1) that an evolutionary learning process does, from time to time, require macrodecisions and (2) that these macrodecisions can be either violent or nonviolent. How might the transition from a violent to a nonviolent form of macrodecision in the global system be engineered?

The premise of this analysis is the "normality" of global wars. In a recent commentary on long cycles and related arguments, Kal Holsti (1985, 682–684) argues that "the great wars of the system were not a consequence of its normal operation" because they were caused by those "who wanted to destroy" the international system. When the system operates normally, he argues, "it does not produce hegemonic war, or at least does so with little frequency"; hence, the "contemporary state system is not . . . a system which will inevitably generate hegemonic wars."

Holsti's argument has two parts: one about the past and the other about the future. As for the past, can it be convincingly argued that the great wars of the modern system were not part of its normal operation? Can wars that are fought to maintain, preserve, and assure the survival of a system be called abnormal? It seems unlikely. Operations of self-maintenance are necessary components of all systems, and it is wrong to dismiss the major conflicts of the past as a form of aberration, especially because their recurrence points to an underlying necessity: the need to reach systemic macrodecisions.

As for the future, we agree that there is no inevitability about the big war. Nothing in the study of long cycles requires—or even implies—that a sixth global war is inevitable. But we find little comfort in the assertion that the system produces such wars with "little frequency." Because one single such war might be quite enough, we maintain that, unless substitutes are developed for the violent components of the macrodecision mechanisms, the tendency for such a war to occur will continue.

The clearest example of a relatively nonviolent, systemic decision mechanism is an electoral process. Global wars strongly exhibit features of such a process: they were contests between rival parties (coalitions) that sought to execute rival platforms for the future of the global system, they were struggles for a perceived vacancy in the office of global leadership, and they ended up with a legitimately chosen occupant for such a position. On the other hand, an election, like global wars, is also in part a trial of strength, and it is the majority (that is, the stronger party) that carries the day. Riots and public disturbances are not unknown in national electoral campaigns or when votes are cast. But in an election, even though the consequences are real, the contest is conducted primarily at the symbolic level; in global wars, however, the combatants believe that each and every instrument of violence, up to and including the most destructive ones, is appropriate. Theory and reflection, therefore, suggest that a shift from violent to symbolic forms of combat needs to be effected within the global macrodecision process. Some of the problems arising from that formulation are discussed in Modelski (1987a), but the basic problem of discovering—or inventing and installing—a viable alternative macrodecision mechanism in the global system remains.

The Nuclear Deterrence Puzzle

Students of international politics have recently been congratulating themselves on the fact that four decades have now elapsed since the end of the last global war. Regarding such a period of general peace as unprecedented in recent international experience they have, as have major political leaders, attributed it to the condition known as nuclear deterrence. Coral Bell (1985, 37), for instance, has distilled from the world's experience since 1945 the following recipe for avoiding hostilities between the "central" powers: "prudent crisis management in a situation of . . . mutual deterrence." Samuel Huntington (1986, 9) congratulates us on "this 40 years of success in preventing nuclear war," viewing it as "one of our few success stories"; he is confident that "we know how to do it."

These views reflect the growing conviction that the mere existence of nuclear arsenals, prudently managed, has preserved general peace, and that the maintenance of such arsenals is a necessary condition of continuing to maintain peace at the global level. Has nuclear deterrence already proved itself a substitute for global nuclear war?

From the perspective of long cycles that verdict must remain "unproven" for at least another 50 years. In the experience of the modern world system, global wars have occurred at intervals of some 80 years, and, therefore, the prevalence of general peace (though not peace at the regional or national levels) in the last 40-odd years is entirely unsurprising. The role of nuclear deterrence in relation to it is unclear:

> Has deterrence induced prudence by great powers since 1945, or has it been that an era of great power prudence has made it seem that deterrence is working? From the long cycle perspective, the most promising period for attempting deterrence would be the post-global-war phase of the long cycle, for that is when major power wars are least likely. Hence the irony in the frequent assertion that, whatever its defects, nuclear deterrence has at least prevented World War III, when this is less the product of deterrence than the consequence of passing through the most propitious phase of the long cycle. In fact, it is not easy to find hard evidence that deterrence really exists and is working. [Modelski and Morgan 1985, 410]

More to the point is the thought that the probability of global war might gradually rise in the next 40 years. If and when that occurs, will nuclear deterrence continue to work? Will it continue to inspire confidence? On those points doubts are entirely in order. Deterrence is not a decision mechanism but, rather, a means of deferring decisions. It is an architecture of stalemate, and a stalemated global system is, in the long run, incompatible with the process of evolutionary learning. The puzzle is this: How can nuclear deterrence be squared with the need for global macrodecision?

How Do We Recognize a Global War Ex Ante?

Of necessity, students of global wars deal mostly with past such events, and, *ex post*, they do not find it too difficult to recognize a global war when they see it. But those who try to think about the future confront this question: How do we recognize a global war when we see it is coming? Is it at all possible to determine more specifically whether, how, and from what direction such a war might be approaching, or must we be on the alert all of the time, watching each and every conflict for the possibility of escalation, ceaselessly scrutinizing the global horizon for every little cloud from which a major storm might descend.

The problem of forecasting global war must obviously be a key element in the strategic planning of all global powers because the degree of readiness of the forces and the intensity of preparation and mobilization must, in part, be a function of the perceived danger of such a war. For instance, in 1932, British war planning shifted to an assumption of a major war "in the next 10 years." That was pretty close, although not close enough because such a war did indeed break out 7 years later. In 1950–1951 U.S. strategic planners forecast a global war within the next 5 years (Prados 1986). This turned out to be wrong. U.S. war plans continue to require readiness to fight at least one major war on fairly short notice, which implies the assumption of a finite, and fairly positive, probability of such an emergency within the planning period.

The methodology of forecasting the next global war is obviously not well advanced, but it could conceivably benefit from the insights yielded by the theory of long cycles. Our approach suggests the following:

1. The "older" or more advanced the long cycle (the higher the number of years elapsed since the end of the last global war), the greater the probability of the outbreak of another global war, with the highest probability at the end of the phase of coalitioning (deconcentration).

2. Conflicts that threaten the stability of the active zone of the global system (including Western Europe and Japan) have a higher likelihood of triggering the next global war.

3. The probability of the next global war must be discounted by the

effect of processes or measures tending to establish a substitute mechanism of global decisionmaking.

All this would suggest that the high war-readiness military postures of the past 40 years may have been unproductive. Their value in the next 40 years will depend on the development of alternatives.

The Kantian Hypothesis

Students of international relations have long been familiar with Immanuel Kant's famous if somewhat sketchy argument for *Perpetual Peace*, published in 1795. Writing amidst global war, in conditions of political instability and, indeed, of revolutionary turmoil, the philosopher of the Enlightenment put forward a hypothesis that might be formulated as maintaining that

> there exists in the world system a self-organizing social process tending to bring about a condition of perpetual peace.

To substantiate this hypothesis, Kant proposed three mechanisms by which, over the long run of system time, such a condition might be effectuated: (1) the formation of republican regimes, (2) a union of free states (that is, no world empire), and (3) the growth of commerce.

Students of long cycles will find these mechanisms quite familiar. The lead powers of the long cycle have been republican regimes in the sense that they lacked an absolute ruler and maintained systems of government that were liberal in complexion. These states have been forming a gradually expanding community of democratic states within which war has been absent and the practice of peace nearly universal. In contrast, their challengers have been, in their main thrust, absolutist and authoritarian, and, as a rule, they aimed at imperial forms of rule. The world powers tended to uphold the independence of states, and they promoted a variety of forms of international organizations and waged wars to secure that aim. Last, the world powers have fostered arrangements conducive to an expansion of commerce; they have been, in their own economies, the motors of innovation and, consequently, of world trade (Modelski 1987b). Is the long cycle the Kantian process?

The arguments, at this point, may not yet be conclusive. A good question to ask is whether or not the Kantian hypothesis can be falsified (and if so, how?). Are the mechanisms Kant specified (republican government and so forth) sufficiently general to account for the process? Are they the only such mechanisms, or are there others? How does the Kantian process fit into the evolution of the world system? Is the long cycle indeed the Kantian process?

For students of long cycles and global wars, these are basic questions needing further specification. But they are also exciting questions that take us beyond the standard and, so far, infertile categories of the search for general peace.[10]

NOTES

1. George Modelski was, in 1987–88, Fellow-in-Residence at the Netherlands Institute for Advanced Study in the Humanities and the Social Sciences (NIAS) at Wassenaar, and in the spring of 1988 he visited the University of Stockholm. His project on "Global wars in the modern world system" was supported by the United States Institute of Peace under grant USIP-130. The opinions expressed in the joint contribution to this volume are those of the authors alone and do not necessarily reflect the views of the Institute.

2. We employ the term global politics not because it is less homely or more holistic than "international politics" but because it enables us to distinguish the politics of the global system from those at the regional, national, and local levels and, therefore, makes for sharper analysis.

3. The labeling of the phases reflects the analytical perspective employed. Here we adopt the labels of the evolutionary learning model, as shown in Table 2.1, and place in brackets the equivalent terms of the original "systemic" perspective (global war, world power, delegitimation, and deconcentration).

4. Levy (1985) contends that we should leave the outcome open ended when defining systemic war and that the definitional emphasis should be placed instead on battle deaths and the extent of participation. A rebuttal to this argument can be found in Thompson and Rasler (1988).

5. In any event, these contrasts have been drawn elsewhere (see Thompson 1988).

6. It should be noted that similar long-term economic fluctuations play explanatory roles in the frameworks advanced by Toynbee's war and peace cycle and the leadership long cycle. They are not quite as critical to understanding the central theoretical argument on warfare in the two other perspectives as they are in the world economy argument. Gilpin (1987), on the other hand, rules out any explanatory role for *Kondratieff*-like fluctuations. Goldstein (1985) and Rosecrance (1987) offer the interested reader different introductions to this subsection of the literature.

7. An earlier world economy discussion of the role of systemic warfare can be found in Chase-Dunn (1981). Thompson (1983c,d) and Chase-Dunn and Sokolovsky (1983) represent a world economy/long cycle exchange on this issue.

8. This question can also be called the "existence" question because it proposes an "existence theorem" of the form "there exists. . . ."

9. For a nonlinear argument on the relationship between instability and deconcentration, see Modelski and Thompson (1987).

10. Readers interested in additional material on global wars are encouraged to consult the following works: Modelski (1984, 1986, 1987c), which provides basic statements on long cycles and global wars; Modelski and Thompson (1987, 1988) offer empirical analyses of the links between global warfare and, respectively, global order and sea power; Modelski and Modelski (1988) focus on the exercise of global leadership with emphases on global war and

the resulting peace settlements. Thompson (1988) compares long-cycle, structural realist, and world economy approaches to global war. Rasler and Thompson (1989) demonstrate the impact of global war on the formation of the major states. Other, more specific topics related to global war are pursued in Modelski and Morgan (1985), Juday (1985), Pearson (1987), and Kegley and Raymond (1987). George Modelski is also currently engaged in a project tentatively entitled *Global Wars in the Modern World System*, which focuses explicitly on the description and analysis of the long cycle's five global wars.

CHAPTER 3

Hierarchical Equilibria and the Long-Run Instability of Multipolar Systems

Manus I. Midlarsky

Rutgers University

This chapter explores a particular aspect of the hierarchical equilibrium theory of systemic war. It is a theoretical structure designed to predict the absence of systemic war; concurrently the violation of one or more of its properties increases the probability of systemic war. Later in this chapter it will be shown that, in addition to the more obvious paths to systemic war traced by violations of the hierarchical equilibrium, there are more subtle and long-term consequences in the form of an inherent instability in multipolar systems. Bipolarity will be shown to be a more stable international structure, at least in regard to the onset of systemic war.

A systemic war is a war entailing the breakdown of the international system as it existed prior to the outbreak of the war. As such, the scope of the war in terms of participant countries and the degree of civilian–military participation (leading to a large number of civilian casualties and battle deaths) must be extensive in order to yield a systemic breakdown. Essentially, the scope of the war and the widespread bloodshed, which also imply a long duration, but not necessarily the converse (for example, Vietnam), lead not only to the rise of new great powers and the decline of older ones but also to later extensive efforts to restructure the system in ways that presumably will prevent the emergence of another widespread conflict of this type (for example, Westphalia, Vienna, Versailles, or San Francisco).

Thus, for purposes of illustration, eight historical instances have been characterized as systemic war. These are the Peloponnesian War, the Macedonian War, the Thirty Years' War, the War of the Spanish Succession, the French Revolutionary Wars, the Napoleonic Wars, World War I, and World War II. For the modern period, excluding antiquity, they correspond almost exactly with those characterized as hegemonic by Gilpin (1981) and, with the exception of the War of the Spanish Succession, are similar to those of Wallerstein (1984). They are essentially paired conflicts in which the first of each pair (Peloponnesian War, Thirty Years' War, French Revolutionary Wars, and World War I) is termed a structural war and the second is a mobilization war for reasons detailed in Midlarsky (1988a, chap. VII).

THE HIERARCHICAL EQUILIBRIUM

Structurally, the hierarchical equilibrium consists of (1) two or more alliances (or other loose hierarchies, such as loosely knit empires) of varying size and composition but clearly with each including a great power and a number of small powers, and (2) a relatively large number of small powers not formally associated with any of the great powers. Note that great powers at the head of each hierarchy can be either approximately equal in power with each other or unequal as the case may be (as well as the hierarchies themselves) as long as the power differentials *within* each hierarchy are substantial. The model effectively incorporates an element of balance-of-power theory, which requires that a relative equality in power among the great powers be achieved through alliances or some other balancing mechanism. In the hierarchical equilibrium, the equality is achieved via the existence of hierarchies for each great power, although neither the hierarchies themselves nor the individual great powers must be absolutely equal in power. Power preponderance stipulates that the existence of general power hierarchies is essential for peace and is found in the hierarchical component of the hierarchical equilibrium model. The model itself, though, was generated initially in postulating an average equality or equilibrium in the number of disputes begun and terminated within any time interval. The greater the accumulation of unresolved disputes, the greater the likelihood of systemic conflict. The hierarchical equilibrium structure was found to satisfy this basic postulate (Midlarsky 1986a) and to have other properties as well that will now be explored.

Hierarchy and Minimum Entropy

There are several interesting properties of the hierarchical equilibrium structure and, specifically, the hierarchy associated with it. First, it is the

only structure that internationally will meet the minimum entropy requirement that has been discovered to be an essential property of stable and
durable domestic political coalitions. Entropy has been associated with the
concepts of uncertainty or disorder. The greater the entropy of the system, the
greater the uncertainty or disorder of that system. It is clear that if a coalition,
whether domestic or international, is hierarchically organized, then it can
provide the clarity associated with "speaking with one voice" that would be
largely absent in a less hierarchical setting. The association between very
large and very small political parties demonstrates both minimum entropy
and cabinet durability in Western-style democracies (Midlarsky 1984a).
There exists a theoretical basis for the expectation of coalition durability
and, at the same time, the absence of systemic war for minimum entropy
coalitions. The hierarchical equilibrium model specifies the minimum
entropy condition of stable coalitions, which also display an absence of
potential for systemic war.

For the initial purpose of exposition, the entropy is maximized when
there is equality in the proportions of capability in an alliance and
minimized when there is a preponderance of capability in one power with
very little in the remaining powers. Thus, the minimum entropy requirement
is satisfied when one very large power exists in association with a small
power. Conversely, the entropy is maximized when the two powers are of
approximately equal capability. The utility of these concepts can be
illustrated by contrasting the outcomes of the 1914 summer crisis and the
1962 Cuban missile crisis.

In the former, Germany and Austria–Hungary were allied in the Dual
Alliance, which soon became the basis for the Central Powers wartime
coalition of World War I. The crisis unfolded very much as a consequence of
the "blank check" given to Austria–Hungary by Germany to do as she
wished with Serbia almost at the outset of the crisis. It was this joining of the
two countries in a virtually fused political entity that gave the crisis its
unique characteristics. One asks why it was that Germany would have
engaged in such risk-taking behaviors.

One can, of course, attribute these behaviors to muddle-headedness or
excessive aggressive intent toward the Entente powers: France, Russia, and
Great Britain (Fischer 1967). An interpretation that emerges from the
maximum entropy formulation is not so much an aggressive posture as an
excessive reliance on Austria–Hungary as Germany's only great power ally.
And the emergence of Serbia in 1913 at twice her initial size prior to the
Balkan Wars, coupled with an aggressive and effective pan-Slavic propaganda campaign aimed at the ever-growing Slavic population within the
Austro-Hungarian Empire, threatened to result in the disintegration of the
empire, as indeed occurred at the end of World War I. Thus, Germany's

only reliable great power ally in Europe would cease to exist as a great power.

To be sure, one can castigate German policy as having eventuated in this circumstance. As early as 1890, the failure to renew the Reinsurance Treaty with Russia began the process of German isolation from the Entente powers because Russia then turned to France and the basic structure of the Triple Entente was formed. Nevertheless, it was probably difficult for policymakers at that time to foresee the forthcoming internal disintegration of the Austro-Hungarian Empire. When it began to be obvious around the time of the Bosnian Crisis in 1908, the German dependence on the Austro-Hungarians was complete. This is the essential characteristic of the maximum entropy coalition, one where both powers are large and, therefore, essential to the continuation of the perceived security interests of both countries.

Contrast this behavior with the Cuban missile crisis of 1962 in which a minimum entropy coalition existed between the Soviet Union and Cuba. As stated earlier, this is a coalition in which a great power predominates in an association with a much smaller country. Instead of the perceived mutual dependence that existed in the maximum entropy Austro-Hungarian–German alliance, the Soviet Union was largely free of any dependence on Cuba. As such, when the crisis broke out in October of 1962, one of the first decisions Khrushchev would reach was the elimination of direct Cuban influence on the conduct of the crisis. Thus, the crisis could proceed as a superpower confrontation without any of the local animosities felt by the Cubans toward the United States. In contrast, the 1914 summer crisis allowed the parochial interests of Southeast Europe, via the maximum entropy alliance, to exert a truly extraordinary and disproportionate effect on the outbreak of World War I.

Positive-Sum Games

The hierarchical minimum entropy requirement for stable peaceful coalitions is to be supplemented by the necessity, or at least enormous desirability, of positive-sum games. In the case of domestic coalitions, there exists a criterion for minimum winning coalitions, that is, 50 percent + 1 vote. Stable national electoral systems are governed by the widely accepted presupposition that winning by at least this amount is a sufficient condition for accession to power. Obviously, no such criterion exists in the international sphere; only the United Nations General Assembly can provide such a bench mark, and clearly the loci of international authority and decision-making do not reside in that institution. A ready possibility for fulfilling this criterion function is the positive-sum game in which two or more great powers can benefit simultaneously from a joint cooperative action. An example is the Polish Partitions of the late eighteenth century. Here, a maximum entropy coalition, the members of which are in potential danger of experiencing a general war (Hötzsch 1909), unite in the positive-sum game of partitioning a weak and largely defenseless state that formerly had been a major power in Eastern Europe. The positive-sum game of all of the concerned great powers benefiting from the joint action is played out with a vengeance.

In a circumstance such as this, the requirement for many smaller countries not in permanent association with any of the great powers comes into play. The existence of these countries makes it far less likely that, for the great powers, positive-sum games need be enacted upon the remains of another country. Instead, there are coincident gains by the competing powers, as in the simultaneous accession to the existing power blocs by newly independent nations in the 1960s or in the virtually simultaneous move by Ethiopia toward the Soviet Union after Haile Selassie was deposed and the movement by the Somalian government toward the West. The dynamics of these processes need not concern us here; the simple existence of these countries in locations that are fairly remote from both superpowers and their fairly loose ties to both superpowers, make it possible for relatively peaceful changes in political association to take place.

Absence of Memory and of Polarization

There is a third level of generality beyond that of hierarchy, entropy, and positive-sum games, one that is generalizable to other forms of conflict in addition to that of systemic war. This level of generality emerges from the requirements for minimum entropy and positive-sum games, which still are at least partially pitched at the structural level. (For that reason they are termed structure based in contrast to the more generalized analytic properties.) Hierarchy and minimum entropy make it possible to minimize the memory of the leading power in a coalition. If the power disparities between it and its allies are great, then there is little need to rely on the small power for security needs; as a result, the past conflicts or memories of the small power need not intrude on the great power's decisionmaking. The Soviet elimination of Cuban influence in the Cuban missile crisis is a case in point, and it stands in contrast to the Austro-Hungarian influence on Germany in the onset of World War I. This property of the minimum entropy coalition will be referred to as the absence of alliance memory.

At the same time, positive-sum games emerging from the existence of large numbers of small independent powers have a generalizable analytic counterpart. The positive-sum game of each side benefiting while not vitiating the neutrality of the remaining powers is equivalent to the absence of systemic polarization. New nations can persist in their nonaligned coalition, some can adhere to one of the competing blocs, or an exchange of allies can occur (for example, Somalia–Ethiopia) that does not lead to a permanent set of alliances in which virtually all countries are allied with one of the coalitions. This, of course, defines the polarized condition as one in which every state is on one side or the other with no neutrals. Precisely because of the continued existence of the nonaligned countries in the hierarchical equilibrium with the possibility of positive-sum games, there exists a core of resistance to a systemic polarization. This condition stands in contrast to the zero-sum game, which is likely to be an ideal candidate for polarizing tendencies in light of the required loss for a leading power upon some gain to an opponent. It has also been shown (Midlarsky 1988a, chap. XI) that the hierarchical equilibrium is the only international structure that incorporates two forms of international learning—context dependent and context independent—that can lead ultimately to the development of international cooperation.

The structural features and corresponding analytic counterparts of the hierarchical equilibrium are shown in the following diagram. The analytic properties are to be treated here as a consequence of the structural condition. The first two, minimum entropy and positive-sum games, emerge directly from the structure itself, but then are generalized in the form of systemic effects or the absence of memory and of systemic polarization. Effectively, the first generalized analytic property is temporal while the second is spatial, thus encompassing the two domains of systemic behavior. It is understood, of course, that these are idealized consequences and, in reality, there will always be some tendency toward the influence of memory or the presence of some degree of systemic polarization, if only in the continued efforts of great powers to increase their influence on the system. It is only required that these factors do not have a serious impact on the course of international conflict behavior.

In addition to the advantages of minimum entropy (the absence of memory, property a of the hierarchical equilibrium) and positive-sum games (the absence of polarization, property b), the hierarchical equilibrium formulation constitutes a general description of international structure that is then susceptible to reductions to more limited structural forms. Put another way, this structure incorporates others within it, others that, under appropriate conditions imposed on the hierarchical equilibrium, emerge from it. For example, if the small powers are removed entirely, leaving only several powers, the classic multipolar structure of $m > 2$ powers is derived.

Hierarchical Equilibrium

Structural Properties	Corresponding Analytic Properties	
	Structure Based	Generalized
Hierarchy in the form of great power–small power coalitions (property *a*)	Minimum entropy	Absence of alliance memory
Large number of independent unaffiliated small powers (property *b*)	Positive-sum games	Absence of systemic polarization

Alternatively, limiting the structure to two hierarchies and removing the large number of neutral small powers yield a bipolar structure with two great powers and allied small powers.

The hierarchical equilibrium then embodies the principles of absence of alliance memory (although not necessarily of individual country memories) and of positive-sum games. It was confirmed empirically for the nineteenth century conflict system and for the post-World War II period [during which, obviously, no such systemic wars occurred (Midlarsky 1986a)] using the Militarized International Dispute Data (Gochman and Maoz 1984) and a set of stochastic equations implied by the hierarchical equilibrium model. The model was obeyed during the nineteenth century and post-World War II periods, but not in the years immediately preceding World War I and during the interwar period. It should be noted that the nineteenth century analysis terminated in 1899 and, for reasons detailed elsewhere (Midlarsky 1981), there is reason to expect that the instabilities associated with multipolarity did not begin to appear until very late in the century.

The remaining analysis of this chapter will explore the consequences of one of these reductions to more basic forms. Specifically, what are the potential consequences of eliminating (1) the hierarchy within alliance systems and (2) the small, independent powers? When these structural deletions are accomplished, we are left with the conditions of bipolarity or multipolarity (depending on the number of initial great powers) and the obvious consequences of the possibility of alliance memory and the presence of zero-sum games in the multipolar condition that are suggested as progenitors of systemic war. These, of course, are the obvious implications of the structural reduction to multipolarity and have been shown to be associated with the onset of systemic war both in the preceding arguments and elsewhere (Midlarksy 1988a). But are there nonobvious, perhaps even counterintuitive implications of this reduction? This is the possibility that will now be explored. For purposes of clarity, multipolarity is taken to mean the "pure" condition of m major powers ($m \geq 3$) existing simultaneously in a recognized community of nations. Bipolarity is the simple reduction to $m = 2$.

We will be exploring the long-term consequences of the transition to multipolarity in several contexts with special emphasis on the approach to World War I. Most of the hierarchical relations in Europe disappeared with the nineteenth century unifications of Germany and Italy. Some of the German states or principalities, when sovereign, allied with Prussia, some with Austria, and others remained largely independent politically vis-à-vis the two leading German powers (Kissinger 1957). This condition, of course, disappeared with the unification of Germany under essentially a Prussian hegemony. Formerly existing hierarchies in Italy under Austrian tutelage disappeared with the unification of Italy during the previous decade or so. Thus, as of 1871 on the continent of Europe, there existed a condition of pure multipolarity with the consequences to be detailed in the following approach to World War I. Prior to that analysis, we will consider which of the systems, bipolar or multipolar, is more stable. The question to be answered, specifically, is this: Which of these two conditions is more likely to yield equitable relations between major powers as measured by newly acquired resources, especially small allies or colonies, to be incorporated within the respective hierarchies of the major powers?

ARGUMENTS CONCERNING POLARITY

The question of polarity in international politics indeed has once again become a concern for students of international conflict. Although unresolved in its entirety after the debates of the 1960s and 1970s, the issue of the supremacy of bipolar vs. multipolar systems with regard to stability has recently become a major focus of inquiry. This is not surprising in light of the emergence of recent concerns over the effective use of historical materials, especially over long cycles of economic and political behavior (which was detailed in the preceding chapter) in relation to major power wars. Clearly, system structure should bear some relation to the onset of a global or systemic war because it is the system itself that is undergoing some purposive transformation by the concerned powers, which in the end likely will yield a transformation of its structural contours. The extensive use of historical materials in connection with this research enterprise probably has sensitized the scholarly community to the matter of system structure in relation to global war.

Perhaps it was the very indecisiveness of the debate's early outcome that led to a hiatus followed by a revival of recent research on polarity. Although Rosecrance (1966) provided a synthesis of the Deutsch–Singer (1964) preference for multipolarity and Waltz's (1979) preference for bipolarity by suggesting that multipolarity was associated with a higher frequency of war and bipolarity with greater severity, and Haas (1970) gave some empirical confirmation for this view, the matter did not rest there. In what has emerged as probably the most extensive and well known statement of a position, Waltz argued forcefully that, in virtually all cases, bipolarity is associated with peace while multipolarity contains inherent instabilities that are prone to war, including instabilities that are likely to lead to very severe wars.

Waltz's arguments are compelling. With only two powers, there can be continuous political adjustments between them. International practice can be "fine tuned," which can obviate much of the uncertainty associated with multipolar systems (which, by definition, contain more than two major actors—frequently as many as six or seven). Even crises can have a pacific effect, because each one can serve as an arena for testing and communicating political intent. In the end, such crises can leave the two actors with a much clearer understanding of the opponent's perspective.

Several recent studies provide support for this view. In particular, Thompson (1986) found that significantly less global warfare was associated with bipolarity than with multipolarity, while Levy (1985) carried out extensive historical analyses that yielded bipolarity as the more stable system for eight of nine indicators of stability involving great power war. Of greatest interest here is the incidence of general war, which can be system destroying. Here, bipolarity was found to be decisively more stable than multipolarity. We shall have more to say on this point later.

Despite Waltz's arguments and the empirical evidence for them, the proponents of multipolarity have much to say for their position. As Morgenthau (1973) and Gulick (1955) suggest, the existence of many different coalition possibilities, not to mention the salutary role of the balancer, can be stabilizing influences in multipolar systems. Deutsch and Singer argue for the stabilizing effect of many different interaction opportunities, especially for the diminution in hostile attention each of the superpowers can devote to the other. The share of attention that one country can give to another in these circumstances can only be a fairly small fraction of the total.[1] In this fashion, arms races and other manifestations of dyadic hostilities are dampened, and there is an associated decrease in the probability of superpower or global war. The proponents of multipolarity also would argue that peace by crisis in bipolar structures is, at best, a dubious and perhaps very dangerous manner of conducting policy in the nuclear era. Only one failure in such crisis management can end the existence of civilization as we know it. Bipolar systems also are inherently zero sum in nature (what you gain I must necessarily lose) and, therefore, are more prone to conflict than the nonzero-sum activity in multipolar systems.

Arguments for multipolarity, then, have a considerable force and logic of their own, yet the evidence is running strongly counter to this theoretical position. When one is confronted with two theories that have approximately equal analytic content and persuasiveness, but one is more strongly supported empirically than the other, then it is likely that one of two conditions holds. Either both theories are in some sense true and they should be synthesized in some fashion, or, failing that alternative, there exists an additional nonobvious theoretical perspective that can shed light on the debate. Given bipolarity and multipolarity as power structures with inherently different attributes (as are two-party and multiparty systems) and the different empirical findings, it is highly unlikely that a synthesis can be accomplished satisfactorily. Far more likely is the existence of the non-obvious and perhaps even nonintuitive perspective that can distinguish theoretically between the two conditions. Such a perspective is called for not only by the preceding arguments but by the need to account for the existence of an important apparent exception to the pattern of the superior stability of bipolar systems. This is the multipolar nineteenth century, which experienced an almost unparalleled history of stability, especially in comparison with the eighteenth century and its many conflicts among European powers.[2] This fairly recent historical experience suggests that multipolarity may be peaceful with regard to both the frequency and the severity of war, and it seems to belie the arguments of Waltz and Rosecrance as well as the related empirical findings.

As we shall see shortly, this is not the case. Multipolarity will be shown to be inherently unstable under certain basic assumptions, while bipolarity will demonstrate a fair degree of stability. The late nineteenth century European experience will be shown to be somewhat exceptional in giving what appeared to be all the indications of stability and durability, but which in reality existed under ephemeral conditions. Multipolarity now will be linked with the emergence of inequality, and three case studies of structural systemic wars presented in support of this relationship. The only structural systemic conflicts not treated here are those of the French Revolutionary Wars because their origin was almost exclusively internal. However, in a separate discussion of this instance (Midlarsky 1988a), there emerges a strong parallel between the internal class divisions of French society and associated scarcities, on the one hand, and the international scenario that is now examined, on the other.

MULTIPOLARITY AND INEQUALITY

I begin the analysis with three basic assumptions. (1) What we generally regard as multipolarity (or bipolarity, for that matter) was situated historically within European and world systems of some fairly widely accepted scope and definition; that is, the units or countries within the setting constituted a system in which the actors were aware of each other as system members and openly acknowledged that membership. (2) Inequalities among system members are more destabilizing than equalities. Envies and political intrigues that can result in war are far more likely under the former circumstance. (3) In the absence of a centralized administration, the system is subject to random processes that impact on the system members.

The first assumption is derived from treatments, such as Gulick's (1955), that posit the historical balance of power as one existing within a common cultural frame of reference. For most of the period under examination here, this was the political culture of post-Reformation Christian Europe. A secular political culture—but one based on fairly widely accepted norms of behavior—emerged in the post-Westphalia period. The Abbé de Pradt (1800, 86–87) found that Europe formed "a single social body which one might rightly call the European Republic." de Vattel (1870, 251) declared that the practices of balance-of-power politics "make of modern Europe a sort of Republic," and von Gentz (1806, 69) called it a "European commonwealth." The shared experience of the European states led to the emergence of common norms that were established within what was commonly held to be a balance-of-power framework. As summarized by von Martens (1795), "the resemblance in manners and religion, the intercourse of commerce, the frequency of treaties of all sorts, and the ties of blood between sovereigns, have so multiplied the relations between each particular state and the rest, that one may consider Europe (particularly the Christian states of it) as a society of nations and states. . . ."[3] Kaplan's (1957, 23) rules of the balance-of-power system are a precise articulation of these norms of system behavior, which are generally acknowledged by all of the system participants (for example, "Treat all essential actors as acceptable role partners").

The second assumption follows from the current and still widely accepted observation that equality is more conducive to political stability than inequality. We find virtually the same equation of justice with equality in Aristotle's *Politics* as we do in Rawls' (1971) second principle of justice, which demands equal access to all social and economic opportunities. Even more directly, entire theories of instability and their empirical confirmation have been based on the premise of severe inequalities. Included among these are theories based on relative deprivation, rapidly declining economic circumstances, and the scarcity of valued commodities.[4] It is the last of these that will directly concern us when evaluating the relevant properties of multipolar systems. Given a particular society of states, equalities among the members—not inequalities—are more likely to yield stability in the long run. The particular dynamics by which the inequality-induced conflicts occur among states will be treated later. For now, we will simply observe that in the modern period the most stable societies by far are those with industrialized economies and their associated equalities; this contrasts sharply with the severe inequalities found in the instability-prone largely agrarian countries.

The last assumption is almost axiomatic in international politics.[5] Without a central administration, the only other significant system forces that can exist, *ceteris paribus*, are random ones.

Formal Distinctions

A bipolar system composed of two major powers now will be formally compared with a multipolar one consisting of three or more major powers. All major powers initially will have no small powers associated with them. The number of powers in the multipolar system will be taken to be five initially in order to conform to the existence of five major powers throughout much of eighteenth and nineteenth century Europe. The case of three major powers also will be treated, but will be shown to demonstrate essentially the same dynamics.

Consider now the existence of k utiles to be distributed among m major powers ($m = 5$ shortly). The utiles are international desiderata or resources, and they can be allies, which generally are smaller powers to be associated politically with the great powers, or colonies, which can be absorbed politically by the great powers. There could also be other international utiles (for example, access to natural resources).

If k items (utiles) are distributed randomly among m recipients (countries) with equal probability for each recipient, then, in the long run after a steady state has been reached, the number of recipients with r items (n_r) is given by the following distribution:[6]

$$n_r = m \binom{k}{r} \left(\frac{1}{m}\right)^r \left(1 - \frac{1}{m}\right)^{k-r} \qquad r = 0, 1, 2, \ldots, k \qquad (3.1)$$

With $m = 5$ and allowing r to assume successively larger values, we obtain the number of powers with r utiles, n_r. Table 3.1 presents these values. For example, with $k = 15$, there is one country with 1 utile and one with 5 utiles; for $k = 30$, one country has 4 and another has 8. Additional

TABLE 3.1
The Number of Countries with r Utiles (n_r) with m = 5 *and Variable* k

	k				
r	15	30	60	120	180
1	1[a]				
2	1				
3	1				
4	1	1			
5	1	1			
6		1			
7		1			
8		1			
9					
10			1		
11			1		
12			1		
13			1		
14			1		
⋮					
20				1	
21				1	
22				1	
23				1	
24				1	
⋮					
32					1
33					1
34					1
35					1
36					1

[a] All values below 0.5 are treated as zero; all values equal to or greater than 0.5 are shown as 1.

calculations were made with $m = 3$ and $k = 15, 30, 60, 120$, and 180 as well as with $m = 7$ and the associated values of k. Thus, we see in Table 3.1 that, with only 15 utilities to be distributed (the left-hand column), a random result is that one of the five countries will receive 1 utile while another receives 2 utiles, and so forth through the fifth country that receives 5 utiles. Compare this with the distribution to be expected when 180 utiles are randomly distributed (the right-hand column). Again, there is a disparity to be expected among adjacent recipient countries of 1 utile difference among them, but now each receives between 32 and 36 utiles. These calculations will be used in the later construction of Figure 3.1.

What is required now is a measure of inequality to reflect disparities in the random allocation of the k utiles. In previous studies of inequality, the difference between allocations to the upper and lower proportions of a society has been used,[7] and this measure also has shown a strong correlation with the Gini index of inequality, which is a fairly standard measure.[8] Using the top and bottom 20 percent for $m = 5$, the country that is lowest in distributed resources or utiles would be compared with the country that is highest. The difference between the two is treated as a percentage of the amount held by the least favored recipient country. Thus, for $k = 15$, the measure is $I = (5 - 1/1) \times 100 = 4 \times 100$, or there is a 400 percent difference between the top and bottom countries in the possession of resources. For $k = 30$, the difference is $(8 - 4/4) \times 100 = 1 \times 100$ (or 100 percent), while for $k = 180$ the difference declines dramatically to approximately 12 percent.

Thus, the relationship between k available utiles and I, the inequality between the least and the most favored recipients, clearly is curvilinear and has an exponential form. The inequality is greatest for a small number of available resources, and it diminishes rapidly as the number of available resources increases in the lower right-hand portion of the table. This relationship was plotted for values of $m = 3$, 5, and 7, leading to the three curves shown in Figure 3.1. The value of $m = 5$ corresponds to the existence of five great powers during much of eighteenth and nineteenth century Europe, while $m = 7$ corresponds to the emergence of a wider global system at the beginning of the twentieth century when three great powers, the United States, Italy, and Japan, were added and an older one, Austria–Hungary, declined. The value $m = 3$ corresponds to a much older instance of emerging tripolarity to be explored shortly.

The relationship indicated here turns out to be a special case of a more general relationship between scarcity and inequality that was identified in an earlier treatment.[9] The exponential approach to greater equality under increased abundance emerged from a general mathematical–theoretical treatment. Here, the approach is more specific, but yields an additional dividend. In the previous study, the exponential formula was of a general nature and could be identified as a measure of inequality only in an abstract way; here, this is no longer true. The exponential inequality measure, I, has a very specific meaning: the difference between the best and the worst off in the context of several international seats of power; moreover, it is consistent with earlier usages, such as that of Chenery (1975) in the analysis of inequality.

What is most striking about these results is not so much the rapid decline of inequality with increased available resources but the contrast with bipolarity because, in that event, there is the equal division of resources

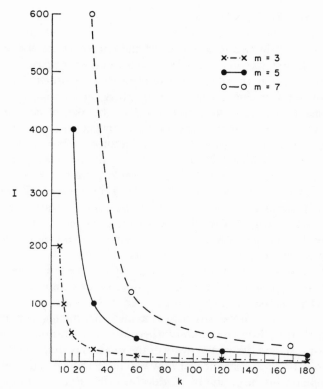

FIGURE 3.1. *The dependence of the measure of inequality,* I, *on the number of available utiles,* k, *for three values of* m.

between the two power centers ($m = 2$) in the long run. This can be easily seen by substituting the value $m = 2$ in Equation 3.1 for any value of k. The equality is independent of the number of resources in the system: it applies equally to $k = 30$ and to $k = 180$. In the former instance, each side receives 15 utiles; in the latter, each receives 90. This is in contrast to the case of $m = 5$ poles where there is a large difference of 100 percent between the most and least favored actor for $k = 30$, but a difference of only approximately 12 percent for $k = 180$. The case of equality for bipolarity may be represented as a horizontal line across the bottom of the figure at $I = 0$.

Another interpretation of these results, then, is that there is little difference between bipolarity and multipolarity for a large number of available utiles (k large) where values of I for multipolar systems begin to approach the horizontal on the right side of Figure 3.1. For a small number of available resources or conditions of scarcity (k small), on the other hand, the strong contrast between the two structural conditions is evident.

HISTORICAL REFERENTS

There are essentially two ways in which the degree of inequality can be increased. The first is by increasing the number of poles or passing to larger values of m (say, from $m = 3$ to $m = 7$ in Figure 3.1). Most emphatic would be the transition from bipolarity to multipolarity ($m = 2$ to 3) because it is here that the qualitative introduction of inequality takes place. The second is by the increasing scarcity of resources or passing to the left, steeply descending portion of the curve for any value of m. A mixture of the two processes also is possible. The first great systemic or general war of the modern period, the Thirty Years' War, began after the transition from bipolarity to tripolarity. The first global war of this century, World War I, and its likely continuation in World War II began after a process of the second type, although it was mixed with some moderate increase in the value of m, the number of great powers emerging at the end of the nineteenth century. Our first example to be treated briefly, the Peloponnesian War, will illustrate generally the relationships expressed in Figure 3.1, especially the important role of colonies as international desiderata.

The Peloponnesian War is important because it constitutes a prototypical instance of the highly destructive systemic war; the importance of the other cases also should not be minimized because they constitute several of the most widespread and destructive wars of the modern period. Our historical instances of structural systemic war now will be examined, although with a greater emphasis on the origins of World War I. The abundance of available materials in the most recent example of World War I coupled with detailed analysis by contemporary historians make it an almost ideal test case.

The Peloponnesian War

The beginnings of the Peloponnesian War can be found in processes similar to those suggested in Figure 3.1. In Hellas, a multipolar system traditionally had existed with each of the Greek city-states maintaining its autonomy, insofar as possible, or allying with somewhat larger city-states to form regional alliances for mutual protection. Many of the future allies actually were colonies spurred by overpopulation in the older Greek cities. This colonization process was in a very advanced stage by the time of Pericles and the onset of the Peloponnesian War. Thucydides (1954, 14), by far the principal source of our knowledge about this war, refers to the fact that "Attica became too small for her inhabitants and colonies were sent out to Ionia." This colonization process was widespread in Hellas and its environs, and it involved many cities such as Corinth and Corcyra. The fact that there were many of these colonies, that they were now outside of Hellas, and that they were repeatedly fought over suggests a scarcity condition. Indeed, the Peloponnesian War began in precisely this manner. Epidamnus, originally a colony of Corcyra, was being absorbed by Corinth, which led to conflict between the two colonial powers, and almost immediately thereafter, Potidae, originally a colony of Corinth but now paying tribute to Athens, revolted against the Athenian overiordship. It was these two colonial conflicts that ultimately drew Sparta and her Peloponnesian allies into a systemic war with Athens and her allies. Corcyra asked for Athenian assistance against the more powerful Corinth, and she assented, defeating the Corinthians at sea and also defeating the Potidaeans and their Peloponnesian allies on land. Corinth and Potidae then asked Sparta to intervene against Athens, which she reluctantly did (Kagan 1969).

The concept of the independence of the small states, which is central to the hierarchical equilibrium, is essentially absent here. Each of the larger cities that gave rise to the smaller colonies laid claim to a tributary status for the smaller colony. Only long struggles between the two could lead to independence for the smaller colony, and even this generally was not permanent.

An earlier equality among the larger Greek city-states was now being violated chiefly by the growth in Athenian power. The analysis of Figure 3.1 suggests this eventual outcome, for at least one of the power centers in such a multipolar setting will stand out from the remainder, especially in comparison with the weaker system members. As Pericles remarked in his final speech justifying his war policy (even in the light of two recent destructive invasions of Attica by the Peloponnesians, which led to talk of relinquishing the empire), "No doubt all this will be disparaged by people who are politically apathetic; but those who, like us, prefer a life of action will try to imitate us, and, if they fail to secure what we have secured, they will envy us. All who have taken it upon themselves to rule over others have incurred hatred and unpopularity for a time; but if one has a great aim to pursue, *this burden of envy must be accepted,* and it is wise to accept it" (italics added).[10] The fact that it is Pericles who makes these judgments is significant because Thucydides regards Pericles as a superb ruler whose decisions were largely correct,[11] especially in comparison with the demagogues who succeeded him (Finley 1972, 25–28).

The Thirty Years' War

The Thirty Years' War began with the famous defenestration of Prague in 1618 and ended with the Peace of Westphalia in 1648. The Protestant rebellion against Catholic rule in Prague began when two regents of Prague and a secretary were hurled from a window in 1618. At that time, the majority of Bohemia was Protestant but under the rule of the Catholic Habsburgs, and the Habsburg dynasty also controlled Austria, Hungary, the Tyrol, Silesia, and Moravia as well as other territories in Central Europe. The other branch of the dynasty, which was in Madrid, governed Spain, Portugal, the Low Countries, and much of Italy. Clearly, the Habsburgs were the dominant power in Europe. They were staunchly Catholic and committed to the restoration of Catholicism as the universal Christian church. The fact that the head of the Habsburgs also was the Holy Roman Emperor and, thus, officially entrusted with the counterreforming crusade, legitimated the nexus between the Habsburg dynasty and absolutist Catholicism.

It is acknowledged that the rise of Calvinism in the sixteenth century helped spark the onset of the Thirty Years' War in 1618. As Pagès (1970, 39–40) has remarked,

> Two facts above all must be borne in mind, for they were to make this crisis inevitable. The first was a direct consequence of the way in which the peace [of Augsburg, 1555] was drawn up. . . . The second fact was the ever-increasing growth of Calvinism, which continued to spread in the Rhineland, in southern Germany, in Upper and Lower Austria and in Hungary. . . . Now the Calvinists had not been included in the peace and the new confession which for the most part spread to the principalities whose prince was a Catholic, could only do so in violation of the principle "cuius regio, eius religio." The members of the Calvinist Church thus formed within the Empire an extraneous body outside the protection of the imperial laws. . . . Consequently, the Calvinist princes took steps to defend themselves, either by uniting or by seeking alliances with foreign princes. They were to be the first to take up arms against the emperor.

It was the "ever-increasing growth" of Calvinism as an "extraneous body" not included within the Peace of Augsburg that makes it an illustration of the processes outlined previously. The Peace of Augsburg was a treaty that directly incorporated bipolarity by recognizing (1) the legitimacy of only two types of states, Catholic and Lutheran, and (2) the principle of "cuius regio, eius religio," which required the population of a principality to be of the same religion as its ruler.[12] Calvinism, of course, was not included within this bipolar arrangement, and yet it continued to spread throughout the regions enumerated by Pagès.

Most important was the recognition that Calvinism was not only a religious form gaining increasing numbers of new adherents, but that it was also represented by powerful states. In particular, Holland was about to embark on an illustrious commercial and naval hegemony in midcentury.

The enormous difficulties experienced by the then strongest power in Europe, Habsburg Spain, in subjugating the United Provinces late in the sixteenth century gave evidence of this soon to be achieved stature. In addition, as early as 1591, a largely Calvinist German Protestant League of Torgau was formed under Christian I of Saxony, John Casimir of the Palatinate, and Christian of Anhalt. This organization was to find a later counterpart in the mainly Calvinist Protestant Union of 1608.[13]

The adherence of each of the principalities to either Catholicism or Lutheranism meant, of course, a zero-sum condition for each of them upon a significant gain to the Calvinists. This is clearly a condition of scarcity in which Calvinist gains could only be made upon losses to Lutherans and Catholics.

An approximate correspondence to the conditions of Figure 3.1 exists because, after the Reformation, the foundations of the Catholic church were so shaken that large numbers of persons were, religiously, "up for grabs." A kind of theological vacuum existed in which (1) the Reformation could proceed largely in its Lutheran manifestation, (2) the Counter-Reformation could gain vigor, thus enhancing the Catholic cause, or yet (3) different forms of Christian faith could gain adherents, as in the instance of Calvinism. An emerging inequality, mainly between Catholic and Calvinist principalities, was occurring in precisely those areas that historically had been Catholic (as had, actually, all of Christian Europe) but had been dislodged from those moorings during the previous century. In Bohemia itself, "nine-tenths of the population, a large majority of the nobility and nearly all the townspeople were Protestant of different shades" (Polisensky 1972, 67). This was the tripolar tension that existed at the time of the defenestration in Prague, which began the Thirty Years' War in 1618.

Although Calvinists and Lutherans (as well as certain other Protestants) eventually fought on the same side during the war, at the outset of the conflict, the Lutherans functioned as a separate entity, for the most part remaining neutral in the conflict. [According to Pagès, they "had perhaps even less sympathy for the Calvinists than they had for the Catholics" (Pagès 1970, 66). Wedgwood (1972, 26) quotes a Lutheran writer who declared that "the Calvinist dragon is pregnant with all the horrors of Mohammedanism".] Further, "the election of a Calvinist as king of Bohemia caused them (the Lutherans) considerable anxiety and deterred them from intervening" (Pagès 1970, 66). John George of Saxony, probably the single most important Lutheran neighbor of Bohemia, actually sided with the Catholic emperor against the insurgents. The envy of the rising Calvinist power is discernible here. The tripolar nature of early seventeenth century Central Europe and, especially, the need for any expanding seat of power (pole) to gain at the expense of another, thus reinforcing the scarcity condition, made the conflict more likely to occur.

The fact that most of Central Europe was identified either as Catholic, Lutheran, or Calvinist meant that such a war also was likely to be a general or systemic war. In the final analysis, Bohemia, "the economic backbone of the power of the Austrian Habsburgs," which "paid more taxes and sent more soldiers against the Turks than any other possessions of the Habsburgs" (Polisensky 1972, 67, 65) and had a population approaching three million, simply could not be allowed to become a Calvinist resource, in the language of this study.

The Approach to World War I

Because of its remoteness in historical time and the absence of detailed historical materials, the preceding discussion of the emergence of tripolarity and the onset of the Thirty Years' War could only be approximate, as indeed was the discussion of the origin of the Peloponnesian War. In the more recent nineteenth century period approaching World War I, we can be more exact even in pinpointing the precise envies and jealousies and their timing consequent upon the emergence of inequality within a multipolar setting. Although the number of great powers increased after the unification of Italy and the later emergence of the United States and Japan, this is not the principal avenue for the emergence of inequality in this instance. Instead, it is the increasing scarcity of colonies or other resources for aggrandizment that characterized the end of the nineteenth century. It is sufficient to mention the Kruger Telegram of 1896 as indicating the first serious conflict between Britain and Germany prior to World War I over southern Africa, or the Franco-German rivalry in North Africa leading to the three Moroccan crises of 1906, 1908, and 1911.[14] The first of these was to lead to the Algeciras Conference, which was to have grave consequences for the onset of World War I. It was here that Germany was nearly isolated internationally as Italy went her own way and, in the end, even Austria–Hungary gave only weak support to her closest ally (Taylor 1971, 450–451). Germany's resolve to never again leave herself in that position may have led to the unconditional support she gave Austria–Hungary in 1908, during the Bosnian Crisis, and again in 1914.

These events followed from an initial confrontation in a colonial context under conditions of rapidly declining colonial opportunities, especially for Germany. One can view the German aggressiveness in the first decade of the twentieth century as, in part, a consequence of the envies of the colonially more favored France and, especially, Britain. ("If we are bled to death," said Kaiser Wilhelm II on the eve of World War I, then "England shall at least lose India.")[15]

In the east, another scenario was being enacted with equally grave consequences, at least according to George F. Kennan (1979) in his magisterial *The Decline of Bismarck's European Order*. The major line of his inquiry explores the reasons for the breakup of the *Dreikaiserbund*, the alliance uniting Austria–Hungary, Germany, and Russia that began in 1881 and was renewed in 1884 for another 3 years. The disintegration of this alliance ultimately opened the way for the Franco-Russian negotiations culminating in the defensive alliance of 1894. It is this alliance that is explored by Kennan (1984) later in *The Fateful Alliance: France, Russia, and the Coming of the First World War*. The Triple Entente, of course, was built on these foundations.

The *Dreikaiserbund* essentially provided for the benevolent neutrality of each of the powers if they should find themselves at war with a fourth power. This pact was a cornerstone of Bismarck's European policy because it united the three powers in such a way as to isolate France diplomatically. Austria–Hungary was given assurance that Russia would not attack her in the Balkans. Russia was assured against combined Austro-German aggression and, in addition, any aid from these quarters to England in the event of another Crimean-like venture. From Bismarck's perspective, most important was that, in the event of a Franco-German conflict, Russia would be forced to remain neutral. In this fashion, French hopes of a successful *revanche* would be small indeed.

Fully one of four parts of the book (220 pages) is devoted to the Bulgarian *gâchis* as Kennan (1979, 103ff.) calls it. It is in this episode that he discerns "the moment of inner commitment to the eventual abandonment of the agreement with the Austro-Hungarian and German Empires which for five years had constituted the cornerstone of Russia's international position; in its place, embarkation on the long and gradual slope that would lead to the signing, some six years later, of the Franco-Russian alliance" (Kennan 1979, 204).

The problem of Bulgaria arose as a consequence of the Russo-Turkish War of 1877–1878, which led to the Congress of Berlin in 1878. As a consequence of that meeting, a nearly independent Bulgaria was created, to be a Russian satellite if that power so wished. In addition, the southeastern part known as Eastern Rumelia was to remain, at least in theory, a Turkish province, albeit with a Christian governor approved by the European powers.

A German, Prince Battenberg, was elected to the Bulgarian throne with the consent of Tsar Alexander II (Kennan 1979, 104). After a period of

some intense diplomatic conflict between Bulgaria and Russia, matters came
to a head in 1885 with a fairly spontaneous uprising in Eastern Rumelia in
favor of unification with Bulgaria. All of the major powers were surprised
by the event, and Battenberg rose to the occasion and assumed leadership of
both halves of Bulgaria even to the point of defending Bulgaria successfully
against an invading Serbian army.

It was clear to the tsar (now Alexander III), however, that the
emergence of a united Bulgaria under a new national hero would not exactly
wed the new country to any great power, including Russia. Indeed, Austrian
power was being felt in the region, particularly in the ultimatum to
Battenberg to cease his pursuit of the now-defeated Serbian army. This was
in addition to the already evident Austrian domination of Serbia, which
presumably also had been arrogated to the Russian sphere after the
Congress of Berlin.

Thus, Russian policy in the Balkans was perceived as having been a
grand failure. One of Russia's ostensible satellites in the region was lost to
Austria, and the other, Bulgaria, was proceeding in the same direction.

It was in December of 1885, just at the end of the brief Serbo-Bulgarian
hostilities, that the first open dissatisfaction over the *Dreikaiserbund*
appeared in the conservative nationalist press. M. N. Katkov, the extremely
influential editor of *Moskovskie Vyedomosti* accused Battenberg of being a
tool of England and identified the Three Emperors' Alliance as a vehicle for
its implementation (Kennan 1979, 144). In an editorial written by Katkov,
Austria–Hungary was perceived as the principal opponent, but it was
Bismarck and the German power in back of Austria that was the real
limitation on Russia's greatness. The editorial opened with "The German
Chancellor has acquired, together with his deserved fame, a certain
mythological quality. His hand is suspected in all the events of our time; he
is viewed as the possessor of the talisman before which all obstacles dissolve
and all locks open. Without his agreement, one is given to understand, one
may neither lie down nor stand up; he runs the whole world" (quoted in
Kennan 1979, 177). It was due to the German Chancellor's machinations
that Russia was being squeezed out of the Balkans. Only when free of the
limitations of the *Dreikaiserbund* could Russia really achieve her true
stature as a great power.

Katkov subsequently was received by the tsar in a personal interview.
"The Tsar (sic) came away . . . persuaded that Katkov's view reflected the
passionate feelings of great and influential portions of Russian society—
feelings of such importance that they deserved deference regardless of how
well or ill founded they were" (Kennan 1979, 261). Further editorials in
Moskovskie Vyedomosti on March 18, 1887 again attacked existing
Russian policy toward Austria, finally sealing the fate of the *Dreikaiser-*

bund. The "long and gradual slope" toward the Franco-Russian alliance had begun.

That these allegations of Bismarck's intentions toward Russia were largely false and had little or no basis in fact turned out to be irrelevant. Bismarck actually wanted to give Russia something of a free hand in Bulgaria, but Austria was reluctant.[16] Being convinced of the widespread belief in Bismarck's perfidy, as well as the tsar's own inclinations in that direction, was sufficient to doom the *Dreikaiserbund* as far as Tsar Alexander III was concerned.

Kennan (1979, 184) summarizes Katkov's position: "It was the combination of these two things—the ignominy of Russia and the success of her German partner—that was intolerable to him. Possibly he could have endured Bismarck's successes if Russia had had fewer failures. He might, conversely, have endured Russia's failures if Bismarck had had fewer successes. *The combination of the two was unendurable*" (italics added). It is clearly the inequality in international resource distribution that Kennan indicates was "unendurable" to Katkov. The range of social comparison within the European multipolar environment allowed, if not encouraged, the making of such comparative assessments by Katkov.[17] In his later volume, Kennan (1984, 33) remarks that Bismarck had been a "formidable rival figure whose successes had aroused in Russia that peculiar form of resentment that only envy can arouse."

Envy may not only have a direct impact on the rupture of alliances such as the *Dreikaiserbund* but may have important indirect consequences as well. It is clear from the foregoing that the Russians badly misperceived Bismarck's intentions regarding Russia and the Balkans. The level of envy may have been sufficient to yield considerable misperception of the German position. Thus, misperception[18] may play an important intervening role between the consequences of inequality such as envy and the deterioration of interstate relations.

What were some of the successes that Katkov and Kennan allude to that had aroused Russian envy? Obviously, one was the "honest broker" played by Bismarck in Berlin in 1878. But this was 8 years before, and much had happened since then. In particular, in late 1884 a conference of 14 nations had been convened in Berlin concerning the colonization of Africa. As a result of the Treaty of Berlin in the following year (the same year as the Eastern Rumelian uprising) the European powers, among other things, agreed to respect each other's incursions into Africa. This, in fact, began in earnest the scramble for Africa.[19]

It is hardly possible that Katkov could have been unaware of this signal event in the history of colonialism with Berlin and Bismarck at its center. Germany briefly had begun to acquire colonies in Africa and the Pacific;

this treaty was now the legitimator and precipitator of such new acquisitions. These were new "successes" for Bismarck to contrast with Russian
"failures" in a similar arena. This is precisely the language of Equation 3.1,
in which "successes" and "failures" are distributed randomly among the
recipients.

I have spent considerable time on Kennan's recounting of these events,
not only because of his eminence as both diplomat and historian and the
similarity of his explanatory purposes to my own, but because of all of the
students of the onset of World War I (for example, Albertini, Fay, Schmitt,
Fischer) Kennan alone chose to focus in such great detail on the decaying
bases of the old order upon which late nineteenth century European stability
was based. Theoretically, it is the slow erosion of the bases of cooperation
over time that is suggested by the emerging inequality in resource distribution indicated in Figure 3.1.

Note that an important assumption embodied in Equation 3.1 that is
not always satisfied (this will be treated at some length momentarily) is
satisfied in this instance. This is the independence of the onset of each of
these events from the others. Clearly, events in Eastern Rumelia, which
precipitated the Bulgarian Crisis, were independent from the race for
colonies in Africa, which was associated with the Congress of Berlin of
1884. Although, the *consequences* of the latter were to affect Russian
nationalists such as Katkov, the onset of each of these events was nevertheless independent of the others. This is all that is required by Equation 3.1.

An additional requirement of Equation 3.1, randomness, is also
satisfied by these events. Kennan (1979, 120–137) goes to great lengths to
show that the rebellion in Eastern Rumelia was not planned by the great
powers and that they were not even aware of its forthcoming occurrence.
The Russians, the Bulgarian government (although probably not elements
of the nationalist population), the Austrians, and the Germans had no
knowledge of its planning or execution until the event occurred. This is the
kind of random event that can set into motion the processes that eventuate
in the inequalities of Figure 3.1.

Comparisons with Bipolarity

Note that in a bipolar structure, these processes would have been greatly
transformed. In the approach to World War I, without the possibility of
German support for her activities in the Balkans, it is likely that the
Austrians would have readily agreed to a Russian predominance in Bulgaria
while securing their own presence in Serbia. This is an illustration of the
equality of distribution in bipolar systems, which is also specified by

Equation 3.1. There can be an alternation over time in gaining access to available resources, or it can occur simultaneously with both gaining access at approximately the same time.

Illustrations of the successful operation of bipolarity along these lines abound. An early instance is the Treaty of Tordesillas of 1494 between Spain and Portugal sponsored by the pope.[20] At his encouragement, these two colonial powers were to divide their activities between east and west. In this fashion, Brazil became a Portuguese colony while all of South America to the west fell to Spain. An equality acceptable to both sides ensued, thus ensuring that future conflicts over these territories would be minimal.

More recently, of course, we have the post-World War II bipolar system that, with the availability of new nations for political competition, has demonstrated a considerable stability, probably more than would be warranted by the nuclear deterrence process alone. Countries such as Ethiopia can leave the Western orbit and join the Soviet bloc, while Somalia does the exact opposite. Chile can cease being governed by a Marxist government, as South Vietnam moves steadily toward incorporation by North Vietnam. As suggested by the dynamics of Equation 3.1, it is constant- or positive-sum processes such as these that allow for an approximate equality in political access for each of the superpowers.

Envy can also arise in bipolar systems, but the mechanisms for moderating its effects are far more direct. It is clear, for example, that the East Germans and, especially, the Soviets were envious of the West German economic and political success in the post-World War II period, successes that, in concert with East Germany's own dismal performance at that time, led so many East Germans to escape to the Federal Republic. The response, the building of the Berlin Wall, was surely an imperfect solution by the Soviets and East Germans, but it nevertheless worked as a means of keeping intact the East German societal infrastructure. Although the West lost easy access and refugees, the propaganda coup of having to build a wall in order to keep a captive population intact was welcomed. Subsequently, without the massive drain of professional talent, the performance of the East German system improved greatly. In this sense, a kind of equality of competitive advantage was achieved in this bipolar confrontation, as suggested by the results of the analysis using Equation 3.1. In contrast, as we have seen, there was no direct means for responding to the misperceptions and distortions occasioned by the immense differences between German and Russian successes and failures in the 1880s, especially in the acquisition of colonies and satellites. The decline of Bismarck's foundations for peace may be dated from that time.

CONCLUSION

I have shown that, probabilistically, multipolar systems engender serious inequalities under conditions of scarce international desiderata. Bipolar systems do not suffer from this limitation, allowing for equality of distribution under all conditions. Historically, counterparts of these theoretical circumstances exist, in some cases strikingly conforming to the theoretical conditions. I do not claim, however, that the conditions of Equation 3.1 are duplicated in the international environment. There are too many instances where nations watch each other closely, thus vitiating the independence assumption (although there are derivations of these random distributions that explicitly violate independence).[21] In addition, many events in the international arena are nonrandom, having been generated by some central direction as, say, at the United Nations. Nevertheless, we have seen that important instances such as the Bulgarian *gâchis* do satisfy these requirements.

Whatever the exceptions or direct satisfactions of the initial assumptions, the consequence is still likely to be systemic instability because the underlying tendencies toward inequality driven by Equation 3.1 would be present, at least to some degree, and would have to be overcome by the great powers in their search for stability. Many important historical processes, such as the Polish partitions (by conference) of the late eighteenth century, came about precisely in order to avoid serious inequalities, such as in an uncoordinated division of Poland, which appeared to the great powers to verge on anarchy and a consequent dismemberment by the great powers individually. One of the most famous aphorisms concerning great power behavior in the partitions explicitly highlights this aspect of equality: "They confused the equity of the action with the equality of shares" (Lewitter 1965, 335).

As a final observation, it can be shown (Midlarsky 1988b) that if the assumption of randomness of distributions is violated and leads instead to a sequential acquisition of resources with several protagonists arriving in sequence at delayed time intervals, then the inequality among the polar actors is even more extreme with the disparity in resource acquisition between the first and last poles much greater than between the first two. Once again, bipolarity reflects greater equality than does multipolarity even under a different and likely more realistic set of assumptions. The conditions depicted in Table 3.1 and Figure 3.1, thus, are probably "ideal" and do not represent the greater inequality inherent in the sequential acquisitions of the real world.

NOTES

1. Deutsch and Singer (1964) base their arguments on the existence of $N(N-1)/2$ possible interactions among the N countries in the system. Thus, as N increases, the number of possible interactions increases disproportionately, thus diminishing the share of attention each country can devote to a dyadic conflict. Deutsch and Singer (1964, 406) do argue in the end for the long-run instability of multipolar systems in absolute terms, but, in comparison with bipolar systems, multipolar systems still are suggested to be more stable, whether in the short or long run.

2. For the evidence on the large number of wars in the eighteenth century and the associated casualties, see Levy (1983b).

3. Quoted in Gulick (1955, 10–11).

4. Probably the best known recent exponent of relative deprivation as a source of political violence is Gurr (1970), while rapidly declining economic circumstances as progenitors of instability are found in Davies (1962). Scarcities and consequent inequalities in the etiology of revolution are explored in Midlarsky (1982), and Midlarsky and Roberts (1985).

5. Raymond Aron (1968, 160), for example, asserted that "The interstate order has always been anarchical and oligarchical: anarchical because of the absence of a monopoly of legitimate violence, oligarchical (or hierarchic) in that, without civil society, rights depend largely on might." On the other hand, theorists of the long cycle such as George Modelski (1983) assert that there are periods of global order with a hegemonic power at the head of the hierarchy. Robert Gilpin (1981) argues for the existence of hegemonies and the periodicity of hegemonic wars.

6. This distribution is given for precisely this type of problem in Johnson and Kotz (1977, 114). Also see Feller (1968, 35).

7. For the use of such a measure, see Chenery (1975).

8. See, for example, Park (1986).

9. Midlarsky (1982, 25–30). The equal probability for each recipient creates what can be called a maximum entropy distribution, which yields the exponential distribution after the imposition of the scarcity constraint. Thus, the circumstances here are, in all important respects, identical to those of the earlier analysis.

10. See Thucydides (1954, 133).

11. See Brunt (1963, XXVI–XXVIII).

12. See Pagès (1970, 35).

13. See Williams (1969, 204, 238) for notations of these historical events.

14. For descriptions of these crises see Thomson (1966, 483–487).

15. Quoted in Zinnes *et al.* (1961, 476).

16. As Kennan (1979, 241) put it, "The urgings he [Bismarck] had given to the Austrians to respect Russian interests in Bulgaria were too numerous to count."

17. The range of social comparison as a variable of importance in understanding people's comparisons of their own rewards with those of others is found in Brickman and Campbell (1971).

18. Relationships between misperception and international conflict are treated by Jervis (1976).

19. These events are recounted in Thomson (1966, 465–466).

20. See Blum, Cameron, and Barnes (1966, 52).

21. Some of these possibilities are discussed in Chatterji (1963). In one instance, the distribution of x conditional upon $x + y$ is binomial as in Equation 3.1, if x and y are Poisson. Other, more applied examples can be found in the operations research literature.

CHAPTER 4

Power Cycle Theory of Systems Structure and Stability: Commonalities and Complementarities

Charles F. Doran

Johns Hopkins University

Epistemologically, power cycle theory is a way of looking at world politics by reasoning from the evolution of individual state foreign policy to the international system and then, given that perspective, from the international system to the foreign policy behavior of the individual state. International systems inherently are defined by configurational and temporal limits and are, therefore, static. Power cycle notions, which are dynamic, enable analysis to bridge systems and, at the same time, to distinguish the elements that contribute to international political stability. Thus, it provides a different perspective, at once more focused and more encompassing, to old dilemmas, as yet unresolved, regarding systems structure and world order.

Ontologically, power cycle theory examines the underlying dynamic of international politics—the cycle of nation-state power and role—and relates this dynamic to the dual questions of systems transformation and the origins of major war. In power cycle theory, systemic structure and stability are understood in the context of the long-term continuous evolution of systems accompanying changes on the various state cycles of power and systemic role. International relations are, thus, the resultant of foreign policy influences operating both on the "horizontal chessboard" of short-term strategic calculation and balance and on the "vertical plane" of long-term upward and downward movement along the state cycles of differential change in power and role. The system reflects an overall dynamic composed of these multiple forces impinging and interacting upon each other.

The question of systems structure and stability addressed by power cycle theory underlies the classical bipolarity–multipolarity debate (Kaplan

1957; Hoffman 1960; Waltz 1964; Deutsch and Singer 1964; Rosecrance 1966; Liska 1967), the contemporary discussion of international political economy (Keohane 1984; Krasner 1985; McKeown 1983), and the extensive literature, which is reviewed here, seeking the causes of war in power distributions and changes. An insight as old and persistent as history itself (Gilpin 1981), the notion that the differential growth of state power is causally related to systemic structure and stability requires a theoretical formulation of the full dynamic, as attempted in power cycle theory, to attain analytic maturity. According to power cycle theory, major war is an outgrowth of certain traumatic changes in the nation's relative power and associated role and security perceptions, and massive, systemswide war is a historical, but not necessary, accompaniment of systems transformation. When many states undergo such "critical changes" in power and role at the same time, policy contradictions long in the making suddenly confront state and system and are responsible for the turbulence that, historically, has been associated with systems transformation. Causation moves from structural change to systemswide war and only secondarily to further structural change. An important key to a just world order is management of the critcal, structural changes producing systems transformation and its trauma, that is, the structural changes reflected in the power cycle dynamic.

Several important studies of major war thus obtain an even broader interpretive significance when viewed in the context of the power cycle dynamic. This chapter reviews the main tenets of power cycle theory as developed and augmented by the contributions of various authors and traditions. Each theoretical contribution has its uniqueness, and the differences in treatment often obscure the convergence of analysis. On the other hand, by examining the different nuances of assumption and interpretation, we might discover commonalities and complementarities that, as Russett (1983b) and Vayrynen (1983) note, offer some hope for theoretical development.

A BRIEF OUTLINE OF POWER CYCLE THEORY

Our brief statement of power cycle theory is, at best, skeletal and not meant to "stand on its own." The muscle that gives support to a theoretical skeleton is detailed, substantive analysis, and for this the reader must turn to the original historical–sociological development of the theory summarized here (Doran 1971), to various empirical and analytic treatments (Doran 1971, 1973, 1974, 1975, 1980, 1983a,b, 1985, 1989a,b,c; Doran and Parsons 1980; Doran, *et al.* 1974, 1979), and, in particular, to the recent volume that combines systematic theoretical development with an analysis of policy implications for the coming decades (Doran 1989a). Nonetheless, this summary, together with the additional aspects of the theory examined in subsequent sections, will suffice for the purposes of this literature review.

According to power cycle theory, most of the leading states in the system have followed a path of systemic power and role—as indexed by their capability *relative* to that of others in the central system—that is marked by ascendancy, maturation, and decline. For most states, absolute levels of capability, which are indexed, for example, by gross national product (GNP) or military spending, increase by some upward-bending function over long time periods. But, relative to the indicators of rivals for influence in the central system, the same indicators, if traced over long enough intervals, tend to follow the pattern of rise and decline of the power cycle.

Regarding the power cycle itself irrespective of any war implications, the reader has perhaps already asked several questions. (1) Are there historical examples that might help explain this cycle of rise, maturation, and decline of relative power? (2) What exactly is meant by *relative* power—what indicators and what operationalization? (3) What specifically is this dynamic of relative power that the generalized power cycle captures? (4) What significance does such a cycle of relative power have for state foreign policy and international relations? These questions will guide our discussion and lead us directly to the implications of the power cycle for systems transformation, major war, and, in turn, for order maintenance.

Historical Examples of the Power Cycle

Since the sixteenth century, at least 12 major countries have passed through segments of such a curve of relative power. Spanish power, for instance, rose throughout the sixteenth century, reached its peak under the reign of Phillip II, and faced pronounced decline by the Peace of Westphalia of 1648. Austria–Hungary was at the center of the European balance of power in 1825 but was already exiting the central system three-quarters of a century later. Described by one classical diplomatic history as the "Swedish meteor," Sweden rose to heights of power under Gustavus Adolphus, only to plummet in the century thereafter (Fisher 1935). The Netherlands passed through the entire pattern of rise and decline between approximately 1650 and 1750, financing most of the major wars against Louis XIV of France, but eventually exhausting itself relative to the emergence of the great industrial countries. French power peaked sometime during the eighteenth century and, like British power that peaked somewhat later, was in relative decline throughout the nineteenth and twentieth centuries. Italy followed the undulating path of a slight rise in power after independence (1860), a slight decline in the face of more rapidly industrializing countries thereafter, and a gradual recovery again by the middle of the twentieth century. Germany was in rapid ascendancy in the last decades of the nineteenth century, reached the apex of its power just prior to World War I, and, despite a much higher actualization of its capability base in the late 1930s than those of its opponents, was already in significant decline by World War II. Both Japan, despite the interregnum of World War II, and China, by the late twentieth century, are in ascendancy. Japan, however, displays characteristics of diminishing marginal returns concerning its growth rate and capacity to compete economically with the newly industrializing countries. The United States has been an ascendant power in the international system since the middle of the nineteenth century and a member of the central system since the first decade of the twentieth century, and empirical evidence suggests that it is at or just past the apex of its power cycle. The Soviet Union has been ascendant since the middle of the nineteenth century, an ascendance that preceded the revolution and has continued in its aftermath.

Requests for historical examples may, perhaps, be less frequent following the recent volume on the rise and fall of great powers (Kennedy 1988), which utilizes the concept of *relative power* developed in power cycle theory.

Definition of Relative Power vis-à-vis Systemic Foreign Policy Role

The power cycle encompasses *state interest* (that to which the government aspires in foreign policy) in the context of *relative capability* or *power* (the national capability and prestige at its disposal for achieving these interests) and *systemic foreign policy role* (the interests that the state has been able to achieve). For a given set of capability indicators, a state's relative national capability is a function both of the very different growth rates on those indicators across states in the "system" and of the particular set or "system" of states to which it is referred. All three aspects of this definition of relative capability—the choice of power *indicators*, the choice of reference (*system*), and the actual *functional form* for relative capability—depend upon the question the state, or the analyst, is addressing. Confusion has understandably arisen because the literature contains many variants of relative capability that are based on different assumptions about these three components (see the following section). Thus, it is not surprising that no general pattern, that was valid across states and time periods had been widely attributed to long-term changes in *relative* capability prior to power cycle theory. Power cycle theory's first task was to introduce order into the concept of relative capability (Doran 1974).

The power cycle notion requires the following choices in its definition of relative capability. The actor and referent set (the system) consists of the central subsystem of major powers (Singer and Small 1972; Levy 1983a). To be a member of this great power subsystem, a state must have a certain percentage of the total capability of the system; it must also have significant foreign policy interactions with the other major powers because the theory deals with *behaviors* and not with capabilities per se (Waltz 1959; Dahl 1957; Knoor 1975). Thus, the system of major actors varies in composition over time as declining states exit the system because they lose capability and role and/or as rising states begin to assume major roles in the central system.

The issue of which indicators best reflect the capability to implement foreign policy broadly—more generally, the issue of determining a "yardstick" for measuring power in the international system—has been subjected to a variety of empirical analyses (Doran 1989a,c). Statistical analyses of the power cycle for the post-1815 period utilized indicators of *size* (iron and steel production, population, and the size of armed forces) and *development* (energy use, in the form of coal production, and urbanization). Although those studies did not use data on GNP because of problems caused by exchange rates and the rate of inflation, iron and steel production correlates very highly with the best collection of GNP data currently available for the post-1815 period (Bairoch 1979). For the most recent post-World War II period, the size of armed forces and urbanization were replaced with defense spending and GNP per capita to obtain the most appropriate yardstick.

Regarding operationalization, the analyst must first determine whether his or her substantive question about relative power involves a comparison that is a "signed difference" or a "ratio." These two formulations of "relative" have completely different meanings. The signed difference meaning is utilized in status disequilibrium, anomie, and various rank theories (Galtung 1964; Midlarsky 1969; Gurr 1970; Wallace 1973). In power cycle theory, the relative power index is a *ratio* reflecting the percentage of total "systemic" (relevant central actor subset) power held by the state at a given point in time. Because the chosen yardstick includes several indicators, the resultant relative power score is the average of the relative capability score for each of these indicators. With this operationalization expressed as a percentage, capabilities are easily compared intuitively across actors and across years.

*Generalized Curve of Relative Power vis-à-vis Systemic
Foreign Policy Role*

The relative capability (power) of a state, as defined previously, is a function
of the very different growth rates of the capability indicators across states in
the system. When a state's relative capability is graphed in a plane, this
functional relationship describes a nonlinear trajectory to and from maturity reflecting the state's political development across history. Early indus-
trializers are overshadowed by latecomers, and/or "smaller" states are
outdistanced by the greater latent capability of "larger" rivals (as compared
on some dimension of size). In addition, when new states enter the central
subsystem (or old states exit), the denominator of each state's capability
ratio may greatly increase (or decrease), an important fact of history
contributing to the pattern of maturation and decline of power and
international political role. The movement along the vertical hierarchy of
relative power change that results from differential power growth among
states in the central subsystem is the source of *structural change in the
system* and, accordingly, of *changing systemic role* for individual states.

    Although there is great variation between states regarding the rates of
change along any portion of this trajectory (so that no two trajectories may
match in period or amplitude even for any given portion of the trajectory), the
general shape and dynamics of the curve are the same across states in the
central system. In this sense, we speak of the "generalized curve of relative
power." Because of the uneven growth rates in national power and the varying
times and levels at which states are able to enter the central system, the curve
of relative power (1) will be concave downward (rise and then decline) for
most states over sufficiently long time periods and (2) will have an inflection
point on both the rising and the declining sides of the cycle that reflects, in turn,
an incontrovertible switch from acceleration to deceleration on each side
respectively. Merely plotting the data on relative capability reveals the basic
aspects of the power cycle dynamic: the accelerating rise in relative power that
ultimately slows down until relative power peaks, and the decline in relative
power that likewise ultimately proceeds at a slower rate. This idealized power
cycle thus reflects a generalized dynamic that is fundamental to the state's
foreign policy role and that, according to power cycle theory, contains important clues to the causes of both systems transformation and major war.

Political Significance of the Power Cycle

Changing relative capability is, to a great degree, a determining and a
limiting condition both for what is possible and for what is demanded in

international politics. This applies at once to the structure of the system and to the systemic role of each member of the central system. In fact, a state's position on its relative power cycle determines, for the most part, its foreign policy role and international political status at any point in time. In addition, the state's decisions and actions that affect the underlying elements of national capability will have a consequent impact on the contours of its power cycle and future role. But a great deal of inertia exists both in the processes underlying changing power and in the decisions of government that must respond to those changes in power. This means that the power cycle dynamic (structure) for the most part determines the foreign policy outlook and function rather than vice versa. This inertia also has important implications for systemic stability.

In particular, power cycle theory examines the impact that changing state power has on the role and security outlook of the state and in turn, the impact of the changed role and security outlook on the stability of the state's foreign policy. For instance, as state power increases (decreases), so does the scope of state interests and responsibilities. On the other hand, the accumulation of foreign policy interests lags behind changes in relative capability (1) because the system is reluctant to yield the state a larger role (or the state is hesitant to assume that role) on the ascendant side of the state's power curve and (2) because the state is reluctant to concede any of its now excessive interest burden (or the system is hesitant to let it yield those tasks) on the descendant side of the curve. A disparity develops between the state's capability and its role in the system. How do changes in relative capability and the accompanying inertia of role change relate to major war?

Power Cycle Theory of Systems Structure and Stability: Major War

Power cycle theory defines major war as war possessing the characteristics of high intensity, long duration, and great magnitude. The most extensive wars were those fought by a "hegemon" seeking to dominate the central system by force and are here labeled "systemic" wars. Thus, while all hegemonic wars were major wars, not all major wars are hegemonic. On the other hand, *all* major wars involved serious questions of role and position and had a direct impact on the security of more than one principal state in the system. When hegemonic war is viewed as major warfare in its most extensive form, a principal cause of the "systemic" as well as the more limited major wars is seen as lying in the very processes of state and system that operate in normal times—the dynamic of state power and role. Power

cycle theory explains when, why, and how the normal operation of this
dynamic is transformed into the abnormal conditions resulting in major
war.

Power cycle theory says that certain points on the power cycle are more
important than others and that they explain the structural causes, psychology, and mechanisms of force escalation and diffusion that result in major
war.

Each power cycle is characterized by four critical points at which the
total *Weltanschauung* of the state is transformed. These four points, or
intervals of historical state experience, are the two turning points and the
two inflection points, and they are far more important to foreign policy
conduct than other points on the relative power curve because they signal a
new trajectory for state power that was not previously experienced or
observed. Straight-line projections of past experience (the slope of the curve)
extrapolated into the future, the most common basis of decisionmaking
from stock market analysis to budgetary estimates, fail at these points on
the curve because change suddenly counters the linear trend. In addition, at
the critical points the disparities between interests and capability become
unmistakable to both state and system as foreign policy adjustment is
suddenly imposed by this precipitous discovery. Reactions of the state to the
system (and, conversely, of the system to the state) are *jointly* responsible
for the misperception and anxiety that heighten the likelihood of involvement in a major war when the state abruptly finds itself in a position that
radically alters its view of where it will stand in the future.

In sum, discovery of a critical point is likely to be a very unsettling event
for both the polity and the system because its security, as well as its status
and position within the systems hierarchy, is suddenly subject to alteration
and may even be at risk. The structural and psychological mechanisms
underlying the process leading to major war will be examined in the sections
entitled "Decisionmaking at the Critical Points" and "Disequilibrium."
Power cycle theory claims that, at critical points on a nation's cycle of
relative power, the state is more likely to become embroiled in major wars
than at other times because of the unique impact critical structural changes
have on members of the central system. At a critical point, long-standing
conditions such as a status disequilibrium, or hegemonic decline, or the
process of power deconcentration suddenly increase in salience. Taken
alone, each of these assessments regarding the causes of major war suffers
from some degree of incompleteness and misspecification. Each assessment
attains fuller causal significance within the context of the complete dynamic
of power and role.

Power Cycle Theory of Systems Structure and Stability:
Systems Transformation and Systemic War

In power cycle theory, *structural change* means movement along the vertical hierarchy of relative power and role that results from differential power growth among the major states in the system. *Critical structural change* occurs when one of these states passes through a critical point on its relative power curve and inverts previous perceptions. In terms of power relations and the implications for future foreign policy role, critical structural change is the most dramatic type of change a state and the system can experience. Because the leading states are continually moving vertically along their respective power cycles, the system is continually in flux; *systems transformation* is the result of massive critical structural change involving several states. Because passage through a critical point on a single nation's power cycle is difficult for that nation and for the system to assimilate and increases the likelihood of major war, the roughly simultaneous passage of several states through critical points on their respective curves (with multiplicative as well as additive effects) is certainly much more difficult for the system to absorb. Perceptual uncertainty and distortion (Wohlforth 1987) greatly increase during critical systems transformation, and the sense of threat is exacerbated if several states have a severe surplus or deficit of interests. When analysis highlights the vertical dynamic, it is clear why massive systemswide warfare has accompanied historical junctures that involve systems transformation. The rapidly changing structure of the international system is a dynamic to which adaptation is difficult using the familiar balancing process that is so successful when vertical changes are less prominent.

Consider the pattern of abrupt structural change and systemic tension in several historical examples of world war. The tension came not so much from upward or downward mobility in the systemic hierarchy, but from a government's sudden discovery that its projected future foreign policy role had dramatically changed. Contrast the outlooks of Charles II of Spain and Phillip II. Although the Spanish–Austrian Habsburgs remained the dominant power in Europe for decades thereafter, Phillip II and his successor suddenly interpreted foreign policy negatively, even arguing that "God had forsaken" them, and became paranoid and belligerent at the same time. Sweden and Holland enjoyed a meteoric rise, abruptly demanding a larger role. Under Richelieu, France began to consolidate its power. This massive transformation of *structure* and *roles* in the international system resulted in the Thirty Years' War.

Similarly, the passage of Louis XIV's France through a first inflection point, which threatened slower growth, led to confrontations with Sweden (an erstwhile ally) and Holland, each of whom had discovered that its relative power had peaked, thus creating severe problems of overextension. Meanwhile, Prussia was rising in the heart of the central European system, and Britain had reconstituted itself to the extent that it was enjoying a renaissance of power growth by the end of the seventeenth century, stimulating it to confront France directly with an army on the Continent. Once again, the wars of Louis XIV, which ended with the Treaties of Utrecht of 1713, resulted from a systemic transformation that saw each of Europe's major players viewing its own foreign policy role in highly altered and more troubling fashion.

French power peaked sometime during the latter eighteenth century in the face of growing British industrial and naval strength. The transformation of the international system that came on the heels of startling declines in power in northern and central Europe saw a belligerent France resisting its systemic fortunes under Napoleon. The contrast between the changing foreign policy outlook of the Russians (as expressed by Alexander I) and of the French (under Napoleon) was an acknowledgment of the failure of Europe to assimilate dramatic structural change without major war. In contrast to the eighteenth century system in which France had played the dominant role, a five-actor concert of shared power, balanced and roughly equilibrated, was emerging.

In these three world wars, the existing system of maintaining order collapsed under the weight of arrangements whose foundations had long since been eroded away (Doran 1971).

An empirical examination of the periods preceding World Wars I and II verified the hypotheses that massive, critical structural change predicts to massive warfare (Thompson 1983a; Doran 1985, 1989a). In the interval between 1885 and 1914, every member of the central system passed through at least one critical point on its power cycle. Austria–Hungary virtually disappeared from the central system, whereas the United States and Japan emerged as new but as yet uninvolved members. Britain and France passed through the inflection point of steady downward power, notwithstanding their unwillingness to yield their systemic role to Germany, which soared to its apex. The Soviet Union passed through a minimum, and two members of the European system, Austria–Hungary and Italy, each passed through two critical points on their downward trajectory while the United States traversed the inflection point on its upward trajectory. Altogether, nine critical points signifying the most abrupt and wrenching form of change on the power cycle were traversed in the 20 years after 1885. Systemic anxieties and perceptions regarding Germany's response to its critical point were exacerbated by the types of critical changes occurring on these other power cycles (Doran 1989a,b). Perhaps few international systems could withstand this degree of structural turmoil in so short an interval.

Implications of Power Cycle Theory for Order Maintenance

A central dilemma for international relations is that each previous transformation of systems has been accompanied by explosive warfare. Were such observations merely extrapolated into the future, there would be cause for unmitigated pessimism. But shifts in power on the cycle and the event of war itself are separable: abrupt change on the power cycle causes war, not the other way around and not deterministically. Massive structural change in world politics that signifies systems transformation is, therefore, not *necessarily* coterminous with major war despite repeated historical experience to the contrary.

The task of the managers of statecraft is to channel systems transformation properly so that state interests and security are preserved while the risk of major war is reduced to a tolerable minimum. In the broadest theoretical and policy terms, this necessitates developing strategies for equilibrium, based upon power cycle dynamics, in which the authority response of the system is appropriate to the specific disposition of the challenger. In the context of contemporary world politics, this observation means that change on the power cycles of the two leading states in the system and of other actors moving rapidly upward and downward may contain the key to the retention of world order in an era that is both the same as, and much more dangerous than, earlier periods and systems (Doran 1989a).

CONFUSIONS HINDERING ANALYTIC CONVERGENCE

Without a priori guidelines for determining analytic paths that will converge, a useful technique is to first identify stumbling blocks that appear to create unnecessary confusion or seeming contradiction. We thus begin by discussing certain assumptions and themes that, we believe, obscure the underlying commonalities of theory regarding systems structure and stability.

Hegemonic Leadership and Dyadic War Assumptions

Many recent studies share a premise that ultimately obscures the complexity of the system and the role of other leading states in both order maintenance and war initiation. This premise results from the coincidence of two separate views that are common in recent literature, neither of which was meant to become a norm of analysis. The *hegemonic leadership view* treats the system as though it was controlled by a single dominant state. It is an easy step from this view to the *dyadic view of systemic war*, which considers massive systemic warfare to be caused by a fight between two dominant states for hegemony or preponderance in the system. Much of the recent literature on political economy argues a hegemonic leadership view of order maintenance and systemic leadership, universalizing ideas put forth by Kindelberger (1973) and offset and qualified in important ways by Gilpin (1975), Krasner (1976), and Keohane (1980). Various notions of systems transformation combine these two views to differing degrees and with different emphases.

Irregardless of how much hegemonic leadership and dyadic warfare assumptions do apply to the current system and a few other systems (for example, 1338–1453, the Hundred Years' War between France and Britain), and irregardless of how valid some of the similarities are to systems in general, applying these assumptions to other systems oversimplifies both the structure of the international system (including the present system) and the dynamics of massive, systemswide warfare.

Analysis of systemic role and process reveals the limits of those assumptions. First, no single state has ever been a "true hegemon" who successfully imposed its power on the system by either military or non-military means. Because power was always pluralistic and shared, no single state was ever dominant in the sense of the hegemonic leadership view. Midlarsky (1986), for example, has persuasively demonstrated the role of nth states in general stability. Second, because the structure of each "hegemonic system" was pluralistic, the system has always been able to prevent such a potential "hegemon" from imposing its own singular concept of world order on the other systemic members. Third, the origins of systemic warfare does not stem solely from the actions of a "hegemonic contender" (whether second, nearly equal, or already preponderant in power); at least as much comes from the cross-systemic consideration of the dynamics of power and role for all of the members of the central system. Fourth, after massive systemic war, no single state so dominated the system that it "wrote" the new rules according to its own preferences [for example, the lesson about rulemaking described in Krasner (1985)] without the consent of the other principal members of the system. In sum, the various members of the central system participate in both order maintenance and massive warfare, and all must be considered when seeking the causal chain. The international system cannot be characterized as a series of hegemonic leaders, and massive war cannot be reduced causally to a dyadic competition for hegemony.

When these limitations on the two assumptions are recognized, the various theories of systemic war readily converge on important aspects as shown in the following section.

Static Structural Conditions versus Dynamic Processes

Unfortunately, the important insight that structure determines systemic stability leads to too much emphasis on static structural conditions and the consequent neglect of dynamic processes. The result is analytic schizophrenia that produces two opposing arguments and conclusions. On the one hand, massive war is seen as resulting when some ideal systemic structure is contaminated and perverted into some less stable form. On the other hand, because massive war separates two "stable" systems, this structural emphasis also leads to the converse argument that the war causes the systems transformation to a new ideal structure, which contradicts the original assumption that structure determines stability. Agreement on the definition of terms such as systems transformation would go a long way toward preventing some of this analytic schizophrenia, but it is not sufficient.

Consider the long-debated question of whether bipolarity or multipolarity is the more stable system. According to the power cycle perspective, systems of varying composition are all stable at maturity. Each has its own regimes and mechanisms of order maintenance, its own configurations of power and value preferences, and its own flaws and incompletenesses such that it is vulnerable to changes that are capable eventually of undermining it. The issue, therefore, should be not which "type" of system is more or less stable, but what change in circumstance or what events move a given system away from conditions of stability. For example, arms races in the medium term threaten the structure and stability of an existing system; "the first shot" is a short-term event challenging that stability. Theory (like the policymaker) must focus on how to manage *whatever* events or conditions challenge the stability of a given system. Power cycle theory argues that the *long-term* structural dynamic itself encompasses the conditions and the events that are *most definitive* in moving a mature, stable system away from both maturity and stability.

It is not surprising that the search for some ideal characteristics of systemic structure that would ensure greater stability has led to inconsistent conclusions across studies. That result, in turn, has led to a sense that the conclusions are dependent solely upon indexation, a sense that takes attention away from theoretical examination of the international political reality. A couple of examples will illustrate this problem for cumulative development.

An early, very influential study showed that major war correlated with a high concentration of power in the nineteenth century but with low concentration in the twentieth century (Singer *et al.* 1972). Another study analyzed the same war data with a different mix of indicators and found that a low concentration (a high deconcentration) of that power index correlated highly with major war in both the nineteenth and twentieth centuries (Thompson 1983a). How are these *differing* conclusions important for *converging* analysis? Convergence of analysis occurs with the equally valid conclusion that the results (1) demonstrate that different indicators yield different degrees of concentration and have different international political meaning and (2) directly support the view that the degree of power concentration (or changes therein) may not be the most important causal phenomenon underlying major or systemic war (Doran 1989c).

Related to this emphasis on some "ideal" concentration of power is the search for some necessary structural constraint. Examples range from the presence or absence of arms races, the presence of a mechanical equilibrator, the number and character of alignments present or absent in the system, an optimal size for the central system, and the comparative absence of ideological division. To argue that an ideal condition or a structural constraint is *necessary* for systemic stability is to reify a relationship between structure and stability that may be spurious or misspecified or, in any case, cannot be guaranteed to occur naturally or be readily constructed. Historical circumstance cannot guarantee any particular characteristic of structure, whether ideal or not. State and system must be able to *adjust* to structural conditions and changes of *any* kind, and attention accordingly must be given to the *process* of changing systemic structure. Structure and process cannot be separate, and each must be free from analytic constraints.

"Who" Relative to "Whom" and Regarding What?

The third issue involves the operational question of the relevant actor set (the system) and the relevant set of indicators for a given theory's concept of relative power and explanation of major war. When considering relative power, "who" is relative to "whom" and regarding what indicators? Many variations exist in the literature, and each is valid for its own purposes. The difficulty arises when trying to compare theories and to determine commonalities vs. divergences. While some of these theories have already been compared with the emphasis on difference of detail (Goldstein 1985), here we seek to show what each theory *can* explain, which in turn depends upon the concept of relative power relevant to the limited questions the theory *seeks* to explain.

Why are there so many variants of relative power in the literature on the causes of war? Implied in international politics is that a state compares itself to its major rivals, meaning not necessarily states with hostile intent but states with sufficient capability to affect its power adversely. For a leading state, this comparison is with the members of the central system, perhaps including states about to enter it and excluding those about to exit it. To study the fuller diffusion of power, the referent may be the international system as a whole. Or a state's one or two principal rivals may be the most important referent against which it measures itself. Thus, depending upon the information desired, the identity of the referent may change. Both the referent and the set of capability indicators are dictated by the substantive question under consideration. The United States may want to examine its capability relative to the Soviet Union and China since 1945 in order to assess the nuances of change associated with the kind and magnitude of power in which the most seems at stake. On the other hand, to discern the full pattern and implications of its power development, long time periods and as much of the ebb and flow of power within the international system as possible should be considered. The basic denominators of comparison for a state regarding its power changes, therefore, are still the central system of leading states (or the international system as a whole) and a mix of indicators that reflects the scope of foreign policy control and influence within that chosen system.

Hence, the questions always arise: Who are the "leading states," what is the "international system," and what indicators are relevant in that system? Compare the different definitions of relative power in power cycle theory and in long-cycle world systems conceptions. For Modelski (1978), the international system has, since its origins, been dominated in turn by Portugal, the Netherlands, Britain, and the United States. All were maritime states with large navies and vibrant capitalist economies at the peak of their influence. Why, asks Zolberg (1983), is Portugal identified as the "leading state" in the fifteenth century when most historians and knowledgeable political scientists would pick Spain? While the question highlights the difficulty of determining relative dominance for states in the early modern system, it also implies that the power cycles of other states have relevance for the system's operation as well and raises the additional issue of the relevance of the indicators used. In any analysis, the process of deconcentration, which reflects the dominant state's decline and which has been identified with major systemic instability from a variety of analytic approaches (including the long-cycle world systems perspective), is *restricted* to the indicator(s) utilized in that study.

Modelski's long cycle involves the "relative power" of a particular type of state (the leading maritime and capitalist state in a period of history) restricted to actualized naval capabilities, which are postulated to reflect global political–economic issues. Whether the reason is solely economic (Wallerstein 1980) or more broadly political, the so-called continental powers with large armies and authoritarian governments do not enter much into the calculations of theories that focus on the ability to dominate on global waters.

Yet if one is interested in overall capability (complete military–strategic as well as economic capability) and the issue of systemic structure and stability, then a *broader mix* of military and economic variables, including latent as well as actualized variables, is essential. A broader mix will reveal (1) that Spain (1540–1648) and France (1648–1815) were at least as determinative of the outlines of modern Europe as were Portugal and the Netherlands and (2) that the Soviet Union was as important as the United States in opposing Germany in the twentieth century. Quite possibly, the states Modelski identifies did exert more global leadership (with their greater global reach) than did the continental polities of the period, but the *scope* of such leadership was limited. The nineteenth century balance-of-power system, for example, was as dependent upon Metternich as it was upon Castlereagh, and it was as dependent on Austrian armies as on the British navy for *equilibrium*. The power cycles of all of the leading states are causally operative in truly systemic (in *scope* as well as *extent*) processes of power concentration and in the nature and degree of systemic instability.

Analysis of the causes of war within the framework of long-cycle theory thus involves this restricted version of relative power and systemic concentration. How the individual power cycles of all of the leading states at a point in time account for the changing structure and stability of the international system is another, quite distinct, task of analysis.

Reality and Remediability of Decline

The final issue hindering the convergence of analysis involves the reality of decline on the state power cycle and its remediability. Necrology is what Kal Holsti (1985) somewhat playfully dubbed the preoccupation with the demise of the nation-state and the war-oriented state system. Of course, while power cycle theory does highlight the relationship between changing relative power and major war, it emphasizes the rise and maturation of states as much as the decline, and it in no way predicts or is predicated upon the demise of the nation-state system. Power cycle theory also heeds

Holsti's explicit warning that, however important the link between shifts on the power cycle and systemic stability, "role" involves far more than security considerations.

In addition, Holsti, like others, implicitly reacts against the possible determinism inherent in an observed decline on the power cycle. Is determinism implied by the statement that the process of growth (as with hegemonic leadership) "sows the seeds" of its own dissolution (Gilpin 1981; Rupert and Rapkin 1985)? Wallerstein (1980), for instance, explains the progressive, accelerating process of leadership erosion as a "scissors effect" of declining capability shares on the one hand and increasing interdependence on the other. And much of the literature on the causes of decline—while encompassing explanations as different as inflation, technological diffusion, increased consumption both public and private, over-extension militarily, or the strategic trap of empire building—almost inevitably turns to the word "inevitably" when describing the process of decline. When Organski and Kugler (1980, 24, 27, 28, 63) insist that the trends underlying patterns of power change are "not reversible" and "not manipulable in response to foreign-policy needs," this sounds like determinism. And, although they acknowledge the short-term role of alliances in affecting some distributions of power, they suggest determinism in the transition theory of major war when they emphasize that, in the long-run, the rising challenger will probably "win" (although perhaps without war) and become the new dominant nation.

It is true that efforts to reverse decline are sometimes counterproductive and contribute to the consequences they are designed to eliminate (Gilpin 1981). Reductions of consumption in the short-run may hurt demand, which in turn can lead to growth reductions and increased unemployment.' Increased taxation to generate greater investment in human capital and technology can drag down economic growth rates, not expand them, if neither domestic consumption nor military spending is also reduced. Examination of the full dynamics of systemic processes involved in power cycle theory, however, indicates that both (1) the notion of strict determinism in the cycle and its systemic consequences and (2) pessimism about "international political engineering" are subject to question. Indeed, treated piecemeal and/or variously within many studies, strategies to recovery of position do promote analytic convergence when classified in three general categories, each yielding a different modification of the downward trajectory of the power cycle (Doran 1989a).

Regarding Holsti's broader concern, much of the work on hegemony has focused on security implications and has assumed the decline of the United States, but other roles have not been ignored. If "hegemony" is equated with dominance, and the concept badly needs more careful definition, then the passing of U.S. dominance may affect the maintenance of international economic regimes as well (Oye 1983; Calleo 1982). Both "hegemony and international regimes," according to Keohane (1984, 240), "can contribute to cooperation," yet neither is essential nor sufficient. Russett (1985) goes further, questioning whether U.S. decline has proceeded as far as some analysts have suggested by pointing to the legacy of "cultural hegemony" that serves to sustain leadership (control over outcomes and benefits) and order even after the material base of power has deteriorated. Distinguishing between collective and private goods, Russett asserts that the United States did not forego much in sustaining international regimes after World War II and that, therefore, even given nascent American decline, analysts of international political economy should not be preparing themselves for the deluge any time soon because the marginal costs are bearable and leadership is likely to continue.

Analysts are therefore probing both the extent of the decline on the U.S. power cycle and the implications for the maintenance of trade, monetary, and energy regimes that have prevailed since 1945 without reaching agreement on the degree of change or its consequences for international political economy. Rosecrance (1986) posits the emergence of a qualitatively new international system in which commerce replaces conquest and the marketplace replaces territory as the new goal of state interaction. Were such qualitative change valid, even in degree, the implication for the declining state is that the military balance can only be sustained by economic renewal; the converse logic, namely that economic renewal is only possible under the shelter of a stable military balance, is, however, also true.

In sum, both the notion of determinism regarding a decline on the power cycle and the assumption of an instant collapse of the U.S. cycle that, for so long, seemed the hallmarks of converging theory are now among the most hotly challenged issues in the literature. Perhaps a new convergence will lead to the view that decline is indeed remediable within certain limits, a view that, in turn, will suggest new leadership options for the United States as it faces decline on its power cycle.

PATHS OF ANALYTIC CONVERGENCE

Having filtered out the assumptions and nuances of analysis that confound diverse contributions to the theory of major war, we can now focus on those theoretical and empirical aspects of these same studies that already indicate clear commonalities of understanding.

The Peak and Other Critical Points as a Locus of Massive War

Gilpin (1981, 186–187) correctly argues that massive war results from fundamental forces at work within the central system that are designed to alter the entire character of leadership: "The disequilibrium in the international system is due to increasing disjuncture between the existing governance of the system and the redistribution of power in the system." Based on the hegemonic leadership assumption, this disjuncture would first occur at what is the apex of the power cycle for the leading state in the system. A rising state "attempts to change the rules" while the dominant state attempts to "restore equilibrium." Likewise, in Organski and Kugler (1980), the greatest systemic confrontation occurs at or after the top of the power curve of the dominant actor as a challenger attempts via war to displace it or to rewrite the rules of systemic operation that the dominant actor is pledged to defend. Focusing solely on the apex and postapex fear of additional relative decline, Levy and Collis' (1985) empirical study of "Power Cycle Theory and the Preventive Motivation" and Levy's (1987) definitional study argue conversely that the dominant actor "initiates preventive action to block the rising challenger while the latter is still too weak to mount a serious threat" (Levy 1987, 84).

Each of these interpretations, however, is limited in two ways to only part of the complete power cycle dynamic underlying systemic structure and stability. Each explains hegemonic war in terms of pairs of states, the dominant actor and a rising challenger, and each is forced to reduce the significance of the power cycle for major war to a single interval or point: the "power transition" point, or the apex of the dominant state's relative power (and postapex fear of impending further decline). We have already argued the limits of assumptions that ignore the role of other leading states in destabilization. An encompassing theory of major war must also probe the significance of the remaining segments of the power curve for major war. It must explore whether other crisis intervals are possible in addition to the apex, whether of the challenger or the dominant actor. Likewise, the challenger's decline and the dominant state's rise may indeed be as important causally as both the challenger's rise hypothesized by Organski and Kugler and the dominant state's fear of further relative decline argued in Levy's preventive motivation hypothesis. Is there perhaps a more general dynamic that encompasses all actors in the central system and all stages of relative power change, a dynamic that underlies each of the previously suggested causes of major war and reconciles their seeming contradictions (Doran 1989b)? What is the actual decision logic or illogic that precipitates disaster for the leading states and the system as they traverse their respective cycles of relative power rise and decline?

Most striking about the apex of the power curve is that it is a point of *nonlinearity*. Both the dominant actor and the challengers realize suddenly that the dominant actor's level of relative capability has changed from rise to decline. Note that this nonlinearity results from important changes in rates of growth. This fact of nonlinearity provides the element of surprise, shock, and unpredictability that is necessary to so unsettle systemic equilibrium.[1] Otherwise, the challenger (the likely initiator for Organski and Kugler) could wait for a more opportune time to take charge peacefully at far less cost to itself. Similarly, the dominant state's fear of relative decline hypothesized by Gilpin and Levy would otherwise be factored into a less threatening cost–benefit analysis regarding war now vs. delay. According to power cycle theory, the fact of unpredictability and shock (a consequence of the *rates* of change) is what precipitates both a reckless effort on the part of the hegemon to recover its lost position and an equally determined effort on the part of challenger(s) to deny that recovery.

Perusal of power cycle dynamics indicates that the apex is not the only point of nonlinearity (of important changes in rates) in the projection of foreign policy role. Despite the focus on transitions, dyadic relations, and the dominant state's apex of power, Organski and Kugler (1980, 61) glimpsed the essential importance of differential growth rates in power:

> The fundamental problem that sets the whole system sliding almost irretrievably toward war is the differences in rates of growth among the great powers and, of particular importance, the differences in rates between the dominant nation and the challenger that permit the latter to overtake the former in power. It is this leapfrogging that destabilizes the system.

Indeed, the rates of growth were more important than the transition scores in the multiplicative relationship "relative power × growth" that led to a prediction of war between contenders at the top of the system. Thus, by stressing growth rates, Organski and Kugler open the door in theoretical terms to the acceptance of other nonlinear points on the power cycle where growth rates change abruptly and, thereby, to the generalizations of power cycle theory. Levy (1987, 97) likewise acknowledges that "the rate at which the power differential is closing may even be more important than its ultimate magnitude." Analysis is converging on this important basic hypothesis underlying the power cycle theory of systems structure and stability.

Although we still postpone the discussion of the mechanics and logic of instability at the critical points until the next section, the issues that arise for the state and system at the four critical points where rates of change have their most compelling effect will be summarized here. The first critical point is at the bottom of the curve when new states emerge as highly nationalistic, newly ascendant actors. At the two "inflection points" on either side of the power cycle, the prior trend of an ever-increasing rate of ascendance or decline is suddenly inverted, setting up the same type of sudden discovery: that past assumptions about role and security position were wrong. For example, the discovery at the first inflection point—that, for the first time in a state's history, its rate of ascendance is collapsing but its interests have not yet matched its growth—is no less unpredictable or unsettling than the discovery at the top of its curve, that now its level of relative power is falling off. Similarly, the discordances released by the discovery that rate of decline at the second inflection point has suddenly reversed itself, thus raising new expectations and placing new demands on the state's foreign policy, is no less problematic for the state and system, both of whom must adjust interests to means. In short, the critical points on the power curve are the points of nonlinearity where change is most wrenching and unpredictable for both the state undergoing the shifts and the other systemic members. It is, at base, an unanticipated structural change of enormous political significance that is responsible for the massive, violent breakdowns of systemic stability, and such change occurs at four points on the cycle.

Thompson (1983a) objects to the foregoing logic of war causation as "too empirical." It is true that empirical evidence rejects the null hypotheses (that the apex of the power curve is the only, or the most important, focus of major war for leading states): each of the critical points on the power cycle seems to precipitate the anxiety and imprudence that precedes major war, and the relationship holds for lesser nations as well as the dominant nation in the central system. It is also true, however, that the historical and theoretical analyses suggesting the importance of all of the critical points preceded the tests by more than a decade. Why the passage of states through critical points on their respective power curves serves to unsettle the global system involves the question of government decisionmaking during such critical intervals.

Decisionmaking at the Critical Points

The power cycle dynamic contains the causal mechanism explaining *why*, *when*, and *how* the propensity is highest for major powers to initiate wars that become extensive. "When" are the four critical points on the state's power cycle, and "why" is the abrupt change in linear role perceptions at those points that engender difficult, pervasive adjustments for the state and the system. Extensive war is not a deterministic process that is set in motion there. A deeper study of that process explains "how" decisionmakers proceed from the perception of a foreign policy dilemma to the actual decision to become embroiled in extensive war. The "how" is directly and incontrovertibly related to the same process that explains when and why.

Studying the decision-making process culminating in major war begins by considering the decision model used most often by most decisionmakers, namely, the straight-line extrapolation of past experience. The problem with linear extrapolation is that it cannot predict real, incontrovertible breaks from the linear trend. Indeed, extensive studies of forecasting (Ascher 1978; Moore 1986; Fischer and Crecine 1980) have reached three striking conclusions about even the most sophisticated methods by which decisionmakers project future trends and plan future policies: (1) *over-optimism* in forecasts, (2) the *inability* to determine a critical point *well in advance* of the event, and yet (3) the *ability* to recognize a critical point suddenly *at or right after* the event (Doran 1989a). Hence, the policy forecasts drawn from a linear extrapolation from past experience will be incontrovertibly wrong at the very points where being wrong is most threatening to continued role and security position. The shock of massive foreign policy adjustment imposed on the state and system by the discovery of nonlinearity (and, hence, massive uncertainty and unpredictability) in future foreign policy outlook is so exacerbated by the suddenness of this awareness and the complete inversion of prior assumptions that both the state and the system become ensconced in an atmosphere of *inverted force expectations*.

The logic of force expectations is inverted for both the potential aggressor and the potential defender. They exaggerate the gains from the use of force and depreciate the costs, even when more objective advice is available, because the stakes seem too high, the threat too certain, and the consequences of inaction too uncertain. The mechanism that accounts for "how" wars become major is this process of inverted force expectations, a process that operates on both horizontal and vertical escalation, a process that expands a minor confrontation to global proportions. The explanation for "why" the mechanism is triggered is the dynamic of the critical interval—the inversions in the dynamic of relative power change and the associated implications regarding state interest and foreign policy role. Analysis is converging to these same conclusions from a variety of perspectives.

In an attempt to capture the decision process itself, several recent studies of war seek new approaches that go beyond the use of mere correlational analysis, which is seen as dealing only with efficient causes and, though postulating mechanisms for the cause, not addressing the goal or purpose and how it will be attained (Dessler 1987). Bueno de Mesquita

(1980) uses a rational choice, expected utility framework, which assumes that interstate war results from a decisionmaker seeking to maximize expected utility. A single decisionmaker calculates such things as the expected utility of fighting or not fighting, the probabilities of winning based on distance-weighted relative capabilities, third-party choices and contributions to the dispute, the risk proneness of the decisionmaker, and uncertainty of several types. Following the criticisms of logical weaknesses and political deductions based on nonpolitical foundations, Bueno de Mesquita and others (Wagner 1984; Bueno de Mesquita and Lalman 1986) have improved and extended the theory. In order to ground the analysis in central features of international politics, McKeown and Anderson (1987) abandon the expected-utility framework and assume instead that the war decision is rooted in the competitive national accumulation of capabilities and is motivated by the state's dissatisfaction with its aspired-vs.-projected share of world capabilities; they achieved predictive success that supports the theoretical importance of the critical points as explained shortly.

Dessler (1987) also explores the relevance of crisis decision-making studies for decisionmaking in the critical interval. Some analysts concur with Heath's extensive experiments on human choice, which demonstrated that even when the constraints on choice differ slightly from the rigid, expected utility assumptions (and the calculations are easily made), behavior is far from utility maximizing (Snyder and Diesing 1977). Foreign policy decisionmakers do not enter the deliberation process with goals, options, and standards already defined. Confronted with a problem and a global goal, they feel their way through by defining a specific goal and policy option and then subjecting it to intensive argumentation and objection until a modified or new proposal is formed. The decisionmakers thus produce a sequence of such goals, options, and decisions, each constraining their own and other actors' further choices. The last step of the process is, sometimes, a decision for war (Anderson 1983).

Furthermore, the *great uncertainty* and *equally great causal significance* surrounding passage through a critical point are key variables in crisis decisionmaking (Dessler 1987). In a crisis, scenarios or simulations are used to assess the probabilities of events which are "low in redundancy and high in causal significance" (Kahneman *et al.* 1982, 207). At the critical points on the power cycle, events that are new, uncertain, and unpredictable threaten the state's power and role. Recent studies also show that scenarios based on nonlinear extrapolations appear implausible, which supports earlier analyses by Jervis (1976) and others (Fishoff 1982) that decisionmakers use linear extrapolations from past trends to project future trends. As the decisionmakers attempt to "assimilate information [on nonlinearity] to preexisting beliefs," they struggle to understand and control the tremendous uncertainty that has arisen from the reversal of the cognitive schema inherent in the existing linear projections (Dessler 1987; Jervis 1976, 143–145).

For example, in the Cuban missile crisis, President Kennedy and his advisors attempted primarily to *control the great uncertainty* facing them and, at succeeding stages in their deliberation, to *reduce that uncertainty* as much as possible (Anderson 1983; Snyder and Diesing 1977). McKeown and Anderson (1985) tried to capture such a bounded rational sequential process regarding war initiation in a series of filters, or imbedded conditionals. Although they used an essentially cross-sectional and linear model, the conditionals capture the inversion in the trend of slope at the two inflection points (Doran 1989b).

Strategic versions of economic theory (game theory, oligopoly theory) and other economic models likewise attempt to capture such interdependence of choice (Dessler 1987). Some models seek the interactive, cumulative aspect of the decision-making process by allowing firms to "learn," to change their behavioral assumptions and strategies as they try to reach an equilibrium (Cyert and March 1963). According to Axelrod (1977, 1984), decisionmakers rarely use specific historical examples to support a line of argument and "novel" arguments carry significant persuasive weight in the decision-making process.

By focusing on the process of decisionmaking in the critical intervals, analysts may, perhaps, gain insight into how decisionmakers can "learn" to avoid the extensive war outcome. Midlarsky (1984b) suggests the prevention of conjoint sets of conflict relationships, (or, perhaps, even the creation of disjoint sets) as a decision-making procedure that could localize instabilities and, thereby, minimize the probability of widespread systemic war. Power cycle theory shows further how world order can be sustained, even during systems transformation, by establishing an equilibrium between power and interests.

Systemic Equilibrium

Persuasive and acute, Haas' (1953) balance-of-power critique almost expunged the equilibrium notion from the dictionary of international relations in the next two decades. Yet, in the absence of centralized rule making, the concept of equilibrium or balance, however abstruse, is immanent in both the thinking of statesmen and the idea of world order.

Gilpin, Organski, and Modelski each focus on the interaction between the dominant actor and the challenger for leadership within the central system as the most determinative factor regarding major war. To preserve systemic equilibrium, leadership must be transferred neither prematurely nor tardily, without loss of security or an outbreak of violence. Although the most central interaction or "dominant game" is that between a dominant state and its rival (or rivals), it is only within the more general and encompassing framework of the full power cycle dynamic that this central interaction can be fully comprehended. The extent of the threat—and, hence, equilibrium—depends as much on the positions of the other members of the system on their own respective power cycles in addition to the entrance and exit of states to and from that subsystem. Stability is facilitated when movement up and down the hierarchies is not excessive or unanticipated. Conversely, it is abrupt, unexpected, structural change for any member of the central system that is difficult for the state and system to absorb and creates conditions that may disrupt systemic equilibrium.

Others argue that an increase in the variety of outcomes, including structural outcomes, increases systemic uncertainy or "entropy" (that is, it decreases known patterns or redundancies) and, thus, increases the likelihood of instability. For Rosecrance (1963), equilibrium exists when regulator activities direct actor disturbances into outcomes that are acceptable to the major actors, so stability may ensue even during systems change when most of the components of the disturbing and regulative forces undergo transformation. Supported by empirical observation that massive war occurred when the disparity in power between dominant and ordinary states dissipated, Midlarsky (1984b) stresses equilibrium within hierarchic structure itself (context-dependent redundancies) such that order maintenance is facilitated by the greater certainty of the decision-making center accompanying a stronger hierarchy. In this view, a small number of hierarchies and an open frontier of small, nonaligned polities that induce cooperation (context-free redundancies) further stabilize discourse between the dominant states of each hierarchy. His conclusion that systems undergoing diffusion (deconcentration) are the most unstable is a static systemic snapshot of the crisis created by critical changes on the relative power cycles of several states (Doran 1988c). According to power cycle theory, what is destabilizing is the sudden inversion in the trend of projections regarding future role and security, and this would occur, irrespective of the degree of concentration, whenever a system undergoes critical changes.

Each of these ideas thus contributes to an understanding of systemic equilibrium from the power cycle perspective. But equilibrium involves one additional essential notion: an appropriate relationship between the means and ends of foreign policy for each state. Apparent predictability of future role and position on the respective power cycles reinforces confidence and stability. Hence, although obtained interests tend to lag behind capability, when these disparities of interest and capability are negligible among the leading actors, the structure of power relationships still appears legitimate politically. The system is said to be "in equilibrium," and "world order prevails."

But if the disparities of interests and capability are not negligible, passage through a critical point will reveal the policy contradictions and uncertainties regarding role and position, pressing massive adjustment on state and system. Both equilibrium and political stability face their greatest challenge.

Disequilibrium: The Problem of Inverted Force Expectations

A final task is to explain the mechanism by which the probability of major war sharply increases as a nation passes through a critical interval on its power cycle. What occurs is an inversion of normal force expectations (Doran 1980, 1989a). To explain this underlying mechanism of systemic disequilibrium, the power cycle idea meshes with the literature on dynamic systems analysis as applied to (1) "inverted markets" in economics, (2) predator–prey behavior, (3) certain voting behavior models, and (4) arms race analysis (Richardson 1960b; Zinnes 1976; Hayes 1975; May 1973; Maynard Smith 1974). All of these substantive areas use the same basic mathematical formulation, including the same conditions for equilibrium. Hence, the inversion of normal expectations that explains the movement from equilibrium to disequilibrium in power cycle theory applies as well to these other areas, and the analogy is instructive.

Consider the economic model. In a normal market, as the price goes up, buyers drop out (demand declines) and sellers become more numerous to take advantage of higher returns (supply increases), thus "clearing the market," forcing the price back down and creating a new equilibrium. But in a runaway market (such as the November 1973 energy market) or in a market collapse (such as the Great Depression), the opposite expectations occur. As the price increases in the abnormal market, buyers may, for example, purchase furiously because they fear that the price will go even higher, and sellers may hold back in anticipation of an even higher price. Price is thus driven further upward into disequilibrium by these inverted expectations rather than returned to normal.

In international relations, therefore, at most points on the power cycle where the future seems predictable and disparities between interests and capabilities are nonexistent or are ignored, normal force expectations prevail. But when a sudden inversion in the trend of slope is reached on the power cycle, the future looks menacing, gross and seemingly immutable disparities between interests and capabilities are discovered, and force expectations may get inverted, which leads to the use of force and escalation into major war.

For the defender, normal force expectations are that force will deter aggression because the force available is a sufficient safeguard for the interests at stake. Likewise for the potential aggressor or challenger, normal force expectations are that force will deter aggression because its own capability does not substantially exceed its perceived interests. Interests and capability are in equilibrium for each actor and for the system as a whole.

Inverted force expectations become likely in the abnormal situations that occur in a critical interval on the power cycle. For instance, a state entering relative decline may suddenly find that its interests exceed its capability for defense and that continued decline is likely to worsen the disparity. Or a state in relative ascendancy may suddenly find that its rate of growth of relative capability has begun to fall off, *and* that this capability substantially exceeds its interests, interests that continue to be denied by the system of states. The frustrated state in ascendancy, rather than responding rationally by pursuing additional interests legitimately or by accepting the constraints on its future role, is tempted to use force to correct what it sees as an irremediable and worsening structural situation. The fearful state in decline may threaten the use of force in order to hang onto a disparity of interests it can no longer satisfactorily defend through its prestige alone. When both states initiate the use of force under these high-stake circumstances, escalation quickly ensues.

When a number of states pass through critical intervals on their own power cycles at about the same time, the prospect of inverted force expectations increases sharply. Abrupt power changes add additional structural uncertainty, and alliances transmit this uncertainty broadly in a way that ensures the expansion of the war. Such systems transformation, accompanied by massive structural uncertainty, is the period in which the inversions of force expectations will have their most cataclysmic impact on the stability of the system. The system is confronting its greatest crisis.

The power cycle explanation is implicit in much of the literature on systems stability. For example, Rosecrance (1973) notes that, in the eighteenth century, what amounts to "normal force expectations" tended to prevail and the international climate was benign. But all of this changed as France and Britain passed through "critical intervals" during the Napoleonic period. Hoffmann (1960) observes that, in the nuclear age, local balances of power (balancing interests and capability) may be more important than the global mechanism for maintaining peace.

The management of world order, therefore, is dependent upon an early adjustment to apparent disparities of interest and capability before these disparities affect many actors and become aggravated in size and crystallized in terms of the expectations and the behavior at the top of the systems hierarchy. Even in the absence of early adjustments, systems transformation can still be disengaged from major war if governments learn to employ the proper mix of accommodation and power balancing in order to mitigate suddenly discovered, deeply entrenched, structural gaps between capability and interests among the leading states in the system. The clue to order maintenance is the cause of these gaps: the dynamic of state power and role.

CHAPTER 5

The Logic and Study of the Diffusion of International Conflict

Benjamin A. Most
University of Iowa

Harvey Starr
Indiana University

Randolph M. Siverson
University of California, Davis

INTRODUCTION: THE POSSIBILITY OF WAR DIFFUSION

This chapter presents a review of the theoretical, data-based research on the diffusion of war, a review that is divided into two main parts.[1] The first part traces the development of the research attempting to capture the nature of the process that best accounts for the distribution of wars across time. As we will show, this research finds that the process seems to be best characterized by positive spatial diffusion or contagion; that is, the occurrence of one war increases the probability of further war. Building upon that finding, the second part explores this within the context of Starr's (1978) conceptualization of "opportunity" and "willingness" in international conflict. These two related ideas will furnish a framework within which, we believe, the current research makes theoretical sense.

IDENTIFYING THE PROCESS OF DIFFUSION

In the late nineteenth century, Galton (in Taylor 1889) pointed out that phenomena tend to diffuse from one locale to another. As recounted by Naroll (1965, 428–429):

> Galton raised his problem at the meeting of the Royal Anthropological Institute in 1889 when Taylor read his pioneer paper introducing the cross-cultural survey method. Taylor showed correlations ("adhesions" he called them) between certain traits; in the discussion which followed, Galton pointed out that traits often spread by diffusion—by borrowing or migration. Since this is often so, how many independent trials of his correlations did Taylor have?

Following Galton, a number of social scientists have attempted to test for the existence of diffusion effects and to assess their explanatory value. For example, researchers have studied the diffusion of race riots (Spilerman 1970; Midlarsky 1978), coups d'etat (Midlarsky 1970; Li and Thompson 1975), alliance formation (Job 1973; Siverson and Duncan 1976), and so on.

In the empirical literature, the earliest explicit suggestion that warfare might diffuse was made by Richardson (1960b, chaps. 10–12). Richardson attempted to construct a mathematical model that would adequately account for the number of nations on each side of a war. The assumptions making up Richardson's best-fitting model were essentially that the number of nations on each side in a war was the outcome of a process heavily influenced by *geography* and modified by *infection*.[2]

Because of the technical limitations faced by Richardson, however, it is possible that he understated the extent to which wars were enlarged by this process. Because his models were complex and his computational aids were primitive (at least by today's standards), Richardson did not include in his analysis those wars in which there was a total of more than four participants. This excluded 17 of the 91 wars in his original data base. Because the 17 excluded wars are precisely those that would be expected to reveal the greatest amount of infection, it is likely that the actual underlying process is more than slightly "modified by infectiousness."

Although Richardson's book reporting these findings was published in 1960,[3] it was not until over 15 years later that several investigators began looking at the problem of infection again. Zinnes (1976) and Wilkinson (1980) both extensively reviewed the contributions of Richardson to the study of war, including a recognition of his work on infection, but this was largely incidental to their more general review.

More recently, inquiry into the possibility of war diffusion has become a central focus of research, and the investigations have moved considerably beyond Richardson's data and methods. The use of other data sets on war has permitted the exploration of the extent to which the process of diffusion is general across different conceptions and measures of warfare. Moreover, better methodologies have allowed the more recent research to demonstrate that apparent "infection" can be produced by any one of several processes, and that some of these are noninfectious in character.

The first question is this: Through what process does war appear to spread? As noted previously, there are several ways to conceptualize "diffusion." Different conceptualizations lead to, and derive from, different models of the diffusion process (see also, O'Loughlin 1986). We will begin, as did Richardson, with those models most closely concerned with "infection" or the growth of an ongoing war.

In one interesting study, Yamamoto and Bremer (1980) used three probability models to assess the tendencies of major powers to enter ongoing wars. This is an important problem because most major power participation in war takes place as a nation joins an ongoing war. Moreover, it is those wars with major power participants that are usually considered to be the most severe because those nations, almost by definition, have the greatest capacity to inflict damage upon others.

The three models Yamamoto and Bremer explored are (1) independent choice, (2) one-way conditional choice, and (3) two-way conditional choice. Substantively, these abstract probability models have very different implications. Under independent choice, each of the major powers is assumed to have the "same constant probability of entering any particular war, and its probability is not affected by whether or not other major powers enter the war ..." (p. 201). Under one-way conditional choice, a major power's probability of entering a war will either be held constant or be increased by the entry of another major power. More specifically, one-way conditional choice leads to either no change or an increase in the probability of a major power entering a war; it cannot lead to a decrease in the probability of that event. Finally, in the situation of two-way conditional choice, the model provides for a major power's probability of entering a war either increasing or decreasing depending upon the choices of other major powers.

> Or, to draw the distinction in a somewhat different way, under two-way conditional choice, the decision of the first power leads to an increase in the probability that the second power will select the same option, regardless of the option chosen, but with a one-way conditional choice process this emulation effect occurs only if the first power decides to enter the war. [p. 203]

When the data on actual major power war entries between 1815 and 1965 are compared to the theoretical distributions generated by the three models, the two-way conditional choice model fits the data much better than the other two. Further examination of the major power record of war entry by Yamamoto and Bremer indicates that the fit of the two-way conditional choice model is stronger in the twentieth century than in the nineteenth century. Yamamoto and Bremer also note that although the two-way conditional choice model fits the data well, the Polya distribution that results from it can also be arrived at from assumptions of heterogeneity. That is, the same distribution of data implied by the model can result from assumptions that major powers have probabilities of war entry that differ from nation to nation and time to time. Such a process could be the result of nations that become, so to speak, war prone.

Although Yamamoto and Bremer demonstrated that major powers apparently influence each other in their propensities to enter ongoing wars, several additional questions of considerable import still remain because of certain limitations inherent in the manner in which they approached the subject. First, is the process of diffusion they observed composed of behavior that is infectious, heterogeneous, or possibly even something else? Second, is the possible diffusion limited to the major powers? Both of these questions have, in fact, been the subject of other research that has been relatively successful in answering them.[4]

The identification of the process through which war has diffused has been the object of inquiry by Davis *et al.* (1978) and Most and Starr (1980). Like the report of Yamamoto and Bremer, these two sets of investigators were interested in exploring the processes through which national war participation increased; these studies, however, were significantly different from each other in terms of data and methods. We will begin with the latter.

Most and Starr (1976) sought to (1) distinguish which of several war diffusion processes was operating and (2) evaluate the extent to which a particular factor contributed to the process they identified. We will discuss the first aspect of this research here and return to the second in the next section. Most and Starr drew upon three data sets on war. Not only did they use the wars between 1946 and 1965 identified by Singer and Small, they also used a combination of data from earlier war lists of Wright and Richardson that was compiled and presented by Singer and Small (1972, 82–128) as well as a list presented by the Stockholm International Peace Research Institute (SIPRI) (1970, Table 4A.1, 365–373).

At the outset, Most and Starr applied what may be termed the traditional approach to the detection of the interdependence of events (such as war): they compared their observed distributions with the theoretical distributions generated by the Poisson and modified Poisson models (Coleman 1964, chap. 10). Such a starting point appears appropriate because one of the key assumptions of the Poisson model is that the occurrence of an event does not alter the probability of a subsequent occurrence, while under the assumptions of the modified Poisson the occurrence of an event does alter the likelihood of subsequent events. Hence, it would appear that if the distribution derived from the standard Poisson model yielded the better of the two fits with the empirical distribution, then there was at least preliminary evidence to support the null hypothesis of no diffusion.

Table 5.1 reports the results they obtained by applying the Poisson and modified Poisson models to the three different data sets on war. The null hypothesis in each test was the proposition that the observed distribution of wars was Poisson or randomly distributed; the alternative to this was simply that the wars were not random. The χ^2 goodness-of-fit tests are reported at the bottom of the table. In the case of the Correlates of War (COW) data, the null hypothesis of random distribution could not be rejected except at the .70 level of significance; at the other extreme, the SIPRI data enabled rejection of the null hypothesis at the .02 level. In the case of the Wright–Richardson data, the results were marginal with rejection being possible only at the .10 level.

A plausible argument advanced by Most and Starr suggests that *different* types of war may exist and that those different types of war tend to result in different diffusion effects. Put more specifically, it seems reasonable to surmise that large-scale international wars may not have tended toward diffusion during the 1945–1965 period, while small-scale civil, guerrilla, and colonial wars may have been much more inclined to diffuse.

Most and Starr, however, note that three aspects of the traditional Poisson–modified Poisson models make them less than satisfactory in studying war diffusion at any level of conflict.[5] First, they are insensitive to the fact that the number of independent states in the international system increased from 66 in 1946 to 125 in 1965. So, in order to not conflate their results, they initially limited their analysis to the behavior of the 59 nations that were present throughout the 1945–1965 period. Hence, any diffusion on the part of the "new" states was omitted.

Second, they note that the traditional approach is insensitive to distinctions among the following: (1) *positive reinforcement*, in which a nation's war participation at time t increases the probability of participation at time $t + 1$; (2) *negative reinforcement*, the reverse of the previous process; (3) *positive spatial diffusion*, in which the participation of a nation in a new war increases the probability that other nations will experience war participation; and (4) *negative spatial diffusion*, in which, of course, the participation of a nation in a new war decreases the probability that other nations will become involved in subsequent wars.

These four types of processes are, of course, fundamentally different, but, as Most and Starr demonstrate, they have frequently been difficult to

TABLE 5.1
Comparisons of Observed, Poisson, and Modified Poisson Distributions of
New War Participations

Number of new war participants	Observed	Poisson	Deviation[a,b]	Modified Poisson	Deviation[a,c]
		COW data, 1946–1965[d]			
0	45	43.18	1.82	46.39	1.39
1	17	18.32	1.32	13.87	3.13
2	2	3.88	1.88	4.07	2.07
3	1	0.55	0.45	1.19	0.19
4	1	0.06	0.94	0.35	0.65
Totals	66	65.99		65.87	
		W–R data, 1946–1963[e]			
0	38	32.38	5.62	41.38	3.38
1	20	23.06	3.06	13.37	6.63
2	4	8.21	4.21	5.80	1.80
3	1	1.95	0.95	2.73	1.73
4	1	0.35	0.65	1.34	0.34
5	1	0.05	0.95	0.67	0.33
6	0	0.00	0.00	0.34	0.34
7	1	0.00	1.00	0.17	0.83
Totals	66	66.00		65.80	
		SIPRI data, 1946–1965[f]			
0	32	21.51	10.49	33.67	1.67
1	17	24.09	7.09	15.67	0.33
2	9	13.49	4.49	7.67	1.33
3	3	5.04	2.04	4.24	1.24
4	1	1.41	0.41	2.00	1.00
5	1	0.32	0.68	1.21	0.21
6	1	0.06	0.94	0.70	0.30
7	1	0.01	0.99	0.41	0.59
8	1	0.00	1.00	0.24	0.76
Totals	66	65.93		65.81	

SOURCE: Most and Starr (1977).
[a] Absolute values.
[b] For COW data, $\Sigma = 6.41$; for W–R data, $\Sigma = 16.44$; for SIPRI data, $\Sigma = 28.13$.
[c] For COW data, $\Sigma = 7.43$; for W–R data, $\Sigma = 15.38$; for SIPRI data, $\Sigma = 7.43$.
[d] $\gamma = 0.424$, $\alpha = 0.353$, $\beta = 0.340$.
[e] $\gamma = 0.712$, $\alpha = 0.467$, $\beta = 0.787$.
[f] $\gamma = 1.120$, $\alpha = 0.673$, $\beta = 0.944$.

distinguish. Analysts, however, must be able to make such distinctions if the study of diffusion is to be successful. Presumably, positive and negative processes ought to be distinguishable. Yet, Most and Starr show that, because their data are aggregated into increasingly long periods of time, the β term in the modified Poisson model (which is usually interpreted as a measure of the degree of diffusion in the events) also increases. The β term is a function of the variance/mean *ratio*, and, for the data utilized by Most and Starr, both increase as the time periods of the data are lengthened. Even if one assumes that this difficulty can be overcome, however, another problem remains. If a positive β term is obtained, no means exist to determine whether it was caused by positive spacial diffusion or positive reinforcement. The same is true in the case of a negative β term.

Several important points can be drawn from the critiques presented so far. The first is that, by differentiating among types of diffusion processes, we see that there can be very different sources of war diffusion.[6] The existence of these different underlying processes also argues against the use of highly aggregated global models or analyses that are inherent in the application of the Poisson model, a point to which we will return shortly. Because all four processes *could* be at work, and because we can find examples to indicate that all four probably are at work, the effects of each could wash out the others at the level of a global analysis. A similar effect is at work in global, cross-national studies of the relationship between domestic and foreign conflict (Starr and Most 1985; Stohl 1980).

As a way to deal with these problems, and because of the need to address both the theoretical and methodological difficulties discovered with the application of the Poisson model, Most and Starr (1980) chose to pursue relatively simple analytical techniques. First they constructed a set of turnover tables showing national war participation rates in two adjacent, nonoverlapping periods. Figure 5.1 illustrates the processes associated with each cell in their tables and Figure 5.2 shows the SIPRI data for the two periods they examined, 1946–1965 and 1956–1965. The data in these figures were then used to construct a set of ratios that could be compared to

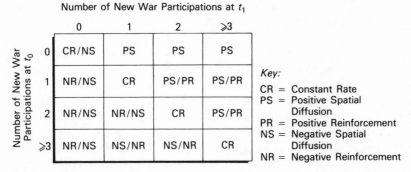

FIGURE 5.1. *Turnover Table: Expected patterns under the different diffusion/reinforcement models. From Most and Starr (1980, 937).*

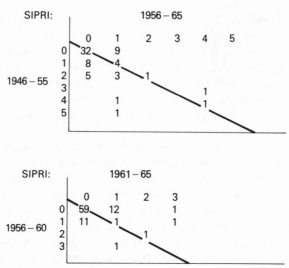

FIGURE 5.2. *Turnover in new SIPRI war participations, 1946–1965 and 1956–1965. From Most and Starr (1980, 938–939).*

several expectations of what would exist in the data if one of the processes was operating. The turnover tables and their ratios gave only slight support to the findings generated from the earlier probability models that diffusion was taking place.

However, the research design's tendency to treat all conflicts as being relevant to all nations—the third general critique of the Poisson—led Most and Starr to pursue the question of the "agent" for the spread of war. Most and Starr argue that one should not reasonably expect war to diffuse throughout the international system as a whole, but rather that such diffusion will be constrained within sets of nations that interact significantly with each other. (This research will be discussed in detail in the next section.)

The work of Davis *et al.* (1978) takes a different combination of approaches to the study of diffusion. Using the Singer and Small data set of all war participants between 1815 and 1965 (not just major powers), they examine the distribution of new warring dyads each year and compare this to the theoretical distributions derived from several probability models that are substantively distinct. The first is the Poisson, which reflects randomness in the emergence of warring dyads. A second model (Poisson with time-varying rate per dyad) could detect heterogeneity over time. A third model (the negative binomial) could detect either heterogeneity over individual nations or addictive contagion. These last two processes are identical except that under addictive contagion each dyad's initiation rate is not constant but, rather, tends to increase with each war. Finally, a model is developed to identify infectious contagion, a process in which a war within any dyad increases the probability that other warring dyads will form. The point of difference between this model and the others is that the dyads in the final model are not independent in their behavior.

Although the initial match of the data to the models reveals that the negative binomial fits best, the fit is very poor. A test of the model of infectious contagion, which *abandons* the independence condition, produces a reasonably good fit. Further analyses lead to the conclusion that wars between 1815 and 1965 grew in size through a process of infectious contagion; that is, one dyad's fighting increased the chances of other dyads beginning to fight. Another way of summarizing these results is to say that variation in war is (1) not random, (2) not due to particular periods being more war prone, and (3) not due to particular dyads fighting a great deal (for example, France–Germany, or, more generally, pairs of neighboring nations).

IDENTIFYING THE "AGENT" OF DIFFUSION: THE OPPORTUNITY MODEL

Although these findings identify a process of positive diffusion (including infectious contagion), they do not identify what might be called the "agent" of infection. That is, we may presume that nations do not pursue war entry in a random manner, but that some factor or set of factors influences their choices once a war begins or seems about to begin. What are these factors?

Interaction and Proximity

One possible answer is to be found in a line of research conducted by Most and Starr (1980; Starr and Most 1983, 1985). Looking at various data on international wars during the 1946–1965 period, they sought, as discussed previously, to first distinguish which of several war diffusion processes was operating and then to evaluate the extent to which a particular factor contributed to the process they identified. Recall that they argue that war should not be expected to diffuse throughout the international system as a whole. They have argued (Most and Starr 1975, 6–7; also see Most *et al.* 1987) that the spatial diffusion of wars is likely to be dependent on the degree of interaction that exists between the nations experiencing war/large-scale violent conflict and potential new war participants (nations at peace that could enter into large-scale violence). To the extent that a war is being waged by nations that have no close ties with other states, we would not expect that war to alter the probability that other nations would begin new wars or join in the initial war.

From the notion that the opportunity for behavior is a necessary condition, Most and Starr also postulate interaction as a *necessary* (but not sufficient) condition for spatial diffusion. This postulate implies that even if international conflicts do diffuse, there is no reason to expect that all nations will eventually become involved in an ongoing war—or eventually go to war—simply because there is war somewhere in the system. Thus, while spatial diffusion may operate at a systemic or global level if all nations have levels of interaction with one another, it is more likely that it would work *within subsets* of states that are somehow linked together.[7]

Interaction, therefore, may be important not only because it is a necessary condition for diffusion, but also because its existence among certain nations may determine the *direction* that such a process will follow. The general implication of this is that some wars may be interdependent if they are waged by nations that are interrelated and that others may be independent of each other if fought by states without interaction ties. A more specific implication is that, because it is unreasonable to posit that all nations in the world are equally interrelated, a consideration of the spatial diffusion of wars requires the development of some measure of the degree to which states interact (see Most *et al.* 1987, 7).

Having thus established the notion of interaction opportunity, Most and Starr argue that one of the primary reasons that nations interact is that they are neighbors, that is, because they share a border.[8] Clearly, nations interact with each other in a number of contexts and along a variety of political, military, economic, and social/cultural lines. It is, Most and Starr admit, an open question as to which of these lines of interaction among nations might be the most useful for delineating the groups of nations within which diffusion operates. However, using Starr's (1978) concept of "opportunity" as the *possibility* of interaction and the social science literature linking proximity to interaction [for example, Zipf's (1949) "principle of least effort"], they hypothesized that diffusion processes might operate most strongly among nations that share *geographic proximity*. To the extent that nations are physically "close," they are likely to interact and perceive their mutual importance. To the extent that a nation is "close" to a large number of other nations, it is faced with a greater risk that it may be threatened or attacked by at least one of its neighbors. The onset of some conflict alters the structural relationships, especially among relevant actors, and a restructured range of opportunities for conflict initiation would result.

To the extent that decisionmakers act to avail themselves of those new opportunities, the initial conflict *may* diffuse. At the same time that proximity may create risk situations, of course, it may also provide potential opportunities for international interactions (see Most and Starr 1985, 22).

They thus reason that borders do not cause violent conflict but instead contribute to it because the more borders a nation has, the *greater* (1) the number of risks and opportunities that confront the nation, (2) the likelihood that the nation or its territories will be conditionally viable, and (3) the level of the nation's uncertainty. Under these circumstances, nations are asserted to be more likely to go to war. More importantly, once a war starts on a nation's border, that nation may find its environment changed in such a way that it either (1) participates in a war it did not intend to participate in or (2) foregoes fighting a war it had intended to fight.

After delineating their measurement of borders (based on six expanding categories of homeland and colonial borders), Most and Starr examine each year between 1946 and 1965 to observe the "existence of a warring border nation as a 'treatment' that nations either did or did not experience" in each year. Using this approach permits them to record the transitions from t_1 to t_0 for any nation (1) from peace to peace (a_{11}), (2) from peace to war, but without the existence of a warring border nation (a_{12}), (3) from peace to peace, but with the existence of a warring border nation (a_{21}), and (4) from peace to at least one new war participation with at least one warring border nation (a_{22}). These transitions are represented in Figure 5.3. The resulting analysis clearly indicates a tendency for conflict to diffuse through borders.

The findings of Most and Starr with regard to the diffusion of war are summarized in Table 5.2.[9] Their approach included the application of three analytical methods to three data sets. Although in some ways—particularly with respect to the turnover tables—their results are mixed, on balance there appears to be some fairly clear indications that war spreads through a process of positive spatial diffusion. This is the same conclusion reached by Davis, Duncan, and Siverson. Most and Starr, however, get their strongest, most striking findings when they examine the impact of shared borders. In other words, they not only identify a process, but also identify a possible

Number of New War Participations t_1 to t_5

		0	$\geqslant 1$
Number of Warring Border Nations t_0	0	a_{11}	a_{12}
	$\geqslant 1$	a_{21}	a_{22}

FIGURE 5.3. *Transition table for treatments. From Most and Starr (1980, 942).*

TABLE 5.2
Tests of the Positive Spatial Diffusion/Warring Border Nation Hypothesis:
Subsequent New War Participations for All Nations at Peace at Each Successive t_0

Row variable (t_0)	Column variable (t_1 to t_5)	a_{12}	a_{22}	Ratio: $a_{22}/(a_{12}+a_{22})$
	Results based on COW data			
1946	1947–1951	0.000	0.364	100.0
1947	1948–1952	0.128	0.500	72.2
1948	1949–1953	0.083	0.393	78.6
1949	1950–1954	0.103	0.343	73.3
1950	1951–1955	0.000	0.098	100.0
1951	1952–1956	0.000	0.082	100.0
1952	1953–1957	0.000	0.078	100.0
1953	1954–1958	0.000	0.077	100.0
1954	1955–1959	0.052	0.130	50.0
1955	1956–1960	0.063	0.105	33.3
1956	1957–1961	0.000	0.000	0.0[a]
1957	1958–1962	0.000	0.027	100.0
1958	1959–1963	0.000	0.026	100.0
1959	1960–1964	0.000	0.026	100.0
1960	1961–1965	0.025	0.000	0.0[a]
	Results based on W–R data			
1946	1947–1951	0.083	0.313	93.8
1947	1948–1952	0.000	0.292	100.0
1948	1949–1953	0.091	0.196	90.0
1949	1950–1954	0.000	0.231	100.0
1950	1951–1955	0.000	0.020	100.0
1951	1952–1956	0.000	0.098	100.0
1952	1953–1957	0.000	0.094	100.0
1953	1954–1958	0.000	0.096	100.0
1954	1955–1959	0.077	0.128	62.5
1955	1956–1960	0.071	0.158	66.7
1956	1957–1961	0.000	0.118	100.0
1957	1958–1962	0.065	0.170	81.8
1958	1959–1963	0.131	0.185	38.5
	Results based on SIPRI data			
1946	1947–1951	0.176	0.300	80.0
1947	1948–1952	0.000	0.209	100.0
1948	1949–1953	0.100	0.163	87.5
1949	1950–1954	0.100	0.217	90.9
1950	1951–1955	0.100	0.061	75.0
1951	1952–1956	0.091	0.167	88.9
1952	1953–1957	0.000	0.170	100.0
1953	1954–1958	0.083	0.200	90.9
1954	1955–1959	0.063	0.172	90.9
1955	1956–1960	0.059	0.180	91.7
1956	1957–1961	0.000	0.123	100.0
1957	1958–1962	0.045	0.172	90.9
1958	1959–1963	0.000	0.237	100.0
1959	1960–1964	0.000	0.186	100.0
1960	1961–1965	0.067	0.226	93.3

SOURCE: Most and Starr (1980, 943).

[a] Zero new war participations occurred in the lagged period. Such occurrences were omitted from the error totals.

agent for the spread of war in shared borders.[10] As we will argue shortly, however, there may be considerably more to this than Most and Starr are able to show with their data. It should also be remembered that their strongest results in favor of diffusion were obtained with the SIPRI data set, the data set that was most sensitive to international conflict (that is, the data set that recorded the lowest level of conflict as war).

Interaction and Alliances

Another approach to the problem of war diffusion also focused upon the extent to which close relationships could be responsible for the diffusion of wars. The close relationships in this case were not borders but alliances.[11] The argument that alliances act as conduits for the expansion of conflict can be applied in two directions: enmeshing smaller, regional alliance partners in major power quarrels or dragging major powers into the regional conflicts of their smaller allies.

Siverson and King (1979, 1980) have explored the extent to which the independent effect of alliance memberships and the attributes of different types of alliances account for the extent and character of war diffusion. Recognizing the work of Most and Starr on diffusion and borders, Siverson and King argued that alliances, unlike geography, result from a deliberate process of policy choice. Nations clearly have much greater latitude in their choice of allies than in the choice of the nations on their borders (although, of course, states may attempt to manipulate their immediate political geography by eliminating or creating neighbors). It is thus important to recognize alliances as *manipulable* interaction opportunities.[12]

Put differently, in the present context it is reasonable to look at alliances as positions of policy preference. In this regard, two nations (or any other number of nations) forming an alliance are indicating, to some degree, that they share policy preferences. This conception of alliances, which was implicit in the work of Siverson and King, is explicitly developed in Bueno de Mesquita's (1981) model of expected utility. From our point of view the most important aspect of this realization is that nations are most likely to interact with nations with whom they share policy preferences. Thus, alliances are a basic, central, and potentially crucial mechanism of the interaction opportunities of states.

Several observers of alliance politics have commented upon their supposed entangling nature. Yet by no means does a consensus about the effects of alliances upon the spread of warfare exist. While Ball and Killough (quoted in Holsti *et al.* 1973, 274) assert that alliances "make it more probable that localized wars will spread," there are many contradictory assertions in the literature of international politics. For example, Liska (1962, 138) concludes that "in themselves, alliances neither limit nor expand conflicts." Similarly, Blainey (1973, 229) observes that it is "doubtful whether it [the alliances spread war hypothesis] fits many general wars."

In order to explore this question empirically, Siverson and King (1979) examined the impact of alliances on subsequent national war participation after two initial nations began the fighting. That is, they were unconcerned with the effect of alliances before any fighting began and only interested in what happened after war was underway. Their first analysis was not too illuminating. Although there was a very weak relationship between alliance membership and war participation, there was also ample evidence that the vast majority of nations with alliances (974, or 90.6 percent) did not join in wars when they took place. Siverson and King argued that many of these nations did not join the wars because they had no reason to do so; that is, the war was not relevant to their alliances. Can we reasonably expect a war involving one alliance to have an impact upon all other nations in other alliances no matter how distant or unrelated. For example, should we expect the war between Spain (a non allied nation) and Peru and Bolivia (allied with each other) in 1879 to have drawn in other aligned nations (for example, Turkey) even though none had an alliance with a belligerent? Probably not. Reacting to this line of reasoning, they then looked at whether or not nations having an alliance with either of the two initial belligerents were drawn into the war. The answer, as shown in Table 5.3, is clearly yes. It may also be noted in their table, however, that alliances could be associated with only 75 of the 188 (or 39.8 percent) national war participations.

While it might appear possible that alliances cannot be held responsible for the large-scale diffusion of war that takes place from time to time, they

TABLE 5.3
Alliance Partnership with Belligerents and War Participation, 1815–1965

	Alliance partnership with belligerent	
	No	Yes
War participation		
No	2150	223
Yes	113	75

Source: Siverson and King (1979, 43).
$N = 2561$, $Q = 0.73$.

TABLE 5.4
Alliance Membership and War Coalition, 1815–1965

		Alliance membership	
		No	Yes
War coalition			
No		52	24
Yes		36	76

SOURCE: Siverson and King (1979, 45).
$N = 188$, $Q = 0.64$.

argue that the critical question is whether shared alliance memberships are present in the coalitions composing the sides in large wars. In other words, many of the nonallied war participants may constitute the respective sides in a *two*-nation war into which *no* other nations entered. If so, as Siverson and King hypothesize, most of the 88 war participants without prewar allies fought without the benefit of coalition partners while those with prewar allies fought as members of a coalition. Their data, shown in Table 5.4, bear out the expectation. To a significant degree, alliances are related to the tendency for a war to expand and include nations other than the two initial participants. It should be noted, however, that Siverson and King did not examine the impact of variables other than alliances on expanding the size of a war. For example, they did not examine the impact of major power participation in a war on its tendencies toward expansion. If the findings of Yamamoto and Bremer were to hold—and it should be expected that they would—this could have been a fruitful line of inquiry.

Siverson and King did follow up a different question. Even if enough alliance partners joined in wars to produce large wars, there were still many that could have joined but did not. Were there identifiable characteristics of alliances that brought some allied nations into a war but not others? Looking largely at the attributes of the alliance itself, Siverson and King (1980) applied discriminant analysis to 290 cases of nations that had an alliance with one of the initial belligerents in a war. The variables they used were (1) the number of allies already in the war, (2) the power status of the allies, (3) the number of alliance partners, (4) the number of alliances, (5) the age of the alliance, and (6) the type of the alliance.

Applying discriminant analysis to the data produced a prediction for each case as to whether it would be among those joining or not joining the war, and the predicted group classification was then compared to actual behavior of each nation. Table 5.5, which displays the results produced by this procedure, shows that 85 percent of the cases are classified correctly.

TABLE 5.5
War Participation and Alliance Attributes, 1815–1965:
Discriminant Classification Results

	Predicted war participant[a]	
	No	Yes
Actual war participant		
No	211 (94.6)	12 = 223
		(5.4)
Yes	32 (47.8)	35 = 67
		(52.2)

SOURCE: Siverson and King (1980, 10).
[a] The numbers in parentheses are the percentages.

The distribution of the accurate predictions, however, is uneven; 94.6 percent of the nonparticipants are classified correctly, but only 52.2 percent of the participants are correctly placed.[13]

When they turned their attention to the incorrectly predicted cases in Table 5.5, Siverson and King introduced a variable not directly related to the character of the alliance and examined the effect of a nation's power status on its proclivities toward entering a war. What they found was revealing. The power status of a nation seems to have a bearing on whether a nation participates in a war or not. Of the 12 nonparticipants, 10 were minor powers, while a majority of the participants were major powers. Thus, it seems that minor powers are better able to avoid being pulled into wars than major powers. They also note that most of the minor power nonparticipation takes place after 1939, suggesting a lessened ability of major powers to control their minor powers allies in a more complex international system.

Siverson and King summarize the results of their research by reporting the alliance characteristics associated with war participation. According to them, nations will be most inclined to join their allies in a war when (1) many of their allies are in the war, (2) the allies they join are minor powers, (3) they have relatively few alliance partners, (4) the alliance in question is a defensive alliance, (5) the alliance is relatively new, and (6) they have a large number of alliances. Considering the third and sixth conditions produces the conclusion that a nation with many bilateral alliances is likely to join a war.

The two sets of research described here, those of Most and Starr and those of Siverson and King, have been concerned with examining the individual effects of borders and alliances, respectively, on the tendencies for wars to expand. Consequently, in many respects their results derive from bivariate analyses. There has been one study designed to compare the effects of borders and alliances on the diffusion process and to explore their interactive effects (Most *et al.* 1987). Looking only at the major power subsystem from 1815 to 1965, the study clearly indicates that the interaction opportunities embodied in warring border nations and warring alliance partners had an impact on the war participation of major powers. While much weaker than the post-World War II findings of Most and Starr, there were consistent indications that "treatments" of having warring border nations or warring alliance partners increased the probability that nations would experience subsequent new war participations. A final but important conclusion for this study is that, for the *major power* sample under analysis, *alliance* impacts were consistently more important than border effects on war initiation and diffusion. It is clear, however, that much more work needs to be done on the interactive effects of alliance and geography, and it must be done within a more inclusive data set than the major powers.

MOVING FROM "OPPORTUNITY" TO "WILLINGNESS"

An alternative approach is to shift the focus of discussion from opportunity to willingness. This shift can be approached from several different directions. In a series of articles, Most and Starr investigated a series of logical problems that have impeded the development of research design, theory, and cumulation in the study of international conflict and international relations in general.[14] One major theme is the confusion of necessary and sufficient conditions. As demonstrated by Most and Starr (1982), case selection and/or conceptual deficiencies often lead to data collections that permit the testing of *necessary* factors, while hypotheses and models are presented in terms of *sufficiency*.

In moving through logical problems of necessity, sufficiency, and research design, the concepts of opportunity and willingness—as necessary and sufficient conditions for the occurrence of international conflict and/or "war" (see Most and Starr 1983)—were used in analyses that clarified the ideas of foreign policy "substitutability," "nice laws," (Most and Starr 1984), and the general relationships between entity and environment. Using the previously cited work on diffusion as a starting point, these contributions investigated the relationships between opportunity and willingness in terms of the relationships between macro- and microanalysis, decisionmakers, and systemic environment. Drawing upon basic concepts provided by the Sprouts—environmental possibilism, environmental probabilism, and cognitive behaviorism (Sprout and Sprout 1969)—they looked at the conflict behavior of various actors or entities as constrained and affected by the "structure" of various environments.

This environmental structure could include the amount, distribution, and diffusion of conflict behavior in other "relevant" actors such as bordering nations or alliance partners. The "treatments" of warring border nations (or warring alliance partners) change the structure of the environment (particularly the "incentive structure") and provide much of the variance in systemic factors. The importance of the systemic context to the study of war resides in such changing treatments and their effects on opportunity, perception, and choice *rather than* the "enduring anarchic character of international politics" that Waltz (1979, 66) considers the central factor in systemic analysis, although it *cannot* explain the variance in foreign policy behavior.

It is not surprising that the general conclusion of the Most and Starr articles is that attention to *both* the macro- and microlevels is required for the understanding of international conflict, or foreign policy behavior in general. The environment, or macro/systemic factors, is shown to structure the possibilities and probabilities of foreign policy behavior. The diffusion discussions outlined previously stress the notion that interaction opportunities (for example, borders) are only necessary factors in the analysis of international conflict. Such systemic structures may, however, be causally important for conflict even though they are neither logically nor statistically sufficient for its occurrence. Structures may be important in the generation of conflict even though different structures and structural changes may not produce changes in the incidence, level, rate, or intensity of conflict. The effects of structures on conflict may not be detectable with standard techniques and approaches. Structures may, nevertheless, be "important" insofar as they delimit the ranges of behaviors that can be produced by decisionmakers—that is, as structures delimit possible opportunities for behavior as part of the "menu for choice" (see, especially, Most and Starr 1987).

Most and Starr (1987) conclude that systemic-level phenomena— polarity, preponderance, and parity, in particular—appear logically to set limits, ceilings or constraints on the amount of conflict that is possible. Because systems have different sizes and numbers of major powers, different systems may set different ceilings. Decisionmakers operate within those structurally defined constraints. While leaders cannot execute options for which they lack the objective capability, the evidence suggests that they are also unwilling to utilize all of the conflict initiation opportunities with which they are presented. Even though certain systems or types of dyadic power distributions may have greater potential for conflict, those potentials may not be—and in the post-World War II were not—exploited. Put differently, microlevel decision processes operate within constraints that may be at least partially defined by systemic-level phenomena.

The arguments developed by Most and Starr are not based exclusively on either a so-called "reductionist" microlevel decision theory *or* a systemic approach. Factors at both levels are important. Structural factors appear to define opportunities and set the "menu" of available options. Insofar as decisionmakers are left with at least the minimal discretion of choosing whether or not they wish to exploit an option or to refrain from its execution, however, it follows that those actors operate within structurally defined parameters and also that how they act—the choices they do or do not make—can be significant.

While both opportunity and willingness are required, the logical analysis provided by Most and Starr (1984, 1987, in particular) suggests that it is willingness, or the process of making choices to take advantage of foreign policy opportunities, that provides the dynamics of foreign policy and that explains variance in behavior. These analyses point to the centrality of the *process* of choice within *layers* of environmental constraints. Thus, systemic structures take on importance as "incentive structures": through cognitive behaviorism environmental possibilities and probabilities are linked to the entity through calculations of willingness or incentives to action. In essence, this means that it is important to study the dynamics and processes inherent in the general family of expected utility.

An Expected-Utility Approach

Thus, let us now turn to an approach that assumes at the outset that wars can diffuse among nations and that this diffusion can be understood as the consequence of a deliberative-choice process in which decisionmakers calculate the effect of various courses of action upon their policies. Working within the theoretical framework of expected-utility analysis, Altfeld and Bueno de Mesquita (1979) propose a model to capture how sides are chosen in war. They begin their analysis by making explicit two important assumptions. First, they assume that decisionmakers are rational utility maximizers. Second, they assume that a war is relevant to all nations, and, hence, all decisionmakers "consider the potential threat to their nation's sovereignty raised by each ongoing war" (p. 88). Without the first assumption there would simply be no way to make the theory of expected-utility work, and the calculations that follow in the article would have no foundation. Note, however, that it is a theoretical assumption; that is, it is an assumption that is required to make the theory viable. The second assumption is not theoretical in this same sense. Instead of being necessary to make the theory work, it is introduced to justify the examination of the expected utility of all nations with regard to a war. As was noted previously and will be elaborated on shortly, this assumption may be problematic.

After stating these two basic assumptions, Altfeld and Bueno de Mesquita lay out the basic elements of the expected-utility calculations of decisionmakers. In their conceptualization, decisionmakers expect that wars may have one of two outcomes: either the initially stronger combatant (O_s) wins or the initially weaker combatant (O_w) wins. For all third nations (C) there are two available strategies: either join the initially stronger combatant (J_s) or join the initially weaker combatant (J_w). All third nations are assumed to have a position with respect to the outcome of a war. Using P to designate probability and U to designate utility, Altfeld and Bueno de Mesquita propose the following algebraic form for the *expected utility for outcome*, $E(U_o)$, for a third nation:

$$E(U_o) = P[(O_s/J_s)U(O_s)] + [P(O_s/J_s)U(O_w)] \\ - [P(O_s/J_w)U(O_s)] + [P(O_w/J_w)U(O_w)]$$

By defining $P(O_s/J_s)$ as the capabilities of the initially stronger combatant plus the capabilities of the third party (C) divided by the total capabilities of the stronger combatant (S), the weaker combatant (W), and the third party (C) and defining all the other probabilities in the same manner, this equation is reduced to

$$E(U_o) = [C/(S + W + C)][U(O_s) - U(O_w)]$$

According to Altfeld and Bueno de Mesquita, there are two main implications of this reformulation. First, if $E(U_o)$ equals 0, then C will remain neutral; if it is positive they will join S, and if it is negative they will join W. Second, it means that

$$E(U_o) = [C/(S + W + C)][U(O_s) - U(O_w)]$$

All other things being equal, this means that very powerful nations are much more likely to join ongoing wars than are weak nations. The interests (or utility for outcome) of great powers need not be as greatly threatened as the interests of small powers before great powers will intervene in a war.

In order to obtain the overall expected utility, Altfeld and Bueno de Mesquita make one other point. They argue that without respect to the outcome of a war, third parties may derive utility from joining an ally in a losing cause because then their other allies are more likely to take their commitments seriously. Hence, there arises the following question: "How much does C value helping its embattled ally?" (p. 91). This is *utility from strategy*, or U_{st}. This leads to *overall expected utility*, $E(U)$, as

$$E(U) = E(U_o) + E(U_{st})$$

Finally, they introduce the idea of uncertainty, in which decisionmakers are considered to be making their judgments in environments having various degrees of uncertainty. When uncertainty is high, they argue that decision-makers are likely to have less confidence in their calculations than when it is low.[15]

Their research design encompasses the period 1816 through 1965 and includes all national decisions to remain neutral or enter into a war. Their data are drawn from Singer and Small (1972), but, unlike the Siverson and King study, are limited to decisions made during the first 2 months of a war. The limit of the first 2 months is imposed because they are not concerned with nations who enter because they are invaded or nations who join because of "possible bandwagon effects" (pp. 94–95).

These constraints produce a set of 40 decisions to enter wars. These 40 cases are nested within three related, but slightly different data sets. The measurement of E_u required estimates of national capabilities. During the period 1823–1965, composite capability data were available for only 1521 of the possible 2214 cases of national choice. A second data set of 2207 cases was derived by using the size of a nation's armed forces as the indicator of capability. Finally, they constructed a smaller data set that consisted of those cases in which either (1) C_s had a bilateral alliance with either S or W or (2) C_s was a nation that lacked an alliance but joined the war. This data set consisted of 144 cases.

Having stated their theory and operationalized the measurement of its components, Altfeld and Bueno de Mesquita then proceed to test it against the three data sets. Table 5.6, a reproduction of their Table 1b, reports the

TABLE 5.6
Predicted and Actual War Choices using the Basic Model

Actual choice	CHOICE			CHOICE$_{allied}$			CHOICE$_{af}$		
	J_w	Predicted neutral	J_s	J_w	Predicted neutral	J_s	J_w	Predicted neutral	J_s
J_w	14	6	0	14	6	0	13	10	0
Neutral	2	481	2	0	104	4	1	2163	3
J_s	1	13	2	1	10	5	1	15	1

SOURCE: Altfeld and Bueno de Mesquita (1979, 104).

results of a classification of the cases by the prediction of the expected-utility model, as generated by a probit analysis, by the actual choices made by the nations. In general, the results of the analysis offer fairly strong confirmation for expected-utility theory as a method of explaining national choices in choosing sides (or neutrality) in a war. The test of the theory, which was based upon the composite-capability measures, classifies 98.5 percent of the cases correctly, and the test based upon a smaller set of cases using only the size of the armed forces as an indicator of P' does slightly better in classifying 98.6 percent of the cases correctly despite the fact that summary measures of the probit analysis indicate that this is the weakest model. The analysis based upon the 144 cases of nations that had a bilateral alliance with a belligerent and the 6 cases of nations that entered without an alliance produces a classification that, although respectable by most standards, is the weakest of the group with only 85.5 percent of the cases classified correctly.

In sum, the general performance of the expected-utility model may be judged a success. Two of the analyses give results that can only be called exceptional, while one is at least as accurate as the best available alternative analysis (Siverson and King 1980). Two aspects of the data selection, however, may indicate a need for caution in evaluating these results.

The number of nations actually joining wars that Altfeld and Bueno de Mesquita have in their data is given as 40 (1979, Appendix). Siverson and King use 67 cases in their analysis. There is a difference between the two studies of 27 cases of nations joining wars. Why such a large difference? At three points Altfeld and Bueno de Mesquita state they are removing cases from their data base, and at another point some cases are missing without an explanation. The first set of cases is removed because they entered the war after the first 2 months and their inclusion would distort the analysis because it could reflect a "bandwagon" effect and, hence, would not be susceptible to the calculations of expected utility. Second, the nations that joined the Korean War are omitted because of the role of the United Nations in that conflict. Third, the entries of Canada, New Zealand, Australia, and South Africa into World War II are omitted because of missing data (p. 112). Finally, although the claim is made that 40 cases will be used, for unexplained reasons only 36 war joiners are present in the CHOICE and CHOICE_allied analyses.

Some observations may be made about this tendency for the data "shrink." It may well be true that nations joining a war after the first 2 months are getting on the "bandwagon." It is not difficult to locate cases to which this might reasonably apply, such as, for example, those nations joining the Allies in the latter part of World War II, nations who not only "won" but, by joining, also became members of the United Nations.

However, it also excludes potentially interesting cases such as the Italian and American entries into World War I and the expansion of a European war into World War II in December of 1941. Whatever one may want to say about these cases, it probably is not that they were nations trying to get on the "bandwagon." Moreover, it also would seem reasonable to include all of the "bandwagon" cases to see if they would fit because if they did not it would be a reasonably easy task to note that late joiners did not fit this particular formulation of the model.

The exclusion of the Korean War because of the role of the United Nations is also curious. Of the nations ultimately involved in that conflict, all but two joined after the first 2 months and would have been excluded under the "bandwagon" criteria. The two who joined within the first 2 months were the United States and the United Kingdom. Although it might be argued that the latter joined because of the approval given by the United Nations, it seems dubious at best to argue that United States policy was guided primarily by the acts of the United Nations.[16]

SOME CONCLUSIONS

Let us now summarize the results of the research we have reviewed. In so doing we will attempt not only to identify what has been established, but also to identify some areas for further research and to note an interesting puzzle.

It is fairly clear that the process through which wars may spread has been identified, as have some likely avenues for the operation of this process. Several of the studies indicate that warfare is contagious; that is, once a war begins there is a positive spatial diffusion process through which nations may be "drawn" into the conflict (Yamamoto and Bremer 1980; Davis *et al.* 1978; Most and Starr 1980).

While the research supports this conclusion, we are inclined to believe that the process by which it actually operates is more subtle than has been captured by the modeling work employed in that early research—even if we did some of it! Put simply, it is entirely clear that all nations are not affected in the same manner. It was this realization that led to the search for the "agent" of contagion. Here, both the work of Most and Starr and Siverson and King emphasize the idea of "interaction opportunity." While they agree upon the utility of that concept, however, they have differing substantive ideas as to how it actually operates in the international system. As related by the previous discussion, it is shared borders that create the communities of interaction for Most and Starr, while for Siverson and King (and, indirectly, for Altfeld and Bueno de Mesquita) it is alliances, not borders, that create interaction opportunities. With only one piece of preliminary research (Most *et al.* 1987) designed explicitly to determine the independent and joint effect of alliances and shared borders on the diffusion of conflict, however, it is difficult to make firm statements regarding the relative explanatory power of these two approaches.

There is another aspect of the differential spread of war that must be presented. Although it is probably correct that nations with both shared borders and mutual alliances have higher levels of interaction among themselves than with other nations, it is not clear from the data that all levels of war diffuse equally through shared borders or alliances. From the previous discussion of Most and Starr's findings, it may be recalled that, although diffusion was ultimately found in all three data sets used, it was most readily detected in the SIPRI and Wright–Richardson data. It was only uncovered in the Correlates of War data after considerable investigation, and, even then, the pattern there was the weakest of the three data sets. Clearly, major powers with global interests, those concerned with a whole range of behavior by its major power rivals and most likely to be central to the large-scale violent conflict reported in the Correlates of War data, are less likely to be affected by a diffusion process involving low levels of conflict than regional powers or minor powers.

A not unreasonable conclusion is that the larger the magnitude of the war, the less the tendency for the war to diffuse through borders. Siverson and King use only the Correlates of War data set, and so we are not able to observe the effects of alliances on the diffusion of wars of various magnitudes. It is clear, however, that within the COW data, alliances did have the effect of increasing the probability of a nation becoming involved in a war. Looking at the problem in this way leads us to suspect that relatively small wars (in terms of their magnitude) may well diffuse through borders, while larger wars, even though they may begin and even initially spread across borders, ultimately spread through the consequence of the political choices involved in alliances rather than the geographic circumstances of a nation. This, then, would constitute a somewhat richer description of how wars spread, one that is composed of two stages: localized onset through geography and more generalized participation through political groupings.

We now turn to an interesting puzzle, one that is not at all obvious: Given the amount of war that begins and the opportunities for diffusion, why does it not spread further? The question of why a spatial diffusion process *stops* or does not spread to all possible actors may be addressed by the concept of "willingness." Recall that interaction opportunities simply create the potential for diffusion and are, at best, necessary conditions. The decisionmakers of states must be willing to go to war given the changed levels of uncertainty and degrees of vulnerability associated with a war affecting other states (bordering states and/or alliance partners). Given the set of criteria for war presented in Most and Starr (1983, 139–140), it should be remembered that they demonstrate that only *1* of 16 possible combinations ensure that war will occur—when both states *i* and *j* have the opportunity ("minimum war-fighting capacity") and the willingness to fight (Most and Starr 1983, Figure 2). Recall also that Most and Starr elaborate the idea of *negative* spatial diffusion (and negative reinforcement). If past war experiences, or the war experiences of others, convey the lesson that the costs of violent conflict outweigh the possible gains, there can be negative diffusion as willingness is reduced (see Starr and Most 1985, 212–213).

Nothing in this discussion is inconsistent with the approach contained in expected utility. For example, within the operationalization of the expected-utility theory put forward by Altfeld and Bueno de Mesquita, alliances are used to calculate the values attached to the variables such as *utility* and *utilitystrat*. In fact, it might easily be argued that the measures of alliance attributes used by Siverson and King are a much less parsimonious (but relatively atheoretical) way of getting at the same thing as the measures of $E(U)$.

This, of course, is not to say that the expected-utility approach is theoretically congruent with the other approaches. It offers an insight into the structure of the factors which influence the choices of decisionmakers. It shifts attention from opportunity to willingness and gives that willingness a particular structure. Given the limitations of the data used by Altfeld and Bueno de Mesquita and the similarity of their findings to those of Siverson and King, it must be said that it is the theoretical cohesion of the approach that marks it as significantly advantageous over other work. The usefulness of the expected-utility approach will be shown in the discussion of the general puzzle identified previously.

For those interested in the spread of war, Table 5.7 tells an unhappy tale. Of the 50 wars contained in the Singer and Small data set, 58 percent showed no diffusion through "infection" while an additional 20 percent attracted just one additional nation. Put another way, tendencies toward such diffusion were modest; toward large-scale diffusion, they were strikingly modest. Indeed, most of the truly significant diffusion (that is, more than 5 nations participating in a war) is found in but 5 cases. The diffusion of warfare appears to be more limited than one might originally have thought.

Moreover, based upon parts of the analysis in the research of Most and Starr and Siverson and King, warfare is more limited in diffusion than either

TABLE 5.7
Size of War Coalitions, 1815–1965

Size	N
1 vs. 1	29
2 vs. 1	8
>3 vs. 1	10
>3 vs. >2	4

SOURCE: Singer and Small (1972).

the borders or alliance hypotheses would indicate. The size of the ratios obtained by Most and Starr in their analysis of the transition rates of nations indicates that there were numerous nations that shared a border with a nation or nations at war and yet did not become involved. Similarly, Siverson and King's data indicate numerous nations with alliances who did not join their allies in war. More precisely, of the 298 nations having alliances with belligerents only 75 (25.2 percent) actually joined in wars (1979, Table 2.2). Sabrosky's (1980) analysis of the wartime performance of alliances also indicates that they were subject to remarkable unreliability. Why do these two factors that have attracted our attention produce, in the end, less diffusion than one might reasonably expect?

Again, moving from opportunity to willingness, we find ourselves back to the calculation of expected utility. Looking at alliances, for example, and centering our attention of the analysis of CHOICE$_{allied}$, by looking back to Table 5.6 it may be seen (leaving aside the choices in such unlikely dyads as China–Bolivia) that the expected-utility model is actually able to specify the cases in which nations allied with an initial belligerent will not enter into the war. The simple answer to the question of why nations did not enter into a war might be expressed as "the nations not joining saw little to gain from their entry." Put slightly differently, and more strategically, the nations not joining a war did not identify their interests strongly enough with the nations fighting to make a choice for entry. As Altfeld and Bueno de Mesquita observe in the opening sentence of their paper "Waging war is the deadliest, and often most significant, political action that decisionmakers can undertake on behalf of their nation" (p. 87). Given the possible costs, the existence of which forms one of the fundamental components of any conceptualization of deterrence or internation influence, is it any wonder that wars were relatively contained?

Coming full circle we can use the structural opportunities presented by factors such as borders and/or alliances and diffusion processes as important—necessary conditions—in calculations concerning the critical decisions to enter war. The low incidence of willingness to take that decision and the relative containment of war support the empirical evidence that war is a relatively rare event. But, for certain types of nations exposed to certain "treatments" and the working of the process of positive spatial diffusion, the probability of war increases. Most and Starr (1980, 942) conclude: "Like lung cancer, wars are rare events. Nevertheless, just as in the relationship between smoking and cancer, having a warring border nation [or a warring alliance partner] *does increase the odds* that a subsequent new war participation will occur...."

The diffusion process has provided us with a useful tool for understanding the interaction of opportunity and willingness and the dynamic by which the probabilities of war increase.

NOTES

1. Partial support for this research was provided to H. Starr and B. A. Most by the National Science Foundation under Grants SES 82-08779 and SES 82-08815. R. M. Siverson was supported by the Institute on Governmental Affairs, University of California, Davis.

2. To clarify usage in this chapter, *infection* will refer to the growth of an ongoing conflict—Richardson was concerned with the process by which states not in a war "caught" the disease and entered *that* war. References to a more general *diffusion* or *spatial diffusion* denote a broader process in which "events of a given type in a given polity are conditioned by the occurrence of similar events in *other* polities at prior points in time" (Most and Starr 1981, 10). Welsh (1984, 3), for example, defines diffusion as "the process by which institutions, practices, behaviors, or norms are transmitted between individuals, and/or between social systems." See Most and Starr (1981) for a review of the diffusion concept and an attempt to reconceptualize diffusion and contagion processes. See also Welsh (1984) and O'Loughlin (1984).

3. The research had been done much earlier, but it was not until 1960 that the edited collection of Richardson's papers appeared.

4. Note also that Houweling and Siccama (1983) used an "epidemiological model" to demonstrate diffusion and that war behaviors were not independent events.

5. These arguments were expanded in Most and Starr (1981, 2–4), where eight limitations of the Poisson model were discussed. Tests based on the Poisson model may be inconclusive, may be misleading, are unable to distinguish *positive* diffusion or reinforcement from *negative* diffusion or reinforcement, are unable to distinguish between positive diffusion and positive reinforcement, are insensitive to changes in the number of potential "initiators" and "recipients," assume similar probabilities across a global sample, yield few insights into the substantive nature of diffusion effects, and fail to suggest how diffusion processes might operate. Only a few of these will be elaborated in the following discussion.

6. See Most and Starr (1981) for an extended analysis that concludes with "Diffusion/contagion research may be usefully seen as a specialized subfield of linkage politics. Diffusion/contagion concerns can be readily reformulated in terms which are congruent with the more general linkage models" (1981, 15).

7. This movement away from global data sets and analyses to subsets of interacting units is somewhat similar to Chaffee's (1975) notion of "nonnormal diffusion" or Eyestone's (1977) concept of "segmented emulation."

8. Commenting on the work of Most and Starr (1980) as well as that of Houweling and Siccama (1983), O'Loughlin (1986) similarly stresses *interaction*. He critiques the use of only "first order, or immediate neighbors," however, going on to argue that "immediate neighbors may be of greatest concern to a state, but spatial effects may also extend to second-, third-, or higher-order neighbors" (1986, 65).

9. As described in Starr and Most in a subsequent contribution (1983, 110–112), two expectations are tested in such a table: "The first expectation compares rates of transition from peace to war under the two different conditions of no warring border nations and at least one border nation. . . . The second expectation is concerned with a ratio—of those nations that went to war, what proportion also had a warring border nation at t_0?" The transition test expectation is that $a_{22} > a_{12}$, where a_{12} represents the ratio $a_{12}/(a_{11} + a_{12})$ and a_{22} represents the ratio $a_{22}/(a_{21} + a_{22})$. The ratio test is based on the ratio created from the number of cell entries and is calculated as $a_{22}/(a_{12} + a_{22})$.

10. The data set on African borders and war employed by Starr and Most (1983, 1985) in the investigation of positive spatial diffusion within the postwar African subsystem was subsequently used by Ward and Kirby (1987) as well. While Ward and Kirby employ more sophisticated statistical tests (such as Moran's I for the measurement of spatial autocorrelation) and suggest more complex design procedures, their analyses also demonstrate the spatial autocorrelation of conflict in Africa. So does the analysis of O'Loughlin (1986), whom they critique. Note also that O'Loughlin utilizes several different border measures, as do Most and Starr. O'Loughlin's results mirror those of Starr and Most (1976, 1983) with significant correlations between border/contiguity measures and war and results that become weaker as the definition/operationalization of contiguity becomes more stringent.

11. The following material is from Most et al. (1987, 7–9).

12. This conceptualization of alliance is additionally important for the development of theory about and including alliances. Most and Starr (1984) argue that because there can be the substitution of foreign policy behavior (for example, security as being enhanced by either arms building, arms transfers, joining alliances, breaking down opponents' alliances, or going to war), scholars must be able to think in broader terms and with more generic conceptualizations than often are found in narrow empirical studies of international phenomena. The alliance literature (Most and Starr 1984, 392) is specifically cited as an example of a theoretical dead end because of its narrow focus and failure to ask what alliances "really" represent in regard to the questions being asked.

13. While this should be of some concern, the proportional reduction of error for the analysis is, nonetheless, a respectable 0.615, which is about the same for the data when they are divided across the 2 centuries.

14. See particularly Most and Starr (1982, 1983, 1984, 1989) as well as Most and Starr (1981). These articles plus additional discussions will appear as a book-length monograph (Most and Starr 1989).

15. The measurement of $E(O_s)'$ and $E(O_w)$ is the Tau B correlation of their alliance commitments with C. This measure is derived from earlier research done by Bueno de Mesquita (1975, 1978). Readers interested in it are referred to those articles, but we should note that $E(U)$ will be high when C has an alliance portfolio similar to either S or W and that, conversely, $E(U)$ will be low for C when its alliance portfolio is unlike S or W. The measurement of $E(U_{st})$ differs from $E(U_o)$ in that the former is derived only if the preferred side wins, while the latter is obtained simply by participating on the preferred side. Hence, $E(U_{st})$ indicates the strategic importance that C attaches to each of the initial belligerents. This measure is simply

accomplished through the use of a "dummy" variable—if C has a defense alliance or an entente with either S or W, then a 1 is recorded; otherwise, a 0 is recorded. The uncertainty of the international system is measured by observing changes in its membership.

16. Less troubling is the omission of the four Commonwealth nations in 1939 because of missing data. What is missing is a record of international alliances for these nations. From the time that they became independent of the United Kingdom in the wake of World War I, none of these four nations had a formal alliance with any other nation. Their relationship to the Commonwealth carried no obligation to defend the United Kingdom. Because these nations were not formally aligned, it is highly likely they would have been predicted to remain neutral by the model; in this case they would have become error cases. The problem here is one of absent indicators and not the theory or research design.

PART II

Minimally Dyadic Theories of War

CHAPTER 6

The Contribution of Expected-Utility Theory to the Study of International Conflict

Bruce Bueno de Mesquita

Stanford University

The study of international conflict has languished without appreciable evidence of scientific progress for more than two millennia.[1] Diplomatic and military histories found in the Old Testament and in the writings of such ancient scholars as Thucydides or Kautilya as well as those of more modern authors such as Clausewitz, Creasy, Richardson, and Morgenthau indicate that good foundations have been laid and give hope that such progress can be made. A common theme runs throughout the classics of international relations. That theme is the self-interested pursuit of gain by national leaders on their own behalf and on behalf of their nations. This is also the theme of research concerned with exchanges in markets. Indeed, Adam Smith's description of the operation of markets as an invisible hand guiding production and investment decisions through self-interested choice is a widely used description of the interaction of nations. Here, I apply a version of that perspective—expected-utility theory—to the study of international conflict.

INTRODUCTION TO EXPECTED-UTILITY THEORY

Expected-utility theory originated as an explanation of microeconomic behavior. Although the subject of some controversy (Tversky and Kahneman 1981), expected-utility theory is widely recognized as being at the core of contemporary microeconomics. Its prominence is partially due to the great success its proponents have enjoyed in predicting the aggregated economic decisions of individuals and partially due to its logical elegance.

The essence of expected utility theory is that

1. individual decisionmakers are rational in the sense that they can order alternatives in terms of their preferences;

2. the order of preferences is transitive so that if A is preferred to B and B p C (where "p" is to be read as "is preferred to"), then A p C;

3. individuals know the intensity of their preferences, with that intensity of preference being known as utility;

4. individuals consider alternative means of achieving desirable ends in terms of the product of the probability of achieving alternative outcomes and the utility associated with those outcomes; and

5. decisionmakers always select the strategy that yields the highest expected utility.

These five conditions can be understood as setting out two straight-forward circumstances. Decisionmakers' choices among opportunities are constrained by the prospects of success and failure and by the utility, or intensity of motivation, they feel for achieving one objective or another. Thus, structural factors and individual psychology come together to shape choices.

Some students of politics believe expected-utility theory provides explanations of political decisions. Probably the best-known efforts to explain political phenomena in this way are concerned with voting (for example, Riker and Ordeshook 1973; Ferejohn and Fiorina 1974), legislative decisionmaking, and campaign strategies (for instance, Shepsle 1972). Others have become interested in the applicability of expected-utility reasoning to the study of international conflict (see, for instance, Bueno de Mesquita 1981; Gilpin 1981; Brito and Intriligator 1985). Particularly noteworthy in this regard are studies of deterrence (Russett 1963; Ellsberg 1969; Kugler 1984; Huth and Russett 1984; Petersen 1986) and of war termination (Wittman 1979; Mitchell and Nicholson 1983). Additionally, several colleagues and I are trying to construct a general theory of conflict using an expected-utility approach (Altfeld and Bueno de Mesquita 1979; Berkowitz 1983; Bueno de Mesquita 1981, 1983, 1985; Kugler 1984; Bueno de Mesquita and Lalman 1986; Bueno de Mesquita et al. 1985; Morrow 1985; Petersen 1986). Of course, it remains to be seen how successful that endeavor will be. I hope to demonstrate that there is reason to be optimistic.

EXPECTED-UTILITY MODELING

Before turning to an examination of specific expected-utility models of conflict behavior, let me briefly review the basic structure of decisions as seen from this perspective. I begin with an abstract example of a choice between a sure thing (which I will denote O_2 for outcome 2) and a risky lottery. Then I turn to an illustrative application of the expected-utility model to a real historical circumstance. Later, I explore the general uses of such a theory in trying to understand conflict decisionmaking.

I posit three outcomes, O_1, O_2 and O_3, such that O_1 p O_2 p O_3. This is equivalent to saying that outcome 1 is valued more highly than outcome 2, and that outcome 2 is valued more highly than outcome 3. Using notation as a shorthand we can say, then, that $U(O_1) > U(O_2) > U(O_3)$ where U denotes utility. Let the probability of attaining O_1 be P, and let the probability of attaining O_3 be $1 - P$. A decisionmaker chooses between accepting O_2 for sure or selecting a strategy that has some chance (P) of resulting in the most desirable outcome (O_1) and some chance $(1 - P)$ of resulting in the least desirable outcome (O_3). The decision to pursue O_1 at the risk of ending up with outcome 3 is called a lottery. In a lottery there are two or more possible outcomes, each of which will occur with some probability, such that *the sum of the probabilities must be 1.0.* That is, some outcome must occur and all feasible outcomes are represented. This is why the probability of O_1 (P) plus the probability of O_3 $(1 - P)$ must equal 1. An expected-utility-maximizing decisionmaker will select the risky lottery between O_1 and O_3 over the sure outcome O_2 if the anticipated return from gambling on the lottery is believed to be larger than the assured value of getting outcome 2. The strategic decision to gamble on getting O_1 can be represented with notation as follows:[2]

$$PU(O_1) + (1 - P)U(O_3) > U(O_2) \tag{6.1}$$

By the same expected-utility logic, the decisionmaker will select the sure outcome (O_2) if

$$PU(O_1) + (1 - P)U(O_3) < U(O_2) \tag{6.2}$$

and will be indifferent between the alternatives if

$$PU(O_1) + (1 - P)U(O_3) = U(O_2) \tag{6.3}$$

Of course, I do not suggest that real decisionmakers *consciously and explicitly* make the numerical calculations implied by the expected-utility model. Rather, the argument is that people inherently act *as if* they make such calculations. This is equivalent to saying that a mathematician could write equations that describe the trajectory of a tennis ball hit with top spin at a specific velocity and aimed at a particular portion of a tennis court. John McEnroe surely would not recognize those equations as being any part of his tennis game. Yet, he acts *as if* he makes such calculations with remarkable precision and frequency.

How might the simple principle illustrated by Equations 6.1, 6.2 and 6.3 help us understand real decisions? Consider, by way of illustration, Miltiades' exhortation to his fellow generals on the eve of the battle of Marathon. They were faced with the choice of initiating or not initiating combat with the superior forces of the Persians. Miltiades argued as follows for fighting in the face of very poor odds:

> Never since the Athenians were a people, were they in such danger as they are in at this moment. If they bow the knee to these Medes, they are to be given up to Hippias [this is equivalent to O_3, the outcome if they do not fight], and you know what they then will have to suffer. But if Athens comes victorious out of this contest, she has it in her to become the first city of Greece [this is equivalent to O_1]. Your vote is to decide whether we are to join battle or not. If we do not bring on a battle presently, some factious intrigue will disunite the Athenians, and the city will be betrayed to the Medes [this is equivalent to O_2, which in this instance is the same as O_3]. But if we fight, before there is anything rotten in the state of Athens, I believe that, provided the Gods will give fair play and no favour, we are able to get the best of it in the engagement. [Herodotus 1954, lib. vi, sec. 109; comments in brackets have, of course, been added for illustrative purposes.]

Here we have the essence of an expected-utility decision problem. While not intended to indicate any special insight that is gained from formalism, let me structure this quotation as an expected-utility analysis to make clear why that perspective leads to the expectation that the Athenians would have fought against seemingly insurmountable odds.

Miltiades' position boils down to the conclusion that defeat in battle did not represent an inferior outcome to capitulation, while engaging in battle held out hope of a superior result. Miltiades' claim was straightforward. If the Athenians "do not bring on a battle presently . . . the city will be betrayed to the Medes." This, presumably, represented an extremely undesirable outcome. If the Athenians fought and lost, then they would again be delivered up to Hippias and the Medes, representing the same undesirable result. Call the utility of that outcome L. Of course, by fighting, the Athenians had some slim chance of winning. Call the utility of that outcome W and denote its probability as P where, as with all probabilities, P is between 0 and 1. Clearly, the utility of L is less than W. The choice facing the Athenians as described by Miltiades was between L for sure and $[PW + (1 - P)L]$. Miltiades made clear that he did not believe P was zero

("I believe that, provided the Gods will give fair play and no favour, we are able to get the best of it in the engagement"). Miltiades' claim was that there was nothing to lose and potentially something to gain by fighting. Symbolically, this is equivalent to the expected-utility statement that $[PW + (1 - P)L] > L$. Therefore, since the value of the lottery was larger than the value of the sure outcome (surrender to the Medes), the Athenians chose to engage in battle.

The particular example of the decision to fight at Marathon is very simple. Indeed, it is evident that the formalism adds nothing new to the interpretation or understanding of the decision of the Athenian generals. But it does help show what the logic is that underlies expected-utility theory. I might, however, have chosen a more contemporary example to show how expected-utility theory does lead to new insights. For instance, we know that great powers engage in warfare far more often than do lesser states, particularly as third-party entrants to ongoing wars. It would be beneficial to have an explanation of this observation that is compatible with a broad array of other phenomena.

The decision to enter an ongoing war is, as I demonstrate formally later in this essay, a function of the intensity of one's preferences for the goals of the combatants. It is also a function of one's perceived prospect of influencing the outcome (Altfeld and Bueno de Mesquita 1979). Great powers, by definition, have a high a priori expectation of being able to influence the outcome of conflicts among weak states. The United States leadership, for instance, seemed to believe that it had a high probability of influencing the outcome of the war in Vietnam. As the perceived probability of success in war increases, the utility for success can decrease and still satisfy the critical threshold level of expectation at which one is willing to commit troops to combat.[3] This means that *great powers have a higher probability of fighting in wars whose outcome is not of great significance to them* than do lesser powers. Weaker states cannot rationally engage in such wars. They are limited to fighting in disputes in which they perceive their stakes to be quite large.

Protests to United States involvement in Nicaragua—as with protests to the war in Vietnam—that depend on claims or demonstrations that political outcomes in those parts of the world are not vital to the national interest are likely to fall on deaf ears. This is certainly one important strategic implication that follows directly from an expected-utility theory of third-party participation in war. Similarly, fears of American involvement in such places as Nicaragua are also warranted by the expected-utility approach. Those who wish to prevent such involvement make a mistake by focusing attention on the absence of vital security risks emanating from Nicaragua. If protestors hope to succeed, they would be better off focusing on the possibility that the President's perceived probability of success may be too high. In Vietnam, the United States miscalculated its chances for success. The danger of such miscalculations is the important lesson from Vietnam for those who wish to prevent the prospect of American combat troops in Nicaragua. And, for those who wish to encourage such involvement, the lesson from expected-utility theory is that they must examine closely the bases for their expectations of success. Claims that Nicaragua is vital to American security interests are not essential to the ultimate decision to become or not become involved in combat there. But, such claims can serve as an effective counterargument to those who maintain that we will not succeed. If the stakes are great enough, decisionmakers will choose to become involved even in a losing effort.

STANDARDS FOR EVALUATING SCIENTIFIC PROGRESS

Most of the remainder of this essay focuses on a general explication of how the expected-utility approach helps bring new insights to the forefront and how it can provide a foundation for accurate forecasting and for policy formation. My goal is to present evidence that shows that an expected-utility approach provides a more comprehensive explanation of generalizable results than do its extant alternatives. At the same time, I hope to show that an expected-utility viewpoint is integrative, encompassing the key insights of many other perspectives, while yielding important generalizations and significant benefits as a precise tool for forecasting and case study analysis.

I will make substantial claims here for the efficacy of a deductive, axiomatic approach to the study of international conflict. At the outset, however, let me be very clear about the important limitations of such an approach and, especially, about the complementarity between mathematical models of conflict and less formal but often more subtle and more detailed studies of particular events. Formal models are not intended to illuminate the rich details and texture of events. Rather, they are designed to specify a simplified, ordered view of reality that reveals internally consistent and externally useful general principles. Formal models are not a substitute for rich information about the events studied. But they can complement the richness of detail, providing more order and strengthening the ability to generalize. In doing so, formal models do sacrifice details for breadth and specificity for generality. When combined with expert knowledge, a powerful synergy results in which the level of insight is often greater than can be gleaned from expert judgment or from formal models alone. Indeed, in several years of close collaboration with area specialists, I have found that expected-utility analyses informed by expert knowledge and interpreted with the expert's eye for nuance yields results not only well beyond those of the modeler's interpretation, but also well beyond those of the area expert working without benefit of the model's structure and logical rigor.

Important limitations of any decisionmaker-oriented perspective arise out of the difficulties of attributing policies to specific leaders. If, as is usually done, we speak of *national* policy, we must be conscious of the assumptions made regarding the aggregation of preferences. Policies are often the product of discussion and compromise among competing elites. Groups of individuals, each behaving in an individually rational way, may produce policies that are contrary to the interests of many, possibly even all. This occurs because cycles yielding intransitive social orderings are possible if issues are multidimensional or, on unidimensional issues, if utilities are not single peaked. The well-known Condorcet paradox draws our attention critically to any endeavor that assumes collective rationality. Behaviors such as bluffing in the face of war may be explicable on strategic grounds, but they may also be the consequence of cyclical preferences among competing elites or bureaucracies. These problems are not insurmountable, but they do remind us of the limitations inherent in applying rational choice theories to collective action.

Other limitations arise out of controversy over the axioms of expected-utility theory (Tversky and Kahneman 1981) and over the assumption of independence across decisionmakers. This, perhaps the most serious short-coming in my research to date, ignores the game-theoretic implications of interactive, contingent behavior. There is an impressive, growing body of research on international relations that relies on a game-theoretic framework (Axelrod 1984; Brams 1985; Morrow 1987; Wagner 1982; and Zagare 1987). Recent developments in the theory of sequential games with limited information (Kreps and Wilson 1982a,b) open up new possibilities of sophisticated theoretical investigations of problems that are particularly well-suited for students of international relations (Morrow 1987). I antici-pate that my own future research will draw much more heavily on the theory of sequential games with imperfect information (Bueno de Mesquita and Lalman 1988).

The main objective behind the construction of a theory is the identifica-tion of lawlike statements. Sometimes, individuals with different epistemol-ogies make the mistake of believing that differences in their intellectual goals reduce to claims about the relative usefulness or meritoriousness of their endeavors. Often this is a problem among students of international conflict. Some researchers are motivated by a desire to explain and understand a specific event and to isolate its unique qualities. Others are motivated by an interest in commonalities across events. Each is an entirely reasonable and important concern, although sometimes each is incommensurable with the other. In this regard, a distinction—not always sharp—should be made between what is meant by science and what is meant by wisdom.

By science I mean the explanation of classes of events through an appeal to logically consistent arguments (lawlike statements) that are parsimonious in the relationship between assumptions and how much they explain and are buttressed by observations of replicable relations among variables without appeal to special (ad hoc) factors in individual cases. Scientific knowledge can be transmitted without the recipients personally experiencing the phenomenon being investigated. Science requires generalizations, and these generalizations must be corroborated by empirical evidence.

Wisdom, as a quality of a wise individual, is an appeal to special or particular knowledge and insight that is not necessarily buttressed by lawlike statements or by multiple observations (or replications) of the relations among variables. Wisdom often depends on personal experience. It does not require corroboration from an empirically diverse base of evidence. As such, personal wisdom is rarely transmissible or replicable, but it is almost always detailed and insightful about individual events.[4] There can be wisdom without science; science almost always proceeds from wisdom.

Scientific progress requires some broadly agreed upon standards for evaluating competing explanations of like phenomena. This is as true in the study of international relations as it is in the study of the physical universe. An interesting feature of most standards of scientific progress is that they require evidence from many events rather than from a single case history. Virtually all widely utilized means of evaluating the gains from scientific inquiries focus attention on the implications that follow from the *preponderance* of evidence. This is as true of studies rooted in the methodology that leads to the accumulation of many case histories as it is of those whose methodology encourages statistical significance testing. The particular standard for measuring scientific progress that I use is that suggested by Lakatos:

> A scientific theory T is *falsified* if and only if another theory T' has been proposed with the following characteristics: (1) T' has excess empirical content over T: that is, it predicts *novel* facts, that is, facts improbable in the light of, or even forbidden by, T; (2) T' explains the previous success of T, that is, all the unrefuted content of T is included (within the limits of observational error) in the content of T'; and (3) some of the excess content of T' is corroborated. [Lakatos 1978, 32]

It is these criteria—that a new theory explains more than rival theories—that I apply in evaluating the contribution of expected-utility theory to understanding international conflict. I begin with a comparison of expected-utility theory to the most prominent theories in international relations, namely those that propose relationships between the distribution of power among states and the incidence of war.

THEORIES OF POWER, ALLIANCES, AND WAR

Two prominent views of war emanate from balance-of-power theories (Gulick 1955; Morgenthau 1973; and Waltz 1979) and from power-preponderance theories (Organski 1968; Organski and Kugler 1980; Keohane 1980, 1984; Gilpin 1981; Modelski and Morgan 1985). These perspectives lead to fundamentally different hypotheses about the factors leading to war (or peace) and the motives underlying the selection of allies. For instance, many balance-of-power theorists hypothesize that

1. a balance of power tends to produce peace and an imbalance of power tends to produce war;

2. alliances tend to be nonideological, power-seeking arrangements; and

3. alliances tend to be short lived.

Some power preponderance theorists hypothesize that

1. a balance of power tends to produce war and an imbalance of power tends to produce peace;

2. alliances tend to be ideological rather than power-seeking arrangements; and

3. alliances tend to be long lived.

These propositions seem diametrically opposed and appear to be incompatible, and there has been considerable debate regarding competing views of the relationship between power distributions and war. An expected-utility theory of conflict choices, however, provides the foundation for deducing the conditions under which each of these seemingly incompatible propositions is true. This is a bold claim. My burden is to demonstrate that this claim is supportable in the face of Lakatos' criteria for assessing scientific progress. Let me turn to a demonstration of this important assertion.

EXPECTED UTILITY, POWER, AND WAR

Let us assume that decisionmakers calculate the expected utility associated with challenging and not challenging a putative adversary. For those in a threatening situation, assume that the probability of them escalating the pressure they bring to bear in pursuit of their objectives increases as a strictly monotonic, differentiable function of their expected utility. The more they believe they stand to gain, the more likely they are to use force in pursuit of their objectives. Then, as has been shown elsewhere (Lalman 1988; Bueno de Mesquita and Lalman 1986), the functional form of the probability of escalation by nations i and j is as in Figure 6.1.

We may now define the probability of various types of conflict in accordance with the probability that i, j, or both choose the strategy of escalation over the strategy of negotiation. Let

$$P(\text{War}) = P^i(\text{Esc}_i) \times P^j(\text{Esc}_j) \qquad (6.4)$$

$P(\text{Intervention})$
$$= \left\{ P^i(\text{Esc}_i) \times [1 - P^j(\text{Esc}_j)] \right\} + \left\{ P^j(\text{Esc}_j) \times [1 - P^i(\text{Esc}_i)] \right\} \qquad (6.5)$$

$$P(\text{Peace}) = [1 - P^i(\text{Esc}_i)] \times [1 - P^j(\text{Esc}_j)] \qquad (6.6)$$

$$P(\text{Violence}) = 1 - P(\text{Peace}) = P(\text{War}) + P(\text{Intervention}) \qquad (6.7)$$

Equation 6.4 says that the probability of war $[P(\text{War})]$ is equal to the product of the probability that i intends to escalate its level of threat against $j [P^i(\text{Esc}_i)]$ and j intends to escalate its threat against $i [P^j(\text{Esc}_j)]$. The probability of an intervention (that is, Equation 6.5 for the asymmetric use of force) is equal to the probability that one nation will escalate beyond a verbal threat while the other nation selects a posture that does not include the use of force. The other definitions have analogous interpretations.[5] It is evident from Figure 6.1 that two points exist in which expectations about the consequences of challenging an adversary (and its coalition of supporters) are balanced. From Equation 6.4 we see that the probability of war is high at the point marked A on Figure 6.1 because the probability of escalation to the use of force is high for both nation i and nation j. At the point marked B, the probability of war is low. Balance-of-power theorists fail to differentiate between these two conditions under which balance has radically different implications. Likewise, areas C and D represent situations of imbalanced expectations in which one adversary expects far more than the other from a conflict. In one such instance (area C) the probability of war is high. In the other instance (area D) the probability of war is low.

Points A and B depict the crucial moment of the "power transition" in which one hegemonic nation is surpassed by another (Organski 1968;

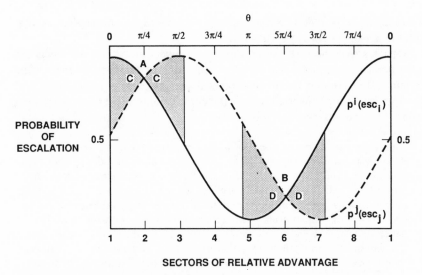

FIGURE 6.1. *The probability of conflict escalation.*

Organski and Kugler 1980, 1986). At point A, *j* overtakes *i*. At point B, *i* overtakes *j*. These two transitions are accompanied also by a high and a low probability of war, respectively. The empirical attention of those supporting a balance-of-power perspective seems focused on situations typified by point B or area C. Power-preponderance theorists seem to have their attention drawn to situations characterized by point A or area D. Preponderance theories do not isolate such circumstances as point B or area C in which balanced expectations lead to peace. Balance-of-power theories overlook conditions under which balance implies war (point A) or imbalance implies peace (area D). The expected utility framework, however, does make these distinctions. Consequently, it has the potential to differentiate between situations when preponderance or balance encourages peace or war. A critical aspect of Figure 6.1 is that it differentiates situations with high or low risks of war as a function of the expectations of gains by adversaries. Most power-oriented theorists make the mistake of assuming that if both sides have the same expectations, each side's probability of victory is 0.5. Subjective and objective probabilities of victory then become confused (Blainey 1973). Of course, *i* may believe its prospects of victory are high at the same time that *j*'s expectations are high (for example, point A in Figure 6.1), or both *i* and *j* may believe that their prospects for victory are very low (for example, point B). In neither of these two examples is it the case that balanced expectations are equivalent to *i* and *j* having a probability of victory equal to 0.5. The historical record should be—and is—consistent with the expected-utility perspective.

Debates over how the distribution of power affects the prospects for peace persist largely because of two limitations of "realist" theories. One common shortcoming of power-centered perspectives is their conviction that understanding power alone is sufficient to comprehend relations among nations. As one observer astutely notes,

> [I]t is dangerous to put in a key position a concept which is merely instrumental. Power is a means toward any of a large number of ends (including power itself). The quality and quantity of power used by men are determined by men's purposes.... The "realist" theory neglects all the factors that influence or define purposes. Why statesmen choose at times to use national power in a certain way (say a policy of "imperialism") rather than in another is not made clear. The ... beliefs and values which account in great measure for the nation's goals and for the statesmen's motivations are either left out or brushed aside. ... Similarly, internationally shared beliefs and purposes are left out. [Hoffmann 1960, 31]

Expected-utility theory shares the view that focusing on power alone is not enough. It takes into account power through the estimation of probabilities of success and failure, but it also takes into account values and purposes through the estimation of utilities.

A second limitation of most power-based theories is rooted in mis-understandings about the actual driving force behind the relationship between system structure and international conflict (Bueno de Mesquita 1978). Theories about the balance of power and war, or about bipolarity and peace, for instance, are not really theories about structural determinants of conflict at all. The assumptions underlying such theories are generally about how people respond to uncertainty and to risks. What makes these theories appear systemic in character is the tendency to assume that everyone responds to risks or to uncertainty in the same way (Kaplan 1957; Waltz 1964; Deutsch and Singer 1964). According to many balance-of-power theorists, for instance, the incentive to wage war is diminished by the belief that the chances for success are only fifty-fifty. This is similar to the statement that decisionmakers facing the choice of waging war act as if they are generally risk averse. Conversely, many preponderance theorists seem to subscribe to the belief that war is most likely when opposed forces are roughly equal, implying that decisionmakers generally act as if they are somewhat risk acceptant. Such assumptions of uniform responses to uncertainty or to risks are very restrictive and certainly inconsistent with the expectations that follow from psychological research or from common observation. Expected-utility theory allows for the possibility that decision-makers may be risk acceptant or risk averse; they vary in their willingness to take chances. The willingness to take risks is described by the shape or curvature of each decisionmaker's utility function. Unlike most power-centered theories, risk-taking propensities are not implied by assumption in expected-utility theory; risk-taking propensities are variable. Consequently, the expected-utility approach demonstrates that the distribution of power—independent of utilities—has no direct theoretical bearing on the likelihood of war. This is easily shown by recognizing that expected utility is always the product of the probability of alternative outcomes and the utility associated with those outcomes.

Assume that the probability of success in war is a function of power, as is asserted by virtually all *Realpolitik* theorists. The expected-utility theory reveals deductively that rational national leader *i* can initiate a war if and only if

$$P_s^i \geq 1 - [U_s^i - E^i(U_{nc})]/[S_j(U_s^i - U_f^i)] \tag{6.8}$$

where P_s refers to *i*'s probability of success, U_s and U_f refer to the utility of success and failure, respectively, and $E^i(U_{nc})$ refers to *i*'s expected utility from not challenging the putative opponent (Bueno de Mesquita 1985).

Equation 6.8 indicates just how small a chance of success a decision-maker is willing to live with before deciding not to challenge a putative adversary. The right side of the expression evaluates how large a proportion of the total stakes (the denominator) in a dispute are representative of potential gains (the numerator). This "law" of conflict decisionmaking reveals that rational actors can choose to wage war even when their subjective (or real) prospects of victory are very small if they care enough about the issues in question.

For any probability of success (and, therefore, for any level of relative power), there is a possible set of utility values such that waging war is preferred to not waging war *or* such that not waging war is preferred to waging war (Hussein 1987). In other words, power by itself is neither necessary nor sufficient for a rational, *realist* leader to choose war over peace despite the arguments of *realist* theorists to the contrary. This is self-evident from an expected utility perspective.

Despite logical inadequacies in theories that link power directly to the likelihood of war initiation, such perspectives persist. Yet even a very simple empirical test demonstrates the superiority, in a Lakatosian sense, of expected-utility theory over, for example, balance-of-power theory. According to Kissinger, for instance, "Throughout history the political influence of nations has been roughly correlative to their military power. While states might differ in the moral worth and prestige of their institutions, diplomatic skill could augment but never substitute for military strength. In the final reckoning weakness has invariably tempted aggression and impotence

TABLE 6.1
Comparison of Balance-of-Power and Expected-Utility Propositions about War Initiators, 1816–1974[a]

Did the war comply with the balance-of-power or expected-utility theory?	Balance-of-power condition satisfied by i?	Expected-utility condition satisfied by i?
Yes	25	31
No	12	6

[a] This table is based on the first column of Tables 5.17 and 5.18 in *The War Trap* (Bueno de Mesquita 1981, 143).

brings abdication of policy in its train. . . . The balance of power . . . has in fact been the precondition of peace" (Kissinger 1979). As is true for so many balance-of-power theorists, Kissinger stipulates that war initiators are more powerful than their adversaries. Expected-utility theory does not impose this restriction, but rather requires that the gains expected by initiators are larger than their expected losses. As Equation 6.8 shows, this may be true even when the probability of success is very low provided that the value attached to success is sufficiently large. Using all wars as defined by Singer and Small (1972), I tested the relative merits of these two propositions. The test is "critical" in the sense that in all the cases analyzed the balance-of-power and expected-utility "rules" could lead to different results. Table 6.1 reports the relative goodness of fit between the two rules and the empirical record.

The expected-utility rule proves superior to the balance-of-power precept. Given the prospects of human error and the limitations of data, it is not surprising that neither provides a "perfect" fit. The strength of the expected-utility result is sufficiently greater than the support for the balance-of-power rule that the difference would have occurred by chance fewer than 1 in 100 times. As suggested by Lakatos, the cases corroborating the balance-of-power hypothesis also corroborate the expected-utility hypothesis, and some additional cases lend added value to the expected utility point of view.

EXPECTED UTILITY, POWER, AND ALLIANCES

The alliance hypotheses of the seemingly contradictory power theories can likewise be shown to be subsets of expected-utility theory. Consider the argument by Organski and Kugler:

> Most of the time alliances are simply not a realistic method of preventing threatening changes in the distribution of world power, given the skewness of relations between the great and the lesser nations, and also among the half-dozen great powers themselves. . . . It is clear that, if the intervals separating the nations in question are as large as we suggest, more probable alliances could affect only the size of the intervals between the strata, but could not alter the fundamental ranking of the great powers dominating the international system. [Organski and Kugler 1980, 25]

This stands in sharp contrast to Morgenthau's argument:

> It is true that the princes allowed themselves to be guided by the balance of power in order to further their own interests. By doing so, it was inevitable that they would change sides, desert old alliances, and form new ones whenever it seemed to them that the balance of power had been disturbed and that a realignment of forces was needed to restore it. [Morgenthau 1973, 197]

The key difference in assumptions about alliances set out by power-preponderance and balance-of-power theorists can be formalized. Let C_i be the power of the most powerful nation or alliance of nations. Let C_j be the power of i's rival j. Let C_k be the power of a third nation or coalition of nations. Organski and Kugler's argument that alliances are ineffectual in wars among the most powerful states is logically equivalent to

$$C_i - C_j > C_k, \quad \therefore \quad C_j + C_k < C_i$$

Given that C_i dominates the combined forces of j and k, alliances are more likely to be motivated by considerations of ideology or world view than by power, making them long-term arrangements. Morgenthau and other balance-of-power theorists, however, maintain that

$$C_i - C_j \leq C_k, \quad \therefore \quad C_j + C_k \geq C_i$$

Given this view, power considerations, rather than ideology, become the major factor in influencing the formation of alliances, making them short-lived, nonideological arrangements of convenience.

An expected-utility view of third-party choices to join side i or side j encompasses the generalizations of both balance-of-power and power-preponderance theorists. Assume that the choice to join i, join j, or remain nonaligned is determined by expected-utility-maximizing criteria. Also assume that the amount of effort third party k makes on behalf of i or j increases continuously and monotonically with k's expected utility for its choice. That is, the more k expects to gain from helping a nation at war, the

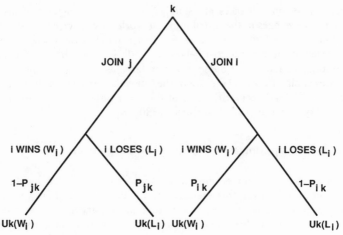

FIGURE 6.2. *Third-party decision problem.*

larger the commitment k is willing to make in pursuit of those gains. Figure 6.2 depicts the decision problem confronting third party k in choosing between side i and side j.

According to the model depicted in Figure 6.2, k's choice between joining i and joining j depends on the probability of i winning given help from k (P_{ik}), the probability of i losing even though k helps i ($1 - P_{ik}$), the probability of j winning (i losing) given that k helps j (P_{jk}), the probability of j losing (i winning) even though k helps j ($1 - P_{jk}$), and the utility—or degree of motivation—k attaches to the two possible outcomes. Let the utility to k of i winning equal $U(W_i)$, and let the utility to k of i losing and j winning equal $U(L_i)$. Expressed algebraically, k's expected utility for joining i or j, as depicted in Figure 6.2, equals

$$E(U)_k = [P_{ik}U^k(W_i) + (1 - P_{ik})U^k(L_i)]$$
$$- [(1 - P_{jk})U^k(W_i) + P_{jk}U^k(L_i)] \tag{6.9}$$

The terms inside the first set of brackets in Equation 6.9 delineate k's expectations if it joins side i. The terms inside the second set of brackets delineate k's expectations if it selects the strategy of joining side j. By subtracting these two expressions we can see if joining i, joining j, or remaining out of the conflict is k's preferred strategy. If Equation 6.9 is positive, k expects more utility from joining i than j, and so k is predicted to join i. If Equation 6.9 is negative, k expects more utility from joining j than i, and so k is predicted to join j, and if the expression equals zero, then k is indifferent between i and j, and so abstains from the dispute. The terms in Equation 6.9 may be rearranged by factoring to yield

$$E(U)_k = (P_{ik} + P_{jk} - 1) [U^k(W_i) - U^k(L_i)] \qquad (6.10)$$

Equation 6.10 helps make clear that k, not surprisingly, always joins the side it prefers. Since $P_{ik} + P_{jk} - 1$ can only be greater than or equal to zero, the sign of Equation 6.10 is determined by the relative magnitude of the utilities or preferences of k for victory by i or j. How much effort k makes depends both on the intensity of k's preference for one or the other side and on k's power. To see this, assume no nation enters a conflict with the expectation of harming the side it chooses to join, so that the a priori probability of i winning if k abstains is not larger than the probability of i winning if k joins i, and, likewise, the a priori probability of j winning is not diminished by k joining j. That is, I stipulate that

$$P_{ik} \geq P_{ib}; \quad P_{jk} \geq P_{jb} = (1 - P_{ib})$$

where P_{ib} and P_{jb} are the respective probabilities of i and j winning a *strictly bilateral* dispute (as estimated by k).

Once P_{ib} and P_{jb} (which together equal 1.0 and represent the probabilities when i and j act alone) are subtracted (as dictated by $P_{ik} + P_{jk} - 1$ from Equation 6.10, all that remains is k's marginal contribution to the probability of the outcome. This can be seen most easily by adding an operational assumption. Let $P_{ik} = (C_i + C_k)/(C_i + C_k + C_j)$, where, as before, C refers to the capabilities or power of the subscripted actor. Similarly, let $P_{jk} = (C_j + C_k)/(C_i + C_j + C_k)$. Then,

$$(P_{ik} + P_{jk} - 1)$$
$$= \frac{C_i + C_k}{C_i + C_j + C_k} + \frac{C_j + C_k}{C_i + C_j + C_k} - \frac{C_i + C_j + C_k}{C_i + C_j + C_k} = \frac{C_k}{C_i + C_j + C_k} \qquad (6.11)$$

Now, under the power-transition condition stipulated previously and with the assumption that effort increases monotonically with expected utility, we see that C_k in Equation 6.11 is small compared to C_i and C_j. Therefore, holding utilities constant, k's expected utility must approach zero for a finite value of $U(W_i) - U(L_i)$ relative to the conditions stipulated for the balance of power (where C_k is *relatively* large). Given monotonicity of effort with expected utility, Equations 6.10 and 6.11 reveal that alliances are less important when third parties are weak compared to initial belligerents and are more important when third parties are relatively strong compared to initial belligerents. Thus, the balance-of-power and power-transition hypotheses are not incompatible at all. Rather, they are each special cases of behavior under the axioms of expected-utility maximization as modified by the assumption of monotonicity. This means that each of these theories can be subsumed under the expected-utility framework, giving us a broader, more general theory. The expected-utility theory differentiates and encompasses circumstances that each of the other theories has to treat as contradictions.

Expected-utility theory satisfies the Lakatos criteria with respect to many balance-of-power and power-preponderance theories, at least with respect to the hypotheses about the likelihood of war and about the efficaciousness of alliances. It accounts for the facts accounted for by each, but excluded by the other. In this way, it has excess empirical content over either. Consider, for instance, the differences in empirical results between an expected-utility explanation of third-party decisions to join one side or the other in an ongoing war and the results reported by Siverson and King using essentially the same data, but a more power-oriented theoretical perspective. Table 6.2 contains the results for the Siverson and King test while Table 6.3 contains the results from Altfeld and Bueno de Mesquita's expected-utility test (Altfeld and Bueno de Mesquita 1979; Siverson and King 1980).

These two tables reveal that the expected-utility model fits better with the historical record, yielding a 66 percent reduction in error (over predicting the modal behavior every time) as compared to Siverson and King's 33 percent reduction in error. Additionally, the Altfeld and Bueno de Mesquita test explains not only whether nations would participate in ongoing wars (the dependent variable for Siverson and King), but also explains which side each third party would choose to join. As indicated by Equation 6.9, third-party choices seem consistent with expected-utility-maximizing behavior. Even with crude data, 16 of the 18 nations predicted to join the weaker side in an ongoing war actually did so, and of the 13 predicted to join the stronger side, 10 did so, suggesting that the theory was very powerful at discriminating who would join, which side they would join, and who would stay out of the fight (104 of 109 predicted to stay out of the war did stay out).

As a final note on expected-utility theory and third-party-alignment behavior, I should observe that other theoretical results can also be derived from Equation 6.10. For instance, equation 6.10 contains explanations of (1) why major powers are more likely to participate as third parties in wars than are minor powers and (2) why major powers are likely to participate in wars, such as the Vietnam War, where they do not have vital interests at risk. So, expected-utility theory provides a vehicle for making consistent the seemingly incompatible propositions of the balance-of-power and power-preponderance theories, does better at accounting for third-party-alignment decisions than do rival theories, and offers additional empirically supported

TABLE 6.2
War Participation Predictions Based on the Siverson and King Model

	Predicted war participant?	
	No	Yes
Actual war participant?		
No	211	12
Yes	32	35

SOURCE: Siverson and King (1980, Table 4).

TABLE 6.3
War Participation Predictions Based on the Altfeld and Bueno de Mesquita Model

	Predicted war participant?	
	No	Yes
Actual war participant?		
No	104	4
Yes	9	27

SOURCE: Altfeld and Bueno de Mesquita (1979, Table 2b).

deductions about major and minor power behavior. While some argue that a separate theory of major power war is required (Modelski and Morgan 1985; Organski and Kugler 1980), much of the evidence from research using expected-utility theory suggests that major power choices can be explained in the same way as minor power choices (but, for an alternative view, see Moul 1987) and that major and minor powers differ primarily in the magnitudes of their respective values on the utility and probability terms.

SOME SURPRISING RESULTS FROM EXPECTED-UTILITY THEORY

Power-based theories have been an important bedrock for accounting for war and peace decisions and for alliance formation choices. A large and closely related body of theory has grown up around the question of deterrence. Using no additional assumptions, expected-utility theory has proven to be a useful tool for explaining the successes and failures of efforts to deter conventional or nuclear war. Huth and Russett, testing a number of formulations to account for successes and failures of deterrent efforts, note that their best-fitting result gives about the same predictions as those from my expected-utility formulation. More interestingly, Huth and Russett observe (1984, 503), "Some research suggests that the defender's previous behavior does not systematically predict either way subsequent behavior, but we still must take it into account in our analysis." The citation for those who claim that previous behavior is not a critical variable is Altfeld and Bueno de Mesquita. The counterintuitive proposition that demonstrations of resolve or other reputational effects are not consequential in the behaviors Huth and Russett examine is supported by *their* evidence. Their empirical investigations lead them to report that "the defender's past behavior in crises seems to make no systematic difference."

Other counterintuitive or seemingly anomalous behaviors are consistent with the expected-utility perspective of conflict decisionmaking. For instance, allies are shown to be substantially more likely to wage war (but not severe wars) against one another than are enemies (Bueno de Mesquita 1981). The potential advantages of nonalignment for a weak nation engaged in a dispute with a stronger adversary that has allies have been demonstrated, while at the same time I have shown that nonalignment can be a liability for a weak nation if the same adversary does not have allies to help it. Conditions under which nuclear proliferation decreases the threat of war have been identified (Bueno de Mesquita and Riker 1982; Intriligator and Brito 1981; Berkowitz 1985), while some circumstances under which arms control exacerbates the risks of conflict have also been isolated. Others have shown that behavior that complies with or deviates from standard norms within international treaty organizations can be predicted using expected utility theory (Berkowitz 1983; Altfeld and Paik 1986). That approach has also proven useful both in predicting escalatory behavior (Bueno de Mesquita 1985; Bueno de Mesquita and Lalman 1986; Petersen 1986) and as an explanation of alliance-formation behavior in the face of threats (Iusi-Scarborough and Bueno de Mesquita 1988; Altfeld 1984; Newman 1985).

A particularly important set of results show that rational conflict initiation and escalation are consistent with decisionmaker misperceptions. Misperceptions are shown to have systematic and predictable effects on the likelihood of war (Bueno de Mesquita 1985; Bueno de Mesquita and Lalman 1986). These results call into question arguments that place misperceptions outside the realm of rational behavior (Jervis 1976). Instead, Lalman and I have shown the circumstances under which decisionmakers engage in actions for which the perceived probability of war is low when, in fact, the likelihood of war is high. And we have shown the conditions under which nations engage in policies they think are highly risky when the actual likelihood of war is low. To see how this is so, refer back to Equation 6.4, which states that

$$P(\text{War}) = P^i(\text{Esc}_i) \times P^j(\text{Esc}_j)$$

Let us define the probability of war *as perceived by* i *and as perceived by* j as

$$P^i(\text{War}) = P^i(\text{Esc}_i) \times P^i(\text{Esc}_j) \qquad (6.12a)$$

$$P^j(\text{War}) = P^j(\text{Esc}_i) \times P^j(\text{Esc}_j) \qquad (6.12b)$$

Equation 6.4 says the probability of war is a function of i's probability of escalating a dispute and j's probability of escalating the same dispute. Equation 6.12a stipulates that i's perception of the probability of war is a function of i's probability of escalating the conflict and i's estimate of j's probability of escalating the dispute; j's perception is derived analogously. Now, suppose i believes the two relevant probabilities are each equal to 0.6 and 0.9, while j believes the relevant probabilities equal 0.8 and 0.6. Then, i perceives the probability of war to be 0.54, j believes it is 0.48, with each viewing the opponent as the more hostile party. The actual probability of war is 0.36, substantially lower than they thought. Suppose i thought the probabilities were 0.9 and 0.6, respectively, while j thought they were 0.6 and 0.9. Each anticipates a 0.54 chance of war, yet the actual likelihood in this case is a much higher 0.81. Finally, suppose i perceives the probabilities of escalation as 0.6 and 0.7, respectively, while j perceives these probabilities as 0.9 and 0.8 respectively. In this case i perceives the situation to have a probability of war equal to 0.42, and j perceives it to be 0.72. In actuality, the probability of war is in between with a value of 0.48.

These examples illustrate the ability of the expected-utility formulation to incorporate perceptual variation in a rational choice framework and to use those perceptions to account for decisions, for instance, to initiate losing efforts. They help lend formal structure to Creasy's important observation: "We thus learn not to judge of the wisdom of measures too exclusively by the results. We learn to apply the juster standard of seeing what the circumstances and the probabilities were that surrounded a statesman or a general at the time he decided on his plan" (Creasy 1851, Preface).

POLICY FORECASTING, INSTABILITY, AND EXPECTED-UTILITY THEORY

A difficult test for any social science theory is its ability to forecast future events. "Explaining" events after the fact is the empirical basis for theory testing, but predicting events before they happen dispels suspicions that "the theory was made to fit the data." The predictive ability of the expected-utility approach to international conflict is particularly difficult to test because hard data do not exist for many of its variables, especially the utility terms. Tests of the theory, therefore, must depend either on proxy indicators of utilities or on implications from the theory that do not require the direct observation of utilities.[6] I have used both methods to test the predictive potential of the expected-utility theory and have done so both in the context of current international disputes and in the broader context of intranational conflict and policy formation. I turn now to the value of the theory as a tool for forecasting policy decisions.

The key problem in applying the expected-utility approach to forecasting policy formation around the world, and the degree of contentiousness surrounding policy decisions, is that there are no preexisting data readily used to approximate probabilities or utilities. As a forecasting tool, the expected-utility model focuses on competition among groups (both within and across national boundaries). In particular, the model requires

1. the specification of the relative power (political, economic, military, or other) of each relevant group;

2. the enumeration of specific policy issues that are indicative of the questions one wishes to answer (for example, what will happen to civil liberties in Hong Kong after the Chinese regain sovereignty, or what restructuring of debt will the Mexican government negotiate with its creditors, or how stable will the new government be in the Philippines?);

3. each group's preferred policy outcome on the issue(s) in question; and

4. the degree of importance or salience each group attaches to the policy under discussion.

Here we have an opportunity to combine the greatest strengths of abstract theory and of detailed expert knowledge on particular situations or places. Data for forecasting purposes are developed in close consultation with area experts. They identify the groups, issues, and other variables required by the model (the policy preferences, or desired outcomes, held by each group on each issue; the relative power to influence decisions controlled by each group; and the salience, or level of importance, each group attributes to each issue).

Experts are not asked for their personal judgments about outcomes or about the contentiousness of the political situation. The model, not a Delphi technique, is used to answer these questions. The model also is used to estimate each group's willingness to take risks and to specify what kind of conflictual relationship (if any) is likely to emerge between each pair of groups. Each group's perceptions about what they can do and about what they believe others can or will do are also derived from the model using only the data specified previously. Indeed, the model allows the analyst to look at the world "as if" through the eyes of each group leader, assessing their perceptions of the situation. Because the methodology for achieving these ends is explained in great detail elsewhere (Bueno de Mesquita, Newman, and Rabushka 1985), it will not be discussed at this point. The key point here is that the model adds considerable information beyond that provided by the experts. Indeed, the model-based forecasts often differ from those of the very experts who provided the input information. When the experts and the model differ, the model's predictions have proven to be more accurate both in terms of the specification of policy decisions and in the delineation of the circumstances surrounding such decisions.

As a forecasting tool, the expected-utility model has proven to be highly flexible and reliable. Included among its successful applications are forecasts of events as diverse as those that follow.

1. It predicted the ascent of Yuri Andropov as successor to Leonid Brezhnev. The forecast was made while Andropov was still with the KGB, before his rise to the Politburo and well before he was viewed as a serious contender by most other analysts (Bueno de Mesquita 1982).

2. It predicted Italian deficit policy, and the attendant fall of the Spadolini government in Italy in 1982. The forecast predicted that Fanfani would succeed Spadolini and that his government would ultimately be threatened by a policy shift of the Communist Party of Italy toward greater support for austerity programs, leading to the rise of Craxi. Spadolini fell several months after the forecast analysis was completed. He was succeeded by Fanfani, who fell to Craxi on the heels of shifting economic policy by the Communists. The model's forecast of the Italian parliament's deficit policy for 1983 was within 99.2 percent of the actual policy, despite wide-ranging speculation at the time that the government would adopt a deficit program anywhere between 60 trillion and 100 trillion lira (Beck and Bueno de Mesquita 1985).

3. Successful elections were predicted for El Salvador in 1981 and again later. The model predicted that the Duarte government would fall to a coalition led by d'Aubisson in 1981, as it did, despite widespread speculation in the American press that the left would prevent the elections from occurring in the first place.

4. The shift in Iran of Rafsanjani from a hardline stand promoting a military solution to the Iran–Iraq war to his stance in favor of economic sanctions and a less bellicose resolution of the dispute was predicted in early 1984 (Bueno de Mesquita 1984). The same article also forecast increasing movement in Iran toward more open, free-market policies in response to pressures from the Bazaaris. Rafsanjani was described in *The Wall Street*

Journal in the summer of 1984 as having surprised everyone by his shift to a pacifist position on the war. And in August of 1984, the *Washington Post* reported that "Revolutionary leader Ayatollah Ruhollah Khomeini has come down firmly on the side of Iran's bazaar merchants in a simmering political and ideological dispute over whether they or the state should control the country's foreign trade. Western diplomats here described his intervention, which steers Iran away from further state monopolies and encourages free enterprise, as a development likely to determine the future course of its Islamic revolution." (the *Washington Post*, August 30, 1984, A38).

5. It predicted a dispute between Chen Yun of the ideological faction of the Communist party of the People's Republic of China and Deng Xiao Ping on the issue of free-market reforms. In *Forecasting Political Events*, my coauthors and I noted that "*the modernizers have seriously misperceived their ability to implement Deng's policies. . . .* [T]he modernizers believe they can resist the demands of the ideologues. . . . However [the ideologues] . . . believe they can successfully counter the modernizers. . . . Such perceptions will produce costly mistakes for Deng's successors among the modernizers. . . . Thus, domestic pressures will ultimately force Deng's successors to compromise with those seeking a more regulated economic system . . .*" (Bueno de Mesquita *et al.* 1985, 149–150; the italics are in the original). In short, the analysis anticipated a serious dispute over market reforms between the ideologues and the Deng faction within the People's Republic of China. The analysis also anticipated a compromise settlement that was more favorable to the modernizers than to the ideologues. That these forecasts were surprising is highlighted by the fact that open disputes of this sort are, of course, rare in tightly controlled societies such as China. Yet, on the first page of the *International Herald Tribune* on September 24, 1985, it was reported that

> The Communist Party of China closed its national conference Monday with an unusual public airing of the policy differences that have created tensions between Deng Xiao Ping, the reform-minded veteran who is the country's paramount leader, and more doctrinaire figures in the party hierarchy. The conference was summoned by Mr. Deng to entrench his open-door economic policies in the five-year plan for 1986–1990. . . . It ended on a discordant note as Chen Yun, a Marxist conservative, made a brusque speech that challenged Mr. Deng's position on . . . the play given to market forces in the economy. . . . With Mr. Deng seated on the podium nearby, Mr. Chen quoted Mao to warn of possible social disorder. . . . Still more sharply he reminded delegates that "we are a Communist country," and said that central planning had to remain the pillar of the economy, not market regulation that meant "blindly allowing supply and demand to determine production."

This sampling of forecasts highlights the ability of the model (1) to predict policy formation and political conflict accurately within democratic and authoritarian regimes in purely domestic, international, or mixed situations, (2) to deal with socialist and capitalist settings for decisionmaking, and (3) to cope with policy decisions in virtually every type of cultural, political, economic, and social setting. As such, it is further evidence of the potential benefits to be derived from the exploration of expected-utility theory as a paradigm for understanding international (and domestic) political conflict.

CONCLUSION

The search for knowledge is a quest for accurate description, explanation, and prediction. The fundamental quality of science is that we cannot know if an explanation is truly correct. We can only know if it "makes more sense" to us than alternative explanations. In the same way, we can be sure that no event is fully described. Reality is infinitely complex. Which facts are essential and which are peripheral in describing an event or a circumstance is a matter of judgment, not a matter of knowledge. So, the task of science is to devise descriptions, explanations, and predictions that *seem* superior to the rivals. This Lakatosian standard is the one I have tried to apply to the expected-utility approach to understanding international conflict.

Reasonable people can be expected to disagree about the quality of any explanation. Explanation depends largely on personal taste. After all, we have no way of discerning what the "right" assumptions are about the world. For those who reject a set of assumptions out of hand, any explanation that follows from them must, perforce, seem wrong. But, agreement should be possible on the consistency between competing explanations and the evidence. Surely the predictive power of alternative theories is not a matter of taste; it is a matter of empirical record. The application of conventional views of evidence lends strong support to my claims for the merits of an expected-utility approach. Many of the main streams of international relations research have been shown to fall within the perview of expected-utility theory. Perspectives that before appeared incompatible were shown to be special cases of expected-utility conditions. Events that seemed like anomalies have been shown to be consistent with more mundane events when viewed from an expected-utility perspective. A high percentage (around 90 percent) of policy forecasts and strategic scenarios, including many counterintuitive ones, have been borne out. The Lakatosian criteria of scientific progress seem to have been satisfied.

The nature of science is that today's theoretical triumph is tomorrow's error. Ptolemaic astronomy fell before the weight of evidence for the Newtonian view. And Newtonian astronomy, likewise, fell before the greater power of Einstein's relativity. Today, the discovery of subatomic particles moving faster than light leads researchers to question Einsteinian physics. One can only speculate about what the future will bring. In international relations, the balance of power has reigned as the principle theory. Perhaps the community of scholars will, in time, conclude that it still reigns. Perhaps they will conclude that expected-utility theory has replaced it. Perhaps they will conclude that some other theory has replaced it. At the moment I can only claim that the evidence for an expected-utility view of decisionmaking about international conflict is too strong to be dismissed. We cannot help but remain conscious of the fact that science compels skepticism. And so, I conclude with the observation of St. Augustine:

> We should not hold rashly an opinion in a Scientific matter, so that we may not come to hate later whatever truth may reveal to us, out of love for our own error.

NOTES

1. I would like to express my gratitude to William T. Bluhm, Bruce Jacobs, and William H. Riker, my colleagues while I was at the University of Rochester, for their many helpful comments on this chapter. I would also like to thank Robert Keohane, Manus Midlarsky, Theodore Rabb, Robert Rothberg, and Robert Powell for their helpful suggestions. This is an extended version of an article published in 1988 by the *Journal of Interdisciplinary History*. The usual disclaimers, of course, apply.

2. I have not made explicit the terms for costs to keep the presentation as simple as possible. These expressions may be thought of in the context of equal expected costs across strategies or, again for simplicity, the costs may be thought of as endogenous to the calculations.

3. Here I make the assumption that the level of effort expected from a third party increases monotonically with its expected utility.

4. Wisdom is also sometimes viewed as "the wisdom of the ages." This Burkian view places wisdom in the context of tradition and culture. That perspective is less closely linked to the sense of the "wise man" in which I use the concept. For the purposes of this discussion, the two meanings of wisdom differ in that the "wisdom of the ages" implies a characteristic that *is* transmissible. It remains true, however, that such wisdom, unlike science, is not dependent on empirically corroborated or testable propositions.

5. As noted earlier, these definitions regarding decisions to escalate a dispute assume that a threat exists. The probability of peace in this context is, therefore, the probability that a threatening situation will be resolved without resort to force.

6. For instance, the proposition that allies are more likely to fight than enemies is testable directly from knowledge of who is allied with whom and how frequently various alignment combinations fight with one another. The test does not require direct measurement of utilities or probabilities.

CHAPTER 7

The Power Transition: A Retrospective and Prospective Evaluation

Jacek Kugler

Vanderbilt University

A. F. K. Organski

University of Michigan

INTRODUCTION

The power transition theory was introduced in 1958 (Organski 1958), and 30 years seems an appropriate period for an initial evaluation of the scientific worth and staying power of a new idea. In such an evaluation, one can use the Lakatos criteria:

> A scientific theory *T* is *falsified* if and only if another theory *T'* has been proposed with the following characteristics: (1) *T'* has excess empirical content over *T*: that is, it predicts *novel* facts, that is, facts improbable in the light of, or even forbidden, by *T*; (2) *T'* explains the previous success of *T*, that is, all the unrefuted content of *T* is included (within the limits of observable error) in the content of *T'*; and (3) some of the excess content of *T'* is corroborated. [Lakatos 1978, 32]

In such an evaluation two sets of things must be asked. Has the new construct, model, idea, or theory provided an explanation more powerful and more parsimonious than what existed previously? Has this way of looking at the problem proven more valid than the alternatives? One can add questions to the ones already posed. Has the new idea influenced the creation of other ideas and the undertaking of new work? Are such extensions successful? It should be kept in mind that the set of ideas that has survived the test of time is a very biased sample. The number of good ideas is very small, and among that set many are ignored for reasons other than their intrinsic merit. An evaluation such as this is inevitably reserved for the lucky few that become visible enough to warrant consideration. Yet, not all is simply a matter of luck.

Clearly, a significant idea will have illumined new ground. It will have suggested what new materials should be dug up, where such materials are to be found, and how the digging can best be done. Significant work makes one of these contributions, excellent work makes two, and path-breaking work makes all three. We know that scientific ideas that induce path-breaking research cannot survive the test of time unchanged. The best, however, will find a permanent niche in the theoretical development of a given discipline. It is by such criteria that we will gauge the impact of the power transition theory on the field of international politics.

THE POWER TRANSITION

The power transition model described the international system in a sharply different way that had been previously conceived. Power transition rejected three fundamental assumptions imbedded in the realist angle of vision about world politics.

First, the international system had been conceived as a world governed by few rules, a world in a state of partial or total anarchy. Power transition sees the international order not as anarchical at all, but as hierarchically organized in a manner similar to the domestic political system. Actors accept their position in the international order and recognize influence based on differences in the power distribution among nations. This fundamentally different assumption separates power transition from preceding realist models.

Second, the power transition conceived the rules governing the domestic and international political system as fundamentally similar. Despite the absence of an enforceable code of international law, there were no major differences in the rules governing the domestic and international arena. Nations, like political groups in the domestic system, were in constant competition over scarce resources in the international order.

Third, power transition conceived international competition as driven by the potential net gains that could be accrued from conflict or cooperation. The objective of nations was not, as the balance-of-power theory argued (Morgenthau 1948), to maximize power; rather, the objective was to maximize net gains. Peaceful competition ensued when parties agreed that the net gains from conflict were inferior to the net benefits; conflict emerged when the opposite was true (Claude 1962; Organski 1958; for a current review of realism see Keohane 1986).

Armed with these few fundamental assumptions, power transition produced a dramatically different view of the workings of the international order than alternate realist perspectives.

Hierarchy, Power, and the Status Quo

To explore the power transition model, one can start with its perspective of hierarchy in the international order. At the top of the hierarchical pyramid is the dominant nation that, for most of its tenure, is the most powerful nation in the international order. Today that nation is the United States, and its predecessor was England (Kugler and Organski 1989; see also Gilpin 1981; Keohane 1980). Below the dominant nation are the great powers. As the name implies, these are very powerful countries that cannot match one on one the power of the dominant nation at a given point in time, but have the potential to do so at a future time. Among them is to be found the eventual challenger of the international order. Below that group are the middle powers, further down still are the small powers, and at the bottom are colonies, which have today all but disappeared. Figure 7.1 provides a sketch of this perspective.

Power transition maintained a strong connection with the realist perspective on international politics by stressing that power is a critical variable shaping the way in which the international order functions. Yet this is not a power-maximization model. Satisfaction with the way goods are distributed in the international order is the second critical determinant of how smoothly the international order operates. Degrees of satisfaction as well as power are critical determinants of peace and conflict. Great nations that support the international order are allies of the dominant nation and help determine how smoothly the system runs. Indeed, peace in the international order is assured by the dominant nation with the support of the great powers that are satisfied with the distribution of benefits and the rules by which it is run. For this reason, power transition conceives of alliances as stable and reliable instruments created to support the international order that cannot be easily altered in the short run (for alternate assumptions about alliances see Morgenthau 1948).

Of course, not all nations are satisfied with the way the international order functions and the leadership of the dominant nation. The elites of some nations are dissatisfied because they do not believe they and their societies are receiving their due from the international order. The number of

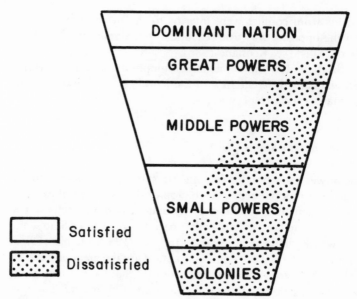

FIGURE 7.1. *Hierarchical distribution of power in the international order. From Organski (1968).*

such countries may be large. Whenever the dissatisfied nations are weak, however, they cannot (in isolation or by combining with each other) pose a threat to the dominant nation and the coalition supporting the international order. Only rarely—when the dissatisfied nation is also a great power that has managed to catch up with the dominant nation—is the setting created for challenges that lead to major conflict.

Challengers are those powerful and dissatisfied great nations who have grown in power after the imposition of the existing international order. Their elites face circumstances where the main benefits of the international order have already been allocated. The conditions for conflict are present. Peace is threatened when challengers seek to establish a new place for themselves in the international order, a place to which they believe their increasing power entitles them.

Note that, as illustrated in Figure 7.1, the conditions for a peaceful international order are present when the dominant nation has a large power advantage over any other single nation and most combinations of countries dissatisfied with the status quo in the second tier. For this reason, during periods of preponderance the international system is peaceful and stable. To ensure the smooth running of the international order, however, it is very important for the dominant nation to have the support of most great powers. As a rule, most great powers *are satisfied* with the way the international order is run. Today, for instance, supporters of the United States-led international order include Germany, Japan, England, France, and Italy. The Soviet Union and China are potential challengers, but they are in direct competition with one another and, very importantly, are also much weaker than the United States (Kugler and Organski 1989). India is still a very weak country unable to challenge the great powers. Clearly, even if only Japan and the European countries support the United States, the preponderance of resources—short of nuclear weapons—favoring the international order is massive (Kugler and Organski 1989). Thus, power transition contends that the international order is, as it should be, stable, as it has been since 1945 because of this massive power preponderance in support of the status quo.

Figure 7.1 indicates that instability is likely only during periods of relative parity among potential competitors. As a dissatisfied great nation approaches parity by growing in power more rapidly than the dominant nation, instability increases and so does the probability of conflict. The closure of the power gap engenders fear on the part of the leaders in the dominant nation that the challenger will (1) surpass the dominant country, (2) become increasingly unwilling to accept a subordinate position in the international order, and (3) challenge the leadership and rules of the international order. And this, in fact, is very likely what the challenger will do. Thus, power transition argues that competition for dominance in the international order is finally joined when the dissatisfied party anticipates greater benefits and privileges if a conflict is successfully waged than if the current status quo is preserved. Concurrently, the dominant nation, recognizing the reality of the changing power relationship, prepares to resist such change. World wars are rooted in such relatively rare conditions (Organski 1968, 364–367).

Before we turn to the empirical tests of some of these propositions, it is useful to contrast power transition with the alternative realist positions.

NOVEL PROPOSITIONS IN THE POWER TRANSITION

To understand how radical a break the power transition theory represents, it will be helpful at this point to compare this view of the international order with that of the balance-of-power theory. When the power transition was first presented, collective security was also a viable, alternate model seeking to account for the connection between the distribution of power and the presence of conflict or stability. Collective security, however, was always far more prescriptive than explanatory and has since lost ground (Carr 1945; Claude 1962; Organski and Kugler 1980). Balance of power, on the other hand, despite very limited empirical scrutiny, was and remains the most widely accepted explanation of the way international conflict and stability emerge in the international order (Morgenthau 1948; Kissinger 1964; Waltz 1979; Siverson and Sullivan 1983; Keohane 1986).

Balance of power, as the label implies, proposed that an equal distribution of power leads to peace and an imbalance brings about the necessary conditions for war. Nations were expected to attack when they were stronger than an opponent. The reason balance-of-power theorists reached this conclusion is that in an anarchic international order all nations wish to increase their absolute power, and the main way in which this could be accomplished was by defeating others and imposing one's preferred outcomes on the vanquished. Hence, instability would occur when one side gained a power advantage.

The function of alliances was to preserve parity of power among the competing coalitions of great nations and provide the weaker states with sanctuary. Under conditions of power equality a great nation could not attack other great powers or their smaller allies and expect to obtain major concessions through war at low absolute costs. A balance of power ensured peace not because nations were satisfied with the status quo—none was— but, rather, because war under conditions of power equality meant that the absolute costs of war could be expected to be very high. In sum, balance of power presented the international order as anarchic and intrinsically competitive, a system in which individual nations seek to maximize power and were restrained from aggression because the opponents were just as strong.

The balance-of-power perspective differs from the power-transition model in fundamental ways. Balance of power views the power of states as largely manipulable through coalitions. Indeed, from the perspective of balance of power, the power of nations remains roughly unchanged, and if any such shifts do occur, they can be easily compensated for by restructuring alliances. A state could marginally expand its power by increasing its military strength, but a government could do very little to alter fundamentally and dramatically a nation's ability to impose its preferences on the rest of the international order (Knorr 1956). Alliances become the key to understanding conflict in the international order because they are the major source of variations in power. This viewpoint resulted in a focus on diplomats and diplomacy as the mechanism that could ensure the key values of international politics: peace and security (Morgenthau 1948; Kissinger 1979). It should be noted that the view that domestic growth could only marginally affect the international order is far more congruent with the preindustrial period than it is with the world today. Prior to industrialization there was little that national elites could do to enhance their power other than to ally themselves with other states.

From the viewpoint of power transition, on the other hand, changes in the international power structure were, in all significant respects, the result of the domestic developmental process. Thus, the significant data for the discussion of power relations were the shifts from primary to secondary to tertiary production, variations in movement of fertility and mortality from high to low rates, the increase in the ability of the political system to mobilize resources, and differences in the social mobility of populations. Maintaining the international order was conceived not as a global chess game where the power of actors is relatively fixed and changes in alliances are critical, but as adjustments to the dynamic changes induced by differential growth rates across countries over time. Because of such different conceptions of the international order, one should not be surprised that, as we will see, the prescriptions for preserving peace also differed radically.

The balance-of-power and the power-transition models also differed in their assumptions of the goals that nations pursue. Balance of power assumes that the central goal is to maximize power and that all nations will take advantage of preponderance to impose their will on others. Power transition, as we have seen, recognized the existence of a power hierarchy that provides structure for the international order and attributes peace to the power advantage of the dominant nation and the support for the international order by the satisfied nations. It is common to think of the differences we have discussed as simply different assessments of the power distributions required for stability and conflict in the international system. But they are more than that. The disagreement regarding the relationship between power distribution and the cause of major war are merely a reflection of the profound differences between the balance-of-power and power-transition theories regarding the willingness of national elites to maximize absolute or net gains. The logical implications of this fundamental difference will be discussed further when we assess the implications of each theory for deterrence. Before we move on, however, a clarification is in order.

The Power Transition and the Overtaking Pattern

This review provides an occasion to address a popular misconception regarding the dual role played by the notion of transition in the theory. The transition is always taken to refer to the overtaking process where a challenger catches up with and passes the dominant nation. When the model was first presented the conception of the "transition" referred to the domestic changes that take place when it moves from underdeveloped to developed status. Organski (1958) postulated that the transition process was composed of three stages. An underdeveloped country is in the stage of power potential: all of the power that its government can derive from modernization lies all in the future. As the country begins to develop, economic changes are accompanied by profound social and demographic changes that increase greatly the pool of human and material resources exposed to governmental penetration and extraction. These are the sources of major power changes that a nation experiences as it passes through the stage of the power transition. When a country is fully developed it reaches the stage of power maturity and slows down in its overall power growth.

As nations move up from stage one, they leave behind the countries that have not begun their development. As new countries develop, they catch up to those that have developed earlier. The reason developed countries in the stage of power maturity are caught by those undergoing the transition is that mature, developed nations have already used up the power potential to be gained through development. If a latecomer is very much larger and grows at faster rates than the nations that developed earlier, it will inevitably overtake the nation that had developed earlier. It is the domestic transition from stage to stage that leads in some cases to the overtaking of one great power by another in the international order, which sets up the conditions for major conflict. Thus, the overtaking process at the international level is an externality of the domestic transition. This conception has left an important imprint on the discipline, particularly in what has now become known as hegemonic stability theory in the new emphasis on political economy. Gilpin (1981), for example, presents a very similar picture of the international order, suggesting that large nations in their youth increase their power but slow down once they become a mature hegemon. Using Olson's collective goods perspective, Keohane (1984) argues that a "hegemon" declines because of the burden imposed on it by the need to maintain the international order. While very distinct paths are used in these newer attempts to explain rate changes in the power of competing nations, in many ways these models appear to differ from the core elements in the power-transition model only by nomenclature. The "dominant nation" is a clear precursor of the "hegemon," the "international order" is the antecedent of an "international regime," and, perhaps most importantly, parity in power is seen by both theories as the condition for major conflict (Organski and Kugler 1980). At this point it seems proper to turn to the empirical record accumulated over the last 20 years regarding power distributions and conflict.

EMPIRICAL EVALUATIONS

The Initiation of Conflict

A fundamental and testable difference between power transition and balance of power concerns prediction about conflict over control of the international order. Despite its influence, balance of power has been exposed to a very limited number of empirical tests, and, with a few exceptions, most of these have produced negative or contradictory results (Ferris 1973; Midlarsky 1981, 1983; Singer *et al.* 1972; Siverson and Sullivan 1983; Bueno de Mesquita 1981).

Empirical tests by Organski and Kugler (1980) show that the insights of the power transition are far more likely to be valid (see also Thompson 1983a and Houweling and Siccama 1988). In Table 7.1, the analysis of relations among great powers that comprises a small set of the possible dyads over the last century and a half shows the power of this inference.

Table 7.1 makes two fundamental points. Preponderance by the dominant power insures peace among great powers, while a balance of power may lead to either conflict or peace. Clearly, the necessary but not sufficient conditions for major war emerge only in the rare instances when power parity is accompanied by a challenger overtaking a dominant nation. The odds of a war in this very reduced subset are 50 percent. No other theoretical statement has, to our knowledge, reduced the number of cases to such a small set, and no other is so parsimonious in its explanatory requirements (for alternatives see Bueno de Mesquita 1981).

One should note that when power parity among major contenders is

TABLE 7.1
Great Powers, Power Distribution, and Major War, 1860–1980[a]

		Relative power distribution		
		Preponderance	Parity no transition	Parity and transition
Major war				
	No	4	6	5
		(100%)	(100%)	(50%)
	Yes	0	0	5
		(0%)	(0%)	(50%)

SOURCE: Organski and Kugler (1980, 42–53, Table 1.7).
[a] $N = 20$, tau $C = 0.50$, significance $= 0.01$.

present, war is avoided two thirds of the time. Major war, however, was never waged in the past 100 years when the dominant power was preponderant. Preponderance appears to provide the most stable condition for the international order.

There are obvious drawbacks to the story presented in Table 7.1. First, the number of major wars is so small that chance may have produced these effects. Because the universe of cases is used for the 1870–1980 period, however, such a question can only be answered as additional historical data become available, particularly for the period of the Napoleonic wars. More importantly, the power transition suggests that, during the rare periods when a challenger overtakes the dominant nation, war will be waged only if the potential challenger is dissatisfied. Tests of the theory thus far, however, have not included explicit measures of satisfaction with the status quo. It is perhaps easy to persuade oneself that Germany was a dissatisfied power prior to the Franco–Prussian War, World War I, and World War II. But did the United States support the status quo when it overtook England in the 1870s? Was Russia satisfied with the international order when it matched England in power prior to World War I? It may well be that when satisfaction with the status quo is operationally defined, a sufficient explanation for major war will be approached. This may not be sufficient, however, because extensions of power transition in the context of deterrence (reviewed later) and the current work on expected utility suggest that, along with dissatisfaction, a separate concept of risk may be required to specify this model fully (Kugler and Zagare 1987a; Bueno de Mesquita and Lalman 1986).

Before turning to an empirical comparison of the implications of balance of power and power transition, we wish to bring up why we think such great differences in interpretation exist between the two models.

The Likely Source of Disagreement between Balance of Power and Power Transition

One is puzzled by the question of how is it possible that scholars, those who espouse the balance of power and those who favor the power transition, see the international order as working so differently. One can only guess why the differences arose. The "reasons" we advance are linked to when each model was elaborated. We think that the key to the different perspectives espoused by the backers of the balance-of-power and the power-transition models is to be found in the moment when the two models originated. Although the balance of power is an ancient idea that goes back to the politics of the Italian city states, was revived and modernized by the British

TABLE 7.2
Percentage Distribution of Gross National Product among the Major Powers,
1870–1980[a]

Year	United States	Japan	Germany	United Kingdom	Russia/ USSR	France
1870	19.6	6.7	16.8	19.3	19.8	17.8
1880	26.1	5.4	16.3	17.5	19.1	15.6
1890	28.2	5.0	15.7	19.3	17.7	14.1
1900	30.6	5.3	16.4	17.8	17.1	12.8
1913[a]	36.0	5.5	17.0	14.3	16.9	10.3
1925[a]	42.5	8.0	12.2	12.6	15.1	9.6
1938[a]	36.3	9.2	15.0	11.7	20.8	7.0
1950	50.0	5.0	7.1	10.6	20.1	7.2
1960	42.5	7.8	9.2	8.6	24.8	7.1
1970	40.7	11.3	11.6	6.3	21.5	8.6
1980	36.6	16.8	11.2	5.4	21.8	8.2

SOURCE: Data for 1870–1960 are based on various works by Angus Madison. Data for 1970–1980 are from the World Bank *World Tables* and National Foreign Assessment Center, *Handbook of Economic Statistics* (1979). For details on adjustments, see Kugler and Organski (1989).

[a] These odd years are used to avoid, as much as possible, the direct effects of mobilization for World Wars I and II and the unusual global distortion introduced by the Great Depression.

foreign office at the end of the nineteenth century. Likewise, while the basis for the power-overtaking idea (with a good deal of imagination) can be traced to the work of Thucydides (1959), Organski proposed the model in its modern version in the 1950s. Table 7.2, a representation of the productivity of great powers (which is used as a rough surrogate for power) in the previous century, can be used to illustrate the reason for the different perspectives.

At the end of the nineteenth century, when the balance of power began to be invoked, two things were true. Most of the European great powers appeared to be very near to each other in power. Moreover, these countries were growing slowly and the overtaking of one by the other was very slow. In short, if one looked at the structure of power at the end of the nineteenth century, the distribution of power appeared in rough balance and the slope of the trajectories that each country was traveling in its growth appeared almost parallel and flat. On the other hand, France and England were very conscious of being overtaken by German growth because Germany had passed France in the 1870s and England in the 1900s. Hence, it appeared as if the balance of power's prescription—that the stronger power was the aggressor—seemed correct.

On the other hand, when the power transition model was first formulated in the 1950s, the dominance of the United States was clear and the interval between the USSR, Japan, and all of the other European nations was also very wide. The hierarchical nature of the international order was in plain view. Moreover, the secular decline of England and France had also become plain. Clearly, the emergence of the United States as the dominant power was due to its fast and continued growth for several decades. Likewise, the position of the Soviet Union as the potential challenger in the system was rooted in the decade of the 1930s, during which fast growth followed the collectivization, industrialization, and urbanization of that country. Given these developments, there could be no question in the 1950s that—aside from the Korean War—the international order appeared peaceful, secure, and clearly connected to U.S. dominance.

Thus, one explanation of the different views of the balance-of-power and the power-transition perspectives on the international order was the actual world state the authors observed at the time each theory was promulgated. The empirical record, however, can be used to assess the overall validity and the generality of each proposition. We now turn to some of these findings that allow us to evaluate the growth and assess the impact that the power-transition model has had on other formulations.

EXPLORING IMPLICATIONS OF THE POWER TRANSITION

The Timing of War

Organski (1968) initially argued that war would be waged as the challenger approached power parity with the dominant nation. Tensions between the two major contenders would mount as the dissatisfied challenger, growing faster than the dominant nation, threatened to catch up and overtake the dominant power. As each actor perceived that the power gap between them was disappearing, conflict would be triggered by the challenger who became impatient and mounted its attack before it was as strong as the dominant nation. This evaluation may have been influenced, in part, by the very vivid outcomes of World Wars I and II, which the challenger lost. Such outcomes could be understood if the challenger attacked before it had achieved parity with the dominant nation and was, therefore, doomed to defeat, as Germany learned painfully in World Wars I and II.

Organski and Kugler's (1980) test suggested, however, that on this point the original power-transition model was incorrect. Their study shows that the challenger did not attack *before* but only *after* it had surpassed the

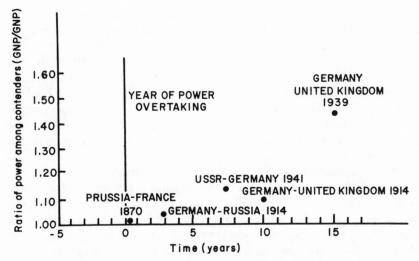

FIGURE 7.2. *Ratio of power between the dominant and the challenging nation associated with war initiation. The challengers are listed first, dominant powers last. At a ratio of 1.00, the contenders are equal in power. From Organski and Kugler (1980, 59, Figure 1.2).*

power of the dominant country. Their evidence prior to every major war since 1870 can be clearly seen in Figure 7.2.

This finding is of major interest to the transition argument not only because it relates the timing of war initiation to a power overtaking but because it implies a different relationship between satisfaction, power, and conflict than was originally postulated. Note that, contrary to original expectations, in each case the conflict started after and not before the parity point. This unexpected outcome could be accounted for without any respecification of the dynamics within the Power Transition in at least two ways.

First, an explanation fully congruent with the original notion attributes this inconsistency to a failure in the measure of national power. Thompson (1983a) replicated the early results using a now-standard measure of power developed by Singer *et al.* (1972). Thompson's work confirms that parity is associated with war, but indicates that major conflicts started, as Organski originally anticipated, prior to the overtaking. Indeed, Thompson argues that when the power measures are adjusted for the performance of the military and industrial components, the timing of conflict conforms with the expectations advanced in the original theory. Organski and Kugler (1980, chap. 2)—as we show later—used an admittedly simple measure of total output in order to approximate power, which, as their own work later shows, may distort the real relation between the main contenders. Their research on power measures now shows that incorporating a direct measure of governmental capacity into the power equation permits an accurate accounting of the outcome of major wars (Kugler and Domke 1987). That work, however, fails to confirm Thompson's findings. Rather, the new measures of power suggest even more definitely that the challenger was stronger than the dominant nation prior to the initiation of major conflicts. There is, again, not enough empirical evidence to settle this issue at this point; there is, however, a second explanation consistent with the early formulation of power transition that may explain why the more powerful country lost the war.

Power transition postulated that alliances were relatively stable and that capabilities were known. In the original statement of the model, however, the effects of allies on war outcomes may have been underestimated. Recall that allies satisfied with the working of the international order are expected to support the dominant nation. Organski and Kugler (1980) show that major allies remain true to their alliance in the major wars under scrutiny, and this finding is generalized by extensive evaluations of alliance performance (Bueno de Mesquita 1981; Siverson and King 1980). Allies of the dominant nation include, as we have seen, the great powers in the international order. The weight of their power immediately after an overtaking would be sufficient to overcome the marginal advantage that a challenger held over the now slightly less powerful but still dominant nation. Thus, as Organski and Kugler (1980) suggest, the reason why the dominant nation succeeds more often than not in major conflicts can be traced to the performance of allies. Despite the marginal inferiority of the dominant nation in relation to the challenger immediately after the overtaking, if conflict is initiated the ultimate outcome tilts in the direction of the dominant power because the great powers that are satisfied with the organization of the international order are able to help the dominant power overcome the challenger and its less powerful alliance (Organski and Kugler 1980, 53–61).

The inclusion of alliances allows power transition to account for the outcome of war after the overtaking. It does not, however, explain why the challenger fails to start the conflict prior to the transition point as originally anticipated. The possible contradiction between original expectations and empirical results led one of the authors to investigate the internal consistency of power transition in the context of nuclear deterrence. From this research a third and perhaps more systematic explanation for the timing of conflict has emerged. Because this work extends the original propositions of power transition and links them to nuclear deterrence, let us discuss it in a separate section.

Power Transition and Deterrence

Before we turn to the specific implications for the timing of conflict, it is important to stress that the advent of nuclear weapons has altered the notion of power in the international order. Few would disagree with the original assessment of Bernard Brodie (1946) that nuclear weapons have so increased the costs of conflict that war can no longer be simply thought as the continuation of policy by other means. Brodie (1946, 1959) then argued that these massive costs made war unwinnable and unthinkable; given these new conditions, he proposed the notion that nuclear weapons could be turned into instruments to frighten an aggressor from its course, and the concept of nuclear deterrence was born.

As nuclear arsenals developed and relative parity of nuclear weapons was attained among the main competitors, maximization of power reemerged as a viable assumption and power parity among the major actors was again associated with peace. Like balance of power did previously, deterrence today, as exemplified by the strategy of mutual assured destruction (MAD), proposes that international stability is assured when nuclear contenders are dissuaded from initiating a conflict because the absolute costs of nuclear war are so high that the parties find them "unacceptable" (Jervis 1979; Hardin *et al.* 1985; Intriligator and Brito 1987). Proponents of MAD now argue that nuclear preponderance will lead to war because when one side gains a substantial advantage, it will impose its preferences by threatening an opponent with nuclear devastation. Indeed, and somewhat paradoxically, proponents of MAD now oppose the Strategic Defense Initiative (SDI) because it would reimpose nuclear preponderance, which is precisely the condition that Brodie addressed.

In sharp contrast with classical deterrence, power transition suggests that the calculus of war and peace has not changed with the advent of nuclear weapons. It is taken for granted that the absolute costs of war have obviously multiplied, but the calculations of marginal gains or losses as a challenger overtakes a dominant nation still provide the necessary conditions for the initiation of war. There is no need to adjust assumptions in the nuclear era. A preponderant dominant nation—the United States— would have no incentive to destroy its potential challenger—the Soviet Union—during the period 1945–1960 when the United States held unilateral preponderance of nuclear power because the United States enjoyed all the benefits of the international order. This stability, however, would be altered and would become increasingly tenuous as nuclear parity is approached and an overtaking by the Soviet Union becomes possible. Thus, in this view, a balance of terror is very tenuous and unstable (Organski 1968; Organski and Kugler 1980; Kugler 1984; Kugler and Zagare 1987a,b; Zagare 1987).

TABLE 7.3
Sufficient Conditions for Peace

	Alternatives offered to j	
Alternatives offered to i	Do not challenge	Challenge
Do not challenge	Status quo (a_1, b_1)	j wins (a_1, b_2)
Challenge	i wins (a_2, b_1)	War (a_2, b_2)

Formal extensions of the Power Transition were constructed to show the conditions under which nuclear conflict could logically be waged. Recall that satisfaction with the international order reflects the value that each participant attaches to the status quo. The dominant nation is the main architect of the international order and is assumed to be satisfied, while the challenger must be dissatisfied. Before we evaluate the power interaction in a competitive setting, we should underline the importance of the assumption regarding the status quo. Zagare (1987, 151) shows that, regardless of their power relationship, two nations satisfied with the status quo in the international order have no incentive to challenge each other and, hence, no need to deter each other. This is simply demonstrated by the generalized representation shown in Table 7.3 of a competitive game used frequently to represent deterrence where the two players, i and j, can either support (a_1 or b_1) or challenge (a_2 or b_2) the existing status quo.

Note that no matter what values are attached to all of the other alternatives, when the status quo is preferred by both actors to the outcome that could be secured by challenging it, the status quo is never challenged. Simply stated, when i and j are satisfied and marginally prefer the status quo to a challenge, war is not possible. Consequently, such an outcome pair does not need deterrence to insure cooperation (Zagare 1987; Keohane 1984). Deterrence is required, however, if at least one party prefers the option of challenging the status quo, and the investigation of different combinations of such values produces a number of complex and interesting deterrence alternatives (Kugler and Zagare 1987b; Zagare 1987). Thus, consistent with the fundamental assumption of power transition, it has now been shown by others that *dissatisfaction* with the status quo is an essential precondition for conflict.

Given the dissatisfaction of at least one party with the international order, let us now explore what power distributions can lead to conflict. Kugler and Zagare (1987b) propose the power-overtaking structure in Figure 7.3 to account for stable deterrence: Under conditions of power

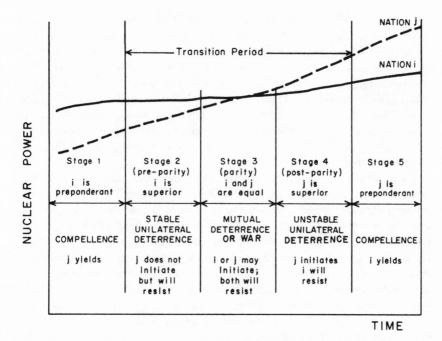

FIGURE 7.3. *Power transition and the dynamics of deterrence.*

preponderance (stages 1 and 5), the power-transition and deterrence theories—unlike the balance-of-power model—suggest that war is unlikely. The weaker power cannot obtain concessions without significant costs, and the stronger party has little incentive to alter the status quo. Power transition adds an additional refinement. When the dominant power is satisfied and preponderant (stage 1), war is unlikely because *i* has no incentive to extract added concessions from potential challengers. When the challenger becomes preponderant (stage 5), however, it will extract concessions that can no longer be resisted by the previously dominant nation.

Power transition differs fundamentally from both balance of power and deterrence in stages 2, 3, and 4. Power transition indicates that the conditions for conflict are present during most of the transition period and are heightened by the growth of the challenger. Contrary to Organski's (1958) original expectations, we find the conditions for stable unilateral deterrence during the immediate preparity period (Stage 1). The challenger, *j*, is able to resist the demands of the dominant nation, *i*, thereby signaling that, at that power level, the sufficient conditions for conflict are met. Because the dominant nation, *i*, is committed to the status quo, however, *i* has little incentive to challenge *j*. After all, the prevailing international order is controlled by and designed for the benefit of the dominant power. Concurrently, *j*'s own incentive to challenge is minimal because *j* is still marginally inferior to *i* and expects to gain no concessions should a confrontation arise. This deduction is consistent with the empirical report that challengers did not initiate major war prior to the overtaking, but instead waited until they were stronger than the dominant nation to make a move (Organski and Kugler 1980). Moreover, this logic provides a clear explanation for the absence of nuclear war since Hiroshima and Nagasaki were devastated.

The Power-transition model indicates that the stability of nuclear threats erodes in the next two stages (Figure 7.4, stages 3 and 4) where this model anticipates simultaneously the conditions for war and peace. Unlike classical deterrence and the balance-of-power models, which argue that parity of power insures peace when the costs of war are very high, power-transition theory proposes that these are the very conditions where deterrence is most uncertain. When power equality is achieved (stage 3), *j* is sufficiently strong to make credible threats and to fight if spurned. Thus, war may be waged precisely because each side has an equal opportunity to achieve net gains with a victory and the dissatisfied party anticipates net losses from continuous compromise. There is also a reverse side to this argument. Parity also suggests the conditions for stability. Congruent with the expectations of the balance-of-power model, power equality is associated with peace when the potential challenger, *j*, is unwilling to take risks and anticipates no gains from a conflict involving nuclear weapons (Kugler and Zagare 1987a,b).

Finally, and germane to this argument, after the challenger, *j*, has surpassed the previously dominant power, *i* (stage 4), the conditions for a major war are present. Unlike the preparity period (stage 2), which is stable because the dominant power is satisfied with the prevailing order, the postparity period is potentially unstable because *j*, now slightly stronger, is still dissatisfied with the status quo but can now anticipate the possibility of marginal gains through conflict. Under such conditions, sooner or later *j*'s frustration will manifest itself in a challenge. When it does, the declining but still dominant nation, *i*, is expected to resist. War can ensue.

What, then, are the implications of the power-transition model for stability in the nuclear age? This exploration shows that the power-transition model extends easily to encompass deterrence without altering the basic assumptions or reformulating the theory as nuclear weapons proliferate. Given Lakatos' concept of generality, power transition's concept of international politics seems to have a definite edge.

The practical implications of this model are, however, sobering. The power-transition perspective suggests that when nuclear parity is reached and a challenger threatens to overtake the dominant nation, perceptions of a "missile gap" or a future "window of vulnerability" can destabilize deterrence. As power transition suggests, this is true only if elites of competing nuclear powers concentrate on the net gains and losses each may achieve from a challenge and are not stopped from action, as Brodie suggested, because of their concern with the absolute costs of a nuclear war. With the perspective of power transition, for example, one can see why Kennedy thought that the deployment of nuclear weapons in Cuba was a radical step that could not be accepted and, to prevent this marginal change, accepted a high risk of a massive nuclear war. It should be noted that much of the new strategic literature now suggests the possibility that parity does not, after all, insure stability. For example, Huntington, whose work was instrumental in the development of classical deterrence, now argues that it is unwise to rely on nuclear equality alone when facing an opponent who is willing to risk more to attain its own ends (Huntington 1982). Indeed, with the deployment of tactical nuclear weapons the possibility of waging and "winning" a nuclear war has reemerged (Gray 1979). Indeed, despite pleas by proponents of continued balance under the mutual assured destruction policy (Jervis 1979; McNamara 1984), it is no longer universally accepted that, with parity, nuclear war is so "unthinkable" that it could not be used to advance policy goals. Note that this is precisely what power transition suggested would happen when parity was reached.

Quite understandably, these two perspectives of international politics produce very different policy propositions in the nuclear field. The most obvious divergence is in the impact of nuclear proliferation. Both deterrence and balance of power permit the inference that the proliferation of nuclear weapons will enhance the stability of the international order. Indeed, Waltz (1981), Intriligator and Brito (1981), Bueno de Mesquita and Riker (1982), and, much earlier, Kaplan (1958) independently developed, from the balance-of-power structure, the idea that nuclear proliferation can increase international stability even in volatile disputes. Each analyst proposes slightly different schemes for the dispersement of nuclear weapons, but, from the simple premise that increasing the absolute cost of war will reduce its likelihood under balanced conditions, all deduce that the proliferation of nuclear weapons should enhance stability and secure peace.

The power-transition framework produces a diametrically opposite conclusion. The high costs attached to nuclear conflicts do not reduce the danger because it is the marginal calculations of gains and losses that lead to challenges. Nuclear parity does not produce assured stability. Rather, the nuclear parity created by proliferation enhances the potential for instability. Indeed, proliferation augments the number of nations that can achieve regional or world nuclear parity and, because of this, expands the number of actors that have the opportunity to consider the risk of nuclear war, increases the chances for an overtaking among competitors that may be willing to take the risk of war, and, therefore, undermines world and regional stability. Note that most balance-of-terror advocates are inconsistent on this point because they concurrently advocate stable nuclear deterrence under equality and vehemently oppose nuclear proliferation (Jervis 1979; Hardin *et al.* 1985).

The development and reformation of power transition show how the theory has produced important extensions in the nuclear age that are empirically and formally consistent with the record of international stability while remaining consistent with the original proposition. Related extensions in the field of comparative politics also support the vitality of this perspective.

Power and Political Capacity

The concern of power transition with national development led to a concept of national power that was radically different from the prevailing view. National power was only partially captured in military strength (Claude 1962), in the mobilization of untapped resources for war purposes (Knorr 1956), or in the many-faceted notion of the will to fight (Aron 1967). The power-transition model suggested that national power was rooted in the development of socioeconomic and political resources. At the core of the developmental process are three interconnected sets of changes: the increase of economic productivity resulting from industrialization, the increase in the demographic pool in the economically active ages due to the demographic transition, and the increase of the capacity of elites to mobilize resources produced by the population. For students of international politics, this specification of the connection between development and power made relevant the data and methodologies of many disciplines.

Initially, power transition suggested a very simple indicator by which national power could be measured and specified an interactive model to do so (Organski 1958). Measures of political capacity were not available, and, while Organski noted this deficiency, he suggested that changes in the economic and demographic structures were sufficient to measure, at least very roughly, the concept of national power. Thus, power was simply

$$\text{Power} = \text{Economic Productivity per Capita} \times \text{Population}$$

The gross national product (GNP) was the measure chosen because it combined the demographic and economic aspects of a nation's productivity.

In empirical tests this parsimonious and robust measure performed as well as the more complex index of power developed by Singer *et al.* (1972), which included demographic, industrial, and military components. Indeed, the same periods of transitions among developed nations were identified with both approaches (Thompson 1983a; Organski and Kugler 1980). Here, the power-transition concept led to a second major innovation. If power was the result of the levels of development in the demographic, economic, and political spheres, it was critical to specify a model of such a relation and measure the capacity of political systems. A concept and a measure of political capacity, however, were not easy to come by. For the purpose of international politics, the fundamental political question can be phrased as follows: Is the political system more productive, more effective, and more efficient than another in its ability to extract resources for its own ends? The problem, then, is how to measure the capacity of elites to mobilize the human and material resources under their jurisdiction.

Relative political capacity (RPC) is a first attempt to approximate the level of political performance through the use of revenue data. As Ardant stated, "The fiscal system is the 'Transformer' of the economic infra-structure to the political structure" (Organski and Kugler 1980, 74). To approach political capacity, then, one must estimate the ability of a political system to mobilize the resources within the polity. The procedure used for such an estimation has been fully described elsewhere, and numerous analysts have added specificity to this general concept allowing RPC to deal with world, regional, and even domestic political capacity (Organski and Kugler 1980; Kugler and Domke 1987; Kugler 1987; Snider 1988; Rouyer 1987). Simply stated, RPC is a ratio that measures the difference between the revenues a government is expected to extract (given its economic performance and resource endowment) and the revenues a government is capable of extracting to pursue its own ends. Power could now be reformulated as

$$\text{Power} = (\text{Economic Production per Capita} \times \text{Population}) \times \text{Relative Political Capacity}$$

Political capacity is used to shrink or expand the original base of power. The validity of this new measure of national power would, of course, be tested. Tests were set to determine if one could "postdict" the outcome of wars among developed and developing nations—including Korea, Vietnam, and the Middle East wars—and if one could concurrently improve on the account of the outcomes of wars among developed nations in conflicts such as World Wars I and II. The new measure proved successful in both environments (Organski and Kugler 1980; Kugler and Domke 1987). The importance of such tests is that, at long last, a parsimonious measure of power that accounts for the outcome of wars with a high degree of accuracy has been developed and validated.

Political Capacity: A Demographic Test

The search for a measure of political capacity had direct payoffs in political demography. The use of demographic variables to explore changes in political behavior has long been a staple of political analysis, but the measurement of the effects going the other way had proven elusive. One could not tell, for instance, what effects the growth of the political system had on the fertility and mortality of populations. Many analysts, of course, suspected that as the capacity of a government grew and state authority was strengthened, internal conflict, which decimated the population, devastated the economy, and caused further death through lack of health care and disease, decreased causing a drop in mortality. And again, with state growth and with governmental rules on marriage, education of women, divorce, ownership of property, education, employment, and access of contraception or abortion, infertility also declined.

To test the effects of state growth on fertility and morality, the measure of political capacity was transformed into a measure of political costs. The theory connecting the measure of political costs and the process of growth of the political system has been outlined elsewhere (Organski *et al.* 1984), and brief synopsis must suffice. The growth of a government's ability to extract political resources is the result of the elites' attempt to gain as much of the resources as they can from their society. The major reason more resources are not extracted from the population is that the ruling elite cannot pay the political costs that the extraction of additional resources would require.

The results of analyzing the effects of political capacity on fertility and mortality had vast implications for our understanding of the process of national development. It has been suspected for some time that the growth of nations was the result of changes in the social, political, economic, demographic, and belief structures making up a national society. A key to this pattern of growth is to be found in the fact that fundamental changes in behavior in one sector brought about changes in other sectors. In the demographic sphere, for example, Thompson (1929) and Notestein (1945) proposed that fundamental changes in economic development caused changes in fertility and mortality. In the absence of economic development, it was not thought possible that fertility could be brought down sufficiently to permit the savings that developing countries required in order to develop. Analyses using political capacity suggest that this view was fundamentally in error. Politically capable countries reduced both fertility and mortality (Organski *et al.* 1984). As the case of China vividly demonstrated, an economically underdeveloped country (with, however, a highly effective political system) could lower the fertility of its population to levels of countries in Europe like Spain. This lowered fertility was part of the unintended consequences of that nation's political growth and started well before any population control programs were instituted (Organski *et al.* 1984). More recent research shows that political capacity indicates when a government-instituted program of birth control will have far reaching effects. The major birth control attempt by Indira Gandhi fizzled out in India, but Rouyer (1987) shows that relative success was directly related to the level of political capacity achieved by the local governments in each of the Indian states that attempted such programs.

The realization that political change by itself could bring down fertility, which permits the necessary savings for economic development (although, of course, such savings need necessarily be channeled into productive investment), suggests a very different prognosis for the economic development of the many remaining underdeveloped countries. If such countries can develop their political capacity, as China or Vietnam have, they can enhance economic growth. Hence, the distribution of power driven by such political changes in domestic structures is very likely to change the world of tomorrow in massive ways.

The introduction of political capacity may also affect comparative politics in areas that had received a good deal of attention in the 1960s and 1970s under the rubric of political development. That effort produced some memorable work but has since died out. We suggest that one of the reasons for this failure is the inability to estimate the capability and productivity of the political system. The measure of capacity is a tool that allows direct cross-national comparisons and suggests that the field of political development should again be at the center of political research.

CONCLUSIONS

We return to Lakatos' criteria to assess the value of power transition. As expected from any novel idea, power transition suggests a number of new assumptions and derives nonstandard hypotheses about the reasons for peace and conflict in the international order. Power transition asserted that an equal distribution of power among key contenders is the necessary condition that bring about major international conflict and that when power is asymmetrically distributed, peace is assured. This proposition was radically different from prior expectations of the realist tradition and has, thus far, been supported by the existing evidence.

Turning then to Lakatos' criteria of generality, the extensions of power transition provide a description of the nuclear world that is consistent with the empirical record and do not require additional assumptions or revisions to develop the general argument of deterrence. Balance of power and its various extensions into deterrence accomplish such ends only by altering assumptions to correspond with changes in the distribution of nuclear resources. Moreover, the debate regarding the stability of deterrence, the value of nuclear proliferation, and the usefulness of defensive systems, which now divide many analysts in the realist tradition of equilibrium, can be understood and directly related to the behavior of practitioners using the perspective of power transition.

Power transition has also influenced the study of world politics by directing attention to domestic developmental processes rather than to international interactions to understand peace and war. The new perspective has clearly influenced writers in the hegemonic tradition who also place development at center stage. Moreover, by refocusing the concept of power away from military force, power transition had a lasting impact on the way power is now measured. Perhaps the greatest cross-disciplinary impact of power transition can be traced to the development of measures of political capacity. Such measures, designed originally to approximate power more effectively, have now acquired a life of their own in the systematic analysis of national behavior. Their promise is that we will understand more fully the process of national development and—for the first time—will be able to compare directly the political capacity of governments regardless of governmental forms.

The survival of power transition as a major idea in the field should be secured by such a record. Reformulations of key concepts under new names and the inclusion of key aspects of the theory under different rubrics may well result in the absorption of this central idea into other constructs. This, of course, is also a measure of success. Regardless of labels that may eventually be used, however, upon completing this evaluation it seems to us that, on the key aspects of Lakatos' criteria (novelty, generality, and empirical support), power transition fares very well because it has focused and added to our knowledge. Perhaps no higher reward can be asked from any idea.

CHAPTER 8

Arms Races, the Conflict Spiral, and the Onset of War

Randolph M. Siverson
University of California, Davis, Davis, CA

Paul F. Diehl
University of Georgia, Athens, GA

INTRODUCTION

> While the [arms race] models are more formal now than in the pre-Richardson days, they all seem to be variants of his basic approach . . . , even . . . more recent efforts, while clearly informed by the scientific outlook, leave us very far from the sort of knowledge we seek. [Singer 1970, 137]

Although these words were written over 15 years ago, they still have a ring of truth today. Scholars continue to devote most of their attention to modeling arms races, with special emphasis on the effects of factors such as reactivity and technology. One need only look at the recent reviews of arms race models (Moll and Luebbert 1980; Isard and Anderton 1985; Anderton 1985) to appreciate both the volume and sophistication of this work. Yet even though many of these models enlighten us on the dynamics of arms races, they tell us little or nothing about their relationship to and effect upon the broader political context in which these competitions take place. When will arms races lead to militarized confrontations? When will they lead to war? Under what conditions can they be terminated in a peaceful manner? Can arms races actually reduce the chances of war? These are only a few of the questions to which Singer alluded.

Most of these questions are relatively unexplored, but in recent years there has been greater attention devoted to studies of the outcomes of arms races. To a considerable extent, these studies are based upon a desire to assess the relative accuracy of two significant, diverging points of view on the consequences of weapons acquisition. One view, put forward most notably by the Roman military writer Vegetius, is that "if you want peace, prepare for war"; this is often referred to as the para bellum hypothesis. Put simply, if a nation acquires sufficient weapons, other nations will be unwilling to attack it because the costs of aggression are far greater than if the nation was not as well prepared. This is the conventional wisdom of deterrence. The alternative view argues that two antagonistic nations will be caught in an arms spiral in which each nation believes it is necessary to either match or exceed the arms level of the other. In the view of some, the resulting "arms race" further exacerbates international tensions and increases the chances of war.

Attempts to assess the extent to which arms races increase or decrease the likelihood of war have created an interesting, often controversial body of literature. This chapter, which reviews and evaluates this research with the purpose of determining whether we are near to the knowledge we seek about arms race outcomes or we are no closer than when Singer made his observation, is composed of three sections. In the first, we consider and compare studies of arms race outcomes along several dimensions, including the strategy of inquiry and measurement. In the second section, we present an extensive critical discussion of the main findings that have been reported. Finally, we present a set of research priorities to chart some paths for future investigation. In conducting this review, it was necessary to limit our contribution to only those works that deal explicitly with arms race outcomes. In doing so, we bypass the hundreds of works on deterrence that are relevant for any study of war but do not specifically address the arms race question.

METHODOLOGICAL FOUNDATIONS

Theoretical Positions

Studies of the arms race–war relationship display the same wide methodological variation found in other areas of international relations scholarship; some are primarily deductive, others are largely empirical, and a few entail some combination of the two. Many of the studies (Huntington 1958; Wallace 1979, 1982; Diehl 1985b) are substantially empirical but without well-articulated models to guide their investigations. The specific propositions tested and the rationale underlying them are rather vague. This is not only a problem in understanding the logic underlying the research design; it is even more troublesome when searching for viable explanations of significant findings. This latter difficulty is discussed in more detail shortly.

As much as empirical studies suffer from a lack of theoretical focus, those in the formal modeling tradition tend to be deficient in the opposite direction. For example, working from well-defined deductive models, Intriligator and Brito (1984, 1985c) elegantly lay out a sequence of assumptions and conclusions that is systematic and replicable. As in the case of other similar models, however, there is no attempt at explicit empirical testing. Many of the formal models of arms races cannot be disconfirmed through empirical tests. Those that define the conditions for nuclear war (for example, Patchen 1986) have no empirical referents and, hence, are difficult to evaluate and (happily!) impossible to test in the natural world. Still others (for example, Majeski 1986a) are not necessarily under the same constraints and seem incomplete without empirical testing. It can, of course, be argued that these models have heuristic and other values regardless of whether or not they are tested for empirical validity. Although we are sympathetic to this method of theory construction, it is critically important that the model be capable of empirical analysis.

Obviously, some of the problems can be remedied by combining the theoretical and empirical approaches. Nevertheless, relatively few scholars have chosen this route. Richardson (1960) and, following his lead, Smith (1980) develop arms race models and test their predicted outcomes. Perhaps the best blend of formal modeling and empirical analysis is suggested by Morrow (1984), who advocates an expected-utility approach to investigate arms races and war. Nonetheless, most studies that combine deductive models and empirical analysis do not concern themselves with conflict outcomes, but rather with the processes of action and reaction.

Point of Reference

Beyond differences in their theoretical positions, studies of arms races and war also vary according to their starting points. Some look at arms races in the context of military conflict, while others look at military conflict in the context of arms races. These are not identical approaches, and each leads to dissimilar strategies of investigation. It makes a significant difference whether the beginning point of reference is the arms race or the war. Some scholars have chosen to identify a sample of arms races (Huntington 1958) with special attention to the outbreak of war within the time period of each arms race. This appears to be the simplest and most straightforward way of approaching the research question. A somewhat more sophisticated variation (Smith 1980) looks at different patterns in the arms competition (for example, stability versus instability) to account for the outbreak of war at a particular point in the arms race.

Although this approach avoids certain pitfalls (which are discussed later) associated with a focus on war, it is not without some difficulties. Many of the studies that select arms races as the points of reference use broad ranges of years to define an arms race period (both the Huntington and Smith studies contain arms races that cover extended periods of time). This tendency leads to a blurring of the distinction between a rivalry and an arms race. A strict definition of an arms race must be used with this approach; if not, rivalries and arms races become synonymous or questionable cases are identified. For example, Smith (1980) unaccountability includes France and Germany from 1961–1977 as an arms race.

The major problem with this strategy, however, is that it isolates the arms race cases from all other conflicts not involving arms competition. In effect, there is no control group in the study. Determining whether or not arms races increase the likelihood of war is exceedingly difficult unless the researcher knows the probability, ceteris paribus, of escalation in the absence of arms competition.

Using arms races as points of reference seems a logical choice, but this has not been the preferred method of all or most scholars. A significant portion of the arms race–war studies focus on conflict in the form of Correlates of War (COW) "militarized disputes." In this approach, arms races are investigated because they center around the occurrence of these disputes. Work by COW researchers Wallace (1979, 1983) and Diehl (1985b) as well as Houweling and Siccama (1981) is indicative of this strategy.

There are several problems with this approach. First, the researcher is unable to detect an unspecified number of arms races that do not involve militarized disputes between the participants. These instances can provide important evidence that arms races do not lead to war or even military conflict; the case that arms races deter war and disputes is, therefore, artificially weakened. Second, this focus provides an unnecessarily narrow view of an arms race. The arms competition is considered only at one static point (for example, the time of the dispute or its escalation). Thus, it is impossible to see if disputes on war occur at the apex of the arms race, at some point of instability, or on a downward trend of intensity. Even those arms race indicators that use data across a range of years are unable to detect these potentially important patterns.

An initial focus on disputes also leaves a scholar the option of which conflict phase to study; these can roughly be classified as the initiation, escalation, and postescalation phases. Most attention has been directed at the escalation phase, determining whether arms races influence the likelihood that disputes will end in war.[1] With this approach, the occurrence of a serious disagreement is at least as important as the arms race in affecting the chances for war (Houweling and Siccama 1981). Only a few efforts (see Diehl and Kingston 1987) explore whether or not arms races have any role as an instigator or early-warning indicator of the dispute. Whether or not arms races influence the conduct of war or its aftermath is virtually ignored (a notable exception is Smith 1985). Few studies, if any, take into account all three phases. Accordingly, the results generated have narrow applicability and require additional study to gain a broad understanding of arms races and war.

Spatial–Temporal Domain

Another dimension with which arms race studies can be compared is their choice of time periods and nations analyzed. Not surprisingly, the United States–Soviet arms competition since World War II is a popular topic (see Intriligator and Brito 1984). Even those works that do not directly address that competition do so implicitly by looking at nuclear arms races and situations that can best be applied to the American–Soviet rivalry (see Patchen 1986). Although a particular focus on the United States–Soviet arms race can be justified on the grounds of importance, it may be unnecessarily limited in scope. Implicitly, this approach assumes that conflict in the nuclear age is different from preceding epochs. Recent work (Gochman and Maoz 1984) indicates that continuity is evident in conflict patterns over time with little apparent change precipitated by the advent of nuclear weapons. Insights gained from studying other arms races are lost if attention is given only to the American–Soviet rivalry, which is critical in that this particular arms race has not experienced war and any conclusions about the likelihood of war are rather speculative.

Some empirical studies have included arms races involving major powers in the nineteenth and twentieth centuries (see Wallace 1979, 1983). In large part, this choice may be attributable to the conflict data sets available, data sets that have tended to focus disproportionately on the major powers. The perceived importance of the major powers (their conflicts having the greatest impact on the international system) might also be cited as a justification for this spatial–temporal domain. Studying the major powers also allows the researcher to consider the American–Soviet competition within the context of other arms races, noting differences when appropriate and strengthening inferences about the contemporary prospects for war.

A common drawback to conflict studies, including works on arms races, is that they all but ignore minor power nations (an exception is Smith 1980). Studying minor power arms races is certainly more complicated than when the focus is upon only major powers. The reasons for this gap are not difficult to locate. First, it is frequently impossible to find accurate, reliable data on minor powers, particularly prior to World War I. Second, the indicators for arms races may have to be different than when studying major powers in the modern era. In arms competition, minor power nations usually rely heavily on arms transfers rather than on their indigenous military production capacity, and technology may be less significant than sheer manpower. Another consideration is that the buildup of arms in a minor power nation may be as much for internal as external security concerns. Finally, minor power nations may be surrogates of their major power benefactors, and the decision to enter a war may not be solely in the hands of the smaller nations regardless of whether there is an arms race or not.

Despite these difficulties, minor power arms races can provide a better picture, under varying conditions, of when arms races lead to wars. Minor power wars in the last 40 years have not had the destructive capacity of a nuclear encounter, yet they have been numerous with a large loss of life and destruction of property.[2] Such wars could also be the beginning of a nuclear confrontation between the superpowers. A credible case can be made that minor power arms races are collectively as important as the arms competition between the United States and the Soviets.

ARMS RACES AND WAR

The Findings Summarized

One of the earliest studies was put forward by Huntington (1958), who identified 11 arms races from 1840 to the current arms race between the United States and the Soviet Union, which began in 1946. Although by no means optimistic, Huntington's analysis of these arms races indicated that several other outcomes were possible in addition to the outbreak of a war. Not only could nations recognize the futility of extended arms competition and enter into arms-control agreements, but they could also offset the competition through alliances with other nations or one nation could realize that overtaking the other was not within its means and, therefore, acquiesce to the other's superiority. Although suggesting several outcomes for an arms race beside war, Huntington does argue that arms races are dangerous, particularly in their early stages when uncertainty and instability are at their greatest. Huntington also contends that arms races involving quantitative (as opposed to qualitative) improvements in stockpiles are more dangerous. Whereas qualitative improvements lead to brief, transitory advantages, competition in the number of armaments allows the nation with the greatest resource capacity to be victorious in the race. Nevertheless, "If the challenged state neither resorts to preventive war nor fails to make an immediate response to the challenger's activities, a sustained arms race is likely to result with the probability of war decreasing as the initial action and counteraction fade into the past" (Huntington 1958, 63).

Earlier research by Richardson (not published in one volume until 1960) was far less sanguine. After setting forward his now famous equations, which capture an armaments race between two nations in terms of various psychological, sociological, and economic variables, Richardson generalizes his theory to N nations and puts forward several extensions and elaborations. His study of the solutions of his equations for armaments races demonstrates that levels of armaments either tend to constant equilibrium values or increase to infinity over time, depending upon the values of different socioeconomic and psychological factors. Richardson reasons that when armaments reach constant equilibrium values, war will not result. If weapons increase indefinitely, however, he reasons that war between the racing nations will occur in the end.

Subsequent research by Lambelet (1975) is in general agreement with Huntington. Lambelet identifies two admittedly extreme hypotheses: (1) Richardson's view that unstable arms races inevitably lead to war and, alternatively, (2) that arms races and war are independent events. Lambelet argues that the resource constraints faced by all nations undermine the idea of an unstable arms race. As he puts it, "At the limit, it is obvious that no nation can maintain a defense establishment that would claim more than the total economic resources at its command" (pp. 123–124). Although this form of the point is extreme, resource constraints, even in limited manifestations, limit defense spending and make significant instability over an extended period an unlikely event. Although it may be unlikely, it is not impossible. Israel, for example, has devoted as much as 35 percent of its gross domestic product to the military (International Institute for Strategic Studies 1984). With regard to the second position, Lambelet musters an argument similar to Huntington's, and he concludes not only that arms races may end in ways other than war, but also that unilateral disarmament or a failure to keep up with the other side may actually increase the probability of war (the latter position is also defended by Weede 1980). Moreover, with specific reference to the nuclear arms race between the United States and the Soviet Union,

Lambelet reasons that the increase in the "stakes" of a war that would ensue are so large that war is further deterred.

Although the arguments advanced by Huntington and Lambelet are persuasive, they are not based upon an analysis of widely gathered systematic data. What, we may ask is, the overall relationship between arms races and war? Fortunately, a number of research articles have appeared recently that attempt to explore the linkage between arms races and the outbreak of war. The next section of this chapter will review and comment upon these studies.

The first empirical studies of the relationship between arms races and war based upon extensive data analysis were reported by Wallace in two related contributions, the first published in 1979 and the second in 1983. These are of interest for two reasons. First, they opened an important topic to empirical research and enlarged our knowledge about the relationship between arms races and the onset of war. Second, Wallace's research has itself been the subject of considerable controversy and attention, and the resulting discussion has further illuminated the issue of arms races and war. After a summary of Wallace's research, we will review the criticisms of it, comment upon them, and then discuss some other studies in this area.

In seeking to understand the relationship between arms races and the onset of war, Wallace initially asked a fundamental question: Does the existence of an arms race between two states significantly increase their probability of going to war? After noting the existence of the two starkly opposed views of the arms race phenomena (that is, the spiral and deterrence views noted previously), Wallace seeks to (1) define an arms race and (2) specify the process through which an arms race might increase the probability of war. This second task is critically important because a significant omission in the work of Richardson and his followers is the identification of the events or processes that might turn an unstable arms race into a war. To be sure, two nations in an arms race can hardly avoid recognizing the possibility of war; what has been missing from the traditional Richardsonian view of an arms race (and almost all of the literature it inspired), however, is an articulation of the process that is likely to transform the arms race into war.

Wallace's conceptual definition of an arms race is that it reflects simultaneous, abnormal rates of growth in military outlays by two or more nations; this is quite similar to the specification by Gray (1971). There are two qualifications accompanying this. Wallace states that the increases must be attributable to the competitive pressure of one nation upon the other nation and not the result of purely domestic factors. More significantly, he states that the nations in the arms race must be interdependent in their security policies; that is, they must be capable of truly harming each other.

This forecloses the possibility of an arms race between, for example, Peru and the United States; indeed, given this requirement, arms races are said to exist only between enemy nations of reasonably equivalent capabilities.

The requirement that the nations must identify each other as rivals for an arms race to exist is quite reasonable, but how are rivalries to be identified by the researcher? By reviewing the historical record to identify the nations that had serious disputes with each other, Wallace is able to locate the population of presumptive enemies. In doing this, however, the original research question changes to this: Do serious disputes between nations engaged in an arms race have a greater probability of escalating to war than disputes between nations that are not engaged in an arms race? In other words, what Wallace is assessing is not the independent impact of an arms race on the onset of war, but rather the intervening impact of an arms race on the escalation of a dispute.

In order to begin the empirical work, Wallace must identify his domain. Drawing upon a list of 99 militarized international disputes between major powers between 1833 and 1965, Wallace is able to use the arms expenditure data of the Correlates of War project to find those pairs of nations that added large increments to their arms expenditures prior to the dispute. Wallace is then able to cross tabulate whether or not the dispute escalated to war with whether or not the nations were in an arms race. The result of his cross tabulation is shown in Table 8.1.

As given, these results indicate that the rapid, competitive growth of armaments by a pair of nations is strongly associated with a dispute between those two nations escalating to war. Wallace notes, however, that the coincidence of the wars and arms races could be related to other factors such as an ongoing tension that prompts nations to arm in a competitive fashion. If so, then the close association in Table 8.1 would be spurious and the entire arms race–war relationship would be open to serious question (and rather different policy implications).

In a reaction to Wallace's paper, Weede (1980) raised three significant objections. First, Weede noted that during three time periods (namely,

TABLE 8.1
Arms Races and War, 1815–1965

	Arms races	No arms races
War	23	3
No war	5	68

SOURCE: Wallace (1979).

1852–1871, 1919–1938, and 1945 to the present) escalation of disputes to war did not take place regardless of whether the arms race index was high or low. Second, he observes that many of the escalations took place in the same war and, hence, might be better attributed to war (for example, World War I) diffusion rather than to the effects of an arms race. Finally, Weede argues that, whatever else it establishes, Wallace's research does not address the assertions by "realists" that the most dangerous event is not a runaway arms race but, rather, status quo powers losing an arms race. In essence, this third criticism accurately observes that Wallace did not test the hypothesis that wars can be avoided through military preparedness, and although his results indicate an association between arms races and war under some circumstances, this is far from necessarily meaning that military prepared-ness, even when increased at rapid rates, leads to war through either the escalation of crises or some other means. As noted previously, Wallace's research design is unable to detect arms races that deterred disputes or wars.

In a response, Wallace (1980) addressed each of these points. He argued that (1) in the periods in which disputes did not escalate, the cases were distributed in accordance with his interpretation and (2) even allowing for the diffusion of war, the findings remained. With regard to Weede's third point, Wallace not only responded, but presented two new studies (1981, 1982).

In exploring more fully the "peace through strength" or para bellum hypothesis (that is, "if you want peace, prepare for war"), Wallace (1982) establishes two types of nations, status quo and revisionist. He then formulates the specific hypothesis "International conflicts and disputes which are accompanied by a shift in the distribution of relative military capability in favor of a revisionist state, or to the detriment of a status quo state, are more likely to result in war than those in which such a shift does not occur" (p. 40, emphasis deleted).

Drawing upon essentially the same set of disputes used in the previous study, Wallace asks this question: Is a great power dispute more likely to escalate to war if the revisionist nation is (1) significantly superior in military capability, (2) gaining in strength relative to the status quo nation, or (3) both growing and stronger? Wallace then identifies the revisionist and status quo nations in each dispute and uses the Correlates of War arms-expenditure data to measure military balances between the two nations for the 3 years prior to the occurrence of the dispute. It might be noted that this formulation bears a close resemblance to the "power-transition" idea of Organski and Kugler (1980).

What ratio of military strength between the revisionist and status quo states should be used to determine superiority? Wallace selects the ratio of 1.5 of revisionist to status quo nations to indicate superiority (that is, the revisionist nation is at least 50 percent stronger than the status quo nation), but it is unclear exactly how this ratio was determined.

Having identified the respective nations and their strength ratios, Wallace is in a position to begin his analysis. First, he examines the relationship of the strength ratio to the escalation of conflicts to war. Table 8.2 reproduces his results and does not provide much evidence for revisionist superiority leading to the escalation of crises.

Wallace next turns to the question of the relative momentum in the power ratios of revisionist and status quo nations. He does this by constructing a ratio of the growth rates of the two nations, with a resulting index that reflects the extent to which the revisionist power was moving ahead of the status quo power. Using the admittedly arbitrary level of the revisionist winning the competition when this ratio indicated that the growth rate of the status quo power was 50 percent less than the revisionist power over a 5-year period, Wallace then cross-tabulates competitions in which the revisionist "won" the competition with crises that eventuated in war. Table 8.3 reproduces his result, and it is apparent that the rates of relative growth have little to do with the outcome of disputes.

Reflecting that his analysis may not have captured the full dynamics of a competition in which the combination of revisionist strength and rapid growth are important, Wallace multiplies his indices of strength and relative change to capture their combined effect. Using unity as the threshold of revisionist threat, Wallace cross-tabulates this against the escalation of

TABLE 8.2
Revisionist's Strength and War

	Revisionist superiority less than 50 percent	Revisionist weaker or more than 50 percent stronger
War outcome	9	17
No-war outcome	19	54

SOURCE: Wallace (1982).

TABLE 8.3
Revisionist Success and War

	Revisionist wins	Revisionist does not win
War outcomes	7	19
No-war outcomes	21	52

SOURCE: Wallace (1983).

TABLE 8.4
Revisionist Threat and War

	Revisionist threat	No threat
War outcome	11	15
No-war outcome	25	48

SOURCE: Wallace (1983).

disputes to war; his result is given in Table 8.4. His conclusion, which is inescapable from the data given, is that military preparedness is not useful in preventing the escalation of disputes to war. Using a logit analysis on essentially the same data, he arrives at the same conclusion in a companion study (Wallace 1981).

To continue his analysis, Wallace returns once again to the question around which his original research revolved: Do arms races lead to war? Wallace begins by setting forth a strict definition of an arms race. Using a smoothed time rate of change for each nation prior to the instance of a dispute, Wallace defines an arms race as "an average annual bilateral predispute growth rate of 10%." Wallace finds this rigorous approach necessary because past research had defined arms races loosely "to include almost any situation of competitive military growth" (p. 44). Given such a definition, Wallace contends that it is, hence, not surprising that these observers did not find a link between arms races and war.

The cross-tabulation of Wallace's index with the outcome of disputes indicates that "almost all disputes accompanied by an arms race ended in war" (p. 45). Reacting to Weede's criticism of his earlier study that all the dyads might not be independent and that the strong results were, therefore, a consequence of war diffusion, Wallace considers merging "all the conflict dyads arising from a single war or dispute" (p. 46). This seems too strict, however, because it would have joined the war between the United States and Japan in 1941 with the war between France and Germany that began in 1939 "despite the consensus of historians that these two outbreaks had little to do with each other" (p. 46). Instead, Wallace adopts the strategy of combining all "dyads in which two or more allied nations entered simultaneously into a conflict with a common foe" (p. 46). This procedure produced the results shown in Table 8.5, and it is clear that even with the more restrictive set of dyads the data are consistent with the hypothesis that arms races lead to war.

As a final analytical step, Wallace explores the effect of various levels of military preparedness on the outbreak of war. He wants to know if an arms race that has the revisionist nation in the lead is more likely to lead to war

TABLE 8.5
Revised Set of Arms Races and War

	Arms race	No arms race
War outcome	11	2
No-war outcome	4	63

SOURCE: Wallace (1983).

than one in which the status quo power remains in the lead. He concludes that the overall tendency shown in Table 8.5 is not affected by the military balance at the time the war starts. That is, when controls for the relative strength of the revisionist and status quo nations are introduced into Table 8.5, no differences are found between the two conditions.

Wallace concludes that "arms races are a danger to the peace of the international system." Nevertheless, before stating that conviction he suggests a number of qualifications. First, he notes that his data are imprecise and preliminary, and, hence, future analysis might lead to some modification of the findings, although such changes are likely to be minor.[3] Second, and more importantly, Wallace recognizes that arms races in themselves do not always lead to war. Because he has focused upon the escalation of conflicts in the presence of an arms race, for Wallace to say that arms races in and of themselves lead to war would necessarily involve a demonstration that arms races lead to conflicts and disputes. Oddly enough, even though the data to explore that possibility are immediately at hand, Wallace does not pursue the idea. A new study by Diehl and Kingston (1987), however, concludes that large arms increases do not make a nation or rivals more likely to be involved in disputes. Their results remained constant despite using three different indicators of an arms race and accounting for national differences, periodicity, and possible delayed effects from the military buildups. This is further evidence that the effect of arms races on war may be indirect.

Just as Wallace's first article was subject to critical commentary by Weede, his second drew an extended set of comments from Altfeld (1983). Altfeld's main misgivings about Wallace's work were, broadly speaking, that (1) his measures of arms races did not match his definition and (2) he continued to overlook the impact of alliances in the diffusion of war.

In his first article, Wallace (1979, 5) defined an arms race as "simultaneous abnormal rates of growth in the military outlays of two or more nations." Altfeld has no quarrel with that definition or with the further restriction that Wallace imposes upon it by requiring that, realistically, we can only think of an arms race between nations that are in some very direct ways interdependent in their security policies. Altfeld notes, however, that there are some potentially significant gaps between the definition and the data. For example, what is abnormal spending? Wallace arbitrarily defined it as an index level of 90; but why is this abnormal? How does it stand as an index level with respect to the normality of spending? Using Wallace's own data, Altfeld finds that the mean index value for all dyads was 100.357 and that the standard deviation was 182.645. Altfeld then argues that abnormal spending might reasonably be thought to occur when the index exceeds one standard deviation greater than the mean, or, to be precise, 283.002. Under such a procedure, a large number of arms races still lead to war; indeed, all wars are preceded by an arms race. Nevertheless, it is also true that many arms races do not lead to war. Altfeld's results are given in Table 8.6. As he states, the data indicate that arms races may be a sufficient condition for war, but are not necessary.

In a response, Wallace (1983) contends that because the arms race index is a continuous ratio, there is really no necessity to dichotomize into normal and abnormal levels at all. Logit, he notes, will permit the assessment of the effect of the arms race index on war in much the same manner as regression analysis. Without making it clear why this alternative was not chosen originally, Wallace then reports the results of a logit analysis indicating approximately the same conclusions as he originally reported. A possible problem with this, however, is that logit chooses the optimal point for constructing the ratio. In other words, the technique finds the best results, and we are again left to wonder at the exact effect of abnormal spending; the meaning of "abnormal spending" is clouded, and its level is statistically contrived rather than theoretically derived. On this point, Altfeld appears to be correct in both his criticism and his reanalysis of the data. Whatever the exact relationship, both Altfeld and Wallace would agree, on this basis, that arms races are apparently capable of making a contribution to the onset of war.

TABLE 8.6
Arms Races and War

	Race[a]	No race	
War	11	15	26
No war	0	73	73
Total	11	88	

SOURCE: Altfeld (1983).
[a] One standard deviation above the mean index value is used as the threshold for the identification of an arms race.

Such a conclusion is warranted only if the data are appropriate, and it is here that Altfeld enters several very serious objections to Wallace's data set. Wallace's data contain a number of cases that may initially strike one as curious and, in the end, questionable. Altfeld notes that eight of the dyads in which disputes escalate to war represent dyads that were already at war with another nation when the war represented in the case occurred. For example, the United Kingdom–Italian dyad that is included represents a war beginning between Italy and the United Kingdom in 1941 when the latter was already at war with Germany. In this regard, it is difficult to think that the armaments being added by the United Kingdom represent much of an arms race with Italy as much as they represent the war with Germany. Similarly, in 1945 the data include a war between Japan and the Soviet Union, both of which had been at war with other nations for a number of years. Furthermore, as Diehl (1983) points out in his critique of Wallace's work, "in cases where one or both disputants are involved in a war, the probability of that war-related dispute escalating is greater than that of a dispute independent of an ongoing war [and] the arms race impact (if any) on dispute escalation is indiscernible from the effects of the ongoing war" (p. 206). A reasonable possibility posed by Weede and Diehl is the spread of war from the initial two parties to their allies with little or no effect from a previous arms race. There is some evidence to indicate that alliances are an important factor in spreading wars (Siverson and King 1979; Altfeld and Bueno de Mesquita 1979). How can one possibly include such cases in the analysis as arms races?

Wallace's response is that he "instituted a modified procedure for those dyads where one or both parties were already at war at the time of the dispute and backdated their data series to the year immediately prior to the first war entry" (1983, 233–234). This, however, does not totally solve the problem because we are, for example, asked to associate the 1945 Soviet–Japanese war with arms acquisitions made significantly earlier. Indeed, in the case of Japan, it is not exactly clear when such a backdating process should begin and end inasmuch as Japan had been at war with China since 1937. It also does not take into account the increased likelihood of escalation stemming from the presence of an ongoing war. These considerations make Wallace's conclusions much less tenable.

Even if alliances are important in spreading wars, however, it is not necessarily appropriate to use them to eliminate the possible effects of an arms race on the outbreak of war by simply attributing war to the process of diffusion. Such a position would argue for the independence of arms races and alliances. A more reasonable approach, one not taken so far, would be to look at the independent and joint effects of alliances and arms races on the escalation of war. Put differently, the same factors that create an arms race may create a search for allies; just because a nation joins an ongoing war on the side of a prewar ally does not necessarily remove the contribution of an arms race to the decision to begin fighting.

Diehl (1983) also notes several of the already observed problems in Wallace's research. Like Altfeld, he also focuses upon Wallace's arms race index, but in a slightly different manner. After noting that Wallace does not attempt to determine if the arms acquisitions of each nation in a dyad were substantively directed at another nation (without such evidence it may only perhaps be said that any one nation was engaging in a military buildup), Diehl notes a peculiarity of the index itself: "By multiplying the products of each side's cardinal spline estimate of military spending, a unilateral buildup by one side might be defined as an arms race" (p. 207).

Diehl then proceeds to reexamine the relationship of interest to Wallace, but because he also lacks data on whether or not particular nations had "targeted" each other, he analyzes the relationship between mutual military buildups and war. Using the revised and updated set of COW disputes, Diehl constructs an index of each nation's rate of military expenditure. A mutual military buildup in the disputes of interest is identified as "any instance of both dispute sides increasing their military expenditures at a rate of 8% or greater for the three years before the dispute. . . ." (p. 208).

Diehl's initial analysis, produced in Table 8.7, produces dramatically different results from those obtained by Wallace because his data indicate no relationship between mutual military buildups and the outbreak of war. Suspecting the possibility that differences over time might be concealed by the aggregation of data, Diehl divided the data into the nineteenth and twentieth centuries. The relationship is slightly stronger in the twentieth century, but it is still not statistically significant. Finally, Diehl considers the possibility that, in the 74 cases in which there was no mutual buildup, a unilateral policy of arms acquisition by one of the nations may have increased the chances of war. Nevertheless, his data show that this is not so.

How can such substantial differences in the findings of Diehl and

TABLE 8.7
Mutual Military Buildup and Escalation

	War	No war
Mutual military buildup	3	9
No mutual military buildup	10	64

SOURCE: Diehl (1983).

Wallace be explained? After accounting for several differences in the two data sets, Diehl concludes that the differences primarily are attributable to the elimination of some 17 cases used by Wallace from his own data set. As he explains it,

> Ten cases which were not independent of ongoing wars, yet exhibited covariation of spending increases and escalation, were eliminated in this study. In addition, the non-dyadic coding method used here resulted in the collapse of ten cases, which fit the escalation hypothesis, into three integrated disputes. In each case, the two World Wars account for almost all the instances. In effect, the strength of the arms race–war relationship cited by Wallace rests heavily on the two World Wars. The relationship seems absent in any other circumstances and gains statistical significance only through an artificial division of an integrated situation. [p. 210]

At this point, one may be strongly tempted to question the value of the research reported by Wallace. The research design, measurements, and cases are, in one way or another, all open to serious question. Nevertheless, in viewing Wallace's results several points deserve consideration. First, Wallace's research represents the first systematic findings to be presented on an important, controversial problem. Under such circumstances, it is no small wonder that problems will be found.[4] Second, although Wallace has defended his findings, he has never suggested that they are definitive; indeed, he has recognized several times that problems may exist and that other interpretations are possible. Finally, it is possible that some of the criticisms of Wallace have gone too far.[5] For example, as noted previously, although alliances may well be responsible for the spread of war, it is by no means correct to assume that there is no relationship between the arms acquisition policies of allies and their entry into war; in fact, there is every reason to believe that all three factors—alliances, arms acquisitions, and war—may be intimately interrelated, especially for major powers.

Although most of the work on arms races and war has centered around the debate over Wallace's work, there are several notable, "independent" efforts. Smith (1980) investigates the Richardsonian concept of "instability," which is defined as the failure of an arms race to establish a point of equilibrium at which change in the process of arms competition ceases. She develops a set of arms race cases, including both major and minor powers, from a much simpler definition than Wallace. All that needs to exist is "the participation of two or more nation-states in apparently competitive or interactive increases in quantity or quality of war material and/or persons under arms" (p. 255). Furthermore, the competition must last a minimum of 4 years and involve explicit statements of government hostility. A race is considered over when spending on weapons decreases over 2 years or a war begins.

Smith concludes that relatively "unstable" arms races are prone to end in war, implying that the relative intensities of arms races might be important in determining peace or war. She speculates that races beginning more slowly might be unstable. "Races showing tremendous early buildups may quickly approach financial or political limits which cause them to level out, while in a slower-growing race, the economy and political attitudes have a greater opportunity to accommodate higher levels of military funding over time" (p. 279). In an extension of this work, Smith (1988) finds this to be the case because arms races that begin slowly and quickly intensify are more likely to end in war.

The concept of stability, however, may not be the characteristic that separates dangerous and benign arms races. Intriligator and Brito (1985c) study a hypothetical (although closely modeled on the American–Soviet rivalry) arms race between two nuclear states. They contend that unstable arms races can lead to either war or peace depending on whether they enhance or detract from the conditions of deterrence. In effect, a runaway arms race may not give an advantage (and, hence, an incentive for war) to either side if both sides have approximately equal capabilities and the race is symmetrical. Morrow (1984) seems to suggest a related situation when he reports that differential rates of arms growth (mitigated or exacerbated by the risk-taking propensities of each side) are associated with the outbreak of war.

Diehl (1985b) looks at arms races within the context of 22 enduring rivalries between major powers in the years 1816–1976. To identify an arms race, he uses an exponentially weighted average of military expenditure increases over a 5-year period. An arms race is "designed as any sequence in which both nations in a rivalry have an index score of 9.0 percent or greater for the year under scrutiny" (p. 336). Diehl also considered the power distribution and defense burdens of the rivals as well as the geographic location of the disputes in the rivalry.

Diehl discovered that war occurred relatively late in enduring rivalries, usually after at least two prior militarized disputes between the rivals (regardless of whether an arms race was present or not). Parity in the nineteenth century and preponderance in the following century were found to be almost necessary, but not sufficient, conditions for war. Another necessary but insufficient condition for escalation is that a dispute arise in an area that is contiguous to at least one of the rivals (and, in the twentieth century, the defense burden of the target is high).

Although military buildups were found to have little direct effect on escalation, they were found to be dangerous under two circumstances. Given the requirement for at least two prior disputes,

> [W]ar soon followed a unilateral military buildup or an asymmetrical arms race that precipitated an escalatory distribution of power (parity in the nineteenth century and preponderance thereafter). Arms races that inhibited a shift in the power distribution away from the escalatory distribution were also followed by war between the rivals. Military buildups did not lead to war when they allowed a shift in power to a pacific distribution (preponderance in the nineteenth century and parity thereafter), or they maintained that pacific condition.... Military buildups are also significant in affecting the defense burdens of potential dispute targets, which in turn influence the likelihood of dispute escalation. [p. 343)

Diehl's model of arms races include several factors (contiguity, power distribution, defense burdens) that are important for war. Only about one-half of his rivalries, however, follow the pattern laid out in his conclusion. Yet, although there are one or two exceptions to each of the conditions for war, no rivalry exhibited an exception to more than one of the general conditions simultaneously.

This exhausts the major empirical work on arms races and war, but several other studies deserve mention for their insights on the subject. In a qualitative analysis, Patchen (1986) argues that arms races involving "offensive" as opposed to "defensive" weaponry are most likely to end in war. An increase in offensive weapons systems makes a nation more inclined to distrust an opponent and acquire more weapons on its own. In contrast, defensive weapons improve the prospects for peace by increasing the costs and decreasing the likelihood of success resulting from an aggressive act. The distinction between offensive and defensive weapons, however, is difficult to make objectively (Levy 1984) and may be all but impossible in an environment of mutual hostility and distrust.

Although he does not address war specifically as an outcome, Majeski (1986a,b) argues that the prospects for future interaction, the payoff structure of the arms competition (assuming a prisoner's dilemma situation), and the desire of each side to win affect whether or not an arms race can produce a cooperative outcome. He further postulates that cooperative outcomes are less likely under the conditions of qualitative technological advances, a position opposite that of Huntington. Majeski argues that the uncertainty associated with innovation makes short-term losses in "the game" very costly.

A Brief Evaluation

If there is any consensus among arms race studies, it is that some arms races lead to war and some do not. This may at first appear to be a less-than-profound revelation. Nevertheless, following World War I, conventional wisdom was that arms races were inherently evil with war being a very likely, if not necessary, outcome. Furthermore, the Wallace studies reported that over 90 percent of militarized disputes preceded by an arms race escalated to war. Both can be interpreted as approaching the absolutist position that all arms races lead to war. The subsequent experience of World War II and the various criticisms of Wallace's work discussed previously, however, have made this position much less tenable.

The bulk of the research on arms race outcomes offers a much more qualified assessment than the absolutist position on when arms races lead to war; in general, the type of arms race and its various surrounding conditions are believed to be decisive factors. Whether the decisive conditions are "instability," as Smith and Richardson would suggest, or the qualitative or quantitative character of the race, as Huntington, Patchen, and Majeski might argue, is at best unclear. The traditional factors used in conflict research to account for the onset of war, as advocated by both Diehl and Morrow, may also play an important role.

Given the uncertainty and diversity in the arms race–war literature, we believe a different line of inquiry is necessary for resolving the arms race debate. We now outline several suggestions that we believe are essential to future progress in this research area.

FUTURE DIRECTIONS

During the past two decades we have witnessed an increasing number and variety of arms race studies. Given the primacy of the topic in contemporary world affairs, this is hardly surprising. We have made progress in our understanding of arms races and war, but it is a cliche to say that we have a long way to go. The consensus in the scholarly literature is tenuous at best, and then it exists only at a very general level: some arms races end in war and some do not. Although any research endeavor will include "brush-clearing" exercises, the next phases of investigation should include broader purposes. Presented here are several suggestions on how future research on arms races and war might proceed. Emphasis is given to changes in the methodological and theoretical ways we look at arms races and war.

Case Studies

At first glance, advocating a case study approach appears inconsistent with the goal of systematic knowledge across a wide spatial–temporal domain. But, too many investigators of arms races begin without detailed knowledge of the history and processes of at least some of the arms races they study. The lack of contextual knowledge of specific cases may result from the ready availability of cross-national data and the scholarly incentives that attend to the rapid publication of findings.

Undertaking several carefully selected case studies yields certain benefits (even if the results are never published). First, it helps the researcher identify the important conditions and hypotheses that require further investigation. Scholars may then cease ignoring relevant factors in lieu of considering only what is traditional or currently fashionable in the study of war.

The case study strategy is more than a heuristic device. In subsequent work, information gained from case studies can be used as a check on all phases of the more systematic studies. Variable measurement (an issue covered later) should make sense in the context of specific arms races. This is also true when interpreting the findings of the study, although it is recognized that individual cases will have their own peculiar characteristics.

Detailed investigations, such as that by Lambelet (1974), should not be ends in themselves. Nonetheless, they are appropriate starting points for more systematic studies, thereby enabling a blend of historical and social scientific insight in our final judgments.

Expanding the Spatial–Temporal Domain

As noted previously, research has tended to concentrate almost exclusively on major powers, in particular the American–Soviet competition. A broader understanding of arms races (and indeed international conflict in general) requires that the empirical domain be expanded. Minor power arms races need to be accorded equal attention to those involving major powers. Minor powers may exhibit the same propensity as their major power counterparts for war during an arms race (although there is some reason to expect otherwise). Yet this should be an empirical determination rather than an a priori assumption.

The expansion of the domain also increases the number of cases, thereby lending greater credibility to the generalizations drawn from the analysis. Although mixing what may be different types of arms races could muddle the aggregate findings, a careful analysis might identify these different types of arms races and the conditions under which they are dangerous. As discussed previously, considering minor power arms races is not without significant difficulties, but the theoretical benefits seem to outweigh the additional problems encountered.

Arms Race Indicators

Another concern in the research design is the indicator used to detect an arms race. Virtually all studies rely on growth in military expenditures as a basis for identifying arms competition. This is not to say that such indicators are necessarily invalid or inappropriate. They are, however, too restrictive and occasionally misleading. Military expenditure data include a wide range of items (among them pensions), and increases in defense spending are not always indicative of an improvement in capability or strengthening of resolve. Indeed, a pattern of normal, annual increases in military spending exists for almost all nations. Thus, what constitutes an arms race is not always distinct from incremental growth in military outlays. Military expenditure data also do not necessarily reflect qualitative competition in weaponry.

Growth in military expenditures as an indicator of arms competition must not be completely abandoned, but this measure must be employed in a more judicious manner. Different indicators may be appropriate for different arms races. In a longitudinal study, indicators need not be identical, but only equivalent. The Anglo-German naval race at the beginning of the twentieth century is only fully apparent when looking at naval budgets and capital ships rather than total defense expenditures. Early periods in the modern state era might be better suited to an analysis of manpower levels, although there is some evidence to suggest that these are insensitive to change until war begins (Mullins 1975). In eras of greater technological sophistication, changes in weapons stocks may best reflect arms competition of rivals (Ward 1984b). In general, it seems prudent to select different arms race indicators according to the types of arms races and the time periods in which they occur.

Alternate Theoretical Framework

The previous guidelines relate primarily to the mechanics of studying arms races and war, but the research design should be a servant to the theoretical framework under which the study operates. It is the framework of arms race studies that needs the most dramatic revisions.

A primary difficulty in arms race studies is their tendency to look at arms races in isolation from the other relevant conditions for war. In effect, researchers forget that arms race studies must be part of a general effort to uncover the correlates of war. The result of this exclusion is that whether or not an arms race is a necessary *and* sufficient condition for war is not tested (Bulkeley 1983). This seems an unreasonable burden for any one variable. The factors that "cause" war are, at best, probably necessary, but not sufficient conditions. More likely, these factors and the various configurations of them vary across different historical epochs and types of nations (see Most and Starr 1983). Considering arms races as necessary and sufficient conditions for war all but inevitably leads us to our current predicament—knowing that some arms races lead to war while others do not and being unable to adequately differentiate between the two.

Perhaps the reason that scholars have studied arms races in isolation is that their theoretical rationale for why arms races lead to war is so underdeveloped. In most empirical studies, why arms races lead to war is inadequately specified, if at all. At one time it was thought that arms races generated tension between nations, precluding an accommodation during a confrontation. Nevertheless, as Singer (1958) aptly noted, it is unclear whether arms races are the products or instigators of interstate conflict (or some combination, such as a nonrecursive relationship). Even ignoring the direction of the relationship, the theoretical links between tension and conflict escalation are somewhat frayed.

Much attention has been directed to how arms races affect the distribution of capabilities between two or more rivals. A particular distribution of power (or configuration of missile inventories) is argued to be dangerous or benign in these works. Given the various distributions at which war has occurred, however, so simple a model seems inadequate (Siverson and Sullivan 1983; Vasquez 1986).

Exactly what should replace these theoretical specifications is not our prerogative. Rather, in the absence of a well-articulated theoretical framework that draws on historical insight and broader studies of war, we are unlikely to make any substantial progress in understanding arms races and war. We may know more about arms races and war than when Singer made his observations, but we can lament that such information is still inadequate for informed policy decisions.

NOTES

1. In a different strategy, Diehl (1985a) looks at disputes that do *not* escalate to war, seeking to find patterns among the outcomes based on whether an arms race was occurring or

not. Arms races were found to be strongly related to capitulation outcomes while having a negative affinity with stalemate outcomes.

2. On the contribution of minor power instability to systemic wars, see Midlarsky (1986).

3. Since the time of Wallace's studies, the Correlates of War Project has identified additional militarized disputes in the period before 1965 and updated the dispute list to include the period through 1976. In addition, it has corrected some errors in that list. The result is a slight weakening of Wallace's findings as noted in Diehl (1983).

4. It must be pointed out that Wallace's findings cannot be replicated with the current Correlates of War files on militarized disputes and military expenditures, which suggests errors in the analysis. This inability to replicate the findings may be the most severe problem with his work.

5. Houweling and Siccama (1981) also present a critique and analysis of Wallace's work. Although they offer valuable insights by pointing out that Wallace only looks at arms races at the time of disputes, their own analysis is seriously flawed. They report that serious disputes are a more powerful predictor of war than arms races. Given the coding scheme for serious disputes and wars used by the Correlates of War project (from whom Houweling and Siccama draw their data), their argument is something of a tautology. *All* COW wars begin as serious disputes, which leads to the inevitable result that disputes are necessary, but not sufficient (because only a small portion escalate), conditions for war. Yet, this is a coding decision and not a causal relationship as Houweling and Siccama imply. If our analysis is correct, why did Houweling and Siccama not find a perfect relationship between disputes and wars (they find several cases of a war not preceded by a serious dispute)? This can be explained by mistakes and the data sets used. They used Wallace's dispute data set, which at the time contained several mistakes and omissions. For example, it did not include a dispute for the Korean War as the revised Correlates of War list of disputes now does. This leads Houweling and Siccama to identify three dyads involving Britain, France, and the United States with China as having experienced a war without a dispute. In fact, *all eight cases* they cite of a war without a serious dispute can be explained in this manner. Had they redone the analysis with the current and correct list of COW disputes, they would find *no* cases of a war not preceded by a dispute. This, however, only indicates the militarized dispute data set is complete, not that such disputes should be used as independent variables that predict war.

CHAPTER 9

Richardsonian Arms Race Models

Michael D. Intriligator

University of California, Los Angeles

Dagobert L. Brito

Rice University

The Richardson arms race model constitutes one of the most important models of arms race phenomena and, at the same time, one of the most influential formal models in all of the international relations literature. This chapter discusses the nature of the arms race, introduces the Richardson model, discusses its later variants, and contrasts it to other models of the arms race.

Models have been used as analytic approaches to the study of arms races in order to describe and to predict the course and consequence of an arms race. Such models can be either descriptive or normative. The original Richardson model is an example of a descriptive model, one with neither an explicit objective nor an assumption of maximizing behavior. Another example of a descriptive model of an arms race is the stock adjustment model. The normative model, with an explicit goal and the assumption of maximizing behavior, represents another type of model that is intended to explain the underlying motivation for an arms race in terms of goal-directed behavior. One such normative model is the Brito model; another is the differential game model. These four models, two descriptive and two normative, can all be interpreted as variants or extensions of the original Richardson model. The Richardson model, therefore, can be given various interpretations that arise from different approaches to the arms race. Another type of model, which also has a Richardson model interpretation, integrates strategic considerations into the treatment of an arms race and thereby provides a synthesis of the various models, with implications for arms races and the outbreak of war. Yet another approach to arms races is that using heuristic decision rules; here, defense planners use certain rules of thumb regarding weapons procurement that are based on optimizing behavior, on strategic considerations, or on institutional aspects of the defense bureaucracy.

We begin by defining our terms and assumptions. By an *arms race* we mean the dynamic process of interaction between countries in their acquisitions of weapons. We shall, like Richardson, treat only two countries, labeled A and B, and avoid such issues as proliferation, alliance formation, multicountry stability, and so on. While these are clearly important issues, they are not addressed for two reasons. First, from a theoretical standpoint, a theory involving coalitions, switching alliances, and so on for three, four, or more countries is intrinsically more complex than one for two countries and, hence, should follow the development of the simpler theory. Second, from an empirical standpoint, much of the observed interaction in arms races is that between two countries or two alliances. In nuclear weapons, there is the United States–USSR superpower arms race interaction [or, more broadly, the North Atlantic Treaty Organization (NATO) vs. the Warsaw Pact], with only relatively insignificant impacts of other nuclear powers, such as France and China. In conventional weapons there are the Arab–Israeli, Iran–Iraq, and India–Pakistan interactions, among others, with other nations (specifically the United States, the USSR, the United Kingdom, France, China, and others) playing roles in supplying weapons to the participants and imposing constraints on the participants but not being active participants themselves in the bipolar arms race. In fact, the roles of these external powers are, to some extent, analogous to the roles played by the basic technological and economic constraints in the superpower arms race. Thus, we concentrate on the bipolar case, but we recognize that, in the future, it will become important to treat the multipolar case.

We also assume, again as Richardson did, that there is a single homogeneous weapon, here called a "missile," where country A has M_A missiles and country B has M_B missiles. (Of course, Richardson, writing in an earlier period, did not discuss "missiles" but rather weapons or military expenditures.) The theory can and should be extended to the more complex case of several weapons types, but, as before, both theoretical and empirical arguments justify this assumption. From a theoretical standpoint, several types of weapons would considerably complicate the basic theory by involving both a portfolio selection, as in the triad of strategic weapons, and changes over time in both weapons capabilities and the capabilities of systems to destroy such weapons. While this is important and there is a qualitative arms race in the development and deployment of weapons systems, it is important to start with the simpler analysis of a single type of weapon. From an empirical standpoint it is possible to aggregate either nuclear weapons or conventional weapons—but not the two together—

into an overall measure of military capability. In fact, several such aggregation measures are available (such as launchers, warheads, megatonnage, and equivalent megatonnage for nuclear weapons), and the theory to be developed can be considered applicable to one of these aggregates.

THE RICHARDSON MODEL

The Richardson model is the best known and most influential model of an arms race (Richardson 1939, 1951, 1960; Rapoport 1957, 1960).[1] It is a descriptive model of the dynamic processes of interaction in an arms race. The model is summarized by two differential equations describing the rate of change over time of missile stocks in each of two countries, A and B. For country A, if $M_A(t)$ is the stock of missiles at time t, then $\dot{M}_A = dM_A/dt$ is the rate of change of missile stocks in country A at time t. According to the Richardson model, $\dot{M}_A$ can be described as the sum of three separate influences. First is the "defense term," where $\dot{M}_A$ is influenced positively by the stock of missiles of the opponent, M_B, and represents the need to defend oneself against the opponent. Second is the "fatigue term," where $\dot{M}_A$ is influenced negatively by one's own stock of missiles, and represents the economic and administrative burden of conducting the arms race. Third is the "grievance term," representing all of the other factors influencing the arms race, whether historical, institutional, cultural, or derived from some other source. In the Richardson model these terms are independent, additive, and linear, resulting in two coupled linear differential equations

$$\dot{M}_A = a_1 M_B - a_2 M_A + a_3 \quad (a_1, a_2 > 0) \tag{9.1}$$

$$\dot{M}_B = b_1 M_A - b_2 M_B + b_3 \quad (b_1, b_2 > 0) \tag{9.2}$$

These equations show the additions to arms levels on each side as functions of the levels of arms held in both countries. In the equation for country A weapons acquisitions (Equation 9.1), the constants a_1, a_2, and a_3 determine, along with weapons stocks in both countries, the size of the defense term (as influenced by the opponent's weapons), the fatigue term (as influenced by one's own weapons), and the grievance term (representing all other factors), respectively. According to the theory, a_1 (and b_1) are positive because the countries are opponents and, therefore, threatened by the weapons of the other side. Also according to the theory, a_2 (and b_2) are positive, because the burden of maintaining existing stockpiles reduces the extent of additional weapons acquisitions. The grievance term, a_3 (and b_3), can be positive or negative.

At an equilibrium point of the dynamic process there is no change in missile stocks, so $\dot{M}_A = 0$ and $\dot{M}_B = 0$, yielding the reaction functions

$$M_A = a_1'M_B + a_3' \text{ where } a_1' = a_1/a_2 \text{ and } a_3' = a_3/a_2 \qquad (9.3)$$

$$M_B = b_1'M_A + b_3' \text{ where } b_1' = b_1/b_2 \text{ and } b_3' = b_3/b_2 \qquad (9.4)$$

These reaction functions give the number of weapons each country holds as a (linear) function of the number held by the opponent, that is, how each country reacts to weapons stockpiles of the other for an equilibrium to be attained. The new coefficients, a_1' and a_3' (and, symmetrically, b_1' and b_3'), are normalized coefficients, that is, coefficients normalized by deflating by the fatigue coefficient a_2 (and b_2), assumed not to be zero. If the grievance terms a_3 and b_3 are positive, then an equilibrium exists; it is stable if the following stability condition on the slopes in (9.3) and (9.4) is met:

$$a_1'b_1' < 1 \qquad (9.5)$$

Then the equilibrium stockpile of missiles for A is given by

$$M_A^E = \frac{a_1'b_3' + a_3'}{1 - a_1'b_1'} \qquad (9.6)$$

and a symmetric equation exists for M_B^E, the equilibrium number of missiles for B. The equilibrium is stable in that small movements away from the equilibrium would set in motion forces that, via the basic equations of the model, would restore the equilibrium. For example, if the stocks on both sides exceed the equilibrium, then the force of the fatigue terms would offset the defense (and grievance) terms to reduce stocks on both sides to the equilibrium level. Conversely, if the stocks on both sides were both below their equilibrium levels, then the defense terms would offset the others to raise stocks on both sides. In the asymmetric case where M_A is "too large" and M_B is "too small" relative to the equilibrium, the force of the fatigue term for A and that of the defense term for B would reduce M_A and increase M_B, restoring the equilibrium.

For the Richardson model, the process of interaction between the two countries results in movement toward a defined stable equilibrium, assuming that (1) the basic "causes" of an arms race, namely defense, fatigue, and grievance, each have independent and additive effects on changes in missile stocks, as expressed in Equations 9.1 and 9.2; (2) all parameters of the model, including the grievance terms, are positive; and (3) the condition in Equation 9.5 (regarding the slopes a_1', b_1') holds, which requires that neither side overreact to the other (that is, neither a_1' nor b_1', which represent the normalized defense terms, can be "too large").

THE STOCK ADJUSTMENT MODEL

While the Richardson model is the most well known and the most influential model of an arms race, it is certainly not the only such model or even the only such descriptive model. Another descriptive model is the *stock adjustment model* (see Boulding 1962; Intriligator 1964; and McGuire 1977).[2] According to this model, each country determines a desired stock of missiles, $M_A{}^*$ and $M_B{}^*$, and the rate of change of missile stocks is assumed to be proportional to the discrepancy between the desired and the actual missile stocks, as in the following two differential equations:

$$\dot{M}_A = a_4(M_A{}^* - M_A) \tag{9.7}$$

$$\dot{M}_B = b_4(M_B{}^* - M_B) \tag{9.8}$$

According to these equations each side acquires additional stockpiles in order to offset and to overcome a perceived deficiency in its stockpile of missiles; the deficiency is given by the gap between the desired and the actual levels of missiles, for example $M_A{}^* - M_A$.

In general, the desired stocks of missiles depend on the level of missiles in both countries. If, as one example, each country desires a certain base level of weapons and, beyond that, wants to match increments of the other side's levels according to a fixed ratio, then the desired stock is a linear function of the levels of missiles held by the other side:

$$M_A{}^* = a_5 + a_6 M_B \tag{9.9}$$

$$M_B{}^* = b_5 + b_6 M_A \tag{9.10}$$

where a_5 (and b_5) are the base levels and a_6 (and b_6) are the fixed ratio of increments of one's stocks relative to the increments in the opponent's stocks. Inserting these in Equations 9.7 and 9.8 yields the equations of a Richardson model. Conversely, any Richardson model, as in Equations 9.1 and 9.2, can be interpreted as a stock adjustment model with the desired stock as a linear function of the missiles held by the opponent.

In the general stock adjustment model, the reaction curves are general functions of the weapons on both sides:

$$M_A{}^* = M_A{}^*(M_A, M_B) \tag{9.11}$$

$$M_B{}^* = M_B{}^*(M_A, M_B) \tag{9.12}$$

while in the Richardson model they become the linear functions in Equations 9.9 and 9.10. More generally, the reaction curves can take various shapes, which, depending on strategic considerations and constraints, leads to a variety of possible outcomes. There may, for example, be multiple equilibrium points, and the outcome may depend on the starting point.

THE BRITO MODEL

A normative model differs from a descriptive model in that it incorporates goal-seeking phenomena in order to explain behavior. In the arms race context, such a model formulates an explicit and specific form for the arms objective of each country and then obtains the conditions necessary to attain these objectives, as in the Brito model. In this type of model rationality is assumed in that both countries are assumed to follow, given their objectives, the conditions necessary for optimization. This assumption may be justified here in terms of the substantial costs involved in not optimizing a system involving weapons with enormous potential for damage, such as nuclear weapons.

In the Brito model each country chooses rates of acquisition of new missiles and levels of consumption so as to optimize overall national self-interest (Brito 1972; Simaan and Cruz 1975, 1976). For country A there is an index of defense, D_A, that is dependent on the missiles in both countries

$$D_A = D_A(M_A, M_B) \qquad (9.13)$$

which measures its well being at any time in terms of security. In general, D_A increases with M_A and decreases with M_B, but, for both, at a diminishing rate. At any instant of time the utility function for A depends on its level of consumption, C_A, and the index of defense

$$U_A = U_A[C_A, D_A(M_A, M_B)] \qquad (9.14)$$

The former provides material well-being benefits, and the latter provides security benefits. The objective of A is to maximize its welfare over all time given the discounted present value of all future utility levels

$$W_A = \int_0^\infty e^{-rt} U_A[C_A, D_A(M_A, M_B)] \, dt \qquad (9.15)$$

Here, W_A, the welfare of country A, is obtained by adding (integrating) the contributions of utility to welfare at each instant of time, appropriately discounted at a rate, r, given as $e^{-rt}U_A(t)$, over all time from the present time, $t = 0$, into the infinite future.

The welfare integral in Equation 9.15 is maximized by the choice of the acquisition of missiles, Z_A, and the level of consumption, C_A. This is subject to the constraints (1) that the net change in the level of missiles is the gross investment in missiles less the resources needed to replace the missiles becoming obsolete and (2) that the level of net national product, which is assumed as given (on the basis of an aggregate production function from the available levels of capital and labor), is divided between consumption and investment in missiles.

With suitable (and reasonable) assumptions on the utility and defense functions [$U_A(\cdot)$ and $D_A(\cdot)$] and the parameters (namely the discount rate and the depreciation rate) for country A and comparable functions and parameters for country B, control theory—in particular, the Pontryagin maximum principle—implies the existence of functions F_A and F_B where

$$\dot{M}_A = F_A(M_A, M_B) \tag{9.16}$$

$$\dot{M}_B = F_B(M_A, M_B) \tag{9.17}$$

which describe the evolution of the arms race between A and B. Thus, the arms race dynamics are derived as a consequence of a behavioral model of maximizing behavior with each side maximizing a welfare integral that is dependent on consumption and defense. The Richardson model, then, is the special case in which the arms race functions $F_A(\cdot)$ and $F_B(\cdot)$ are linear; Equations 9.16 and 9.17 simplify to Equations 9.1 and 9.2.

Control theory also implies the existence of equilibrium levels of missiles for this model, M_A^E and M_B^E, that satisfy

$$F_A(M_A^E, M_B^E) = 0 \tag{9.18}$$

$$F_B(M_A^E, M_B^E) = 0 \tag{9.19}$$

Comparable equations for the Richardson linear variant yield the reaction functions in Equations 9.3 and 9.4. These equilibrium levels are stable if both countries act in a myopic manner, if they do not overreact to new information, or if one or both attempt to behave as a Stackelberg leader, that is, an agent determining optimal choices of its strategic variables given that the other agent is expected to behave in a naive fashion.[3]

THE DIFFERENTIAL GAME MODEL

The differential game model is a variant of the Brito model that uses control theoretic methods to solve a dynamic optimization problem (Gillespie and Zinnes 1975; Gillespie *et al.* 1976).[4] Thus, it is also a normative model in which behavior is derived from a maximizing hypothesis. This model uses a utility function of the form

$$U_A = U_A(M_A, M_B, Z_A, Z_B) \tag{9.20}$$

in which utility depends on the levels of missiles and the acquisitions of missiles in both countries. The welfare integral is

$$W_A = \int_0^\infty e^{-rt} U_A(M_A, M_B, Z_A, Z_B)\, dt \tag{9.21}$$

and W_A is maximized by the choice of Z_A subject to constraints on net increases in missiles being the gross acquisitions less depreciation. This model can be solved using differential game concepts. In particular, in the zero-sum case where the welfare of B is the negative of that of A (so $U_A + U_B = 0$), if it assumed that the U_A function is quadratic, then the problem is of the quadratic–linear variety, that is, a problem with quadratic utility functions and linear constraints. The solution to such problems is obtained as a linear decision rule of the form

$$Z_A = a_{11}M_A + a_{12}M_B + a_{13} \qquad (9.22)$$

$$Z_B = b_{11}M_B + b_{12}M_A + b_{13} \qquad (9.23)$$

where the acquisition of missiles depends linearly on the missiles in both countries. Combining these linear decision rules for the choice variables with the investment equations for missiles, which state that net increases equal gross increases less depreciation, yields a linear system that is the same as the Richardson model in Equations 9.1 and 9.2. In particular, the defense term coefficient is the coefficient of the opponent's missiles in the linear decision rule equation, which stems from the quadratic–linear zero-sum nature of the differential game. Thus, the differential-sum formulation in the quadratic–linear zero-sum case yields the Richardson model. Conversely, any Richardson model can be interpreted as if it were the solution to an appropriate differential game model of arms interactions.

STRATEGIC CONSIDERATIONS IN THE ARMS RACE

A criticism that can be lodged against all four models introduced so far is that they treat an arms race from the "outside," in terms of a mechanistic model, rather than from the "inside," in terms of the decisions of defense planners (Intriligator 1975; see also Wohlstetter 1974a,b; Liossatos 1980; Leidy and Staiger 1985). They all ignore strategic considerations—in particular, the roles of weapons in both deterring and conducting a war. Taking such factors into account connects the acquisition of weapons to their use in both peace (via deterrence) and war (for warfighting). This section develops a model that connects the strategic considerations as perceived by defense planners to the dynamics of the arms race and arms control initiatives.

In both country A and country B at any time t, the political authorities will generally require the military authorities to justify their proposed budgets, which generally call for certain increases in the level of missiles (which are used generically here to represent all weapons systems). They may also question the existing levels of missiles in terms of their danger and/or expense. The military authorities would typically seek to justify both their budgetary request for missile acquisitions and their current inventories of missiles in terms of national security considerations by showing their potential for deterrence or waging war. Both the deterrence and the war-waging roles of weapons can be addressed by considering a hypothetical missile war involving either war gaming or the simulation of strategic interchanges.

A simulated missile war that starts at the present time can be described by the time paths both for missiles and for casualties in the two countries. These time paths can be considered as the solutions to a system of differential equations and boundary conditions at the present time for the four state variables, namely, the missiles and casualties in both countries, which provide a dynamic model representation of the hypothetical or simulated missile war (Intriligator 1967, 1968, 1975; Saaty 1968; Brito and Intriligator 1972, 1973, 1974; Intriligator and Brito 1976a, 1984, 1986a,b; Mayer 1986; Wolfson 1987).[5] In this dynamic model the stock of missiles starts at the current level and declines for two reasons. First, each country fires its missiles, so that there is a decline in missiles due to its own firing decisions. Second, each country's missiles are destroyed due to missiles launched against them by the other side. Casualties start at zero and rise due to countervalue missiles launched by the other side.

The evolution of the simulated war is determined by the number of initial missiles (which is the only actual, as opposed to simulated, factor determining the outcome), strategic decisions concerning the rates of fire, strategic considerations concerning targets, the counterforce effectiveness of missiles against enemy missiles, and the countervalue effectiveness of missiles against enemy cities. It should be emphasized that this is a model of a *hypothetical* war (for example, in a war game or a computer simulation), not an actual war. In particular, it is a model of a simulated war that could be used by the military authorities to justify their proposed budgets and force levels to the political authorities.

The simulated war can be used by the military authorities to justify current budgetary requests and force levels; in particular, it can be used to justify the force levels and weapons acquisitions needed to deter an actual war. Deterrence, in this context, refers to the ability to deter the opponent from initiating a war, so it is necessary to consider what happens in the hypothetical war if the enemy initiates the war at the present time. From the vantage point of country A, suppose B initiates the war at time t by attacking A. It is reasonable for A to assume that B launches its missiles at the maximum rate of fire and that it targets only A missiles, because such strategic choices have the greatest effect in reducing the retaliatory capability of A.[6] Country A cannot respond instantaneously but only after a delay, so, over this "window" time interval for the first strike of B, it cannot launch its missiles. Country A retaliates by launching its missiles at the maximum rate of fire at B cities over a window time interval for its response because such strategic choices have the greatest effect in terms of retaliation.[7] It is then possible to calculate the number of casualties A can expect to inflict on B in retaliation for B's initiation of the war from the differential equation model.

If the military authorities in A are seeking to deter B from striking by threatening to inflict upon it an unacceptable level of damage on a potential retaliatory second strike, and if the military authorities believe that the minimum unacceptable damage to B that would deter it from initiating the war in the first place is a certain value, then they should have enough missiles to inflict this level of casualties. It is then possible to solve for the minimum level of missiles required for country A to deter country B by inflicting this level of casualties. This minimum number of A missiles needed to deter B turns out to be a linear function of the number of B missiles. It is, in fact, a linear reaction function, as in the Richardson model, of the same form as Equation 9.3 where the slope coefficient, a_1' and the intercept coefficient, a_3' can be obtained as explicit functions of certain underlying strategic, technical, timing, and social–psychological factors, namely, the maximum rates of fire, the counterforce and countervalue effectiveness ratios, the window time intervals, and the minimum number of B casualties needed to deter it (as estimated by the military authorities in A). Thus, the Richardson model coefficients can be interpreted as the consequences of underlying strategic and related factors.

In the case of both countries each acting to deter the other, a stable equilibrium for the resulting arms race exists if the condition in Equation 9.5 is met, which, in terms of the underlying strategic and other factors, can be expressed as a certain condition that is likely to be met if it takes, on average, more than one missile to destroy an enemy missile. It is then possible to solve for the equilibrium levels of missiles on each side; these levels depend on the maximum rates of fire, the window time intervals, the missile effectiveness ratios, and the minimum casualties believed to be required for deterrence. To give a numerical example, assume that, in the symmetrical case, the maximum rate of fire is 10 percent per minute, that it takes two missiles to destroy one enemy missile, that one missile inflicts 250,000 casualties, that the first strike initiation interval is 15 minutes, that the second strike retaliation interval is 10 minutes, and that the number of casualties required to deter the other side is 40 million. In this case, the solution for the equilibrium level of missiles held by each side is 414; that is, with 414 missiles, each side has enough to deter the other side. At this level on both sides, either side can absorb the 15-minute first strike of the other and still have enough missiles left to inflict the required number of 40 million casualties on the other in the 10-minute retaliatory second strike.[8]

Geometrically, the two reaction curves are shown in Figure 9.1 as the line marked "*A* deters" and the comparable line for *B*, marked "*B* deters." At points to the right of the *A*–deters line, country *A* has a sufficient number of missiles to deter *B*, while at points above the *B*-deters line, *B* has sufficient missiles to deter *A*. The two reaction curves intersect at *E*, which is the equilibrium level of missiles, (for example, 414 on both sides in the previous numerical example). The shaded cone of mutual deterrence is the region in which each side deters the other. As long as the levels of missiles remain in this cone, each side deters the other and the situation will be relatively stable against the outbreak of war. Arms control through arms limitations or reductions is feasible as long as the situation remains in the cone of mutual deterrence. Such arms control measures could include bilateral reductions

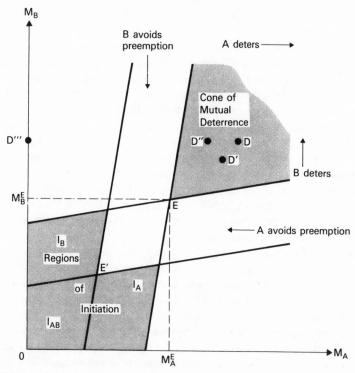

FIGURE 9.1. *Reaction curves.*

(illustrated by the movement from D to D') or unilateral reductions (as in the movement from D to D'' by country A). The point of minimum mutual deterrence, E, represents a floor below which arms reductions could entail strategic instabilities.

Another goal of military authorities could be to avoid a preemptive strike by never having so many missiles relative to those on the other side that it may appear to the other side that an attack could be successfully carried out. If the other side believes that such an attack could be carried out, it might be forced to make its own preemptive strike in order to take advantage by using the element of surprise, of being the first to move. If the number of casualties inflicted on B in retaliation for its initiation of the war were sufficiently large, then A would not fear an attack by B and B, therefore, would avoid a preemptive strike. From the model, the maximum number of B missiles for B to avoid preemption is a linear function of the number of A missiles. It is again a Richardson reaction function, and it is parallel to the A-deters line in Figure 9.1 because it refers to the same scenario of B initiating and A retaliating. It is indicated by the B-avoids-preemption line in Figure 9.1. A similar analysis for A yields the A-avoids-preemption line, which shows the maximum number of A missiles for which B will not stage a preemptive attack.

In Figure 9.1 the shaded cone of mutual deterrence is included in the area of the somewhat larger cone (with its vertex at E') for which both sides avoid preemption. The figure also shows the regions of initiation as the lower, shaded, sawtooth-shaped region in which one side (or both) neither avoids preemption nor deters the other side. For example, in region I_A country A does not avoid preemption because it has enough missiles to attack B with impunity, and neither has enough missiles to deter the other. Thus, A will be forced to attack or B will be forced to preempt; either of which will lead to war. Region I_B is the obverse case in which either B attacks or A preempts. Region I_{AB} is the most dangerous region of all: because each side can successfully attack the other, neither can avoid preemption and neither can deter the other. Each is forced to initiate the war in order to take advantage of striking first.

Bilateral disarmament, which is interpreted geometrically as a movement to the origin in Figure 9.1, inevitably entails movement through the region of initiation. The movement to the disarmed state need not necessarily lead to initiation, but a movement *from* the disarmed state may be highly explosive. In such a situation, either country could acquire a small inventory of missiles that could enable it to attack the other with impunity. In fact, the danger of war may be greatest if one side detected that the other was starting to rearm because, in such a situation, the missile levels move through regions of initiation in a crisis atmosphere.

Unilateral disarmament, which is interpreted geometrically as a movement by one country to a zero level of missiles, may not lead to the outbreak of war if the other side has enough missiles. For example, if B has enough missiles, then A could unilaterally disarm from D to D'' or even to D'''. At this point, A avoids preemption, A is deterred, and, while B does not avoid preemption, there are no missiles for A to use to preempt. Of course, at this point A does not deter B and, thus, would have to trust B's intentions. If B had a level of missiles significantly less than that of D''', however, then B would be forced to initiate.

ARMS RACES AND THE OUTBREAK OF WAR

Figure 9.1 can also be used to study the effects of arms races on the outbreak of war (that is, strategic stability) (Intriligator and Brito 1984, 1985a, 1985b, 1986a).[9] Arms races are, in terms of Figure 9.1, movements in this plane that represent changes in the weapons levels of both sides. An arms race in the usual sense of increasing levels of weapons on both sides would be represented by a movement up and to the right, while a disarming race would be represented by the opposite movement—down and to the left. Other types of arms races can also be represented, such as one in which one side was increasing while the other was decreasing its levels of weapons. The shaded areas indicate the likely effect on the outbreak of war. For example, a movement from the disarmed state at the origin (0) up into a region of initiation, such as I_{AB}, would represent an arms race that is likely to lead to war. It results in an explosive situation in which neither side can deter and both can preempt. It is precisely this potential arms race that shows the danger of a completely disarmed situation; rearming from this point in a crisis atmosphere without the stabilizing influence of mutual deterrence could lead to the outbreak of war.

Not all arms races, however, lead to the outbreak of war. Consider, for example, an arms race that starts in one of the regions of initiation, such as I_A. If both countries increase their levels of weapons via an arms race from a point in I_A to one in the cone of mutual deterrence (say, to point D), then the arms race has the effect of *reducing* the chance of war by the stabilizing influence of mutual deterrence. In fact, this type of increase may be one interpretation of the United States–USSR nuclear arms race. In the late 1950s and early 1960s, the American–Soviet military balance was characterized by the instability of relatively low numbers of missiles that were not sufficient to deter either side. There was, furthermore, asymmetry in the situation in that the United States, country A in the diagram, did not avoid preemption while the USSR, country B in the diagram, did avoid preemption. Thus, the situation was in region I_A, one of initiation. The fundamental instability in the situation was seen by repeated crises that culminated with the 1962 Cuban missile crisis. In the mid and late 1960s, however, there was a considerable buildup of Soviet weapons, which substantially increased M_B and some buildup in U.S. weapons, which increased M_A. As a result, by the 1970s there was a more stable situation of mutual deterrence. Thus, the arms race resulted in movement from a region of initiation to the cone of mutual deterrence. Such an arms race had the effect of reducing the chance of war, as illustrated historically by the fact that there have been no crises comparable to the Cuban missile crisis or the other crises of the late 1950s and early 1960s since mutual deterrence was achieved. Both sides have become, by necessity, more restrained and less willing to "go to the brink" due to the existing mutual deterrence relationship.

Figure 9.1 can also be used to study disarming races, that is, movements reducing weapons stocks. A disarming race that stays in the cone of mutual deterrence could be desirable in signaling peaceful intentions and building confidence, as in the movement from D to D'. A disarming race that went "too far," however, in moving out of the cone of mutual deterrence could be dangerous and increase the chance of war, particularly if it would result in levels of weapons that are in one of the regions of initiation.

Another approach to the relationship between arms races and the outbreak of war treats the redistribution of resources as an alternative to war (Brito and Intriligator 1985, 1987a,b). In this approach, two countries act as rational agents concerned with both consumption and the cost of a war. The countries can either consume or build arms in the first period, and they can threaten the use of force in the second period in order to reallocate resources. If both countries are fully informed, then there will be no war but, rather, a voluntary redistribution of resources that is dependent on the arms they have accumulated. In this case there are reaction functions that show how the arms acquired by each country depend on the arms acquired by the other side; these functions constitute discrete time analogs of the Richardson model reaction functions in Equations 9.3 and 9.4 in describing the dynamics of the arms race. As in the Richardson model, equilibrium levels of weapons exist that are consistent with both reaction functions, but, in this case, the equilibrium depends on the allocation of economic resources between the countries. In the case of asymmetric information in which one country is fully informed but the other is not, however, a war can occur if the uninformed country precommits itself to a positive probability of war in order to prevent bluffing by the informed country in the latter's attempt to redistribute resources in its favor.

HEURISTIC DECISION RULES AND THE DYNAMICS
OF THE ARMS RACE

A realistic treatment of the arms race has to account not only for strategic considerations but also for the institutions of defense decisionmaking. Because these institutions are large, complex, and bureaucratic, they must rely on rules of thumb or, more generally, heuristic decision rules with regard to weapons procurement. These rules may be based, in part, on some type of optimizing behavior or on strategic considerations, but they may also be based on history, the attitudes of decisionmakers, interservice rivalry, or other institutional aspects of the defense bureaucracy.

An example of a heuristic decision rule was British naval policy in the period preceding World War I when the navy was the principal component for projecting force worldwide. British naval policy at that time was to have a navy capable of defeating the combined fleets of the two next-largest naval powers. This decision rule was based on institutions, history, and strategic factors. Another example is recent U.S. policy on conventional force capabilities, which calls for forces sufficient to fight one and one-half wars at the same time, that is, a major conflict plus a separate local conflict. A third example is recent U.S. policy on strategic capabilities, which calls for sufficient force levels to enable the U.S. to survive a Soviet first strike and to inflict unacceptable levels of damage on the Soviet Union in a retaliatory second strike. In all three cases, decisions on weapons procurement can be described in a two-stage process involving (1) a bureaucratic–political decision to establish a certain rule or goal and (2) an economic decision on the procurement of weapons to satisfy this rule or to achieve this goal.

An important example of a heuristic decision rule is one in which the acquisition of missiles is proportional to the gap between the desired and the actual levels of missiles, as in the stock adjustment model (Equations 9.7 and 9.8), where the coefficients a_4 and b_4 are the adjustment coefficients (Intriligator and Brito 1985a). If the heuristic decision rule is one in which the desired level of missiles is a linear function of those held by the opponent, as in Equations 9.9 and 9.10, the result is a Richardson model. But suppose that the particular heuristic decision rule chosen is the deterrence one in which each side seeks only enough missiles to deter the other. The result is an arms race in which there is movement to the point of minimum mutual deterrence, point E in Figure 9.1. This point is an equilibrium of the resulting process if both sides use a deterring decision rule, and it is a stable equilibrium. In this case each country moves toward its deterrence line; for example, country A acquires missiles if it is to the left of the A-deters line, and it destroys missiles if it is to the right of this line.

Consider, alternatively, the case in which both sides use an attacking decision rule. In this case country A acquires missiles to the left of the A-avoids-preemption line in an attempt to be able to preempt by attacking B with impunity. If country B also uses an attacking decision rule, then it builds its weapons up to the B-avoids-preemption line. In this case the outcome depends on whether the starting point is in the region of initiation or above this region. If the process starts in the region of initiation, then the dynamics of the process drive the levels of missiles down to the origin. If, however, the process starts above the region of initiation, then the result is not equilibrium but an unstable arms race that moves to higher and higher levels of missiles on both sides. Thus, the outcome is either a movement to the origin through the region of initiation or an unstable arms race trap—that is, either instability against the outbreak of war or arms race instability.

A third case is the asymmetric one, where one country seeks to deter and the other seeks to attack. The result is an unstable arms race trap, but in the region of stability against war initiation. Instead of equilibrium, there is a continuing arms race with a low chance of war outbreak.

These cases of heuristic decision rules in which countries seek either to deter or to attack the other side point to a fundamental difference between arms race stability and crisis stability, that is, stability against war outbreak (Intriligator and Brito 1986a). In the case of two deterrers there can be both arms race stability and stability against the outbreak of war at the point of minimum mutual deterrence, but in the other cases treated there is *either* arms race stability or stability against the outbreak of war, not both. In the case of the superpower arms race between the United States and the USSR, each side may profess to acquire weapons only to deter the other, but their weapons employment policy is more salient than their declaratory policy and each side believes that the other is, or could be, seeking weapons to attack it. The result is an unstable arms race that moves weapons levels to higher and higher levels, but the race is stable against the outbreak of war because the situation moves higher and higher into the cone of mutual deterrence and further and further away from the region of initiation. In this case, which perhaps comes closest to describing the American–Soviet arms race, there is crisis stability but arms race instability.

CONCLUSION

This chapter has developed the basic Richardson model and several variants of this model, including another descriptive model, the stock adjustment model, and two normative models (the Brito model and the differential game model). While these models are useful in understanding the inter-action processes in an arms race and the possibility of a stable equilibrium, they tend to be mechanistic, treating the arms race from the outside and ignoring the actual or potential use of these arms. The model based on strategic considerations in a hypothetical war, by contrast, explicitly treats the use of arms in deterring the enemy and avoiding a preemptive strike. Reaction curves obtained using this model can be interpreted as Richardson reaction curves in which the coefficients are not given in an ad hoc way but are themselves given as explicit functions of strategic, technical, timing, and social–psychological factors. This strategic model determines the equi-librium levels of missiles as explicit functions of these same factors, and it can be used to analyze both bilateral and unilateral arms control and dis-armament initiatives and the effects of arms races on the outbreak of war. Another useful approach is that involving heuristic decision rules, which implies, for certain important cases such as the United States–USSR arms race, the presence of an unstable arms race that is stable against the outbreak of war.

NOTES

1. Lewis Fry Richardson's seminal work became available in 1947–1949 on microfilm and was published in book form in 1960. Rapoport (1957, 1960) provides a review and appreciation of this work. For applications of the Richardson model to arms races in the missile age, see Burns (1959), Boulding (1962), Kent (1963), Schelling (1966), Caspary (1967), Saaty (1968), Pitman (1969), Sandberg (1974), Intriligator (1975), Intriligator and Brito (1976a,b, 1984, 1985a), Lambelet *et al.* (1979), and Majeski and Jones (1981). See Isard and Anderton (1985) and Anderton (1985, 1986) for a detailed survey and bibliography. For references to other arms race models and to other differential equations models in conflict theory, see Intriligator (1982). For empirical studies of the Richardson model, see Lambelet (1971, 1974, 1976), Luterbacher (1975), Rattinger (1976), McGuire (1977), Hollist (1977a,b), Smith (1980), Cusack and Ward (1981), and Ward (1984a,b).

2. A basic reference for the stock adjustment model is Harberger (1960).

3. For formal statements of existence and stability conditions and their proofs, see Brito (1972). For a discussion of the nature of a Stackelberg leader in economic models of duopolistic competition, see Intriligator (1971). The Brito model, it should be noted, treats the maximiza-tion of national self-interest, which need not necessarily entail overall maximization in terms of global welfare.

4. For a general discussion of differential games, see Intriligator (1971).

5. For a related model, see Kupperman and Smith (1972, 1976).

6. The optimality of such strategic choices for the opening phase of a missile war was shown by Intriligator (1967) and discussed by Intriligator (1968). See also Intriligator and Brito (1976a).

7. In their simulation of a missile war, the military authorities in *B* would assume such strategic choices using "worst case" analysis. Furthermore, the optimality of such strategic

choices for the middle phase of a missile war was shown by Intriligator (1967) and discussed by Intriligator (1968).

8. For a discussion of the sensitivity of the equilibrium levels of missiles to changes in the strategic, technical, timing, and social–psychological parameters, see Intriligator (1975).

9. See also Huntington (1958), Gray (1971, 1976), Lambelet (1975, 1985), Smith (1980), Mayer (1986), Intriligator and Brito (1986b), and Wolfson (1987).

PART III

State-Centered
Theories of War

CHAPTER 10

Public Opinion and National Security Policy: Relationships and Impacts

Bruce Russett
Yale University

Thomas W. Graham
Harvard University

There are four possible interpretations of the relationship between public opinion and national security policy.[1] One is that public opinion is *controlling*: policy obeys the dictates of popular opinion, as stated in the extreme versions of democratic theory and mythology. The second is that public opinion is *controlled*: policymakers basically shape and manipulate opinion; the democratic mythology is false, and ruling elites persuade the populace to support whatever the leaders wish to do. A third is that the two are mutually *irrelevant*: leaders neither obey nor control public opinion; policy and opinion go their separate ways. The fourth is that opinion and policy *interact*: each influences the other, depending on the political and social context.

Obviously the first three interpretations are extreme. In reality, there is a bit of truth as well as exaggeration in each of them, which leads us most closely but imperfectly to the fourth. We shall review evidence for each interpretation, drawing on data and analyses about conflict and war, foreign policy, and public opinion in general.[2] We shall then deal with the special case of the relationship between public opinion and legislators' behavior, and then with the degree of, and reasons for, changes in public opinion. We shall conclude with a discussion of the structure of belief systems and make a key point missed by all existing theories; namely, that in a pluralistic system with multidimensional opinion structures, policy-making coalitions may be unstable even if public opinion is substantially unchanging. We shall also suggest that the combination of increased polling on foreign policy by many survey organizations, better access to data at several archives, and the prospect of analysis through new formal models provides many opportunities to reevaluate old theories and test new ones.

It must be said at the outset that the connection between public opinion and war is not direct and immediate in the sense that governments, even democratic ones, initiate war simply because a majority of the public favors war or abstain from war just because the majority favors abstention. Obviously, many other influences—the nature of the adversary, crisis dynamics, the perceptions and interests of decisionmakers—play major roles. But questions of when and how public opinion influences decisions to fight remain important. Even if one were to contend that, once an international crisis has arisen, public opinion becomes a minor factor compared with the others, public opinion may be very important if it helps determine whether the government will initiate crises in the first place. Similarly, public opinion may be expected to influence a government's decision on whether or not to continue a war, or perhaps how to conduct it (for example, by aiming for a quick rather than an extended struggle). Hence, an examination of the role of public opinion in a rather broad range of foreign policy decisions becomes necessary.

PUBLIC OPINION AS IRRELEVANT

We begin with the view that the mass public is uninterested and, to all intents and purposes, irrelevant.[3] Public opinion is often thought to be basically permissive on foreign policy issues; that is, the mass public has little information about or sustained interest in foreign policy. A substantial body of work supports part of this proposition (Caspary 1970; Leigh 1976). Concern with international affairs as the country's "most important problem" varies, with domestic problems dominant for long stretches (Smith 1985). A comprehensive review of public knowledge about arms control and nuclear weapons policy finds that the public is poorly informed about specific facts (Graham 1988).

Knowledge of foreign policy, however, is not the same thing as awareness of or interest in it. While scholars have known that the public lacks detailed knowledge of foreign policy, a new direction of research has emphasized patterns of awareness and knowledge and their relationship both to various attitudes and to impacts on policy. For example, public knowledge about nuclear weapons is higher than about arms control, and public knowledge varies enormously depending on the issue and specificity of the question (Graham 1988).

Mass preferences on security policy can long be ignored if they run counter to elite consensus. For example, majorities in 10 Western European countries have for decades favored a policy of de facto no-first-use of nuclear weapons. More recently, a similar preference has emerged among most Americans (DeBoer 1984; Russett and DeLuca 1983; Graham 1989a; Kramer *et al.* 1983). Their governments, however, have refused to countenance the idea on the grounds that it might be dangerous policy and might fail because of a public unwillingness to pay the economic price that a nonnuclear defense of Western Europe would entail.

Instead of simply ignoring popular preferences as weakly held or unenforceable, elites may recognize that, in many instances, members of the public are willing to accept any of several alternative policies in pursuit of a general goal like "peace and security." One of the clearest examples is the range of policy options that were approved during the early years of the Vietnam War (Verba *et al.* 1967). Majorities could be found for bombing North Vietnam (but not China) and sending more U.S. troops, but also for negotiation and even allowing Viet Cong participation in the South Vietnamese government. President Johnson chose to move primarily in the direction of military action, but, if the survey data are to be believed, he alternatively could have found majority support for a negotiated settlement. Public opinion thus need not have constrained policy. If it was not quite irrelevant, at least it could be used to support and legitimize a wide range of policies.

PUBLIC OPINION AS CONTROLLED

Conventional wisdom has long been that the president could use foreign policy to get people to "rally 'round the flag" and support presidential actions. The "rally" effect was first labeled and well documented by Mueller (1973), revised slightly but basically reconfirmed by Kernell (1978), and further documented by Brody (1984). Recent work, however, shows it is a mistake to suggest that all foreign policy actions or events increase presidential popularity. If other political leaders are critical of the president's action, the rally may be reduced or entirely absent (Brody and Shapiro 1987). When asked in opinion surveys about hypothetical occasions to use military force, most people disapprove (Benson 1982). But their immediate reaction to an actual use of military force is almost invariably favorable, in instances including Lebanon, the Dominican Republic, the *beginnings* of the Vietnam War, the Mayaguez affair, and the bombing of Libya. One careful study concluded that threats, the actual use of military force, or talking tough to the Soviet Union were worth about 4 additional percentage points in presidential job approval (Ostrom and Simon 1985). By contrast, cooperation with the Soviet Union seems to have carried a typical penalty of 1 or 2 points in the job performance rating (with the penalty least apparent at times when most people did not consider foreign affairs a "most important problem"). On their face, these findings would imply a permanent bias in American public opinion toward a confrontational foreign and military policy. Moreover, if leaders actually are constrained and controlled by public opinion, a similar bias would apply to policy as well.

That conclusion nevertheless should be held in abeyance. First, much survey evidence indicates, in conformity with the preferences for Vietnam policy mentioned above, that a majority of the population can be led to support either confrontational or conciliatory policies, as long as both are in moderation. Strength, toughness, and deterrence all are popular; but so too are conciliation and negotiation. About half the people explicitly combine the two if given a chance: "We should take a strong position with the Russians now so they won't go any further, but at the same time we should try to reestablish good relations with them." The public, therefore, seems to synthesize "realist" views of world politics (the importance of power and self-help) and "idealist" ones (the need for negotiation and cooperation, even with adversaries) (Schneider 1984, 1987, 49; Eichenberg 1989). In January 1985, three-quarters of the population believed that "the United States should negotiate a nuclear arms limitation agreement even if there is a risk that the Soviets would cheat" (Schneider 1987).

Second, different leaders operate under different kinds of popular expectations and may get popular approval for behaving opposite to those expectations. For example, Jimmy Carter was widely perceived as a dove; when he talked or acted tough (for example, the abortive Iran hostage rescue operation or the post-Afghanistan sanctions against the Soviet Union), his approval rating rose. President Reagan, by contrast, was generally seen as a hawk. His confrontational rhetoric was not so popular, and while the public approved of his military action in Grenada, they also approved of his withdrawal of troops from Lebanon and negotiation of arms control with the Soviet Union. Carter's ratings systematically rose with tough actions; Reagan's rose with pacific ones (Nincic 1988). While the number of examples is small and few other presidents have had such clear "dovish" or "hawkish" public images as those two, the results are intriguing. They suggest why President Reagan's political advisers, to the consternation of some senior military officers like General Bernard Rogers, counseled him to conclude a European nuclear arms control agreement at a time in 1987 when his popularity was badly faded. It appears that the public is more willing to accept negotiated arms control at times when it feels secure about its own country's military strength and when the agreement is proposed by a president who normally takes a hard line (Kohut 1988).

Finally, the popularity to be derived from threatening or using military force abroad is brief, even ephemeral—it lasts only a month or two (Mueller 1973; Lee 1970; Kernell 1978; Benson 1982; Brody 1984).[4] The long-term consequences are almost always negative, and the effects of substantial and, especially, long-term military conflict on a leader's popularity are particularly severe. Wars are not popular, either in prospect or in retrospect. World War I, Korea, and Vietnam (but not World War II) are all regarded by the public as "a mistake" (Erskine 1970; Smith 1971).

PUBLIC OPINION AS CONTROLLING

War—costly, often protracted, and usually dangerous—is very different from a quick demonstrative or coercive use of military force. The popularity of Truman, Johnson, and Nixon was damaged by war. The political punishment is real. Perhaps after a brief spurt of national unity, wars typically produce a loss of social cohesion and popular morale that are manifested in higher rates of strikes, crime, and violent political protest (Stein 1980; Stohl 1975). Governments lose popularity directly in proportion to the length and cost (in blood and money) of the war. Least healthy for a leader is, of course, to lose a major war; all great power governments to have lost a major war in the past century have been overthrown from within if not by their external enemies (Stein and Russett 1980). But even the leaders (and their parties) who start and *win* costly wars are likely to be punished rather than rewarded by their electorates. All of America's wars of the past century have shown this pattern; this is true even of World War II, which was widely perceived as just and popular (Cotton 1986). Thus, public opinion can be seen, in some sense, as controlling.

Herein lies the risk for a leader who is tempted to garner short-term support by initiating foreign policy belligerence. A threat to use military force may lead to an international crisis, and the crisis may get out of hand and lead to a serious military engagement; military engagements may escalate and become prolonged. The temptation is nevertheless there, and leaders do yield to it. Both Vietnam and the earlier Bay of Pigs fiasco have been called instances in which leaders "were driven into policy failures . . . by the conflicting imperatives of acting wherever the Communist challenge was raised, but adhering to the constraints of peace and keeping the war at the lowest possible level. The result was policies of bold commitment but compromised means" (Destler *et al.* 1984). Any interpretation holding that public opinion does not affect policy is clearly and seriously an exaggeration.

OPINION AND POLICY INTERACTION

Political leaders, especially in a democracy, live a precarious life in which the demands made always exceed the leaders' capacity to satisfy them. They are expected to solve numerous—and contradictory—social problems, to provide employment and prosperity without inflation, and to combine peace with strength. They know that they will be rewarded or punished at the polls in proportion to the rate of economic growth in the year or so preceding the election.[5] As a consequence, they try to stimulate the economy so as to produce the necessary popular support. "No president can have an economic policy; all his policies must be political. Economic policies are only means to the end of maintaining the president's power and prestige" (Rose 1985, citing Neustadt 1960). But modern economies are complicated systems, often beyond ready control, and government interventions will help some people and hurt others. Thus, leaders may be unable to buy electoral popularity by filling their constituents' pocketbooks.[6] In the absence of an ability to control the economy, leaders can then turn to foreign policy as a means of increasing their support.

Enter the rally 'round the flag effect. According to Stoll (1984b), American presidents are more likely to use military force if they are seeking reelection during a developing or on-going war—that is, when a president knows that voters will be more concerned than usual about foreign affairs and, therefore, more likely to hold it against him if the war goes badly. Another study showed that presidents have been more likely to use force when the economy is experiencing high inflation or high unemployment in the months preceding an election. They also found that a president was more likely to use force when his popularity rating was in the "critical" 40–60 percent range rather than very high or very low—in other words, when he most needed the popularity boost (Ostrom and Job 1986).[7]

The most substantial evidence for economic and electoral incentives to use force is provided by Russett (1989a). Over the past century, American presidents have been more likely to use or threaten to use military force internationally in years when the economy was doing badly or when there was a national election. This was especially true when poor economic conditions and an election (particularly a presidential election) coincided. These results fit nicely with a model of a rational president trying primarily to maximize the chances that he (or his party) will retain the presidency and secondarily to maximize the number of his supporters in Congress. Although the data base on presidential use of military force following economic decline and before elections necessarily remains small, the body of evidence is at least as strong as that for presidential manipulation of the economy in accordance with the electoral cycle. "The desperate search is no longer for the good life but for the most effective presentation of appearances. This is a pathology because it escalates the rhetoric at home, ratcheting expectations upward notch by notch, and fuels adventurism abroad" (Lowi 1985, 20).

Similar results emerge with regard to economic conditions in some other democratic countries, particularly great powers—like Britain through most of the past century—who have relatively greater control than small states over when they will engage in international conflict. A cross-national analysis of the post-1953 era added several measures of domestic political conflict; it found only a weak relationship between international conflict by democracies and economic downturn, but a much stronger one between international conflict and both protest and government repression. It was related to repression in the previous as well as the current year, which suggests that if preceding attempts at repression failed to prevent protest, participation in international conflict becomes an alternative state policy for dealing with protest (Russett 1989a). Because economic downturn is but one—albeit very important—cause of political protest, research employing the latter variable directly may, with a set of equations in carefully specified models, still prove rewarding.

This fits with another recent study that found that countries experiencing political turmoil were less likely to engage in cooperative international behavior (which might be unpopular at home) and more likely to engage in foreign conflict over issues of international security and status (Hagen 1986). Countries more often get into international military disputes when periods of domestic political turmoil coincide with opportunities abroad. Threatening a foreign enemy offers not just an opportunity to divert discontent, but also a chance to strengthen centralized political control[8] (James 1987). Once into a crisis, leaders are more likely to escalate the crisis into a war at times when domestic economic difficulties coincide with positive expected utility from initiating a war (James 1988).

Authoritarian states, where leaders are not so directly and immediately bound to popular approval, are not more likely to engage in international conflict when the economy does poorly; if anything, they seem to do so after the economy has been growing for a while—perhaps as a result of deliberate preparations for war. But they are more likely to engage in conflict after experiencing protest and rebellion (Russett 1989a). Even in authoritarian states, leaders' perceptions of their own public opinion matter; Fagen (1960) showed how the German government in 1914 saw public opinion as a constraining, active, and coercive force.

Leaders in a real sense interact with public opinion, both respondin *it and manipulating it.* By the logic of the previous paragraphs, they re by doing what will be popular in the short run (using or threatenin military force internationally) when domestic, economic, and political conditions encourage short-term vote maximization. They manipulate it in the sense that they increase their popularity without correcting the under-lying causes of mass discontent that endangered their popularity in the first place. This is, perhaps, a perverse form of democratic responsiveness.

An emerging body of research suggests that democracy may work in other ways as well: successful leaders work with and around public opinion in tactical ways. To see this link, scholars must review both public and private polling conducted for most presidents and analyze primary source documents. President Roosevelt closely watched public opinion before Pearl Harbor in order to determine the tactics he used to move the United States into World War II. He first chose greater military spending and lend-lease—not the draft or direct intervention—because these instruments offered the greatest potential for domestic approval (Cantril 1967; Steele 1978). Concern for public opinion greatly influenced the selling of the United Nations (Riggs 1960; Chittick 1970). Similarly, Ronald Reagan developed an extensive organization to watch public opinion and used its information in making decisions (Beal and Hinkley 1984). A review of the positions taken by seven presidents in negotiating nuclear arms control agreements with the Soviet Union concludes that public opinion played an important role both in framing the debate and in determining outcomes (Graham 1989b).

OPINION AND LEGISLATIVE RESPONSIBILITY

If presidents and others responsible for the execution of foreign policy can be said to respond to public opinion, can the same be said for legislators? Here the evidence is even more fragmentary. In a systematic review of public opinion and government policy change in the United States, Page and Shapiro (1983) found that the government was more likely to change in response to a shift in public opinion than vice versa and that the change was in the direction preferred by the public.[9] Other comprehensive studies of the interaction between attitudes toward defense spending and congressional decisions to increase or cut the president's military spending proposals have found a strong relationship between opinion and subsequent policy (Jacobson 1985; Ostrom and Marra 1986). Public attitudes toward defense spending are quite highly correlated with changes in actual spending during the subsequent year (Russett 1989b).

If so, does this mean that members of Congress respond primarily to conditions in their own constituencies, or that they are more nearly representatives of shifting opinion in the body politic at large? When they and their constituents turn against long and costly wars, for instance, what is the linkage between a member of Congress and the citizens in her/his district? There is little evidence specifically on the matter of war and peace, but some evidence exists on more general relationships between voters' attitudes, by constituency, and those of their representatives on a range of issues including foreign policy.

The classic study is by Miller and Stokes (1966), which found that constituents' foreign policy attitudes seemed to have little impact on members of Congress. The correlation between representatives' foreign policy voting records and the surveyed attitudes of their constituencies was very weak, and it was even weaker between representatives' voting and their perceptions of their constituents' foreign policy views. This study has been subjected to many attempts at replication and refinement, with mixed results. In Sweden, voters and legislators' opinions were similar on defense policy but not on more general matters of foreign policy (Goldman et al. 1986). Erikson (1978) found a discernible, though still weak, relationship between constituency opinion and both representatives' attitudes and roll call voting on foreign policy. Page et al. (1984) reported a somewhat stronger relationship between constituents' survey responses and congressional roll call voting, but had no foreign policy issues in their sample. In Miller's earlier study (1964), representatives, whether Republicans or Democrats, from closely contested districts tended to vote very much alike, which suggested that electoral competition tends to make representatives more responsive to constituency opinion. Achen (1978), however, reported that winners of contested elections were no more representative of their constituents' opinions than were losers, and that they were neither more nor less so on foreign policy issues than on other dimensions.

The conclusion from these studies, such as it can be, seems to be that the idealized (but not Burkean) vision of constituency representation is but distantly approached, especially on foreign policy and security issues. Perhaps this is not surprising in an era of weak local party organizations and nationally organized campaigns and fund-raising.

PUBLIC OPINION: STABLE OR VOLATILE?

Political leaders respond in some degree, although weakly and variously, to public opinion; they also try to mold opinion. But is public opinion on vital issues of national security stable enough to provide a reliable basis for steady public policy? In the early days of survey research, fears were often expressed that mass opinion on foreign and security policy issues would be highly volatile, with whims changing in response to every contradictory international event. These fears have proved groundless. Almond's (1950) "mood theory" of volatility was effectively challenged by Caspary (1970) and essentially destroyed by Shapiro and Page (1988). Whereas the rally 'round the flag effect suggests some opinion change, remember that typically less than 5 percent of the population responds with a more favorable view of the president and that even this effect usually wears off in less than 2 months. Most experts agree that a major change in attitude takes place only in relation to dramatic and, usually, repeated real world events (Deutsch and Merritt 1965; Brody and Page 1975; Jacob 1940). The media can shape the form of this attitude change and influence its magnitude—on the margins—but the media alone cannot initiate significant opinion change (Iyengar and Kinder 1986; Munton 1984; Page et al. 1987).

Attitudes toward military spending are consistent with a model of "normal" opinion stability and rational attitude change in relation to events. They proved quite stable through most of the 1950s and 1960s, with about a quarter of the population wanting to spend more on defense, about a fifth wishing to spend less, and the rest expressing no desire for a change. Attitudes did shift thereafter, as did national and international conditions. Because the cumulative impact of the Vietnam War produced an aversion to things that were military, at the beginning of the 1970s half the population wanted to spend less on defense. Some observers (for example, Russett 1974; Allison 1970–71) thought this represented a semipermanent change; they were wrong. By the beginning of the Reagan era, the portion of the population wanting to spend less on defense had fallen to 10 percent— recently, it has risen again to a level approximating that during the Vietnam era (Russett and Starr 1985, 243). In effect, defense spending came to be seen in a more favorable light during a period when American military budgets continued to drop as a fraction of the gross national product (GNP) while Soviet strategic weapons acquisition proceeded apace, detente faded, the Russians invaded Afghanistan, and the Iranians humiliated the United States.[10] But then, as the Reagan military budget soared, opinion shifted once more toward the conclusion that the defense buildup had gone far enough and it was a time to emphasize other priorities. While opinion changes certainly occurred, they were neither sudden nor frequent, and they seem to have responded well to changes in the world.

Attitudes toward the Soviet Union and China provide a basic backdrop to attitudes about when and for what purpose resorting to military force is desirable. These attitudes also have changed substantially over the postwar decades, but they have moved slowly and in ways that reflect external events. Attitudes toward both countries were very negative until the early 1970s. Then, in the era of detente and the official policy of opening to

China, they warmed; in the case of China they became, on balance, more positive than negative by the beginning of the 1980s. Attitudes toward the Soviet Union, however, became negative again under the impact of events of the late 1970s and the Reagan rhetoric. The rise of Mikhail Gorbachev, warmer American–Soviet rhetoric, and no major Soviet provocations resulted in unprecedented levels of popularity for a Soviet leader and about a 15–20 percent improvement in attitudes toward the Soviet Union from the early 1980s to 1987 (Russett 1989b; see also a survey by Marttila and Kiley in 1987).

A new study cogently posits that opinion stability is the rule and that when change occurs it happens in logical patterns in relation to world circumstances (Shapiro and Page 1988). This study examined over 400 foreign policy items that had been repeated in national surveys at various times over a nearly 50-year period. The authors found that slightly over half of those items showed no statistically significant opinion change at all, that half of those that did change showed shifts of less than 10 percentage points, and that there was very little fluctuation in the direction of change in foreign policy items. Foreign policy items, and particularly war-related items, did, however, show more rapid *rates* of change than did domestic policy items. The authors regard these as appropriate changes in response to rapid alterations in the international environment as interpreted by the American media and political leadership. Thus, American citizens "have formed and change their policy preferences in a rational fashion—in a manner worthy of serious consideration in deliberation about the direction and content of U.S. foreign policy."

This major study is supported by an earlier one of attitudes in four European democracies. This study found that sentiment toward foreign countries was generally stable and consistent with measures of conflict and cooperation with those countries; short-run changes in policy sometimes were reflected in attitude changes, but the relationship usually was not strong (Abravanel and Hughes 1975). Attitude stability can occur over long periods of time even when one might think change should have taken place. Public opinions concerning the feasibility and desirability of building defensive strategic systems—either the anti-ballistic-missile (ABM) system or the strategic defense initiative (SDI)—have been remarkably stable over a 40-year period (Graham 1986).

MECHANISMS OF OPINION CHANGE

Mass attitudes, of course, respond not only (or even primarily) to "objective" international conditions, but to how these conditions are interpreted for them by the elites and the mass media. The standard wisdom, especially on issues of foreign and security policy, has long been that there is a two-step flow of communications, first from the policymakers and the media to opinion leaders in communities and then to the mass public; similar views postulate movement downward from the "top dogs" or center to the "underdogs" or periphery (Katz and Lazarsfeld 1955; Galtung 1967).

Recent work, however, suggests that the process is more stratified and that those who regularly follow politics in the mass media talk primarily to each other and not to those who have a low level of political information and interest; political discussion is stratified and the trickle-down effect is weak (Neuman 1986, 147). Research into opinions on issues such as defense spending, the presence of American troops in Lebanon, and aid to the Nicaraguan contras indicates that the content of the electronic media is an excellent predictor of opinion within a very short time frame. Indeed, the lag between media message and opinion response may well be less than a day, and the effect may no longer be discernible after a week. Such a very short response time suggests little time for a two-stage process of discussion and dissemination; at least in the television era, the media effect seems more direct (Fan 1988).

If so, more attention needs to be given to this direct influence of the media on mass opinion in the areas of foreign and security policy that often are remote to most citizens. Because of their remoteness they become prime examples of symbolic politics, events to be interpreted for people by the media (Sears et al. 1980). Public opinion seems to respond to the views of prominent television commentators and to testimony by ostensibly non-partisan experts as reported on television. It also responds to the media efforts of popular presidents, but not to the efforts of presidents scoring below 50 percent in polls on presidential job performance (Page et al. 1987). However, "even *intensive efforts over several months by highly popular* presidents appear to bring about changes in opinion poll results of only some 5 or 10 percentage points, hardly a tidal wave" (Page and Shapiro 1984, 659, our emphasis). Again we have evidence for opinion stability, not volatility.[11]

Insofar as change does occur, it results from differences in the exposure of individuals to the media and their levels of knowledge, the credibility of particular leaders or media figures with different individuals, individuals' levels of information and policy interest, and the social network of individuals' direct personal contacts. Such a list of influences sounds rather like an epidemiological model of the determinants of the spread of a disease within a population. Individuals who are differentially exposed by their placement in social networks are differentially susceptible or immune on ideological or personality grounds when exposed. As highly susceptible persons become exposed, the disease may spread at exponential rates; later, because those who are the most vulnerable and exposed have already contracted it, the rate of spread decreases and large segments of the population may be spared. The distribution of the likelihood of contracting the disease may be bimodal: a large portion of the population may be highly vulnerable and another large portion may be only minimally so. Good mathematical models exist for this in attitude research as well (for example, see Abelson 1964).

Something like this may be seen in the popular attitudes toward China and the Soviet Union, which were referred to previously. In the 1960s the vast majority of the population held highly negative views of both countries. The opinion shift in the 1970s was not uniform across the population, but rather was concentrated in a part of the population—those who were more educated, had a higher social status, presumably were more interested in and informed about foreign affairs, and were led by changes in national policy—adopted a slightly positive evaluation. The distribution across the full range of possible attitudes, from highly negative to highly positive, became distinctly bimodal. For China the positive mode shifted even further toward the positive end and became dominant, leaving only a few diehards at the negative pole. Opinion and policy toward China have achieved remarkable harmony, sometimes with one leading, sometimes with the other leading (Kusnitz 1984). Harmony has also applied in the case of the Soviet Union. Toward that country, however, the "disease" of more positive attitudes was contained as American official policy and rhetoric shifted; the positive mode shrank and the negative mode substantially recovered in the early 1980s (Russett 1989b). In both cases the content of the media linkage between policy and mass opinion needs systematic study.

The persistence of a bimodal distribution suggests important polarizations in mass communication networks: people tune in largely to opinions with which they already agree. If peoples' expressed opinions are to change, people must perceive that the general climate of opinion makes their own opinion acceptable. Noelle-Neumann (1977) uses the term *public opinion* to refer to the set of controversial opinions that an individual can express without feeling isolated. If an individual believes that his or her opinion is not socially acceptable, he or she will not express it and, in a "spiral of silence," will make it less likely that others will be willing to express that same opinion.

If we conclude that attitudes change at different rates throughout the population and that the general public is not dependent on elites for top-down learning to take place, this has important theoretical implications for the relationship between public opinion and policy. Research into attitude change on the Vietnam War concluded that people who first opposed the war were relatively low in social and economic status and education (Hahn 1970; Lunch and Sperlich 1979; Bryen 1980). The grass roots turned against the war before the Tet offensive, whereas the elites—which closely follow the media—changed their opinion after Tet. With both parts of the public moving in the same direction for different reasons, the administration had to respond (Moyers 1968).

THE STRUCTURE OF BELIEF SYSTEMS

This notion of separated networks of opinion transmission also helps explain the phenomenon of consistency or structure of attitudes across several issues. Converse (1964) argued that belief systems, in general, would be more structured and more stable among the elites than among the mass for reasons that included logical, psychological, and social sources of constraint as well as lower levels of information in the mass public. Converse's findings have been subject to sharp challenge, but the most recent evaluation (Achen 1983) concludes that, while methodologically flawed and exaggerated in its conclusions, Converse's findings were probably basically correct. Elites are, for example, more likely to take a differentiated view of which countries the United States should assist militarily if they were invaded; members of the general public are more likely to give the same answer—yes or no—for all countries (Reilly 1983, 31). Nonetheless, some studies conclude that "the mass public has maintained a coherent and remarkably stable set of foreign policy beliefs in the post-Vietnam decade" with substantial information and interest (Wittkopf 1986, 434).

Structure and consistency of attitudes may be derived from cognitive processes of logic or psychologic. Structure may also result from differences in the salience of various issues for different individuals, coupled with varying intensities of communication. For example, if we had what appeared to be a single dimension of combined foreign and domestic policy attitudes with one end composed of people who are both hawks and domestic conservatives and the other composed of those who are both doves and domestic liberals, it might be because those who care about foreign policy and are hawks are largely in the same social networks with those who care primarily about domestic policy and are conservatives. If so, those for whom foreign policy is most salient and are hawks are likely to persuade those domestic conservatives who don't care much about foreign policy to be hawks also; similarly, the foreign-policy-oriented people are likely to adopt the domestic policy views of those they talk to regularly who are more interested than they are in domestic policy. The pattern of social communication, rather than a deliberate effort to achieve cognitive consistency, would thus account for most of what "consistency" appeared (Abelson 1979). This phenomenon fits with the conclusion noted previously that most people have basically very low levels of knowledge on security policy issues. They "tune in" to issues in a rational fashion and depend on trusted social contacts or communications media to provide an orientation on issues to which they do not normally give much serious attention.

As characterized in the preceding paragraph, structure in belief systems implies a single underlying dimension of foreign *and* domestic policy with individuals distributed along the continuum of hawk–conservative to dove–liberal. In fact, however, it is doubtful that the situation is usually so simple. Decades ago, Westerfield (1955) found domestic policy and foreign policy to constitute quite distinct voting dimensions in Congress; a representative's position on one only weakly predicted his or her position on the other. Russett and Hanson (1975) later reported a substantial degree of merging of the two dimensions in an elite opinion sample; indeed, they found that domestic political ideology was a much better predictor of foreign policy attitudes than were various measures of economic interest. They also summarized various other studies, largely of Congressional behavior, that provided the same conclusion during the Vietnam War era. Kriesberg and Klein (1980) found much the same, and Holsti and Rosenau's latest work (1988) suggests this phenomenon may be operating in the mid-1980s.

Yet in all their studies, Holsti and Rosenau (1984, 1986, 1988; Holsti 1986) documented a fragmentation in foreign policy consensus among American elites in the sense that a single attitude dimension cannot characterize most people's attitudes. This fragmentation is most evident on the advisability of using military force abroad. A lack of consensus appears most clearly in their survey conducted in 1976, but it continued almost as strongly in their 1980 and, to a somewhat lesser degree, 1984 surveys. Wittkopf (1986, 1987) and Hinckley (1988) modify these findings in substantive detail while supporting the fragmentation thesis. For example, Wittkopf speaks of two kinds of "militant internationalists." Both support a militarily interventionist foreign policy, but some also support the cooperative aspects of postwar internationalism, such as support for international organizations, while others, the "hard-liners," rely primarily on military instruments and prefer to "go it alone." Similarly, he finds "accommodationists," who advocate international cooperation but not military intervention abroad, and true "isolationists," who oppose both. Fragmentation of mass opinion along more than one foreign policy dimension, although with somewhat different analytical categories, is shown by Modigliani (1972), Wittkopf and Maggiotto (1983), and Wittkopf (1987).

MULTIDIMENSIONAL ATTITUDES AND POLICY INSTABILITY

If opinions at the mass and, especially, the elite levels are structured but multidimensional, the implications for stable national policy in a democratic political system are profound and disturbing. Much of the "blame" for instability in the policy of a democracy is typically laid at the feet of allegedly volatile public moods and fickle changes of opinion that are rooted in superficial public information and understanding. We noted such a perspective previously and found that public opinion on the major issues of security policy actually has not been terribly unstable. Yet the inability to form a stable majority *in support of policy* need not be rooted in instability of *opinion*. From the public choice literature (see especially Miller 1977), we know that stable majorities are likely to exist only when preferences are distributed over a single dimension.[12] But if preferences are distributed over more than one dimension, there will be *no stable majority coalition even if individual preferences remain fairly stable over time*. Rather, there will be shifting (technically, cyclical) majorities with different winning coalitions; any temporarily "winning" coalition can readily be replaced by another. This would be the case not just in a democracy with a mass franchise, but in any pluralistic political system lacking a dictator who regularly enforces his or her will.

This puts a new light on the connection between national security policy and public opinion. One may well look at the past 25 years of American security policy and judge it to be volatile in a way that has been unpredictable to Americans, allies, and adversaries alike. It began with the breakdown of cold war internationalism during the Vietnam War, shifted in the first half of the Carter administration, then moved toward a more hard-line policy in the second half, and was followed by an additional hard-line lurch and ultimately returned to moderation during the Reagan years. These shifts could well be accounted for by the multidimensionality of policy preferences, especially among the elites, and could have little to do with changing attitudes among the voters. More effectively insulating policy formation from popular influence would then be quite irrelevant as a "solution" to the problem of policy instability.

If a finger of accusation for volatile policy is to be pointed, it should first be directed toward the elites.[13] The elites themselves are divided and unable to produce a coherent perspective on the means and ends of American foreign policy. According to the shifting majority explanation given previously, policy instability can be reduced only when, intellectually or psychologically, coherent belief systems emerge to array relevant attitudes along a single dimension—if, for example, most "internationalists" support both multilateral cooperation and military intervention and most "isolationists" oppose both. That may have been so between World Wars I and II, when isolationists were dominant, and during the first cold war decades, when internationalists were in command. But in the complicated contemporary world such a reordering of beliefs does not happen easily, and sometimes traumatic international events promote rather than reduce opinion fragmentation (Holsti and Rosenau 1984). Perhaps the change in American foreign policy orientation wrought by World War II was the last policy shift attributable to a clear shift in elite *and* mass opinion along a single dimension.[14]

CONCLUSION

The past decade has seen innovative and important new research on the relation among public opinion, foreign policy, and war and peace. A new research program is emerging from the earlier theory established in the 1950s and 1960s. Public opinion is more stable than many observers previously thought. While levels of knowledge are generally low, the pattern of knowledge and its relationship to attitudes is complex and deserves to become an important topic of research. Models of differentiated attitude change seem to fit intuitive ideas of our complicated society and research on the diffusion and impact of mass media. In forming constraints and providing incentives, public opinion is not purely passive and has a more important and intricate relationship to foreign policy decisionmaking at the presidential level than previously suggested.

Taken together, all of these findings suggest that the significance of work in this area is increasing. They also indicate an additional weakening of the realist paradigm of international relations theory. The "unitary actor" assumption of that paradigm has been modified in mainstream research by emphasizing bureaucratic politics. This review challenges both as incomplete and inadequate; both require a fundamental reexamination of their reigning theoretical perspectives.

Research opportunities in this field are expanding commensurately.

More survey research is being conducted, more material is being placed in archives, and more methodological issues are being discussed in ways that will facilitate the analysis of existing surveys. The material is becoming easier to use as indexes are published and as data bases become easier to search.[15] All of these developments should encourage scholars to renew their efforts.

New data resources can and should be combined with the greater use of mathematical modeling techniques. While public opinion research often has made good use of multivariate statistical techniques, the use of complex models of attitude transmission or of reciprocal influences in this field is much rarer. Some of the most important problems, including those of the interplay between opinion and governmental policy, require complex systems of simultaneous equations. In principle, the necessary data—on opinion, on governmental acts, and on the content of the mass media—are available or could be made so. To bring together the data, the models, and these important questions concerning governance in democratic political systems is a major challenge.

NOTES

1. B. Russett wishes to thank the United States Institute of Peace for their support in his work on this chapter. Of course, only we bear responsibility for the product.

2. Previous studies (for example, Cohen 1973; Hughes 1978) simply do not point to a clear conclusion. For a comprehensive bibliography, see Graham (1987).

3. A large literature reviews the concepts of issue publics, the attentive public, and the general public. The most definitive reexamination of the topic finds little evidence that approximately 20 percent of the public is attentive. Rather, only 5 percent of the population can be considered politically active, 75 percent constitute a middle mass that moves in and out of politics, and 20 percent are apolitical (see Neuman 1986).

4. Sanders et al. (1987) report the same effect for Prime Minister Thatcher in Britain after the Falklands/Malvinas dispute. However, Norpoth (1987) contends that there was a discernible positive effect of that short and successful war even a year later.

5. This phenomenon is well established and familiar to all students of voting behavior in the United States and other industrial democracies. For the classic study, see Kramer (1971); some of the more recent examples are cited in Russett (1989a).

6. This was best documented for the United States by Tufte (1978), and it undoubtedly is a common phenomenon. A good discussion of how it works in Israel is given by Mintz (1988). The difficulties in identifying an electoral connection as the major variable influencing economic growth rates, even in election years, are well presented by Alt and Chrystal (1983).

7. A subsequent analysis by the same authors, however, one with a more complete specification of the external conditions promoting international conflict, found no relationship to the electoral cycle (Job and Ostrom 1986).

8. See the contribution on diversionary theories of war by Jack S. Levy in chap. 11 of this volume.

9. It is possible, of course, that policymakers might first form a new opinion and then persuade opinion leaders in the media, who in turn persuade the mass public so that, finally, the very people in government who initiated the change can then "respond" to public opinion.

10. After the Iranian hostage crisis, the public not only approved greater military spending but increasingly supported the use of force and, for a while, wanted the United States to gain superiority over the Soviet Union in military and nuclear strength (see Free and Watts 1980; Gergen 1980; Russett and DeLuca 1981).

11. When the right kind of dramatic event and an intensive media strategy are combined, however, a president can create a short-term improvement in public opinion up to 25 percentage points, as occurred with the Grenada invasion, President Reagan's speech, and media coverage of returning rescued American students.

12. The situation is most stable with a single-peaked preference distribution, but it can be stable even in a double-peaked distribution if one peak is substantially larger than the other and remains so over time.

13. Several studies have shown that elite attitudes are more likely to change than are general public attitudes if government policy changes. Also, elites often favor strong military action and have supported nuclear deterrence more than has the general public (see Modigliani 1972; Gamson and Modigliani 1966; Hamilton 1968; Eckhardt and Lentz 1967).

14. Mass and elite opinion surely changed sharply during the Vietnam War, but, according to Holsti and Rosenau (and Mandelbaum and Schneider 1979), by becoming multidimensional.

15. While the Roper Center at the University of Connecticut remains the most important public opinion archive in the United States, scholars should review collections at the Inter-university Consortium for Political and Social Research (ICPSR) at the University of Michigan and the Harris Data Center at the University of North Carolina. In Europe, there are important collections at the University of Essex and ZUMA, University of Mannheim. For indexes, see the series produced by Hastings and Hastings (1987) and the Opinion Research Service (1987).

CHAPTER 11

The Diversionary Theory of War: A Critique

Jack S. Levy

University of Minnesota

The idea that political elites often embark on adventurous foreign policies or even resort to war in order to distract popular attention away from internal social and economic problems and consolidate their own domestic political support is an old theme in the literature on international politics.[1] Generally referred to as the scapegoat hypothesis or diversionary theory of war, it is one of the few societal-level theories besides the Marxist–Leninist theory of imperialism to attract much attention in the theoretical literature on international conflict.[2] This hypothesis has served as the basis for the interpretation of numerous historical cases, and it also has generated a considerable amount of quantitative empirical research on the linkages between internal and external conflict. This study aims to (1) survey the theoretical, quantitative empirical, and historical literature bearing on the diversionary theory of war, (2) identify some important conceptual problems with this work, and (3) further develop the theoretical linkages leading from the domestic political interests of key elites to the outbreak of war.

Numerous scholars have noted the use of belligerent foreign policies by political leaders in order to solidify their domestic political positions. Four centuries ago Shakespeare (1845) suggested to statesmen that "Be it thy course to busy giddy minds/With foreign quarrels," and Bodin (1955, 168–169) argued that "the best way of preserving a state, and guaranteeing it against sedition, rebellion, and civil war is to ... find an enemy against whom [the subjects] can make common cause." Two of the leading theories of imperialism emphasize the domestic political interests driving external expansion. Lenin (1935, V, 123) viewed World War I as an attempt by the imperialist classes "to divert the attention of the laboring masses from the domestic political crisis," and Marxist–Leninists argue more generally that imperialism and war are instruments by which the capitalist class secures its political position and guarantees its economic interests against revolutionary forces internal to the state. Schumpeter (1939) argued that imperialism and war serve the interests not of the capitalist class but of the military elite, which has used war and the threat of war to rationalize and maintain its dominant position within the state.[3]

More general forms of the scapegoat hypothesis have been endorsed by numerous modern international theorists. Wright (1965, 727) argues that one of the most important causes of war is the perception that war is a "necessary or convenient means . . . to establish, maintain, or expand the power of a government, party, or class within a state." Haas and Whiting (1956, 62) argue that statesmen "may be driven to a policy of foreign conflict—if not open war—in order to defend themselves against the onslaught of domestic enemies," particularly against enemies arising from the inequities generated by rapid industrialization and social change. Rosecrance (1963, 306) argues that the domestic insecurity of elites is one of the most important causes of war and that "domestic stability and internal peace [is] the vehicle of international stability and external peace."

The inherent plausibility of the scapegoat hypothesis, in conjunction with its apparent support from numerous historical cases, has led to its acceptance by many political scientists. Wright (1965, 257) asserts that "the direct relationship between political revolution and war, whether as cause or effect, is in fact such a historical commonplace as to need no elaboration." More recently, however, there have been numerous efforts to subject the hypothesis to rigorous and systematic empirical tests. Most of this literature links the scapegoat hypothesis to the in-group/out-group or conflict–cohesion hypothesis in sociology, which provides a theoretical explanation for the hypothesized relationship.

THE IN-GROUP/OUT-GROUP HYPOTHESIS

Simmel (1956), the first to treat the subject systematically, argues that conflict with an out-group increases the cohesion and political centralization of the in-group. Extending the hypothesis to international relations, Simmel (1956, 93) suggests that "war with the outside is sometimes the last chance for a state ridden with inner antagonisms to overcome these antagonisms, or else to break up definitely." Simmel recognizes, however, that war may also lead to discohesion, for it "appeals to those energies which are common to the discordant elements of the community. . . . [War] might either cause domestic quarrels to be forgotten, or might on the contrary aggravate them beyond reconciliation" (Simmel 1898, 832).

Simmel's conflict–cohesion hypothesis is adopted by Coser (1956), who attempts to elaborate further on the conditions under which external conflict increases or decreases internal cohesion.[4] Drawing upon the work of Williams (1947), Coser (1956, 93–95) argues that external conflict will increase the cohesion of the in-group only if the group already exists as a "going concern," has some minimal level of internal cohesion, perceives itself as a group and the preservation of the group as worthwhile, and believes that the external threat menaces the in-group as a whole and not just one part of it. In the absence of these conditions external conflict will exacerbate internal conflict, perhaps to the point of disintegration, rather than moderate it.

The in-group/out-group or conflict–cohesion hypothesis, now generally associated with Coser rather than Simmel, has been so widely accepted among social scientists (although often without acknowledgment of the Simmel–Coser qualifications) that Dahrendorf (1964, 58) suggests that it has acquired the status of a general law: "It appears to be a general law that human groups react to external pressure by increased internal coherence." This proposition has been widely used to explain, among other things, the common observation that the popularity of American presidents generally increases during a crisis regardless of the wisdom of his policies, which is often referred to as the "rally-round-the-flag phenomenon" (Mueller 1973; Polsby 1964, 25; Waltz 1967, 272–273).

The cohesion-building consequences of external conflict are recognized by group leaders who often attempt to use this phenomenon to their own advantage (Simmel 1955, 98). Thus, Coser (1956, 104) argues that "groups may actually search for enemies with the deliberate purpose or the unwitting result of maintaining unity and internal cohesion," and Wright (1965, 1516) argues that "War or fear of war has often been used to integrate states." Similarly, the anthropologist Kluckhohn (1960) suggests that if aggressive impulses within a society are sufficiently strong and disruptive, that society may attempt to preserve its cohesion by initiating an external war to displace that aggressiveness.

The in-group/out-group hypothesis has generated a considerable amount of systematic empirical research by social scientists. An excellent review of the research in sociology, anthropology, and psychology can be found in Stein (1976), and for this reason I will only briefly summarize his conclusions before moving on to the political science literature. There is substantial support for the group cohesion hypothesis in the literature but only under certain well-defined conditions that are quite similar to those suggested by Coser (1956). The group must be an ongoing one with some minimal level of cohesion prior to the external conflict, and the external conflict must involve a threat that is believed to menace the group as a whole and that is perceived as solvable by group effort. Although there are analytical problems in extrapolating from small group behavior to that of larger collectivities (and even in defining what constitutes a "group"), these findings from other disciplines do provide a source of hypotheses that might help inform the study of the relationship between the domestic and foreign conflict behavior of states.

THE POLITICAL SCIENCE LITERATURE

There is less convergence in the political science literature on the relationship between a state's internal and external conflict. Sorokin's (1937, chap. 14) longitudinal study of ancient Greece and Rome and of the leading European powers over 14 centuries revealed no relationship between internal disturbances and international war, although his aggregation of the data by quarter-century periods did not permit a very discriminating analysis. The most influential study of the domestic–foreign conflict relationship was Rummel's (1963) cross-sectional study of 77 states for the 1955–1957 period. His factor analysis of 9 measures of domestic conflict and 13 indicators of foreign conflict (including a frequency-of-war indicator) revealed that "foreign conflict behavior is generally completely unrelated to domestic conflict behavior" (Rummel 1963, 24). This finding was confirmed by Tanter's (1966) replication of Rummel's study with data from the 1958–1960 period and by others (Haas 1968; Burrowes and Spector 1973; Zinnes and Wilkenfeld 1971; Wilkenfeld 1972). Thus, there is substantial agreement among these studies that there is no overall relationship between the domestic and foreign conflict behavior of states.

Most of the early studies based on the Rummel paradigm were basically bivariate in nature, however, and made no attempt to incorporate the effects of other variables that might affect the relationship between domestic and foreign conflict. This limitation has been addressed in subsequent studies, which have attempted to control for the effects of other variables. The type of regime has received particular attention. Wilkenfeld (1968) found some positive relationship between war and "revolutionary" activity for centrist (authoritarian) regimes and between war and "domestic turmoil" for polyarchic regimes. The importance of governmental structure for this relationship has been confirmed in subsequent studies by Zinnes and Wilkenfeld (1971) and by other studies in Wilkenfeld (1973). Hazelwood (1973) took a different focus and found that war is associated with the combination of population diversity, ethnic diversity, and domestic turmoil.

There are numerous other studies of the link between internal and external conflict, and the interested reader is referred to excellent reviews by Stohl (1980) and Zinnes (1976, 160–175).

Although the results of some of the controlled studies are somewhat more encouraging, few of the correlations indicate strong relationships. Moreover, there is still little convergence among the findings of different studies using different measures of internal and external conflict, different data sources, different temporal spans, and different statistical techniques.[5] One fears that this mass of unstructured and often contradictory findings may be the artifact of particular data sets, measurement procedures, or statistical techniques. Although the type of regime appears to be important, this has yet to be explained theoretically. Different dimensions of internal conflict are related to different dimensions of foreign conflict for each type of regime, and no theoretical framework has been proposed to integrate the observed patterns. Thus, Zinnes (1976, 170–175) concludes that if the type of regime is considered, the "internal–external conflict hypothesis has some meaning," but she concedes that "exactly how these variables interact requires considerably more research."

It is generally agreed that a decade and a half of quantitative research on the relationship between the internal and external conflict behavior of states has failed to produce any cumulative results. We have a set of findings that are scattered and inconsistent, and these inconsistencies have yet to be resolved or explained. The failure of quantitative empirical research to uncover any indication of a strong relationship between the internal and external conflict behavior of states is disturbing for a number of reasons. It is in contrast with the empirical findings from other social science disciplines, which provide considerable evidence as to the validity of the conflict–cohesion hypothesis for small groups. Because of the far greater complexity of decision processes in the nation-state than in small groups, however, one cannot directly extrapolate from the latter to the former. The gap between these quantitative empirical findings and the theoretical literature is of greater concern. As Hazelwood (1975, 216) notes in developing a point made by Burrowes and Spector (1973, 294–295), "in no other instance do the arguments present in international relations theory and the results recorded through systematic empirical analysis diverge so widely as in the domestic conflict–foreign conflict studies."

This gap between theory and empirical research is all the more disturbing because evidence from a large number of historical cases suggests that decisions for war are frequently influenced by the domestic political interests of political elites facing internal challenges to their political authority. Here I will mention only a few of the more widely cited cases. With regard to the French decision for war in 1792, Michon denies the existence of an external threat and argues that "War was willed solely to act as a diversion from the social problems. . . . [War] would give the government dictatorial powers and would allow it to eliminate its detested enemies. For these groups war was a grand maneuver of domestic politics" (in Blanning 1986, 71). The Crimean War has been interpreted by many in terms of Louis Napoleon's attempt to increase his political support at home, particularly among French Catholics, by aggressively supporting the Catholics in Jerusalem against the Russian-backed Greek Orthodox. As Marx said, Louis Napoleon "has no alternative left but revolution at home or war abroad" (Mayer 1977, 225). The origins of the Russo-Japanese war of 1904 have also been traced to the scapegoat motivation. As stated by the Russian minister of the interior at the time, "What this country needs is a short victorious war to stem the tide of revolution" (White 1964, 38; Langer 1969, 29; Lebow 1981, 66).[6]

State behavior in the period leading up to World War I is also commonly interpreted in terms of the scapegoat hypothesis. A. J. P. Taylor (1954, 529) argues that the leading European statesman in 1914 believed "that war would stave off their social and political problems." German imperialism under Bismarck, her naval expansion at the turn of the century, the hostile tariff policy against Russia, and other German policies leading up to the war have all been interpreted in terms of the attempt by the traditional ruling classes to block or co-opt the forces of social democracy and hang onto the reins of power (Kehr 1970; Wehler 1985; Fischer 1975; Mayer 1967, 1977; Berghahn 1973). Fischer (1975) argues that "large-scale industry and the *Junker*, the army . . . and the civil service . . . viewed world policy and national power politics essentially as a means of dissipating social tensions at home by campaigns abroad" (in Wehler 1985, 196). In fact, one recent review suggests that "a far-reaching consensus now agrees that German foreign policy after 1897 must be understood as a response to the internal threat of socialism and democracy" (Kaiser 1983).[7]

It is difficult to generalize from individual case studies, of course, and some historical studies have adopted a comparative methodology in an attempt to establish a more general relationship between international war and the perceived domestic interests of the political leadership or ruling class. Mayer (1977, 220) argues that, under conditions of internal crisis (which he claims applies to most of the period since 1870), "the primary motives, preconditions, and causes of war are political. The governors opt for war for reasons of domestic politics rather than of foreign policy and international politics." Their aim is "to restabilize political and civil society along lines favorable to the hegemonic bloc, notably to certain factions, interests, and individuals within that bloc." Mayer (1967, 1977) argues that this hypothesis applies not only to all of the great powers in 1914 but also to most of the major wars since 1870—including the Franco-Prussian War (1870–1871), Russo-Japanese War (1904–1905), and the two world wars—as well as to the French Revolutionary Wars and Crimean War before then.

In a more detailed comparative historical study, but one guided by a different theoretical orientation, Rosecrance (1963) examines nine distinct European systems in the 1740–1960 period. He concludes that the primary determinant of international stability and peace was internal stability and the resulting security of political elites, whereas domestic turmoil and elite insecurity were associated with war. Rosecrance finds that this relationship holds regardless of the political structure or ideology of the regime. Similar findings emerge from Lebow's (1981, chap. 4) comparative study of 13 "brinkmanship crises" over the previous century in which states initiate major challenges to an important commitment of the adversary in the hope that the adversary will back down. Lebow finds that only 5 of these crisis initiations can be explained by deterrence theory—by weakness in the adversary's capability of defending its commitment, the credibility of that threat, or its communication of that threat to its opponent. Lebow finds that the other crises were initiated by political elites in part as a response to their own sense of domestic political vulnerability and in the hope of buttressing their political positions at home through a diplomatic success abroad. Once initiated, several of these crises escalated to war largely for domestic reasons.[8]

Thus, there is a striking gap between quantitative empirical studies and historical case studies regarding the validity of the scapegoat hypothesis. It would be valuable and, in fact, necessary to examine each of these historical cases to determine (1) whether the scapegoat interpretation actually does have greater empirical support than the leading alternative interpretations and (2) whether these studies taken together systematically demonstrate the superiority of the scapegoat hypothesis over alternative theories of the causes of war. On the surface, however, the supporting evidence is plausible enough, particularly in conjunction with the theoretical literature emphasizing the importance of the diversionary use of force, to suggest that much of the explanation for the observed discrepancy between the historical and the quantitative literature can be traced to flaws in the quantitative literature itself. We shall now examine this literature in more detail while reserving judgment on the question of the validity of the historical literature dealing with diversionary processes.

Some of the reasons for the failure of quantitative empirical studies to confirm the hypothesized relationship between internal and external conflict may be methodological. The limited temporal domain of most of these studies is particularly troubling. The 1955–1960 period upon which nearly all of these studies have been based is not only too narrow to permit an adequately controlled empirical study, but it also coincides with an especially peaceful period of international politics. Even if one were to accept the validity of the finding of the absence of a relationship between domestic and foreign conflict for various groups of states in this period, there would be little reason to believe that this is a general relationship applicable in a wide variety of historical circumstances. This is particularly true if one is interested in the domestic sources of war involving the great powers because there were no great power wars during this period.

There are a number of additional methodological questions that might be raised about various aspects of the research designs guiding these studies, particularly the difficulties in coding events data. These include the comparability of nominally similar events in different political and cultural systems, the trade-offs between using single sources and multiple sources, the problem of counting numbers of events (especially if multiple sources are used), and the weighting (if any) of inherently unequal events. Another set of problems concerns the different units of temporal aggregation and the different time lags utilized by the various studies. The interested reader is referred to the critiques by Scolnick (1974), Mack (1975), Vincent (1981), and James (1988) for an analysis of these and other problems. The most serious problems confronting these studies are theoretical rather than methodological, however, and our attention will be focused primarily on these.

The basic problem, one that is widely recognized in the literature, is that few of the quantitative empirical studies of the relationship between internal and external conflict behavior of states have been guided by any coherent theoretical framework. As Stohl (1980, 325) argues, "the continuing lack of theoretical foundation has worked against the cumulation of evidence. Rather, what has resulted is the accumulation of isolated bits of information supporting neither theoretical argument nor conventional wisdom."

These studies appear to be driven by method and data availability rather than theory. They have been more concerned with duplicating or disconfirming Rummel's (1963) findings for different spatial or temporal domains in the post-1945 period than with asking the question of whether or not the research design guiding those studies is appropriate for the theoretical questions supposedly being asked. This literature has focused on the operational question of whether or not an empirical association between internal and external conflict exists with little regard for the causal processes that might generate such a pattern. There has been little concern with the direction of the relationship between internal and external conflict, alternative explanations for any such relationship, the precise form of the relationship, or the conditions under which it is likely to hold. As a result, the models being tested are technically misspecified, and it is conceivable that important empirical patterns are being obscured by inappropriate research designs. Let us explore each of these problems in more detail.

THE DIRECTION OF THE RELATIONSHIP BETWEEN INTERNAL AND EXTERNAL CONFLICT

Most quantitative empirical studies of the internal–external conflict relationship simply attempt to determine if there is a correlation between the levels of domestic and foreign conflict (conceptualized along several dimensions) at a given point in time. They fail to distinguish between two distinct processes: (1) the externalization of internal conflict, in which internal conflict has a causal impact on external conflict, as predicted by the scapegoat hypothesis, or (2) the internalization of external conflict, in which independently generated external conflict has a causal impact on internal conflict.[9]

The importance of the internalization of external conflict is recognized in other bodies of literature. Laqueur (1968, 501), for example, argues that "War appears to have been the decisive factor in the emergence of revolutionary situations in modern times . . . [because] the general dislocation caused by war, the material losses and human sacrifices, create a climate conducive to radical change." Although this occurs in victorious as well as defeated states, it may be particularly likely in the latter: "In a defeated country authority tends to disintegrate, and acute social dissatisfaction receives additional impetus from a sense of wounded national prestige." Similarly, Tilly (1975, 74) identifies two main paths by which external war generates internal conflict: (1) the exaction of men, supplies, and particularly taxes for the war effort induces resistance from key elites or masses, and (2) the weakening of a government's capacity for domestic repression by war, coupled with a decline in its ability to meet its domestic commitments, encourages its enemies to rebel.

Although some (but not all) quantitative empirical studies recognize that the internalization of external conflict may occur, what they generally fail to recognize is that the different causal mechanisms involved in the two distinct processes mean that the operational indicators appropriate for tapping one process may not adequately tap the other one. Rummel's (1963) use of the number of foreign protests, ambassadors recalled, negative sanctions, and the like may be useful measures of external conflict resulting from internal scapegoating, but they are less adequate as independent variables in predicting internal conflict. In addition, because the conditions under which internal conflict leads to external conflict are different than the conditions under which external conflict contributes to internal conflict, the analyses of these two different processes require the incorporation of different contextual or control variables. One might hypothesize, for example, that democratic regimes may be more prone to scapegoating than authoritarian regimes because of electoral accountability, but that democratic regimes are less likely to suffer from internal conflict as a result of external war.

More importantly, there may also be a reciprocal relationship between internal and external conflict. Domestic conflict may lead to external conflict, which in turn may further increase the level of domestic conflict along lines suggested by Tilly (1975) or decrease domestic conflict by unifying the society against the external threat. The existence of the second scenario would seriously complicate any empirical test of the hypothesis, for whether it predicts a positive or negative relationship between internal and external conflict would be critically dependent on the times at which these variables are measured. This temporal dimension cannot be captured by the cross-sectional analyses of the domestic–foreign conflict relationship that basically follow Rummel's original research design.

One example of the seriousness of the problem is illustrated in Stohl's (1980) review of this literature. He notes that "the most common form of the hypothesis in the conventional wisdom . . . is that foreign conflict behavior should be inversely related to domestic conflict behavior, that is, that increases in foreign conflict behavior lead to decreases in domestic conflict behavior" (Stohl 1980, 311). Thus, Stohl treats external conflict as an exogenous variable predicting an increase in domestic cohesion and a decrease in internal conflict, but ignores the sources of external conflict.

The scapegoat hypothesis, however, is not the same as the in-group/out-group or conflict–cohesion hypothesis as Stohl conceptualizes it. The basic point of the scapegoat hypothesis is that external conflict cannot be treated as an exogenous independent variable leading to internal conflict. The scapegoat hypothesis is fundamentally dynamic and reciprocal in nature. It suggests that internal conflict at time t will generate an increase in external conflict at time $t + m$, which in turn reduces internal conflict at time $t + n$ $(n > m)$.[10] Consequently, the absence of studies producing negative correlations, which Stohl laments, may not necessarily be inconsistent with the scapegoat hypothesis.[11] It all depends on the points in time at which the variables are measured.

The use of lagged variables in a regression analysis, which might capture a simple model of one-way causation, would not be as appropriate as some form of causal modeling procedure or simultaneous equation model, as Stohl (1980, 327) recognizes. The problem of specifying time lags would remain, however, because there is no solid theoretical basis for discriminating among essentially arbitrary time lags. The problem is particularly serious for a large N aggregate study because there is little reason to believe that there is one set of time lags appropriate for a large number of states under a variety of international and domestic conditions. What is clear, however, is that the attempt to test a hypothesis that is temporal, dynamic, and causal with research designs that are cross-sectional, static, and correlational is flawed from the start.

THE EXTERNALIZATION OF INTERNAL CONFLICT:
ALTERNATIVE EXPLANATIONS

Even if we were to restrict our attention to the relationship leading from internal conflict to external conflict, we would have to recognize several distinct causal mechanisms that could be involved. Conflict within state A may lead A's political elite to attempt to solidify its domestic political support through diversionary actions abroad, as suggested by the scapegoat hypothesis. Alternatively, conflict within state A may generate internal weaknesses, or perhaps be a symptom of such weaknesses, which may tempt state B to intervene militarily. B's intervention may be motivated by the desire to exploit a temporary window of opportunity created by the disruptive effects of A's turmoil on its military power, as illustrated by Iraq's attack against Iran in 1980. Alternatively, it may be designed primarily to influence the outcome of the struggle for political power in A, as illustrated by the Soviet interventions in Czechoslovakia (1968) and Afghanistan (1980), the U.S. intervention in the Dominican Republic (1965), and numerous other interventions by the strong in the internal political affairs of their weaker neighbors.

One can also imagine situations in which both of these processes are operative. Internal conflict may weaken A and tempt B to attack, which then provides a real external threat that can be exploited by A's political elite for its own domestic political purposes. This can be particularly useful for a revolutionary regime, as demonstrated by the cases of France in 1792, Russia in 1918, and Iran in 1980 (Skocpol 1979).[12]

These alternative mechanisms leading from internal to external conflict are only occasionally acknowledged in the quantitative empirical literature on the internal–external conflict relationship (Gurr and Duvall 1973; Weede 1978; Ward and Widmaier 1982), but there appears to be substantial evidence that this process is historically important. Blainey (1973, chap. 5) constructs a list of over 30 international wars between 1815 and 1939 that had "visible links" with civil strife and concludes that, in most cases, the war was not initiated by the strife-torn nation, contrary to the predictions of the scapegoat hypothesis. Internal conflict leads to international war, Blainey argues, not by scapegoating but instead by weakening a state internally, upsetting a stable dyadic balance of power, and creating the opportunity for an attack from the outside.

Internal conflict does not always provoke external intervention, however, and Blainey (1973) attempts to identify some of the conditions under which this is most likely to occur. He hypothesizes that civil strife in the stronger state is most likely to disturb the peace because it muffles the existing hierarchy of power and undermines deterrence. Civil strife in the weaker state, on the other hand, tends to preserve peace because it reinforces the existing dyadic balance of power. This is illustrated by the historical phenomenon of "death-watch" wars (Blainey 1973, 68–70), in which the deaths of monarchs led to a succession crisis, the dissolution or weakening of defensive alliances that rested on personal ties, a general shift in the balance of power, and often led to war.[13]

Although Blainey's (1973) empirical analysis is not sufficiently rigorous or systematic to provide definitive support for his hypotheses, his arguments and his examples must be considered seriously in any analysis of the relationship between internal and external conflict. An important theoretical problem with Blainey's analysis, however, is that he fails to recognize that external intervention in the weaker state is not always motivated by the aggressor's desire to seize territorial or economic resources, or more generally to increase its own military power and potential relative to that of its weakened adversary. Civil strife is often the manifestation of a struggle for political power, and external interventions may be designed primarily to influence the internal political processes and struggle for power in the strife-torn state. For this reason, civil strife in weaker states rather than in stronger states may be most likely to trigger external military intervention.[14]

Although great powers are more likely than other states to initiate such interventions because great powers have more extensive interests as well as greater military capabilities to defend those interests (Levy 1983b, chap. 2),[15] intervention in the internal political affairs of weaker states is not limited to the great powers. This is illustrated by Israeli and Syrian interventions in Lebanon as well as by numerous other cases. The likelihood of intervention is increased if there are ethnic, religious, and political cleavages in the strife-torn state that provide the external state with ideological as well as power-political motivations to support one particular internal faction over another, which is again illustrated by the Lebanese case.

This discussion makes it clear that although most of the quantitative empirical literature on the internal–external conflict relationship as well as most reviews of that literature suggest that this relationship is equivalent to the scapegoat hypothesis, it is not. There are several distinct causal mechanisms, of which the scapegoat mechanism is only one, leading from internal to external conflict and vice versa. Consequently, the observation of an empirical relationship between the internal and external conflict behavior of states would not necessarily confirm the scapegoat hypothesis. Such an empirical association could reflect (1) the internalization of external conflict, (2) the externalization of internal conflict through the intervening mechanisms of (a) a shift in the dyadic balance of power or (b) external intervention in the political affairs of another state. The first could be differentiated from scapegoating through the use of time lags, but the second two could not. Identifying the initiator of the war would not always solve this problem because the diversionary action may not necessarily be war itself.[16] It might also be actions short of war that provoke or otherwise lead the external target to initiate the actual war. In addition, we have seen that the scapegoat hypothesis also differs from the in-group/out-group hypothesis in that the latter usually treats external conflict as an exogenous variable and posits one-way causation, whereas the scapegoat hypothesis posits a dynamic and reciprocal relationship leading from internal conditions to external conflict and then back to internal conditions.

There is another reason why the scapegoat hypothesis is analytically distinct from the relationship between domestic and foreign conflict. Internal "conflict" is not a necessary condition for the diversionary use of force against another state if, by conflict, we mean demonstrations, riots, general strikes, purges, major governmental crises, or other activities that are used to define conflict in the quantitative literature. Other conditions can contribute to elite insecurity and to the temptation for the diversionary use of force even in the absence of overt internal conflict. It has been suggested, for example, that democratic states are particularly likely to use force externally during an election year, especially when the election occurs at a time of economic stagnation (Ostrom and Job 1986; Russett 1989a). Thus, the key question is not the connection between internal and external conflict, but the kinds of internal conditions that commonly lead to hostile external actions for diversionary purposes. We will return to this question in the next section.

THE FORM OF THE RELATIONSHIP BETWEEN
INTERNAL AND EXTERNAL CONFLICT

Another problem with the quantitative literature on the domestic–foreign conflict hypothesis is the lack of attention given to the form of the relationship. Nearly all of these studies measure the relationship between internal and external conflict through factor analysis, regression analysis, or related statistical methods that assume a linear relationship between the two variables. Much of the theoretical literature on group cohesion suggests, however, that the relationship is neither linear nor even monotonically increasing. As Coser (1956, 93) hypothesizes,

> The relation between outer conflict and inner cohesion does not hold true where internal cohesion before the outbreak of the conflict is so low that the group members have ceased to regard preservation of the group as worthwhile, or actually see the outside threat to concern "them" rather than "us." In such cases disintegration of the group, rather than increase in cohesion, will be the result of outside conflict.

As we have seen, Coser's hypothesis has received some support from empirical work in psychology and anthropology. Although these findings cannot be directly extrapolated to the behavior of states in international politics, there are enough historical cases to suggest that this is at least a plausible hypothesis. The German, Russian, and Austro-Hungarian Empires were each beset by serious internal problems in 1914, and it has been widely argued that an important factor influencing the foreign policies of each of these great powers was the attempt of conservative forces at home to strengthen their position through an aggressive foreign policy and, perhaps, even war (Kehr 1970; Fischer 1975; Mayer 1967). The consequences of the war, of course, were precisely the opposite: the war contributed to the disintegration of each of the empires and, in fact, strengthened the forces of revolutionary change in those states in the postwar world.[17]

These examples suggest that the internal consequences of external war may be a function of the outcome of the war as well as the preexisting level of internal conflict, although this possibility is rarely acknowledged in quantitative empirical studies of internal–external conflict linkage.[18] As Solzhenitsyn (1974, 274) suggests, "whereas governments need victories, the people need defeats." The argument is developed by Mayer (1977, 219–220), who argues that "victory (success) and defeat (failure) result in opposite outcomes." Mayer also emphasizes the interaction effects between the outcome of the war and the preexisting level of internal stability, for which he uses a threefold classification. If the government and society are relatively stable, "victory has the unintended but not unwelcome effect of further solidifying the existing structure of class, status, and power, while defeat weakens incumbent governments and ruling classes, though not to the point of endangering the regime itself." If the government faces a limited "inorganic" crisis, the internal effects of war are somewhat greater. And if the government and society face a more serious "organic" or general crisis, victory reunifies and relegitimizes the regime, whereas a serious defeat can lead to revolution (Mayer 1970, 220).

Political elites often recognize these dangers and, under such conditions, are less inclined to engage in the diversionary use of force. Whereas some German leaders in 1914 sought war as a means of unifying the country, Chancellor Bethmann Hollweg feared that "a world war with all its unpredictable consequences is likely to enhance the power of the Social Democrats" and undermine the existing political order (Mommsen 1973, 33).[19] Mayer (1969, 295–296) generalizes from this and other cases and argues that political leaders generally refrain from war if "internal disturbances and tensions are so acute that they cannot rely on the loyalty of critical segments not only of the working and peasant population but also of the armed forces" because that creates prohibitive risks. Under such conditions they often prefer to postpone war until internal conditions are more conducive to successful external scapegoating.

If these arguments are correct, the diversionary use of force should be a nonlinear function of the level of internal conflict, with scapegoating being most likely at moderate levels of internal conflict and less likely at both very low or very high levels of internal conflict. This view is reinforced by some additional arguments by Blainey (1973, 81). He argues that, under conditions of open civil war, states are more likely to seek external peace rather than war so that they can turn their full attention toward their internal problems. From his list of over 30 international wars linked to significant civil unrest, he argues that governments facing grave internal tensions tend to direct their military forces against the rebels rather than against an external scapegoat. Moreover, serious internal problems weaken the state militarily and reduce the chance of victory in an external war. He notes that scapegoat interpretations have more often been applied to states suffering from mild tensions than open civil war, and he suggests an inverse relationship between the need for diversionary action and the positive benefits from such actions: diversionary actions are most useful where they are least necessary and most likely to boomerang where they might be the most helpful.

These are plausible arguments, but the linear model of diversionary processes cannot be so easily rejected. As Mayer argues, in apparent contradiction to the passages quoted previously, "strained and unstable internal conditions tend to make elites markedly intransigent and disposed to exceptionally drastic . . . [and] extravagantly hazardous preemptive solutions." Beleaguered and vulnerable governments "seek war, or do not exert themselves to prevent it, in spite of the high risks involved." They adopt a "fortress mentality [and] are particularly inclined to advocate external war for the purpose of domestic crisis management even if chances for victory are doubtful" (Mayer 1969, 295; 1977, 220–221).

Restated in the language of decision theory, Mayer is suggesting that political elites are risk acceptant when faced with nearly certain losses. When decision-making elites perceive that their political authority is becoming increasingly tenuous, they are inclined to take particularly drastic measures to maintain control. The greater the internal threat, the less elites have to lose from risky measures and the more likely they are to gamble. This hypothesis is reinforced by some recent experimental and theoretical work in social psychology, which demonstrates that individuals tend to be risk averse with respect to gains but risk acceptant with respect to losses (Kahneman and Tversky 1979).[20]

In addition to emphasizing the risk-seeking behavior of elites faced with a deteriorating political climate, Mayer (1977, 220–221) emphasizes the likelihood of misperceptions contributing to the tendencies toward the diversionary use of force. The misperceptions include not only the over-estimation of one's military capabilities relative to those of the adversary, but also the underestimation of the political pressure and will for war in would-be enemy nations.[21] Thus, there is a tendency to exaggerate both the likelihood of diversionary actions short of war being successful without escalating to war and the probability of victory in the event of war (Levy 1983b, 1989; Blainey 1973, chap. 3).[22] In fact, the motivated biases (Jervis et al. 1985, chap. 2) that help generate these misperceptions are particularly likely to occur under conditions of internal (or external) crisis. The greater the internal crisis and the greater the need for an external diversion, the greater the tendency toward motivated biases that convince elites that diversionary action would be successful both externally and internally and that it would involve minimum costs and risks. Mayer (1977, 201–202) also argues that ruling elites also have a tendency to exaggerate the seriousness of the internal crisis, the frailty of the institutional apparatus of the existing political order, and, therefore, the need for extraordinary action. Mayer (1977, 201–202) concludes that resorting to external war and internal repression is often the result of "overreaction to over-perceived revolutionary dangers rather than any calibrated and hazardous resistance to enormous and imminent insurgencies."[23]

Thus, both the linear and nonlinear versions of the scapegoat hypothesis can be supported by plausible theoretical arguments and, undoubtedly, by well-selected historical examples; which (if either) is correct is ultimately an empirical question. Before these models can be tested—either against each other or against the null hypothesis of no diversionary action under any domestic conditions—more attention needs to be directed to the questions of what kinds of domestic conflict are likely to lead to diversionary actions and what kinds of foreign conflict serve as useful distractions for internal unrest. These questions have been touched upon in the literature in that internal and external conflict are each conceptualized along several different dimensions. These have not been integrated into any larger framework, however, and much more work needs to be done.

Different foreign responses involve different costs as well as different probabilities of effectively distracting attention from domestic difficulties, and whether each brings net benefits is a function of the nature of domestic conflict and its threat to the interests of the elite. As Hazelwood (1975, 224) notes, "nations using diversion mechanisms to reduce domestic conflict will generally engage in that type of foreign conflict which is sufficiently intense to divert attentions from domestic to external matters but which is also sufficiently limited to control the costs to the regime." Moreover, as Blainey (1973) reminds us, there are internal as well as external means of reducing internal conflict. Presumably, whether elites resort to internal or external solutions for domestic unrest depends on the relative expected utilities of the best internal and external responses (Bueno de Mesquita 1980, 394–395).[24]

An example of the application of a cost–benefit framework to the domestic/foreign conflict problem is provided by Hazelwood (1975), who recognizes that the form of the domestic–foreign conflict relationship is a function of the nature of the domestic conflict. He identifies three distinct categories of domestic conflict: mass protest, elite instability, and structural war, which provides a more differentiated typology than Mayer's (1977) distinction between inorganic and organic crises.[25] Mass protest refers to popular dissatisfaction with existing policy orientations or programs and involves demands against the incumbent regime. Elite instability refers to significant cleavages among the elites and disagreements over policy, procedures, and role occupancy. It constitutes an important challenge to the incumbents and is generally more intense and violent than mass protest. Structural war is the most extreme form of domestic conflict and refers to violent and widespread attempts not only to overthrow the government and change current policy, but also to change other substructures of society and establish a new order (Midlarsky 1988a). Each of these dimensions is measured by a different set of operational indicators.

Hazelwood (1975) also categorizes the dependent variable into disputes, conflicts, and hostilities (following Barringer 1972, 20), which involves an ascending scale of seriousness and violence. He argues that mass protests are likely to generate diversionary mechanisms only if the protests are chronic and persisting, and he posits an increasing exponential relationship between foreign conflict (of all types) and the intensity of mass protest. He argues, however, that diversionary actions are more likely responses to divisions in the elite. He suggests a monotonically (concave) increasing relationship that turns slightly negative after a certain threshold because if elite instability is too great, internal "encapsulation" processes are more likely responses. The hypothesized relationship between foreign conflict and structural war is similar but with a much sharper decline after a certain threshold, which reflects the fact that the ability to use diversionary actions is severely constrained if a society is beset with open civil war.

These are intriguing hypotheses and a significant conceptual contribution to the literature on the linkages between internal and external conflict. Many of these hypotheses, however, are not supported by the results of Hazelwood's (1975) quantitative empirical analysis of 75 countries for the 1954–1966 period. Mass protests, not elite instability, are the best predictor of foreign conflict. Because extreme elite instability is often associated with foreign conflict rather than internal responses and foreign conflict is more likely at high levels rather than lower levels of structural war, Hazelwood concludes that there is no evidence of a curvilinear relationship between internal and external conflict. Moreover, there is little evidence of proportionality or balance between the nature and intensity of internal conflict and the intensity of foreign conflict behavior. Mass protest is as likely to lead to serious hostilities as to lower level disputes, and structural war is more closely associated with disputes than with hostilities. While these findings are intriguing, it should be emphasized that the 1954–1966 temporal domain of Hazelwood's study seriously restricts our ability to generalize about the relationship between internal and external conflict at other times and in other systems. In other words, Hazelwood's empirical analyses may not be as damaging to his hypotheses as they might appear.

OTHER CONDITIONS FOR DIVERSIONARY ACTION

I noted earlier that one of the most serious limitations of quantitative studies of the domestic–foreign conflict linkage is their general failure to specify the conditions under which the hypothesis is likely to hold. We have already discussed the question of whether or not the relationship holds under conditions of high levels of preexisting internal conflict. The focus here is on other conditions contributing to the diversionary use of force. There is good reason to believe that sweeping analyses that fail to control for these contingent conditions may be masking some significant empirical patterns.

One variable affecting the relationship between internal and external conflict that has received some attention in the literature is the type of regime. We have seen that Wilkenfeld (1973) and others have found that, by controlling for regime type, some significant relationships between internal and external conflicts emerge. In the absence of a more coherent theoretical framework, however, it is not clear how to interpret a variety of findings involving different types of relationships between different types of internal and external conflicts for different types of regimes. Russett (1989a) also emphasizes the importance of regime type—particularly the differences between democratic and nondemocratic regimes. He emphasizes the vulnerability of governments in industrial democracies to electoral punishment following economic downturns, notes the temptations for scapegoating, and finds (in an empirical analysis spanning more than a century) that the likelihood of the involvement of these states in international disputes is somewhat greater during periods of economic decline. For nondemocratic states, however, involvement in international disputes is greater in periods of economic expansion rather than decline.[26] These relationships disappear, however, if the focus shifts from involvement in international disputes to the escalation of disputes to higher levels of conflict, including war. Recall here that Rosecrance's (1963) comparative historical study of the previous two centuries suggests that the tendency of political elites to resort to external *war* in response to their internal problems holds true regardless of the nature of the political system.

The domestic–foreign conflict linkage and the propensity toward scapegoating are also affected by external constraints. Because the internal impact of external diversionary actions, particularly war, depends on the success of those actions, militarily more powerful states are freer to engage in scapegoating than are states with lesser military capabilities.[27] Thus, Russett (1989a) finds that the linkage between economic downturns and involvement in international disputes is stronger for major powers than for minor powers and is particularly strong for the leading great powers. Failing to control for these and other external conditions can introduce a serious bias into the analysis of the domestic conditions contributing to the external use of military force.[28]

The rate of change in military capabilities (as distinct from the existing dyadic balance of military power) is another important variable affecting whether or not political elites engage in the diversionary use of force beyond their borders. A decline in military strength relative to a particular adversary may lead to war directly by creating the temptation for a "preventive war" in an attempt to block or retard the rising challenger (Levy 1987).[29]

Systemic decline may also interact with domestic variables to increase further the likelihood of war. Decisionmakers in declining states who are also faced with serious internal political problems may be particularly willing to gamble on a war that might solve both sets of problems simultaneously; thus, they may be driven to war by the combination of preventive and scapegoat motivations.[30]

The impact of external decline and the internal problems confronting elites are not necessarily independent, of course. They may both be the product of the same underlying processes. Economic decline generates social conflict and, therefore, political problems for the ruling elite at the same time that it undercuts the military power of the state, which intensifies the incentives for scapegoating as well as for preventive war. In addition, political and ethnic divisions can affect the strength and reliability of the army as well as the internal cohesiveness of the state. This is illustrated by the Austro-Hungarian Empire in 1914. Berghahn (1973, 213) concludes that Germany's ruling elites "were increasingly haunted by the nightmare of impending internal chaos and external defeat so that an offensive war appeared to be the only way out of the general deadlock." This view, which is shared by Fischer (1975) and numerous other historians, is applied to Austria–Hungary as well as to Germany (Ritter 1970, vol. 2, 227–239; Fischer 1975, 398; Levy 1988c).

PLURALIST MODELS

Most of the discussion up to this point has assumed the existence of a relatively homogeneous political elite or ruling class that attempts to bolster its domestic political position through the diversionary use of military force abroad. Scapegoating can also arise under conditions in which political elites are divided. One faction may be tempted to engineer a foreign confrontation or push for the use of military force as a means of advancing its own interests in the intraelite struggle for power. Lebow (1981, 74–79), for example, argues that the attempts to expand Russian influence in Korea, which ultimately led to the Russo-Japanese War in 1904–1905, resulted in part from the deliberate efforts of the navy and the so-called Bezobrazov clique to undermine the political influence of Witte, the foreign minister.

Although the intraelite struggle for power might appear to reflect bureaucratic politics rather than domestic politics, the two may be very difficult to separate in many cases, particularly in democratic political systems. Appealing to public opinion can be an important source of influence in bureaucratic politics (Art 1973; Halperin 1974), and appearing as the strongest defender of the "national interest" through a hard-line foreign policy may serve as a useful means of increasing one's public support. The calculations of elites regarding the domestic impact of foreign policy actions may focus on the population as a whole, but they may also focus on particular subgroups of society. These subgroups may be defined ideologically, with scapegoating being motivated primarily by the desire to appeal to those on the right of the political spectrum. Diversionary actions may also be designed to boost a particular elite's standing among certain economic interest groups or ethnic groups. Diversionary actions, whether directed at the population as a whole or at certain subgroups within it, may be affected by a current political issue, especially in democratic states during election years. The dominant elite's main concern may be to deny potential opponents a key political issue. Scapegoating by U.S. presidents in the cold war period, for example, has occasionally been designed to counter the potential charge that one is "soft on communism."

The domestic interests perceived by contending elites are not always incompatible. Several different factions may simultaneously perceive that a foreign policy of confrontation or war would advance their own domestic or bureaucratic political interests, and they may support such a policy to further those interests. A good example is revolutionary France, where nearly all of the major factions (except the extreme radicals) sought war for different reasons. In this case it was only the perceived interests, not the "objective" interests, of the different factions that were compatible. Their respective preferences for war were based on mutually inconsistent expectations regarding the likely consequences of a war, and many of these expectations were based on wishful thinking and serious misperceptions of military strength (Blanning 1986).[31]

The objective domestic political interests of different factions need not be fully incompatible, however. Snyder (1987) constructs a theory of imperial overextension driven by coalition politics and strategic ideology. He demonstrates how coalition building among groups with different but not mutually incompatible interests can generate a logrolled outcome leading to both external expansion and internal harmony, particularly when those perceived interests are reinforced by rationalizations based on strategic ideology. The consequences, however, are often a more aggressive foreign policy than is desired by any single domestic group and the creation of more external enemies than can be managed by existing national resources and diplomatic arrangements. A classic example is the coalition of "iron and rye" in Germany in the decades before 1914.

Snyder's theory of imperial extension based on coalition politics and strategic ideology is, in many repects, more plausible than alternative theories of diversionary war that focus on the domestic interests of a single dominant elite.[32] It also raises a critical issue that is rarely explored in other discussions of scapegoating: Exactly how does a belligerent foreign policy or war work to consolidate the domestic support of a political elite? Nearly all discussions of scapegoating—and, in fact, the very concepts of scapegoating or of diversionary mechanisms—assume that some form of psychological mechanism is at work. This is not surprising in that the same assumption is made by the conflict–cohesion hypothesis. The outcome is explained by the inherent psychological propensities of in-groups toward cohesion in response to out-group threat, in conjunction with the forces of modern nationalism. In addition, these tendencies can be further manipulated by the elite because of their influence over the media and instruments of propaganda.[33]

It is interesting to note that the scapegoat hypothesis implies that diversionary policies are adopted because they are expected to serve elite interests but that they work because of the response of the mass public to symbolic politics rather than their real interests. It is not clear, however, why elites but not the mass public, are driven by their private material or political interests. Why do elites give priority to their domestic political interests, whereas others give priority to the national interest and are so easily seduced by symbolic psychological scapegoating? One could presumably construct an explanation for this based on the higher degree of concentration of elite interests (while costs are diffuse) as opposed to mass interests (Olson 1982; Snyder 1987) or on the basis of some alternative framework. My point, however, is that this is something that needs to be explained but that is rarely, if ever, addressed.

The possibility that the externalization of internal conflict may work because it serves the interests of masses as well as elites reinforces a point made earlier: the adoption of an aggressive foreign policy by political elites for the primary purpose of advancing their domestic political interests is analytically distinct from the in-group/out-group or conflict–cohesion hypothesis. The conflict–cohesion hypothesis specifies one possible mechanism through which elite interests might be served by an aggressive foreign policy, but there may be others.[34]

This was recognized by Lenin. Although I previously cited Lenin's statement suggesting that diversionary mechanisms were involved in the processes leading up to World War I, his primary argument in *Imperialism* (1939) is that imperialism serves the interests of the capitalist class (for a time, at least) because it also serves the material interests of the upper strata of the proletariat and divides the working class. Imperialism succeeds in propping up the falling rate of profit and increasing the pool of surplus value for paying off the labor aristocracy (Lenin 1939, 104–108). Snyder (1987) develops this idea further by incorporating the material and political interests of various elites and interest groups into a theory of coalition behavior reinforced by strategic ideology.

It should be noted, however, that Snyder's dependent variable is imperial expansion, not war. If our concern is to explain not just imperial expansion but also the phenomenon of interstate war, the linkages from imperial expansion to war must be specified. This raises the more general question of how the dependent variable in diversionary theories is to be conceptualized.

THE NATURE OF THE DEPENDENT VARIABLE

Most of the literature on the diversionary theory of war exhibits a puzzling lack of attention to the question of the nature of the dependent variable. Although much of the theoretical literature surveyed earlier speaks explicitly about *war* as a means of distracting attention from internal problems (Wright 1965; Haas and Whiting 1956), most empirical studies of scapegoating have focused on various forms of foreign conflict short of war rather than on war itself. The incidence of war, for example, is only one of about 13 measures of external conflict utilized by Rummel (1963) and others in their quantitative empirical studies. Moreover, the research designs guiding nearly all of the quantitative studies are further biased against the analysis of war as the dependent variable in another sense: the 1954–1960 period covered by most of these studies is characterized by the relative absence of war, and certainly the absence of major war. Even Lebow (1981) is more concerned with the domestic sources of crisis initiation than with the escalation of those crises to war, although he gives some attention to the latter.

This focus is not unreasonable because, on theoretical grounds, we would expect more diversionary actions short of war instead of war itself: actions short of war are generally more cost effective in achieving the desired internal effect than an actual war, and political elites are further driven by their own motivated biases to believe this. If political leaders have calculated correctly, their actions will not lead to war. In other cases, however, diversionary actions undertaken with little expectation of war can inadvertently lead to war by triggering a conflict spiral driven by misperceptions (Jervis 1976; Levy 1983c), by precluding certain diplomatic commitments that are necessary for stability, or in other ways.[35] The Argentine occupation of the Falklands/Malvinas in 1982, for example, was motivated largely by domestic politics but was undertaken without the intention or expectation of war (Hastings and Jenkins 1983).

In these and similar cases an explanation for the causes of the war would be incomplete without including the diversionary actions and the domestic interests that generated them. Not all diversionary actions lead to war, however, and an important question is whether those that do (and those that do not) follow any particular pattern. That is, we need a theory that specifies the conditions under which certain types of diversionary actions help lead to war (directly or indirectly) and the processes through which this is likely to occur.[36] This raises another point. Whether or not diversionary actions short of war lead to war depends not only on the actions of the scapegoater but also on the behavior of the target and, perhaps, of other states in the system. That is, the diversionary theory of war is not really a theory of war. It is a theory (although an incomplete one) of the foreign policy behavior of an individual state with respect to one particular issue area. War, on the other hand, generally involves the strategic interaction of two or more states.[37] Thus, the diversionary theory of war is logically incomplete unless it is incorporated into a broader theory of strategic interaction and international politics.

CONCLUSION

I have argued that there is a considerable discrepancy between the theoretical and historical literature on the diversionary theory of conflict, on the one hand, and the quantitative empirical literature on the other. Whereas the theoretical and historical literature suggests the importance of the diversionary use of force by political elites to bolster their internal political positions, the quantitative empirical literature in political science has repeatedly found that there is no consistent and meaningful relationship between the internal and external conflict behavior of states. Although a careful examination of the validity of the historical evidence of diversionary processes is needed, the focus of this study has been on the limitations of the quantitative empirical literature.

This literature deals with an extremely important theoretical question and a level of analysis that has generally been neglected by political scientists studying war. It has generated a compilation of data that are based on rigorous and systematic coding procedures and have involved an enormous amount of scholarly effort, and it has utilized sophisticated statistical methods to analyze this data. The basic problem, I have argued, is that there is too poor a fit between the hypotheses supposedly being investigated and the overall research design guiding the empirical analyses. There is no well-developed theoretical framework guiding what are basically descriptive correlational analyses. Little attention is given to questions of under what kinds of conditions what kinds of states resort to what kinds of external conflict in response to what kinds of threats to the security of political elites. Consequently, there is a significant risk that large numbers of correlations between many variables for large numbers of states without any form of scientific control may be masking significant relationships that hold under a more restricted set of conditions.

Although most of these studies refer explicitly to the scapegoat hypothesis based on group cohesion theory and present their empirical studies as a means of testing that hypothesis, they fail to recognize that the scapegoat hypothesis or diversionary theory of war is not the same as the relationship between internal and external conflict. Consequently, operational models of domestic–foreign conflict linkages are often not congruent with the hypothesized theoretical relationships supposedly being tested. Inadequate attention is given to the direction of the relationship between internal and external conflict and to the causal mechanism driving the relationship, and there is a failure to introduce controls that could differentiate scapegoating processes from others that might produce some similar empirical patterns. Neither static linear models based on one-way causation between internal and external conflict nor cross-sectional research designs are appropriate for analyzing the dynamic and reciprocal relationships involved in diversionary processes. A causal modeling perspective, and particularly a longitudinal research design, would be more useful.

Diversionary actions are more likely to occur under some domestic and internal conditions than others, but these conditions have yet to be analyzed. Internal conflict is not a necessary condition for diversionary action, and attention should also be directed. to other conditions under which political leaders seek domestic gains through forceful external actions. Of particular interest here are the questions of what *kinds* of domestic political stability, or what kinds of threats to what kinds of elite interests, are more likely to lead to diversionary actions. More attention also needs to be directed to the dependent variable. What types of external behavior are driven by internal political considerations, and are certain types of internal conflicts or conditions linked to certain forms of external behavior? Some of the quantitative empirical literature (for example, Hazelwood 1975) has suggested certain useful categories, but far more work needs to be done here. Classifications of internal variables based only on behavioral indicators of domestic conflict (riots, protests, and so on) are particularly inadequate.

A more complete theory of scapegoating would also require additional analysis of the causal mechanism through which aggressive foreign behavior advances the domestic political interests of decisionmakers. Does scapegoating work because an external threat increases the cohesion of the in-group and because of nationalism, or do aggressive external actions also serve the more concrete interests of various domestic constituencies? There also has been little concern with how diversionary processes actually contribute to war. Political elites are probably more inclined to diversionary actions short of war than to war itself because the former are far less risky domestically as well as internationally. But under what conditions do what types of diversionary actions lead to war? This can be understood only by integrating the scapegoat hypothesis of foreign policy motivation into a dyadic or systemic-level theory of strategic interaction and bargaining.

In addition to these theoretical issues, more attention needs to be given to the question of how these relationships can best be tested empirically. There must be a clearer specification of an operational model consistent with hypothesized theoretical relationships. There must also be greater sensitivity to the question of what classes of behavior we want to generalize about and what empirical domains should be analyzed for these purposes. The 1954–1960 period used by many of the existing quantitative studies is far too narrow and unrepresentative of the larger universe of international conflict, particularly if one wants to focus on war as the dependent variable and even more so if one is interested in wars involving the great powers.

The extension of the temporal domain is one possibility. The events data used by most existing studies are confined to the post-1945 period. It would be very costly and time consuming to extend the data enough to incorporate a sufficient number of major wars, although Leng's work on crisis bargaining in 40 historical cases since 1815 demonstrates the feasibility and utility of using events data to analyze conflict in earlier periods (Leng 1983; Leng and Singer 1988). Another possibility would involve the use of aggregate indicators rather than events data. The utility of this approach is illustrated by the Ostrom and Job (1986) and Russett (1989a) studies of the impact of electoral and economic cycles on the use of force.

Another possibility would be the application of the methodology of structured, focused comparison in a more intensive analysis of a smaller number of cases (George 1982). This would permit a more focused analysis on war as the dependent variable and also a more careful examination of the motivations of decisionmakers, which is a central concern in the theory. Structured, focused comparison might also be used to validate some of the findings of historical case studies mentioned earlier, but from a perspective that is more explicitly driven by key theoretical questions and more sensitive to the methodological problems of comparative analysis. The potential utility of constructing a research program involving several different methodologies should also be considered. Russett (1970) suggests the advantages of combining correlational and case study methodologies. There are undoubtedly other approaches as well. What is clear is that we need new methodological approaches that go beyond the previous generation of studies based on the Rummel paradigm and research designs that are more closely related to the theoretical questions being asked.

NOTES

1. This research was supported by the Stanford Center for International Security and Arms Control, the Carnegie Corporation, and by a Social Science Research Council/ MacArthur Foundation Fellowship in International Peace and Security. The views expressed here do not necessarily represent those of the supporting agencies. The author is grateful for many helpful comments and suggestions from Bud Duvall, John Freeman, Alexander George, Pat James, Brian Job, Robert Pape, Joe Scolnick, Jack Snyder, and David Sylvan.

2. Elsewhere I have emphasized the contrast between the lack of attention given by political scientists to domestic sources of international conflict and the primacy given to these factors by many contemporary historians (Levy 1988a; Iggers 1984). Note that recently there has been a revival of interest in the Kantian concept of a "pacific union" among liberal democratic states (Doyle 1986). See Levy (1989) for a general review of societal-level theories of war.

3. Schumpeter (1939) argues that although war was once functional for the development of the modern state, it was now "objectless" and "atavistic." In a widely quoted passage regarding the machinery of war and the military elite whose interests it served, he stated that "created by the wars that required it, the machine now created the wars it required" (in Art and Jervis 1973, 296).

4. For a good discussion of Coser's (1956) modifications of Simmel's (1956) thought, see Sylvan and Glassner (1985, chap. 2). They argue that Coser's theory is more mechanistic than Simmel's theory, that it is less sensitive to contextual variables affecting the conflict–cohesion hypothesis, and that it is also more functionalist in orientation.

5. The statistical methods used include correlation, regression, and factor analysis (Rummel, 1963; Tanter 1966), Markovian models (Zinnes and Wilkenfeld 1971), and canonical analysis and path analysis (Hazelwood 1973). Some of these studies introduce time lags and others do not.

6. The validity of this evidence for the Russo-Japanese case is questioned by Blainey (1973, 76–77).

7. There are similar interpretations of British social imperialism in the four decades prior to World War I (Semmel 1960).

8. For a critique of Lebow's emphasis on domestic political variables in these cases, see Orme (1987).

9. The concepts of the externalization and internalization of conflict are suggested by Ward and Widmaier (1982), but I define these concepts differently. Ward and Widmaier (1982, 78) define the internalization of external conflict as a situation in which one state, *A*, becomes the target of another state's military attack because internal conflict within *A* creates weaknesses and an opportunity for an external aggressor. But this process results in external conflict between states, and the antecedent conditions generating this conflict is internal conflict within one state, even if the causal mechanism involved is different than scapegoating. For this reason I classify this as one form of the externalization of internal conflict. I define the internalization of external conflict as any process through which external conflict has a causal

impact on domestic conflict. These internalization and externalization mechanisms may have a negative as well as positive effect, so external conflict may decrease as well as increase domestic conflict (and vice versa). In addition, these two processes may be characterized by reciprocal interaction.

10. The last link in the chain, the actual reduction in internal conflict, can be excluded from the model if one's focus is limited to decisions leading to scapegoating rather than its actual effectiveness in reducing internal conflict. Decisions for the diversionary use of force are based on expectations of its domestic political impact rather than the accuracy of those expectations.

11. Stohl (1980) reports only one study (Kegley *et al.* 1978) finding a negative relationship between internal and external conflict.

12. Conflict in *A* may also provide an opportunity for its rival *B* to attack *C* on the assumption that *A* is too weak or internally involved to respond, which in turn could conceivably lead *A* to intervene either for diversionary or balance-of-power reasons (Levy 1982).

13. Examples might include the War of the Spanish Succession (1700–1713), the War of the Polish Succession (1733–1738), the War of the Austrian Succession (1740–1748), and the War of the Bavarian Succession (1778–1779).

14. The conditions under which internal conflict is most likely to lead to scapegoating may be precisely the opposite: stronger states are probably more prone than weak states to the diversionary use of force precisely because their strength minimizes the external military risks. The differences in the conditions under which these two processes are most likely to occur reinforce the need to distinguish between different causal mechanisms driving the hypothesized relationship.

15. Note that there may be political or economic instruments of policy that are more cost effective than military intervention for the purposes of shaping the outcome of struggles for power in other states.

16. The question of how to define the initiator of a war involves a very difficult analytical problem. This problem has received far too little attention in the literature. Blainey (1973), for one, ignores it.

17. Another clear case of scapegoating that boomeranged on a political elite is the Argentine attempt to occupy the Falkland/Malvinas Islands in 1982 (Hastings and Jenkins, 1983).

18. For an exception, see Sorokin (1937, 489–492).

19. Where some see risks in war, others see opportunities. Marx and Engels, after observing the revolutionary consequences of defeat in the Franco-Prussian War (the Paris Commune), came to see war as a possible vehicle for social progress. Similarly, Jaurès anticipated (by 1905) a world war and thought that there was a good chance that it would strengthen the forces of revolution and advance social democracy in Europe, but he also recognized that it could result in counterrevolution, dictatorship, and militarism as well (Mayer 1977, 215, 223).

20. That is, given a choice between a certain gain x and a lottery involving an expected value $y > x$ (in typical experiments, x and y differ by 20–30 percent), individuals generally choose x. But given a choice between a certain loss x and a lottery involving an expected value $y < x$ (a larger expected loss), they tend to gamble and choose y. Although these findings emerge from studies of individuals in experimental situations, they are fairly robust in that they are valid over a range of individual characteristics and a range of external situations. Thus, in these situations individuals do not act to maximize expected utility.

21. This is consistent with the fundamental attribution error of exaggerating the external constraints on one's own behavior while minimizing the external constraints on one's adversary (Kelley 1972).

22. It is interesting that while Blainey (1973, chap. 3) emphasizes the importance of military overconfidence and other forms of misperception in the processes leading to war, he does not incorporate misperceptions into his critique of the scapegoat hypothesis.

23. There are important contradictions in Mayer's arguments regarding the likelihood of the diversionary use of force under conditions of profound internal crisis.

24. An expected-utility framework, therefore, provides a useful way to conceptualize the problem. Unless the costs of domestic unrest and the costs and probabilities of the success of all of the internal and external options can be specified, however, this framework cannot generate any predictions as to the conditions under which states are likely to resort to various forms of the diversionary use of force.

25. These can be compared with Rosenau's (1964) three types of internal war: personnel, authority, and structural war.

26. There is also a lively debate on the question of whether the United States' use of force externally has been greater during election years (Ostrom and Job 1986; Job and Ostrom 1986; Stoll 1984; Russett 1989a).

27. The important consideration here, of course, is the dyadic balance of military power. Note, however, that although the risks of diversionary military action are reduced if the adversary is militarily weak, so are the potential benefits. Weaker adversaries are less of a threat and are, therefore, less useful as an external scapegoat. Scapegoating against stronger targets, while risky, is potentially more useful internally (witness the Iranian regime's use of the United States as a scapegoat). The internal utility of scapegoating against weak adversaries (with minimum risks) cannot be entirely dismissed, however, as demonstrated by the case of the United States and Grenada.

28. This does not mean that military superiority over a particular adversary is a necessary condition for diversionary action or that the likelihood of such action is a direct and monotonically increasing function of the relative military strength of the state. Weaker states with stronger allies may be in a good position to engage in the diversionary use of force. Moreover, domestic problems may create such strong incentives for diversionary action that such actions are taken in spite of their military risks (Lebow 1981; Stein 1985). In fact, empirical studies provide strong evidence that an expected-utility model provides a better predictor of the use of force than a dyadic balance-of-power model (Bueno de Mesquita 1981) and that the outcomes of disputes are determined more by asymmetries of motivation than by the military balance (George and Smoke 1974; Maoz 1983; Levy 1988b). For an interesting effort to combine external expected-utility considerations with internal conflict variables, see James (1988, chap. 5).

29. Preventive war is only one of several possible policy responses to a decline in one's military power and potential. For an analysis of the conditions under which declining power is most likely to generate pressures for preventive war, see Levy (1987).

30. Note that the risk-acceptant tendencies of political elites facing a deteriorating domestic situation is intensified if they are simultaneously confronted with external decline relative to other states.

31. For example, Lafayette and some others in the military wanted war because they expected a short victorious war over Austria that would bring a restoration of the monarchy and increased influence and prestige to the military. The Girondins and Jacobins wanted war because they expected that it would discredit the king, consolidate the revolution, and bring lucrative contracts to the bourgeoisie.

32. Note that Snyder's theory is not necessarily incompatible with scapegoating. Many agree with Kehr (1970, 39–40), for example, that the coalition of iron and rye was basically an "agrarian–industrial condominium against social democracy."

33. One question that is raised (but rarely addressed) by all of this literature concerns the

precise identity of the political elite or ruling class that is doing the scapegoating or (more generally) is using the foreign policy of the state to further its own political interests.

34. This raises the following question: Should the concept of scapegoating or diversion be used to refer to any aggressive foreign policy behavior designed primarily to advance the domestic political interests of internal groups, or should it be conceived more narrowly to refer to one particular causal mechanism through which this is accomplished—one involving a psychological response to external threats and the manipulation of political symbols? It would probably be best to retain the broader meaning of scapegoating or diversionary actions (1) because any purely interest-based response would presumably be reinforced by psychological and symbolic mechanisms—particularly to appeal to some mass groups whose interests were not served by aggressive external actions; (2) because precisely *how* hostile external actions work may be less important than decisionmakers' expectations that they will work, at least for questions concerning the causes rather than the internal consequences of foreign policy behavior; and (3) because the concept of scapegoating is probably too deeply ingrained to be redefined in a more narrow manner. The question of the specific causal mechanisms through which scapegoating is effected, however, should not be ignored.

35. The German tariffs against Russian grain and the exclusion of Russians from German financial markets precluded Russian diplomatic support that would be essential for the effective conduct of a *Weltpolitik* that was certain to alienate Britain (Kehr 1970; Gordon 1974; Kaiser 1983). In this way, hostile actions undertaken without any desire or expectation of war contributed to the polarization of alliances and the isolation of Germany, which played a major role in the processes leading to war.

36. Such a theory would not be equivalent to a dyadic or systemic-level theory of strategic interaction. The hostile impact of *some* diversionary actions may be dampened if the target accurately perceives that such actions were driven by domestic concerns.

37. The only exception is if the political authorities of one state prefer war to any set of concessions that might plausibly be offered by the adversary and consequently initiate or provoke a war for that reason. Although technically the target can choose to surrender rather than fight, this is not much of a choice. For all practical purposes, it is possible for one state to start a war, contrary to Blainey (1973).

CHAPTER 12

Lateral Pressure in International Relations: Concept and Theory

Nazli Choucri

Massachusetts Institute of Technology

Robert C. North

Stanford University

OVERVIEW

In the study of international relations, lateral pressure is defined as the extension of a country's behavior and interests outside of its territorial boundaries (and, in some circumstances, the extension of the boundaries themselves). The theory of lateral pressure is an explanation of the determinants and consequences of extended behavior, and it accounts for immediate as well as less proximate sources and outcomes. Despite the focus on state behavior, the core elements and processes of lateral pressure are not state centered, but derived from and applicable to all conglomerations of populations at all levels of analysis.[1] The theory draws primarily upon the established literature of international and global politics, but it borrows from other fields and disciplines as needed.

The theory is anchored in core concepts that include the interactive effects of demand and capability—both of which are required for effective behavior. These phenomena are conditioned, in turn, by three "master variables" (population, technology, and access to resources) whose interactions define the essential characteristics, or basic profile, of each state in the international system. The population variable includes all demographic features, technology encompasses both mechanical and organizational knowledge and skills, and resources refer to arable land, water supplies, minerals, metals, fibers, fuels, and other raw materials. These variables combine to form the central processes that help to shape the behavior patterns of actors on all levels of organization.

Designed initially as a "partial" theory of conflict among nations, the lateral pressure approach has been expanded to identify links between individual, state, international, and global systems. Within this framework, the only thinking, feeling, deciding, and acting units are individual human beings. The state and the international systems consist of individuals acting within formalized relationships identified as coalitions, organizations, and institutions. Whereas individuals, states, and (to a lesser extent) alliances can be treated as actor systems, the international and global systems (encompassing the other systems) lack unifying patterns of expectations (or regimes of their own) and are treated as interactive environmental systems rather than actor systems.

Lateral pressure theory is a process-based specification; time is an essential element. All actor units are constrained by the interaction of internal and external phenomena, but all actions originate within and depend upon domestic capabilities and direction. The theory is derived from the premise that actors with superior capabilities and resolve tend to use more resources, exert more leverage, and expand their activities and interests farther (and with greater impact) than weaker actors. Conditions under which the lateral pressures of states generate propensities for competition, conflict, alignments, counteralignments, provocative acts, escalations, and war are elaborated by a set of theoretical linkages.

For conceptual articulation, empirical analysis, and modeling, we distinguish *sources* of lateral pressure (demands and capabilities), *disposition* or tendency, *manifestation* of actual behavior, and *impacts* of activities on external actors or environments (Choucri and North 1975; Choucri and Bousfield 1978). Of central importance in the lateral pressure process is the security dilemma. Activities undertaken by one country to enhance its economic, political, and military security may be seen by another nation as threatening to its own security. Additionally, once a conflict has begun to escalate, some other nation is likely to interpret a conciliatory move by the adversary as a subterfuge or as an opportunity to be exploited. This dilemma is an important requisite for war.

To date, the empirical and quantitative research agenda accompanying our theoretical work is composed of four phases. Phase 1 was the model and analysis of six major European countries before World War I (Choucri and North 1975). Phase 2 was the dynamic simulation of the respecification of this initial model using system dynamics and forecasting the U.S. case from 1930 to 2000 (which was reported in a series of articles). Phase 3 was a more detailed model, which was based on the original, of the respecified structures and focused on the transformation and behavior of one country, Japan, over a 100-year period from the Meiji restoration to the present (Choucri and North, in preparation). And Phase 4, currently in its initial stage, adopts a global perspective by expanding our empirical coverage and analysis worldwide.

DYNAMIC LINKAGES IN THE LATERAL PRESSURE PROCESS

Core Elements

The process of lateral pressure is rooted in the fact that every human being requires some minimal amount of basic resources (food, water, air, and living space), and these requirements increase multiplicatively with the size of a country's population. Human beings are constituent elements of the international system, and the global environment is the source of life in all its forms. To obtain resources, people develop technology (knowledge and skills), which enables them to obtain new resources and apply old (and more abundant) resources to new purposes (Choucri and North 1975, 15–17; Ashley 1980, 23). The development and the application of technology, however, also require resources (raw materials, tools, machines, energy, and structures), and over the millennia of technological advancements, the amounts and ranges of needed resources have increased commensurately. The more advanced the technology, moreover, the greater the demands for raw materials, goods, and services that people have *thought* they needed above the minimal levels required for survival. Although technological advances have provided spectacular improvements in the efficiencies of tools and machines, they have also vastly increased the possible technological applications; as a result, pressures on resources have tended to increase exponentially (Choucri and North 1975, 18–19).

Acting to satisfy their needs and requirements, people make demands on themselves and on their physical and social environments.[2] A demand, which may not be communicated successfully or effectively satisfied, is defined as an "expression of opinion" coming from a need or desire to close a gap between a perception of fact ("what is") and a perception of value ("what ought to be") (North and Choucri 1983, 445). Demands combine with capabilities to produce action. The simplest activity cannot be accomplished unless an appropriate capability exists for accomplishing it. Constraints of the physical and social environments—together with the level of mechanical and organizational knowledge and skills relative to the numbers of people—establish "the upper bounds to human well-being, but do not themselves determine how successful human beings are within these bounds" (Boulding 1956, 11ff). (This notion of "demand" is broader than that of the economists, who define the concept strictly in terms of "willingness to purchase.")

Capabilities can be increased in two major ways: by drawing upon available technology for the development of specialized capabilities (agricultural, financial, commercial, industrial, military, and so forth) (Ackerman 1966, 621–648); and by bargaining and applying leverages in order to persuade others to assist or cooperate with them.

The political assumptions embedded in lateral pressure theory are derived from bargaining and coalition formation: to strengthen the probability that their demands will be met, people (at the individual or at the state level) increase their capabilities by utilizing available capabilities and/or by bargaining in order to persuade others to assist or cooperate with them. This bargaining introduces volatility, voluntarism, and deviation from an otherwise deterministic view of state action (that is, action shaped uniquely by master variables).

Bargaining and Leverages

Lateral pressure theory assumes that political behavior is essentially interactive and anchored in bargaining, leverage, and coalition formation. Thomas Schelling referred to bargaining processes as verbal and nonverbal interchanges in situations where the ability of one actor to gain his or her ends is, to an important extent, dependent on the choices, decisions, and actions that the other actor undertakes (Schelling 1966, 5–6). Inherent in a bargaining move are three critical elements: a contingency (if . . . unless . . .), a demand (an indication of the response that is expected from another actor), and an inducement, incentive, or leverage (the advantage, reward penalty, coercion, or punishment that is awarded, promised, threatened, or inflicted in order to "persuade" the other actor to close the "bargain").

All state activities, including applications of leverage, depend directly or indirectly upon the national economy for effective implementation. National economies and polities are interdependent in other ways. Just as economic leverages can be used to influence political actions, political leverages can be employed to intervene in economic activities (Hirschman 1969, 14).[3]

The strength of a given leverage can be assessed "objectively" in terms of the costs (time, money, other resources, human lives, and so forth) that the initiator has been willing to incur or subjectively in terms of the way the leverage move is perceived and assessed by others (including the initiator, whose assessments of the costs and benefits may differ from those of a detached observer). Leverage can also be assessed according to its impact or outcomes. Whatever the feelings that actors harbor towards each other, the quality of their interactions—accommodative, cooperative, competitive, conflictual, violent—and the outcome will be shaped by the quality and form of the leverages employed.

In addition to exchanges of goods and services and other behaviors, bargaining and leverage can lead to the formation of coalitions and coalitions of coalitions (including states and other "molar" or higher level organizations) as well as to the establishment of adversarial relationships (see Snyder and Diesing 1977; Riker 1962). (Often, the establishment of one coalition or coalition of coalitions, possibly a state, contributes to the formation of a countercoalition or a coalition of countercoalitions.)

To the extent that cooperative efforts are mobilized for a common purpose and more or less stabilized, a coalition is established. Constrained by their relative capabilities, participants normally bargain with and apply leverage to each other, including their leaders. Linkage networks function within and between coalitions and coalitions of coalitions (including states) (Rosenau 1969, 44–45).[4] Group and organizational (including national) decisionmaking can be seen as a process of establishing a coalition around a particular action, policy, or course of activities. Viewed from "above," a national or other collective actor system resembles "an interconnected and interrelated set of subsystems which ultimately lead to the individual" (Brody 1966, 324). [While horizontal and vertical networks of bargaining and leverage can help to hold a society together (see, for example, Befu 1977, 255–281), there are also conflict networks shaped by contending alignments, for example those linking the United States, the Soviet Union, and their respective allies.]

Political Regimes: Capabilities and "Power"

Some coalitions and coalitions of coalitions, both public and private, establish political regimes (including "legitimate" and "sovereign" governments), with varying degrees of authority, that consist of rules, regulations, laws, law-making institutions, and leaders and bureaucrats who think, plan, and act in the name of the organization.

In the realist tradition, state-level systems are usually viewed parsimoniously as acting to maximize or optimize power—much as "economic man," commercial and industrial organizations, and whole economies are assumed to pursue the maximization or optimization of wealth. While the word *power* has a number of different meanings, we are concerned with the implications for capability and influence. What might be referred to as "power$_1$," which is power measured in terms of gross national product (GNP) (or GNP per capita, military expenditures, troop levels, armaments, or other indicators), is virtually synonymous with economic, political, military, or overall capability. "Power$_2$," in contrast, refers to one actor's influence over another. This usage implies a retrospective assessment: during the Vietnam War, for example, the United States had more power on economic, political, and military dimensions than did North Vietnam or the Viet Cong. In the end, however, the United States did not have enough power$_2$ (influence, "persuasion") to achieve its goal in the struggle. The third use of the word, "power$_3$," refers here to country actors: the great powers, the superpowers, and so forth.

States draw on power$_1$ in order to enhance power$_2$, and they use both sets of capabilities to maintain domestic "law and order" and to strengthen national economic, political, and military security. These realities contribute to the double-sided security dilemma or paradox in which one country's move for economic, political, and military self-defense is interpreted by its adversary as a threat, and a conciliatory move by either side is perceived by the other as a deception or as evidence of a weakness to be exploited.

Leaders and their bureaucracies "aggregate," transform, and allocate needs, wants, desires, resources, technology, and the efforts and compliance of others in order to increase their own capabilities and bargaining and leverage potentials. Combining ballots (or merely compliance) with extractions (tax and other levies), national leaders and bureaucrats transform these aggregations into regulative, police, military, and other capabilities and bargaining and leverage potentials. Such transactions can be viewed as outcomes of more-or-less institutionalized bargaining and leverage relationships between the leaders and the led in which the dominant status of the "regime" is normally established and social order is maintained (Keohane and Nye 1977, 21).

Manifestations of Lateral Pressure

Any tendency for a people to extend their external activities (including positive and/or negative leverage in any form) and their interests can qualify as *lateral pressure*—a concept similar to that of outward expansion as used by Simon Kuznets (Kuznets 1955, 334–348). One manifestation of lateral pressure is the tendency of a society to reach for resources beyond its home borders. To meet demands that are rising as a result of a growing

population, an advancing technology, new expectations, or security requirements, a society can be assumed to draw on local resources first, if only
because they are close at hand and likely to be less costly to obtain than
those from farther away.

If resources in demand are not domestically available, however, or can
be acquired cheaper from abroad (because of rising labor costs at home or
depletions of more readily available domestic supplies), a society faces two
main possibilities: it can develop a new technology in order to obtain old
resources at lower costs (or to find new and cheaper substitutions for old
resources) or it can reach out for (and, if feasible, protect its access to)
resources from abroad through trade, territorial expansion, or both.[5]

The search for resources is only one manifestation of lateral pressure.
Other factors contributing to the expansion of a country's external activities
and interests include exploration; territorial acquisition; the establishment
of overseas colonies; the search for markets, investments, and cheap labor;
the extension of religious, educational, and scientific activities; economic
and military assistance to other countries and the dispatch and maintenance
of troops and bases overseas; the exploitation of the continental shelf; and
the exploration of the ocean depths or space (Choucri and North 1975,
17–18).

An additional manifestation of lateral pressure is the large-scale movement of people across national borders. There are "push" and "pull"
explanations of international migrations,[6] and recent history has shown
what happens when the process comes to full cycle (that is, "push" out of
the home community, to the "pull" of the recipient region, to a subsequent
"push back" from the recipient community to the home country, as in
Western Europe or the Gulf region of the Middle East). Distinctions also
must be made between voluntary and coercive population movements,
between state-sponsored or state-chartered migrations and those that are
undertaken privately, between migrations of private persons who maintain
political obligations to and remit a substantial part of their earnings to their
countries of origin and those who sever (or ignore) such obligations and are
absorbed by the country of destination (see, for example, Choucri 1987).

For generations, emigrants from all over Europe contributed to the
growth and development of the United States and the expansion of its
demands, activities, and interests. Since World War II, jobs and higher
wages in northern Europe and in the United States and Canada have
attracted migrant workers from the Mediterranean region, Latin America,
Africa, and Asia. Some of these, providing industrialized countries with
labor or brain power, have commonly remitted large proportions of their
incomes—and have eventually returned—to families back home. Others,
like millions of pre-World War II immigrants, have taken up residence,

sought citizenship, and accepted long-term responsibilities in their countries of adoption. The establishment of Israel, a small but remarkably powerful pressure society, is an indication of how a concerted movement of large numbers of relatively high-technology people can generate high lateral pressures in an environment of limited resources and transform the economic, political, and security dynamics of a whole region. Alternatively, the transference of laborers and small merchants from India into the narrow confines of Fiji in the late nineteenth and early twentieth centuries has pitted entrepreneurally oriented Asians against horticulturally inclined Melanesians and ignited a social, economic, and political *implosion*.

In sum, the concept of lateral pressure encompasses the expansion of both private and governmental activities and interests beyond home borders. Unlike Marxist concepts of imperialism, it is not contingent upon "bourgeois capitalism" or class conflict, but on generic growth, rising demands, and increasing capabilities. Elsewhere such manifestations have been called the "modes" of lateral pressure (for an example of a case study of international trade, see Pollins 1985).

Intersections or Collisions

The expanding activities and interests of a powerful state may be expected to intersect or "collide" with the activities and interests of other states of different sizes, capabilities, and bargaining and leverage potentials. When the lateral pressures of a powerful state encounter those of a substantially weaker state, the effects are likely to be penetrative; that is, the impact—whether diplomatic, economic, or military—tends to be registered in many different sectors of the society that is penetrated. The result may (but need not) include the domination, exploitation (intended or otherwise), conquest, occupation, or annexation of the weaker state by the stronger power.

When the expanding activities and interests of a major power or superpower intersect or collide with those of another major power or superpower, the leverages employed by either or both sides may be predominantly positive, negative, or a combination of both. As indicated in *Nations in Conflict*, lateral pressure itself seldom triggers a war. Sometimes it does no more than bring two or more countries into closer relations with each other (Choucri and North 1975, 18–20). In general, intersections are most likely to turn violent when relations between the states involved are already hostile or at least one of them (rightly or wrongly) perceives the in situ bargaining and leveraging activities of the other as dangerously competitive, threatening, coercive, menacing, or overtly violent. The subsequent study, focusing on Japan over the past 100 years, shows the sources and manifestations of lateral pressure in a state characterized by low resource endowments, rapidly growing technological capabilities, and a large and increasing population (Choucri and North 1988; Minami 1986).

Competition and Conflict

In economic theory, the role of competition is to discipline the various participants in economic life to provide goods and survive skillfully and cheaply. In political competition, contenders vie for resource and other accesses, power, influence, authority, status, privilege, or comparative advantage. All of these different manifestations of competition overlap and interact; they are, to a considerable extent, interdependent. In competitive situations the efficient tend to be rewarded, and the inefficient risk penalty or elimination in the currency of whatever game is being played.

Uneven growth and development within and between states contribute to power distributions and differential lateral pressures, and they often create conditions for—but seldom trigger—war. The proximate stimuli for crisis and war often emerge from subjectively generated perceptions, affects (fears, distrust, hostility, and so on), and human decisions (conditioned by and in response to situations shaped by processes of growth and competition).

Although the boundary between them is often difficult to define or recognize, competition tends to be transformed into conflict as leverages become negative, coercive, threatening, and violent. A conflict may emerge whenever two or more actors seek to possess the same object, occupy the same space or the same exclusive position, play incompatible roles, maintain incompatible goals, or undertake mutually threatening security measures. Whether or not such a trend is transformed into violence may depend upon whether or not the parties see themselves as basically compatible, whether or not the adversaries consider the stakes important, and whether or not they take concrete measures to resolve (or at least to reduce) their differences by switching from threatening, coercive, or violent leverages to more accommodative leverages (Smoke 1977, 278). Clearly, there can be conflicts over means as well as ends. It is not unusual for a "means" conflict to become so acute that it achieves more saliency than the initial disagreement over goals.

States, through their leaders and bureaucrats, bargain over and apply leverage in the implementation of policies (means) in pursuit of national ends. This observation may be as critical as it is obvious: In contrast to monocausal explanations of war and other conflictual (as well as cooperative and peaceful) outcomes, this perspective suggests multilevel (molecular–molar) hierarchies of explanation (hierarchies of what Popper viewed as "plastic" (that is, indeterminate) "causes" and "effects" (Popper 1979, 206–255). Predictions are thus severely limited by the consideration that—at whatever means/end level—B's response to A's leverage cannot be predicted or explained except in probabalistic terms. This dilemma draws attention to the conflict spiral, that part of the lateral pressure process most conducive to overt violence. Following a brief discussion of the lateral pressure phenomenon in comparative contexts, the conflict spiral and its dynamic components are traced in the next section.

THE CONFLICT SPIRAL

The phenomena of uneven growth, differential capability, demand, bargaining, and leverage can be visualized as fluctuating, interactive, converging variables—a dynamic "pyramid," so to speak, of interconnected empirical variables (with strong psychological components). When heads of state and other decisionmakers at the "peaks" of two such pyramids confront each other in an adversarial relationship, an action–reaction (or escalatory) process is likely to be set in motion, a process that can trigger large-scale violence. All of these variables originate with individual human beings responding to (and acting on) physical and social environments in recursive ways.

Action and Reaction Processes

Action–reaction phenomena, such as arms races, crises, outbreaks of war, and the transformation of limited wars into "all-out" wars, can be conceptualized as escalations of negative leverages applied by two (or more) adversaries in a conflict situation in which each side's field of expectation changes with the leverages applied at each step of escalation, each side's expectations and intents are not fully known to the other, and cognitive and psychological processes "filter" actions and intents. The arms race is a special type of escalation process in which an increase in A's military capabilities—whether undertaken as a form of deterrence or as a routine defense measure—is viewed by the leadership of rival state B as a threat to its security. When the military capabilities of B are increased in order to reduce or close the gap, A's leaders, perceiving the increase as a threat to their country's security, act to increase A's capabilities, and so the competition spirals. As the tendencies of A and B to respond in this way now become "intense and reciprocated," the bilateral competition processes tend to "interlock," thus yielding the action–reaction or escalation process (Huntington 1971, 499–531; Richardson 1960a, 15), in which suspicion and fear may be expected to multiply with the armaments (Wallace 1979, 242).

Studies of the arms race phenomenon can generally be classified into two groups: those emphasizing competitive action–reaction processes and those emphasizing domestic factors such as technology and bureaucratic or interest group pressures. Which perspective is closer to reality has become a source of debate. Empirical evidence suggests that both types of processes are significant (Choucri and North 1975, especially chap. 13). In terms of the security paradox, uneven development, lateral pressures, and the interactivity of states, however, it appears self-evident that the domestic factor and the action–reaction process are not necessarily antithetical. "Indeed, the explanation having the closest match with empirical observations may incorporate components from each" (Hollist 1977, 504). It is also possible that the action–reaction process may be the dominant explanation of a particular race at one stage, whereas domestic factors may dominate at some other stage. It would not be surprising to find such variability taking place within the same escalation through time and across countries.

From Escalation to Crisis and War

However the phenomenon of international crisis is defined, it almost always meets the criteria for an escalatory or action–reaction process. Thus, in an international crisis situation, escalatory interactions come about in part because the leaders of one country, *A*, perceive an action of country *B* as aggressive or threatening and undertake counterleverage in one form or another, which is then perceived as a threat by the leaders of *B*. If the leaders of *A* perceive *B*'s response as threatening, then they are likely to undertake further coercive action in hopes of deterring *B* and, thus, bringing relief. Or they may expect early changes in the crisis situation to be punishing but necessary enabling steps toward a more rewarding situation in the future. The expectation of such a reward may involve the avoidance or elimination of a punishing situation rather than an outcome that might be viewed as intrinsically rewarding (Moll and Luebbert 1980, 157; Hollist 1977, 504). Under the pressure of intense interchange, each response is likely to be "automatic and mindless," and each move is so swift that it can scarcely be distinguished from a reflex. It is under such circumstances that statesmen start saying, "We have no alternative" (von Bülow 1931, 165).

For every crisis that escalates into war, however, there are many others that "cool down" or deescalate. An action–reaction process may be expected to continue as long as at least one side perceives that the costs of deescalation exceed the costs of continued escalation; conversely, for a reversal of action–reaction process to occur, the costs of continued escalation must be assessed as exceeding the costs of deescalation by at least one side. Similarly, once a war is initiated, it can be expected to continue until at least one side decides that the risks and costs of additional hostilities outweigh the benefits.

LATERAL PRESSURE IN HISTORICAL AND CONTEMPORARY FRAMES

Origins of State Systems

Uneven growth and development, lateral pressure, bargaining and leverage, and the security dilemma may have contributed to the emergence of the state and thus helped to shape the war-prone characteristics of the modern state system. The origin of pristine states has been explained in various ways—some voluntaristic, some coercive. Within a growth-and-development framework, anthropologist Robert Carneiro's essentially coercive theory of the emergence of the state helps to clarify its "nature" and identify the sources of its power, the underpinnings of the security dilemma, and the adaptive development of the international and modern global systems (Carneiro 1970, 733–738). Carneiro postulated that, during prehistoric times, certain loosely organized, essentially voluntaristic kinship societies with growing populations (combined with advancing technologies) in several widely separated parts of the world circumscribed by mountains, deserts, seas, and/or high-density neighboring populations—in other words, societies experiencing severe pressure on resources—may have rallied behind war chiefs in order to plunder crops, seize land, and reduce their neighbors to slavery or serfdom.

As a result of such victories, a successful war chief could allocate conquered lands (and defeated villages) among leading members of his retinue and assign them the privileges of demanding tribute and levying taxes. Insofar as he commanded sufficient resources to retain a permanent retinue and a standing army (which was available for the maintenance of domestic "law," "order," and economic, political, and military "security")—a war chief could be well on his way to becoming a king or emperor.

By creating security dilemmas for adjoining societies, the presence of one such kingdom in a given locality sometimes inspired the establishment of rival kingdoms or of federated communities, some of which may have evolved into republican city-states.

Ancient state systems were plagued by a fundamental contradiction: Agrarian-based empires, although militarily strong, were able to retain the active loyalty of only a small proportion of their inhabitants, whereas city-states, while attracting the loyalty of their citizens, lacked the ability to extend their power and influence very far beyond their urban limits (Gilpin 1981, 116–118).

Beginning in the tenth and eleventh centuries, population increases combined with new technologies (many of them borrowed from Asia and the Middle East) contributed to a new commercialism (the foundations of capitalism) and new concentrations of power in the hands of European rulers. Fragments of the old Roman Empire began acquiring and putting together new surpluses—usually under the shrewd administration of an ambitious warlord—and economic activities increased. Western European populations expanded, and significant new technologies (many of them, such as the Indian concept of zero, accounting and credit practices from the Middle East, the mariner's compass, and others borrowed from other cultures) were put into practice. A new "spirit of enterprise" prepared the way for early capitalism and an aggressive mode of statecraft (McNeill 1982, 12–21, 150–151, 541–542). Perceiving a need for larger tax revenues as an instrument of power, monarchs of the time were persuaded to encourage and extend trade, which created a disposition toward enforcing property rights over greater areas (and, thus, expanding state control over quasi-independent feudal lords) and finding ways of internalizing some of the costs of long-distance commerce" (North and Thomas 1974, 35).

The joining of intense loyalty with administrative and legal control over large expanses of territory during the emergence of the nation-state made the international system as we know it today possible (Gilpin 1981, 116–118). Successive advances in technological change—such as shipbuilding and improvements in navigation—contributed to unprecedented lateral pressures. Distant regions of the globe were "discovered" and "explored" by Westerners. Areas were "opened" for colonization and exploitation, and the acquisitions included silks and spices from the East and gold and silver from the West. At about the same time, new military technologies, new organizational techniques, and modes of discipline—plus the availability of funds to hire mercenaries—provided a succession of European kings with an ability to concentrate their domestic capabilities, encourage trade according to the emerging tenets of mercantilism, and expand their territories, activities, interests, and power over much of the globe. Thereafter, with the close of the Thirty Years' War (1618–1648) and the Congress of Westphalia

(1648), the nation-state, the Western states system, and a continuing trend towards "globalization" were firmly established (Russett and Starr 1981, 47; Gilpin 1981, 29; McNeill 1982, 150).

Historical and Contemporary Expansionism

The expansion of the world's great empires from the remote to the more recent past provides examples of lateral pressure by territorial acquisition, as does the westward expansion of the United States and the eastward expansion of tsarist Russia. Since World War II most of the great overseas empires have disappeared, territorial expansion has been limited, and most lateral pressure has been manifested through economic activities (trade, aid, investment), routine diplomacy, the support of (or opposition to) revolutionary movements abroad, troops overseas, bases on foreign soil, espionage, and a wide range of covert operations.

Bargaining and leverage processes tend to be near the center of most lateral pressure phenomena—both private and governmental. In general, the expansion of private activities and interests tends to involve economic (agricultural, commercial, banking, investment), professional, and associated activities of individuals, family groups, professional associations, or corporations. The lateral pressures of government include bargaining and leverage activities pertaining to routine diplomatic interchanges, the implementation of national foreign policies, the protection of private and public activities and interests abroad, and, insofar as feasible, the extension of the national power *outreach*.

Configurations of Power

Balance of power is an ancient, venerable, but illusive concept that is still relied upon almost universally (Friedrich 1938, 119). As is well known, however, Ernst Haas identified several different meanings of the term (Haas 1971, 258–259), and according to Inis Claude, a balance-of-power statement conveys only the idea that states will always be in a power relationship with each other, either balanced or unbalanced (Claude 1962, 54). Not uncommonly, the term is used in a number of different ways (sometimes even by the same author in the same publication). A part of the difficulty comes from attempting to apply relatively static concepts to real-world relationships and structures that are "emergent," intensely dynamic, and derived from outcomes of a "totality of processes and vice versa" (Jantsch 1980, 41).

Determined to avoid reductionism, Kenneth Waltz and other neo-realists have excluded all second image factors that contribute to war except power (Waltz 1979, 73, 97–99) (in effect invoking a reductionism of their own) and have insisted upon an "outside-in" approach (Keohane 1986, 190–191) that places a heavy burden upon power distribution as a "cause" of war and other third image outcomes. Because sources of power and changes in power distribution are not specified or accounted for, this approach is not dynamic. In contrast, with the assumption of multicausality traceable through the interplay of a number of variables on both second- and third-image levels, an uneven-growth-and-development, bargaining-and-leverage lateral pressure approach avoids reductionism and allows for both "horizontal" (cross-national) and "vertical" change through time.

At any particular moment the prevailing configuration of "power" in the international system is an outcome of (1) uneven growth and development, (2) the relative and constantly shifting capabilities of countries (and coalitions) in the system, and (3) their bargaining and leverage activities (both positive and negative and continually subject to adjustments and possible transformation). In these terms, international structures may be viewed as asymmetrical and fluctuating relationships between nations of different capabilities with different bargaining and leverage potentials and activities. State structures, in turn, amount to asymmetrical relationships among individuals and coalitions of differing interests, capabilities, and bargaining and leverage potentials and activities. From this perspective, the existence and characteristics of an international structure—including any particular configuration (balance of power, bipolar, multipolar, or whatever)—must be viewed as an empirical consideration that can be investigated and demonstrated rather than "prespecified" (Haas 1982, 242).

Does a balance of power favor war or peace? Leading scholars in the field (as well as policymakers) can be found on both sides of this question. Because it is widely presumed that human relationships are seldom mono-causal, one might expect the implications of a balance-of-power or other configuration to vary according to its interplay with other relevant variables in a particular conflict situation. This observation draws attention to the variables that, in combination with power configurations, seem most likely to affect war-prone tendencies.

NATIONAL PROFILES AND THEIR IMPLICATIONS
FOR LATERAL PRESSURE

Domestic Capabilities and Constraints

Uneven growth and development within and between states contribute to differences in their "size," which economists and political scientists identify as a major factor in determining their relative capabilities and potentials for influencing each other. Used in this context, size is assessed in a number of different ways. Sometimes it means territorial extent, sometimes economic capability, and sometimes political or military power and influence. One way of assessing the relative size and capabilities of states is to compare their profiles, that is, the relationships between their respective levels and rates of change of population, technology, and resource availabilities (the extent and richness of its territory, for example, and/or the extent and strength of its trade network).

The following profiles are used as "ideals" or archetypes; they should not be taken too seriously. In using population density and per capita indicators (GNP per capita, imports and exports per capita, and so forth) we recognize that averages "hide" distributions and thus can be dangerously misleading. Profiles, moreover, are "horizontal" representations, high-speed snapshots, so to speak, of relationships at one cross-section of time, whereas each of the major dimensions—population, technology, territorial size, and so on—is subject to almost continual change (each at its own rate). The metaphor that comes to mind is that of a horse race in which the riders are the decisionmakers and the horses correspond to the national economies, polities, and capabilities of grossly varying sizes and potentials. For convenience we have designated the front-runners as Alphas, at least two of which are competing for the number one position. Behind them come the Betas, Gammas, and Deltas, each with its own problems, ambitions, and goals. Spread over the field behind are the also-rans, the Epsilons, Zetas, and Etas. Some of these are competing for positions among themselves; a few are pushing to industrialize and, thus, to achieve power, influence, and a higher standard of living (Betas, Gammas, or Deltas); the rest are struggling to stay in the race—staving off starvation, raising more food, improving public health and education, modernizing and gaining security and status in the world.

Crude and limited as it obviously is, this metaphor is useful for underscoring the advantages of power-transition theories as contrasted with balance-of-power and other static configuration approaches. If a rigorous definition of the concept is formulated and used consistently, a balance-of-power theory would seem to require provisions within it for dynamic and specifically interactive change. Short of such a formulation, available power-transition theories seem to provide a more promising basis for explaining and predicting the contribution of power differentials to issues of war and peace.

Profiles of Industrialized States

Overall, the "field" can be divided into two sets of profiles that are most conspicuously relevant: those that are characteristic of high-capability, strong lateral pressure, industrialized states at or near the "core" of the international system (the Alphas, Betas, Gammas, and Deltas) and those that are characteristic of the relatively low-capability societies (the Third World or developing Epsilon, Zeta, and Eta states of today) that have been targets, historically, for deep penetration, domination, exploitation, and often reduction to colonial or at least client status by more powerful states.[7]

ALPHA PROFILE: UNEVEN LEVELS AND COMMENSURATE RATES
OF GROWTH AND DEVELOPMENT IN POPULATION,
TECHNOLOGY, AND RESOURCE ACCESS
Countries with populations, technologies, and resource accesses that are "large" and advancing commensurately—that is, technological advancement maintains a substantial lead over population growth—are typically high lateral pressure states, the most powerful and influential in the international system. Pursuing economic, political, and strategic hegemony, Alpha countries may be expected to extend their trade, diplomatic activities, and strategic "defenses" further and further beyond their original boundaries. During their colonial periods, the British, French, and other Western European empires expanded their activities and interests over much of the globe. By the early twentieth century, however, Britain and France reached their apogees and were increasingly challenged by a newly united Germany and, in terms of population growth, technological advancements, and demonstrated capacities for expansion, by the United States and Japan.

BETA PROFILE: GROWING POPULATION, ADVANCING
TECHNOLOGY, AND INADEQUATE RESOURCES
The growing population of a Beta society is large (relative to its territory), and its technology is advancing commensurately, but access to resources is perceived as significantly impeded because (1) the domestic resource base appears to be too limited or inadequately endowed, (2) trade capacities do not seem to provide adequate resources from abroad, and (3) efforts to

expand trade and/or its resource base (by exploration, conquest, purchase, or other means) have not been taken or have been assessed as inadequate. Because of its rising demands for both consumer goods and raw materials for its manufactures, a society with this profile may be expected to feel economically insecure and under continuous pressure to expand its trade or, if that recourse is impeded or otherwise insufficient, to expand its territory by one means or another. Britain, France, Germany, Japan, and other empires of the past approximated the Beta profile prior to and during the early stages of their imperial expansion. Israel's profile is Betalike.

GAMMA PROFILE: DENSE POPULATION, ADVANCING TECHNOLOGY,
AND EXTERNAL RESOURCE ACCESS

A Gamma society differs from a Beta society to the extent that, although its domestic resource base remains severely limited, an extensive, high-volume, reasonably balanced trade network has been established and remains effectively secured. Britain, France, and Germany, all former Alpha countries, can be classified as Gamma countries today. Since World War II, Japan has achieved a Gamma profile by moderating its population growth, additionally developing its industrial technology, and expanding its imports, exports, and investments worldwide.

DELTA PROFILE: LOW DENSITY, ADVANCING TECHNOLOGY,
SECURE RESOURCE ACCESS

A state in which population has remained low relative to advancing technology and access to resources can be seen as having achieved a "moving" equilibrium (or dynamic steady state). Its Delta profile may be presumed to have come about because, in addition to its limited population growth, (1) the territorial base is rich in resources and/or (2) an effective trade network has been maintained and/or (3) technology has been used considerably for production (as opposed to consumption) and available resources have been managed in ways that have created new resources. Delta countries rank at or near the top in quality of life indicators and tend to avoid war unless invaded. Norway and Sweden approximate Delta profiles.

Profiles of Industrializing States

The low-capability societies of the world tend to fall into three major categories. Two of these—Epsilon and Zeta societies—are characteristically poor, developing, and vulnerable. Eta countries, by contrast, are rich but still "developing."

EPSILON PROFILE: DENSE AND GROWING POPULATION,
LAGGING TECHNOLOGY, LIMITED ACCESS TO RESOURCES

A country with a large and growing population approximates the Epsilon profile to the extent that its technology is lagging and its access to resources is limited either because its territorial base is limited or poorly endowed or because existing resources cannot be extracted (or even located, perhaps) with available knowledge and skills. During the nineteenth and early twentieth centuries the colonial possessions of the European empires (and later Japan) tended toward Epsilon profiles. Bangladesh, and El Salvador are examples of modern Epsilon states.

ZETA PROFILE: LOW DENSITY, "PRIMITIVE" TECHNOLOGY,
LIMITED RESOURCE ACCESS

In addition to the underdevelopment of their knowledge and skills and their poor access to resources, a sparsely populated Zeta-profile society possesses an extremely limited labor pool and lacks the critical mass of professional specialists needed to facilitate effective development. Possibilities for the expansion of activities and interests are severely constrained relative to those of societies with more favorable profiles, and starvation and disease are often endemic. Zeta states today include Chad and Mauritania.

ETA PROFILE: SPARSE POPULATION, RECENTLY IMPORTED
TECHNOLOGY, RICH RESOURCE BASE

An Eta country differs from a Zeta country in two critical respects: under one arrangement or another, it has acquired an advanced technology and the specialists required to operate it have been admitted from abroad. As a consequence, oil or some other valuable and hitherto unavailable resource has been obtained in large quantities, and the GNP has reached an extremely high level. Kuwait, Saudi Arabia, and the United Arab Emirates are current examples of Eta countries.

Profiles and Behavior

Identifying a country as belonging to one or another of these profile categories will reveal some of the major constraints shaping its behavior. Time-series analyses of the changing profiles and the behaviors of states of different profiles should provide a useful map of global system dynamics that can be used as a basis for estimating future growth, development, and conflict trends within the global system.

COMPETITION FOR POWER, INFLUENCE, AND GLOBAL DOMINANCE

Who Gets What, When, and How

To a large extent all countries compete for resources and for power and influence within the international system. There are vast differences, however, between the majority of countries, which are struggling to "catch up" in terms of social, economic, and political development, and the industrialized (and rapidly industrializing) states, which rely upon Third World nations for raw materials, cheap labor, and mass markets but compete, to a large extent, among themselves. Beyond this, characteristically, the two or three most powerful states engage in a specialized competition—a "king of the mountain" struggle—for dominance in the international and global systems. This "game" is illustrative of the power-transition phenomenon, the lateral pressure process, and the conflict spiral (Most and Siverson 1987; Doran 1983, 420; Rasler and Thompson 1983, 489–516).

Commonly, the second most powerful state challenges the "hegemon" (and its "security regime") while lesser states achieve and maintain a position on the slopes of the "global mountain" that reflects their relative capabilities. Insofar as a state's establishment of hegemony imposes its own characteristic bargaining, leverage, and disciplinary structures upon other states, a challenger's threat may be expected to initiate a period of instability, intense competition, and potentially disruptive conflict within the system. A number of theorists have been looking in particular for connections between economic cycles in the global (or "world") system, periods of war (and peace), and hegemonic successions.[8]

Virtually by definition, hegemons are high-capability, high lateral pressure states (or empires) characterized by large and growing populations, high and advancing technology, and substantial access to resources acquired either domestically, through an extensive trade network, or both—in short, Alpha states. True hegemons possess superior production, commercial, financial, and military capabilities. Challengers may also be Alpha states or Beta or Gamma states that are rapidly growing and developing and expanding their activities, interests, and power outreach.

The probabilities of hegemonic war may be expected to escalate insofar as (1) the leaders and influential sectors of the hegemon's population perceive their country's economic, political, and strategic dominance and security mortally threatened by the increasing capabilities and negative leverages of the challenger nation and (2) the leaders and influential sectors of the challenger's population who, aware of the hegemon's vulnerabilities, perceive an unprecedented opportunity for achieving economic, political, and strategic security for their own country by destroying the dominance of the hegemon.

A full-blown power transition (Organski and Kugler 1980, 19, 22, 25–27, 54, 244, fn. 8) occurs when the incumbent lacks the economic and/or political and/or military will and/or capability to defend and maintain its dominance against the thrust of its challenger(s). Notably, however, the initial challenger (Germany in 1914 and 1939, for example) may fail in its struggle for dominance, which may be achieved, in fact, by a power that did not overtly pursue hegemony (as the United States did in 1945, if not before).

The extent to which hegemonic wars and hegemonic successions are closely correlated with global economic cycles is an empirical question that remains to be settled satisfactorily. The "objective" circumstances conducive to the convergence of these two sets of perceptions may be expected to occur as the incumbent hegemon, having passed well beyond its apogee, suffers a decline relative to the expanding capabilities, activities, and interests of its challenger.

Power-transition concepts seem to go a long way toward accounting for the rise and fall of hegemons (Organski and Kugler 1980). If competition between a dominant state and its challenger is accepted as the primary determining factor, however, it is difficult to explain why neither World War I nor World War II was initiated by the United States, the country with the greatest potential for challenger status. Why was World War I "not waged between the United States and Great Britain, and World War II from the beginning between Germany and the United States?" (Värynen 1987, 334–337).

From a lateral pressure perspective, the answer would be that the main thrust of expanding U.S. activities, interests, and power outreach was westward and southwestward across the continent and eventually into the Pacific Basin. Not surprisingly, then, it was not until U.S. merchant shipping collided with German U-boats in the Atlantic that the country was drawn into World War I. Nor is it inconsistent that collisions of U.S. activities and interests with those of an expanding Japan should provide a rationale for the latter's attack on Pearl Harbor (Choucri and North 1988, especially chap. 14). The global patterns of extended U.S. and Soviet activities, interests, and respective power outreaches at war's end went a long way toward defining the hegemonic and challenger roles of the two countries, the shape of their alliance and client-state relationships, and the sectors of the globe where Cold War collisions were most likely to occur.

Individual states do not last forever. In the past, every great power has, sooner or later, suffered decline and extinction (the Roman Empire), transformation (the Chinese empires), or severe losses of territory, capability, and influence (the Spanish, Portuguese, French, British, and other major powers of recent times). Sources of decline include population growth without adequate technological advancement, overexpansion, a radical shift from capital to consumer industries, excessive military investment (as compared to investment in basic research and production, education, health, and the like), and the spread of organizational as well as production inefficiencies. Severe endemic inflation has often provided a reliable indicator of decline.

War Propensity and the Peace Paradox

High-capability, high lateral pressure countries (Alphas, Betas, and Gammas) fight more wars *per country* than developing nations (Epsilons, Zetas, and Etas), but more wars are fought in developing or Third World regions than in the more industrialized parts of the globe. High-technology, low-population (Delta) countries seem to fight the fewest, and when they *are* involved, they tend to have been invaded (as Norway was in World War II). There is a long history behind these tendencies. Although the nineteenth century is commonly referred to as a period of relative peace, from a global perspective it was far from peaceful. Quincy Wright listed 95 wars occurring in the course of the nineteenth century; 60 of these were fought in what are now referred to as the Third World regions of the globe, and many were civil wars, revolutions, border conflicts, and surrogate wars in which major powers were directly or indirectly involved (Wright 1968, 699, 956; Coser 1968, 231).

Because investigators often differ with respect to the criteria (casualty levels, for example) used to distinguish between crises, incidents, border conflicts, wars, major wars, all-out wars, and so forth, it is not as easy as one might expect to count and compare wars. Currently, a comparison of sources indicates that something over 130 wars of 1000 or more casualties were fought during the four decades following the termination of World War II. Except for the Soviet intervention in Hungary, all of these wars were fought in developing countries (see Sivard 1986). There is always the risk that a localized conflict, perhaps no more than a terrorist act, may escalate into a global war as major powers become involved—recall that World War I was triggered by the assassination of the Archduke Francis Ferdinand in Sarajevo.

From the lateral pressure perspective, the elusive characteristics of peace can be explained in part as corollaries of the security dilemma. To the extent that action taken by one country, A, to ensure its economic, political, or military security tends to be interpreted and responded to by another country, B, as a threat to *its own* economic, political, or military security, any move by one party to accommodate, compromise with, or "appease" the other runs the risk, to a comparable extent, of being interpreted either as a deception (to be wary of) or as a weakness (to be taken advantage of).

Is there any way to avoid or break out of this dilemma? For the purpose of reducing the probabilities (or the levels) of violence there appear to be two critical intervention points—one long range, the other more proximate.

In a global system of nations with grossly unequal capabilities, leverage potentials, and access to resources, one would expect conflict and predispositions toward violence to be endemic. To expect the achievement of profile changes sufficient to eradicate such inequities would be a chimera. Population management programs, however, combined with more even diffusions of technology and more equitable access to resources might alleviate the longer-term pressures substantially and, in the future, create more accommodative interstate relations and a more favorable global environment.

The more proximate intervention points will be located in the course of interactions between adversaries wherever one or the other is contemplating or deciding upon a move directed toward the other. In recent years a number of theoretical protocols have been advanced for application at such choice points. Within an extended lateral pressure context the problem is how to avoid or reverse an escalation of negative leverages.

In the early 1960s George Homans proposed "the secret of successful human interchange" as follows. A offers B behavior that he thinks will be more valuable for B than it is for himself in return for behavior that he thinks will be less valuable to B than it is to himself. To the extent that B responds reciprocally, the two have put in motion a process that, if pursued, may be expected to uncover compatible interests and induce further reciprocations (see Homans 1961, 62).

Overlapping and supplementing this formulation in specialized ways are social psychologist Charles Osgood's graduated reduction in international tension (GRIT) strategy (Osgood 1962; see also Mitchell 1966, 73–86) and Robert Axelrod's (1984) computerized tit-for-tat strategy. GRIT provides protocols for bargaining with an adversary without a loss of advantage prior to the achievement of a verifiable reciprocation. These and other bargaining, leverage, and negotiating strategies offer possibilities for testing in both laboratory and "real-world" conflict situations, for codifying, and, conceivably, for integrating appropriate protocols into a prescriptive theory useful for institution building and conflict containment and management.

LATERAL PRESSURE: LIMITATIONS AND POTENTIALS

Comparisons of Theoretical Orientations

One way of assessing the contributions and limitations of lateral pressure theory is to compare it briefly with major paradigms in the development of the field, namely, mercantilism, liberalism, Marxism–Leninism, and realism. The first three of these are political economy paradigms.

Mercantilism placed major emphasis upon the close relationship between wealth and power, the interdependence and ever-changing relationships between a state and its economy, and the central importance of expanded manufactures, foreign markets, and access to external resources. Political aspects of mercantilism were broadly generalized, however, and the interplay with economic considerations, which is, by implication, essentially zero sum, was not rigorously identified. As a theory, lateral pressure specifies such interconnections of economic and political factors and is not zero sum.

Classical liberal theory, emerging from comparative advantage (rather than zero-sum) assumptions, proceeded from a view that the nature of international economic relations is essentially harmonious and adaptive. Liberal theorists have tended to treat economics and politics as relatively separable and autonomous. Like mercantilists, liberal theorists have not paid much systematic attention to growth and capability changes within and across countries or the implications of competition for conflict and violence among states. Lateral pressure theory rejects the presumed autonomy of politics and economics and recognizes the conflict potentials of state interactions.

Marxism–Leninism is a dynamic theory, but the dialectic—the source of its dynamism—is difficult to specify rigorously. In a real-world situation, for example, it cannot be determined "scientifically" (but only dogmatically) which is the "thesis" and which is the "antithesis" in a conflict situation (as in the Sino-Soviet conflict when each side cited Marx and Lenin in support of its own position and charged the other as dominated by capitalist remnants). Further, the "economic determinism" of Marxism–Leninism allows no room for political leverage, bargaining, or coalition formation, which may reduce the constraints of economic factors (or, alternatively, increase them). Lateral pressure theory recognizes and makes explicit the interplay among these phenomena and the plasticity of actions, but makes no assumptions about the intentions of actors or the determination of specific outcomes (except probabilistically).

Realism, the dominant paradigm in the study of international relations, is rich in elements and theories of part (balance of power, bipolar, multipolar, imperialism, hegemony, and so forth). Because much of the conceptualization is not generic, however, there is widespread disagreement about meanings, the parts are seldom linked systematically, and the paradigm as a whole is notably splintered. Although power is located at the center of realist (and neorealist) theory, neither its sources nor its dynamics have been made sufficiently specific to allow the systematic comparison or persuasive testing of central hypotheses or component subtheories.[9]

Lateral pressure theory addresses the problem of the sources and consequences of power head on. Because it provides a framework of generic elements and processes, lateral pressure in its extended version is capable of encompassing key concepts of classical mercantilism and liberalism, as well as their modern variants, along with those of contemporary realism and neorealism. The "partial theory" is intensely dynamic. The framework accommodates (and allows the connection of) such processes of change as growth, decline, decision (conditioned by cognitions and affects), bargaining, leveraging, coalition formation, competition, adversarial identification, and conflict (violent and nonviolent). The dependence of all social undertakings on the intense interaction between economic and political processes can be made explicit. Similarly, warmaking and peacemaking can be accommodated within the framework, and their processes can be systematically linked.

Empirical Analysis

The challenge in submitting lateral pressure theory to the empirical test lies in the fact that the theory stresses the dynamic relationship between national attributes (profiles) and international activities. Because the theory seeks to articulate the strong interdependence, the feedback relationships, and the time-dependent processes, the analytical and methodological techniques appropriate for such contingencies must be utilized. Furthermore, in its verbal statement the theory stresses the nonlinearities in interstate interactions and the complexities of equifinal and multifinal realities, that is, many paths to the same outcomes and multiple outcomes due to similar sources. These complexities of the "real world" are difficult to capture.

The methodology we have adopted at the core of our research agenda is composed of three steps: first, the formulation of the theory in testable terms, by estimating a system of *simultaneous* equations; second, the simulation of the system of equations to "replicate" empirical reality; and third, to "exercise" the system or experiment with a variety of counterfactuals (that is, what would have happened if . . . ?). In terms of specific technique we principally have used econometric estimation, but we have also experimented with methods of simulating continuous complex systems (that is, system dynamics).

The choice of estimating and simulating a system of *simultaneous* equations represented an effort to apply economic methods to international relations. The estimation is driven by the belief that an appropriate representation of the relationships posited by the theory of lateral pressure was an essential and necessary first step in validation. The simultaneous estimation procedure allows—and forces—the analyst to specify the *components* of the system (that is, the particular modules or "pieces" of the model) that are supported by the attendant dependent and independent variables and then pulls the components together into an identifiable *system*. In this system the same variable can serve as an independent variable in one component and as a dependent variable in another. (Military expenditures, for example, can explain alliance formation as an independent variable and, *at the same time*, are influenced by alliances and other variables as well.) This interdependence (and, in many instances, the feedback relations) constitutes a more appropriate and realistic way of representing aspects of lateral pressure theory than does emphasizing of correlations alone or using single equation formulations with one dependent variable and several independent variables and no references to, or connections with, other components of the reality at hand.

Estimation is only the first step. The second is simulation, which seeks to recapture and recreate the characteristics of the system of estimated simultaneous equations. Because errors usually accumulate easily, simulating a system of *simultaneous* equations is not an easy task; it entails simulation without reference or resort to empirical or historical data. The *only* empirical observation is the first data point of each variable in the system of equations. *All* of the other observations are estimated simultaneously and *all* are simulated accordingly.

Once estimation and simulation are successfully completed (that is, with very small errors), the third step is to "exercise" the simulated system and to experiment with "what if" questions. (For example, what would be the effects on a country's military expenditures if it were not confronted by hostile alliances, or if the alliances were becoming increasingly strong or increasingly hostile?)

In terms of substance, our research agenda has proceeded in three phases, each phase reflecting our improved specification of the "theory" and an enhanced application of "methodology." The first phase ended with *Nations in Conflict* and tried to represent the elements of lateral pressure in econometric terms, estimating and simulating the parameters of a simultaneous equation. Studies of the European states prior to World War I and of the Scandinavian countries over the span of a century (1870–1970) provided clues to the differences between propensities for war and "peace systems."[10] Our concern has been less with specific events, such as the outbreak and conduct of war, than with general trends and processes. The analysis in *Nations in Conflict* focused explicitly on the sources of lateral pressure and on the impacts of expansion on military competition, alignments, and arms races. The procedure was to specify (1) the components of the model, (2) the description and rationale, (3) the measures used, and (4) the system of simultaneous equations. Then we estimated the coefficients for the simultaneous system and simulated the entire structure as a prerequisite for policy analysis and exploring counterfactuals in terms of "what if" questions.

The procedure for moving from verbally articulated theory (through the written word) to formal representation and empirical analysis (through equation specification, estimation, and simulation) are sketched out briefly in Table 12.1 and in Figure 12.1. Table 12.1 presents the steps to be taken *prior to quantitative* analysis for the research reported in *Nations in Conflict*. These involve specifying the *components* of the model (because the theory addresses complex relationships, both internal and external), the description or rationale for *decomposing* the system as we have done (that is, providing the theoretical justification for the specification of the system of *simultaneous* equations), and the *measure* or indicator used to depict the dependent variable in this particular component, that is, with the full expectation that this variable may be (and, in fact, often is) specified also as an independent variable in another equation. Figure 12.1 depicts the relationships in the model in diagram form. Clearly, the diagram is a highly parsimonious rendition of complex processes; nonetheless, this mode of inquiry generated several important findings and insights.

Table 12.2 represents the econometric equations whose parameters are then estimated empirically; after the parameters are estimated, the system is simulated and a variety of theoretically driven questions are explored. These equations correspond to the diagram in Figure 12.1 and can be thought of as a fourth column in Table 12.1. We emphasize that the equations in Table 12.2 are derived step by step through the procedures outlined here. Therefore, inferring the theory from only a reading of the equation could be tantamount to misplaced empiricism. The equations and the coefficients estimated represent and depict a theory about reality. The equations themselves are signals of reality; they are not the reality itself.

The second phase in our research agenda focused explicitly on simulation and forecasting. The purpose was to model the highly interactive features of the lateral pressure process by first stressing the major feedback loops, then forecasting over the data base, and then forecasting beyond the

TABLE 12.1
Description of the Quantitative Analysis Reported in Nations in Conflict

Components of the model	Description–rationale	Measure[a]
Expansion	Demands resulting from the interactive effects of population and technological growth give rise to activities beyond national borders	Colonial area
Conflict of interest	Expanding nations are likely to collide in their activities outside national boundaries; such collisions have some potential for violence	Metricized measure of violence in *intersections* (conflicts specifically over colonial issues) between major powers
Military capability	States, by definition, have military establishments; these grow as a result of domestic growth and competition with military establishments of other nations	Military budgets
Alliance	Nations assess their power, resources, and capabilities in comparison with other nations and attempt to enhance themselves through international alliances	Total alliances
Violence–behavior	Nations engage in international violence as a consequence of expansion, military capability, and alliances	Metricized measure of violence in actions directed toward all other nations[b]

SOURCE: Choucri and North (1975, 25).
[a] Data are established for *each* nation and aggregated *annually* for the years 1870–1914. See Appendix A for details on measurement and sources of data.
[b] Target nations include not only the six major powers in the study, but all states.

existing record. The emphasis was on future developments of the system (see Choucri and Robinson 1978). Studies of the U.S. case (1930–1970) illustrated the essential interactions between the demand and capability components of lateral pressure, "pushing" the system outward. In the course of this work we learned the essential differences and contributions of each mode of modeling, simulation, and forecasting by experimenting with system dynamics as a methodology in contrast to econometrics estimation and simulation (Choucri and Bousfield 1978).

The challenge of modeling system dynamics lies in representing appropriately the characteristics of a system and the positive and negative feedback relations that shape its behavior. This is rather difficult to do; the analyst first specifies the major and minor loops, primarily on theoretical grounds

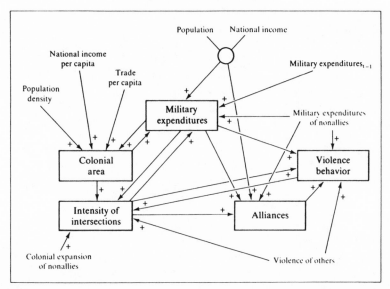

FIGURE 12.1. *Dynamics of international violence: the model. From Choucri and North (1975, 245).*

and the nature of the signs, and then the impacts in terms of the behavior of the system over time. The ingenuity, in this case, is to determine how realistic the model behavior is and how viable these relationships remain over periods of time. The essence of this phase of our research is analyzing the *dynamic* relationships—the interconnections of the complex realities regarding national profiles and external activities that are represented in a simplified way by the theory of lateral pressure.

The third phase in our research agenda focused on the transformations of national profiles over time and the implications for patterns of international activities. National attributes change over time—some nations grow and expand, others may decay and deteriorate—and their activities are, according to the theory of lateral pressure, intimately related to and dependent upon their population/resource/technology profiles. The case we have chosen to explore in great depth is Japan over a 100-year period (Choucri and North 1986). Still in prepublication form, the Japan study developed a system of simultaneous equations to represent the process of lateral pressure during three phases over the span of the century: (1) from the Meiji restoration to World War I, when Japan gradually transformed itself from an Epsilon profile into a Betalike profile, (2) from World War I to World War II, when Japan exhibited all the characteristics of a Beta profile, and (3) from the end of World War II to the contemporary global economic

TABLE 12.2
The Japan Model: 1876–1941

Component of the model	Description and rationale	Measure	Equation
Growth	National productivity resulting from economic performance, population activity, and domestic resource exploitation	Exports of finished goods	$\alpha_1 + \beta_{11}$ (imports of raw materials) $+ \beta_{12}$ (percentage of industrial laborers in total labor force) $+ \beta_{13}$ (production of coal) $+ \beta_{14}$ (previous year's balance of trade) $+ \beta_{15}$ (proportion of colonial imports to total imports) $+ \mu_1$
Resource demand	Demands for raw materials resulting from interactive effects of population growth, technological development, economic productivity, and domestic resource exploitation	Imports of raw materials	$\alpha_2 + \beta_{21}$ (exports of finished goods) $+ \beta_{22}$ (proportion of colonial imports to total imports) $+ \beta_{23}$ (population of Japan proper) $+ \beta_{24}$ (previous balance of trade) $+ \mu_2$
Military capability	States, by definition, have military establishments; these grow as a result of internal and external pressures and as a consequence of the pursuit of national objectives and valued scarce and valued resources	Army expenditures	$\alpha_3 + \beta_{31}$ (Russian military expenditure, a dummy variable of Russia as a potential enemy) $+ \beta_{32}$ (colonial area) $+ \beta_{33}$ (proportion of colonial imports to total imports) $+ \beta_{34}$ (previous year's army expenditures) $+ \beta_{35}$ (government revenue) $+ \mu_3$
		Navy expenditures	$\alpha_4 + \beta_{41}$ (U.S. navy expenditures, a dummy variable of the United States as a potential enemy) $+ \beta_{42}$ (British navy expenditure, a dummy variable of Britain as a potential enemy) $+ \beta_{43}$ (imports of raw materials) $+ \beta_{44}$ (colonial area) $+ \beta_{45}$ (proportion of colonial imports to total imports) $+ \beta_{46}$ (previous year's navy expenditures) $+ \beta_{47}$ (government revenue) $+ \mu_4$
Expansion in trade mode	Resource demands result in expansion of behavior outside national boundaries in search for external control and resource acquisition	Proportion of colonial imports to total imports	$\alpha_6 + \beta_{61}$ (tonnage of merchant marines) $+ \beta_{62}$ (national income) $+ \beta_{63}$ (military expenditures) $+ \beta_{64}$ (colonial area) $+ \beta_{65}$ (food imports per capital) $+ \mu_6$
Expansion in territorial mode	Extension of behavior outside territorial boundaries results in control over alien territories; such control occurs to the extent that there are demands to be satisfied and capabilities to pursue these demands	Colonial area	$\alpha_5 + \beta_{51}$ (military expenditures) $+ \beta_{52}$ (imports of raw materials) $+ \beta_{53}$ (imports of food per capita) $+ \beta_{54}$ (population of Japan proper) $+ \mu_5$
		Government expenditures for administration of controlled territories	$\alpha_7 + \beta_{71}$ (government revenue) $+ \beta_{72}$ (proportion of colonial imports to total imports) $+ \beta_{73}$ (colonial area) $+ \mu_7$

dominance, when Japan became transformed into a Gamma society (Choucri and North 1988).[11] Japan is particularly instructive in that it illustrates *changes* in a national profile and their implications for forms and modes of lateral pressure.

The methodology we have pursued is analogous to, but much more theoretically sophisticated and with greater empirical specification than, *Nations in Conflict* because it combines historical analysis and quantitative methods (estimation, simulation, and counterfactual analysis). From this study we have enriched our theoretical understanding of shifts in modes of lateral pressure and explored what would (or could) happen if Japan had adopted different policies or had been confronted by different adversaries. However, we have yet to model rigorously the connections between short-term events, such as a provocative act, and their underlying long-term causal structure relating national profiles to international activities.

Some comparative—and illustrative—findings from the World War I (1870–1914) and Japanese (1878–1914, 1914–1941) cases have contributed to our understanding of the different sources and modes of lateral pressure, including the ways in which different explanatory variables in varying combinations have contributed to similar outcomes across countries and through time.

In general, the findings of *Nations in Conflict* and the Japan study were comparable with respect to the exogenous variables leading to lateral pressure, that is, (1) those variables reflecting growth, domestic demands, and capabilities and their impact on external expansion which is indicated by territorial expansion, and (2) results relating to military and naval competitions (as indicated by Japan's military and naval expenditures and those of its adversaries) and arms and naval races.

Our study of the origins of World War I focused on one particular mode of lateral pressure: colonial acquisitions. From 1870 to 1914, British colonial expansion was best explained by population density, technology (national income per capita, but only in the earlier years), and (subsequently) by military expenditures and (for the whole period) a coefficient representing colonial size in 1870. The fact that technology was significant only during the earlier years and military expenditures were significant especially during the later years suggests a transition from domestically driven lateral pressure to a "mix" of arms competition.

For Germany, Britain's major competitor during pre-1914 decades, colonial expansion was best explained by population density and national income per capita—although for most of the period, population density was more important. The fact that military expenditures were not significant seems to indicate that German colonial expansion was not driven predominantly by military competition.

Although Japan played a relatively minor role in World War I, the Japanese had been acquiring colonies for two decades, and the country's patterns were roughly similar to those of the other three countries. Home population and national income did not contribute directly to Japanese colonial expansion, but population growth had a major positive impact on imports of raw materials, which was the main predictor of colonial area for the 1878–1914 period.

Between 1915 and 1941, on the other hand, military expenditure was the only significant variable predicting Japanese colonial area. This shift in pattern suggests a transition from lateral pressure generated by resource demand to a pattern of military investment in the face of perceived Soviet and U.S. opposition to Japanese territorial expansion (*in pursuit of raw materials*). During this period, at least, Japanese military expenditures appear to have contributed more strongly to colonial expansion than in the European cases; such expenditures played only a minor role in explaining British colonial area and failed to be significant in determining German colonial expansion.

Treated as "causal" variables, military and naval expenditures function as major precursors of war, and in all cases the influence of domestic factors—growth and bureaucratic pressures—were determinants of expenditure levels. In the British case military expenditures were explained during the earlier years (1871–1890) by the interactive effects of population and technology (indicated by national income) and, to a lesser extent, by an indicator of the hostility level in the intersections of spheres of influence with other powers. During later years (1891–1914) the influential variables were the bureaucratic effect (the military expenditures of previous years) and the military expenditures of nonallies (countries not allied with Britain).

The intersections and the military spending of nonallied countries were not significant variables in the German case, but Germany's military expenditures for the whole 45-year period were shaped by population combined with technology (national income) and the bureaucratic effect (military expenditures at $t - 1$). Also important was a coefficient representing an initial level of expansion that could or would have been reached if the explanatory variables had not been constrained in the "real" world.

Japan's military spending could be traced to lateral pressure together with competition for territory (and armed conflict off and on after 1905) with Russia/the USSR, arms race behavior, and intersections with the expanding activities and interests of other powers including Britain, Russia, and the United States.

The naval race patterns of Britain, Germany, and Japan were also comparable. Overall, the influence of internal factors was especially strong in the British and German cases. Britain's naval expenditures were shaped primarily by domestically driven bureaucratic process (previous naval spending) and, to a much lesser degree, by population times national income and intersections, neither of which was statistically significant. Germany's naval expenditures were best explained by the interactive effects of population and technology (national income). The level of intersections was a significant negative predictor of military expenditures. The intercept term was positive and significant, reflecting an already strong influence of naval allocations during phases of the overall period.

Japanese naval expenditures for the whole period (1878–1941) were best explained by U.S. naval expenditures (when the United States was perceived as a potential threat), its government revenue, and its past naval expenditures. Raw material imports and colonial area surprisingly showed a strong *negative* influence on the country's naval expenditures. The negative sign may indicate an increasing reliance on land warfare as Japanese colonial holdings (and access to raw materials) expanded and dampened elements (a negative feedback loop that constitutes a small but conceivably important component in the overall model). When this link is integrated into the overall picture (Figure 12.2), the spiraling dynamics leading to conflict appear much stronger than the discrete, negative, dampening linkages.

With respect to simulation and exploring what could have happened under alternative conditions (that is, the counterfactuals), we found that removing Japanese perceptions of Russia/the USSR as a threat greatly altered Japan's army expenditures: no buildup occurred during the 1930s when the model was simulated with "Russia as a threat" set at zero. By contrast, removing the "United States as a threat" had little or no impact on Japan's navy expenditures. The latter experiment suggests that the conflict spiral and armament levels were influenced largely by factors other than perception of adversaries. Japan's own budgetary variables were more important than responses to the adversary. Noteworthy is the finding that, prior to 1941, Japan's response to Russia/the USSR was strong, but its sensitivity to the United States navy prior to 1941 was significantly less so.

There is only one period in which we can compare directly the results of simulation for Japan and Great Britain: prior to 1914. We found the impact of bureaucratic momentum to have been more influential in the case of Britain than in the case of Japan. While increasing the coefficient of previous years' military expenditures in the British model led to a massive increase in the simulated level of military spending, analogous increases in the level of the military expenditures $(t-1)$ in the Japanese case had less impact overall and very little impact on the simulated levels of spending for later decades. Other variables influencing military (specifically army) spending in the Japan model—colonial area, imports from the colonies, and especially

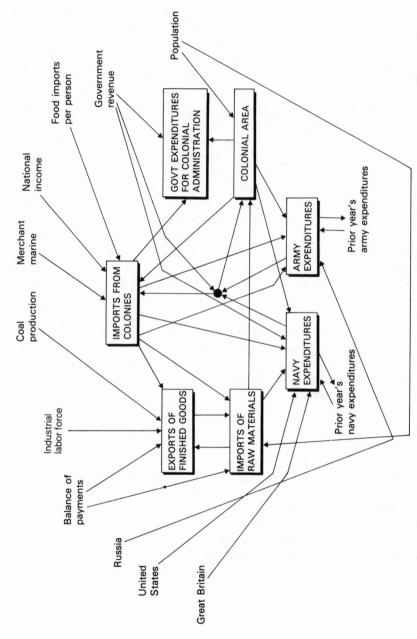

FIGURE 12.2. *The Japan model from the Meiji Restoration to World War II: An overview of the entire system.*

the "Russian threat"—seem to be stronger. Overall, we have found the simulation results to be fairly robust (that is, nonvarying) against changes in the level of previous military spending. This means that the path or trajectory of expenditures was very strong, resisting change in the type of policy experiments (or counterfactuals) we have explored.

The fourth phase of our research agenda is our current work on global analysis. By taking into account all entities in an international system as well as flows of an environmental nature, we expect to obtain a more comprehensive view of the processes of growth, expansion, and conflict.

Review and Assessment

The first two phases of our research program have been reviewed by a number of scholars since publication of *Nations in Conflict*. In retrospect, we see these critiques as falling into two general categories. First are those criticisms that we consider essentially trivial and nonilluminating, such as disagreements over a particular coefficient or a variable or debates over functional form. There is always room for improvement, but the criteria for judgment and evaluation must be rendered explicit, and this is what we have tried to accomplish. By contrast, there are critiques that are derived from attempts to replicate our analysis but that, in fact, do not actually undertake what would be considered a replication. Specifically, because the theory of lateral pressure stresses the interconnections, the dynamic linkages, and the feedback relations and simultaneities of influences linking internal and external factors, any replication efforts or tests of the theory must involve the use of methodology appropriate to the theoretical directives. The use of bivariate linear equations to test our theory or to replicate our work is simply incorrect. The models we have developed are explicitly formulated in a *dynamic, simultaneous system of jointly dependent variables*. We view inferences drawn from bivariate correlation coefficients as logically and methodologically indefensible for testing or assessing the work we have done. In some cases, critiques of our work have even more seriously confused multicolinearity among variables (that is, a high degree of positive correlation in the model) with a system of simultaneous equations.[12]

Second are those criticisms that have focused on the theoretical underpinnings of lateral pressure and reflected on the conceptual problems.[13] These we recognize and greatly appreciate.[14] We are especially grateful for the observations given to improve theoretical specification and to help generate a more elegant theoretical structure. However, occasional allegations of "determinism," we believe, are misplaced because they obscure the interaction at every stage of activity between factors that shape

and constrain a nation's profile (population, technology, access to resources, relative capabilities, and so forth—factors in which human decision
is implicit), on the one hand, and the policy choices that can be undertaken
at critical points, on the other.

Our more important self-criticisms, many of them presented in *Nations
in Conflict*, are theoretical and analytical.[15] We have yet to examine the
data more fully (reporting in greater detail on patterns displayed by
discrepancies between the hypothesized and the actual results, for instance,
the residuals) and improve on the specification of the relations between the
national profile, the form of lateral pressure, and the conflict spiral. The
system of simultaneous equations described here requires considerable
improvement. Initially, we had a tendency to aggregate key relationships
(such as combining imports and exports in a total trade variable). Some of
our indicators could be improved upon, and the quality of available
historical data often leaves much to be desired. So far we have investigated
only bits and pieces of the overall dynamic system we hope to explore. But
the more we probe, the deeper is our conviction that these relationships are
not simple and can only be examined with appropriate techniques that
recognize and accommodate these complexities.

Finally, we share with our colleagues in this field (and others) the
limitations of human possibilities for ascertaining "objective knowledge."
The investigator, like any other observer, must recognize the extent to
which the only access any of us has to "reality" is through our central
nervous systems and the extent to which observing and investigating an
aspect of reality tend to alter reality. Karl Popper stated that all objective
knowledge of human affairs was more "cloudlike" than "clocklike" and,
hence, indeterminate, "plastic," equifinal, multifinal, and probabilistic. It
seems to follow that *all* theories in the social sciences are, at best,
approximations. This recognition need not (indeed should not) inhibit our
investigations. With appropriate caveats, even simplified models can help us
understand indeterminate realities, but conclusions must remain tentative.
We are inclined, therefore, toward the Lakatosian view of "progressive
problem shifts" in which the possibility always exists that two or more
theories (or elements thereof) may cumulate, recombine, and undergo a
transformation to yet another level of understanding.

We believe that with the analytical tools and modes of analysis currently
at hand, the extended lateral pressure framework still remains too inclusive,
extensive, and loosely joined to be fully tested as a general theory. Its major
strength, in our view, lies in the fact that the processes disputed by most
international and global theories can, in principle, be identified and located
within this broader framework. The framework remains sensitive, moreover, to the testing—*within it*—of existing ("quasi," "partial") theories. A

comprehensive framework is, for us, extremely helpful in reminding us of the lay of the land and pushing for internal consistency among its components. When major theoretical inconsistencies or empirical contradictions or inconsistencies arise, the challenge becomes one of recognizing and explaining these discrepancies. For the time being, at least, we assume that this will be the most useful way to proceed; for example, testing two or more contradictory propositions or theories within the extended lateral pressure framework may force theoretical reformulation, enrich the generic framework itself, and lead step by step toward a more parsimonious synthesis. While recognizing that the indeterminacies of international and global politics cannot be eliminated, we *do* expect the lateral pressure approach to reduce their range substantially and to help us appreciate what we do and do not "understand."

Among the candidate theoretical orientations most relevant for "testing" and identifying contradictory or supportive results are theories of arms race and competition, theories of hegemonic stability, and theories of power transition. Each of these theoretical approaches addresses a *particular aspect* of the relations among nations that is articulated in the theory of lateral pressure. In so far as these theories intersect, to some extent they are only partially competitive with each other. It is a challenging research task to determine both theoretically and empirically, for example, when and under what conditions theories of hegemonic stability are more (or less) parsimonious explanations of the relations among nations than are theories of power transition. The modular approach to theory building and theory testing, which was labeled decades earlier as "islands of theory" (Guetzkow 1950) is particularly applicable because the theory of lateral pressure enables systematic incorporation, comparison, and testing of contending "pieces" of a broader puzzle of causes of war and conditions for peace.

NOTES

1. This chapter reports on the lateral pressure theory only in reference to international relations, but the process specified by the lateral pressure theory is general and operative at every level and context of analysis. We are grateful to Sung Joon Roh for his insightful research assistance and to Elizabeth McLaughlin for assistance in manuscript preparation.

2. For an analysis of evidence on the relationship of population and conflict, see Choucri (1974) and (1984).

3. For example, Albert Hirschman, in distinguishing between the supply effect (foreign trade undertaken for commercial, industrial, and consumer purposes in general) and influence effect ("carrot" and "stick" trade manipulations), examined the application of economic leverages by the Nazis in their expansion activities in World War II.

4. The word *linkage* is defined as "a recurrent sequence of behavior that originates on one side of the boundary between two systems and becomes connected in some way with phenomena on the other side in the process of unfolding."

5. The international oil and energy markets and the conflicts in them are illustrative. For a simulation model of international exchanges in energy resources, see Choucri and Ross (1981).

6. These explanations have focused on domestic migration from the economic perspective and are largely based on wage differentials; the treatment of international migration, therefore, has been scanty (see, for example, Lucas 1981; Bohning 1983, 1984). For a new interpretation of international migration from the vantage points of international relations and political economy, see Choucri (1987).

7. This labeling procedure is used only to reduce the affect bias in characterizing states.

8. Long wave or cycle theories can be classified in terms of (1) long-term economic fluctuations such as capital investment (Kondratieff 1928; Forrester 1979), technical innovation (Schumpeter 1939; Freeman *et al.* 1982), capitalist crisis (Trotsky 1923; Mandel 1980), and war (Silberling 1943) or (2) their relationship to war (see Modelski 1978, 1981, and Thompson and Zuk 1982, with respect to "leadership cycle"; Hopkins and Wallerstein 1979, Bousquet 1980, and Vayrynen 1983, in terms of "world system"; and Organski and Kugler 1980, Doran and Parsons 1980, and Gilpin 1981, as to "power transition"). For a summary of the debate and some empirical tests, see Goldstein (1985).

9. For a recent reinterpretation of realism and neorealism, see Keohane (1986).

10. For a discussion of the "peace systems" exhibited by these states, see Choucri (1972).

11. The purpose of model is to formalize and then estimate the relationships between the domestic sources of lateral pressure, on the one hand, and the modes of lateral pressure, on the other, as well as sensitivity to other competing states.

12. For an example of the reviews that contain methodological criticism of this kind, see Zuk (1985).

13. Special recognition is accorded to Hayward R. Alker, Jr. for his continued critique and contribution to theory development.

14. In a seminar at Harvard University in 1986, Ernst Haas made perceptive reference to a critical feature of lateral pressure theory, namely, that it "confounds Rousseau" by addressing the problem of national "happiness" leading to "international unhappiness." The subtitle of *Nations in Conflict* alludes to the generic dilemma.

15. For early self-criticism and a progress report of methodological development and theorizing, see Choucri and North (1975, 278–282) and Choucri and North (1972, 115–122).

Bibliography

ABELSON, R. P. 1964. Mathematical Models of the Distribution of Attitudes under Controversy. In *Contributions to Mathematical Psychology*, eds. N. Frederiksen and H. Gulliksen. New York: Holt, Rinehart.
———— 1979. Social Clusters and Opinion Clusters. In *Perspectives on Social Network Research*, ed. P. W. Holland and S. Leinhardt. New York: Academic Press.
ABRAVANEL, M., and B. HUGHES. 1975. Public Attitudes and Foreign Policy Behavior in Western Democracies. In *The Analysis of Foreign Policy Outputs*, ed. W. Chittick. Columbus, OH: Charles Merrill.
ACHEN, C. 1978. Measuring Representation. *Public Opinion Quarterly* 42:455–510.
———— 1983. Toward Theories of Data: The State of Political Methodology. In *Political Science: The State of the Discipline*, ed. A. W. Finifter. Washington, DC: American Political Science Association.
ACKERMAN, E. A. 1966. Population and Natural Resources. In *The Study of Population*, ed. P. Hauser and O. Duncan. Chicago: University of Chicago Press.
ALLISON, G. 1970–71. Cool It: The Foreign Policy of Young America. *Foreign Policy* 1:144–160.
ALMOND, G. 1950. *The American People and Foreign Policy*. New Haven, CT: Yale University Press.
ALT, J. E. 1979. *The Politics of Economic Decline*. Cambridge: Cambridge University Press.
ALT, J. E., and K. A. CHRYSTAL. 1983. *Political Economy*. Berkeley, CA: University of California Press.
ALTFELD, M. 1983. Arms Races?—and Escalation? A Comment on Wallace. *International Studies Quarterly* 27:225–231.
———— 1984. The Decision to Ally: A Theory and Test. *Western Political Quarterly* 37:523–544.
ALTFELD, M., and B. BUENO DE MESQUITA. 1979. Choosing Sides in Wars. *International Studies Quarterly* 23:87–112.
ALTFELD, M., and W. PAIK. 1986. Realignment in ITOs: A Closer Look. *International Studies Quarterly* 30:107–114.
ANDERSON, P. A. 1983. Decision-Making by Objection and the Cuban Missile Crisis. *Administrative Science Quarterly* 28:201–222.
ANDERSON, P. A., and T. J. McKEOWN. 1987. Changing Aspirations, Limited Attention, and War. *World Politics* 40:1–29.
ANDERTON, C. 1985. A Selected Bibliography of Arms Race Models and Related Subjects. *Conflict Management and Peace Science* 8:99–122.
———— 1986. *Arms Race Modeling: Systematic Analysis and Synthesis*. Ph.D. thesis, Cornell University, Ithaca, New York.
ARON, R. 1967. *Peace and War*. New York: Praeger.
———— 1968. *Progress and Disillusion: The Dialectics of Modern Society*. New York: Praeger.

ART, R. 1973. Bureaucratic Politics and American Foreign Policy: A Critique. *Policy Sciences* 4:467–490.

ART, R., and R. JERVIS, eds. 1973. *International Politics*. Boston: Little, Brown.

ASCHER, W. 1978. *Forecasting: An Appraisal for Policy-Makers and Planners*. Baltimore: Johns Hopkins University Press.

ASHLEY, R. K. 1980. *The Political Economy of War and Peace: The Sino-Soviet-American Triangle and the Modern Security Problematique*. New York: Nichols.

AXELROD, R. 1977. Argumentation in Foreign Policy Settings. *Journal of Conflict Resolution* 21:727–756.

———— 1984. *The Evolution of Cooperation*. New York: Basic Books.

BAIROCH, P. 1979. Europe's Gross National Product: 1800–1975. *Journal of European Economic History* 5:273–337.

BARRINGER, R. 1972. *War: Patterns of Conflict*. Cambridge, MA: MIT Press.

BEAL, R. S., and R. H. HINCKLEY. 1984. Presidential Decision Making and Opinion Polls. *Annals of the American Academy of Social Science: Polling and the Democratic Consensus* 472:72–84.

BECK, D., and B. BUENO DE MESQUITA. 1985. Forecasting Policy Decisions: An Expected Utility Approach. In *Corporate Crisis Management*, ed. S. Andriole. New York: Petrocelli.

BEFU, H. 1977. Social Exchange. *American Review of Anthropology* 6:255–281.

BELL, C. 1985. Managing to Survive. *The National Interest* 1:36–45.

BENSON, J. M. 1982. The Polls: U.S. Military Intervention. *Public Opinion Quarterly* 46:592–598.

BERGESEN, A., ed. 1983. *Crises in the World System*. Beverly Hills, CA: Sage.

BERGHAHN, V. R. 1973. *Germany and the Approach of War in 1914*. New York: St. Martin's.

BERKOWITZ, B. 1983. Realignment in International Treaty Organizations. *International Studies Quarterly* 27:77–96.

———— 1985. Proliferation, Deterrence, and the Likelihood of Nuclear War. *Journal of Conflict Resolution* 29:112–136.

BLAINEY, G. 1973. *The Causes of War*. New York: Free Press.

BLANNING, T. C. W. 1986. *The Origins of the French Revolutionary Wars*. London: Longmans.

BLUM, J., R. CAMERON, and T. G. BARNES. 1966. *A History of the European World*. Boston: Little, Brown.

BODIN, J. 1955. *Six Books of the Commonwealth*, trans. M. J. Tooley. Oxford: Basil Blackwell.

BOHNING, W. R. 1983. International Migration: A Suggested Typology. *International Migration Review* 122:641–650.

———— 1984. *Studies in International Labor Migration*. London: Macmillan.

BOULDING, K. E. 1956. *The Image*. Ann Arbor, MI: University of Michigan Press.

———— 1962. *Conflict and Defense*. New York: Harper.

BOUSQUET, N. 1980. From Hegemony to Competition: Cycles of the Core? In *Processes of the World-System*, ed. T. K. Hopkins and I. Wallerstein. Beverly Hills, CA: Sage.

BRAMS, S. 1985. *Superpower Games: Applying Game Theory to Superpower Conflict*. New Haven, CT: Yale University Press.

BRICKMAN, P., and D. T. CAMPBELL. 1971. Hedonic Relativism and Planning the Good Society. In *Adaption-Level Theory*, ed. M. H. Appley. New York: Academic Press.

BRITO, D. L. 1972. A Dynamic Model of an Armaments Race. *International Economic Review* 13:359–375.

———— 1973. Some Applications of the Maximum Principle to the Problem of an Armaments Race. *Modeling and Simulation* 4:140–144.

———— 1974. Uncertainty and the Stability of the Armaments Race. *Annals of Economic and Social Measurement* 3:279–292.

BRITO, D. L., and M. D. INTRILIGATOR. 1972. A General Equilibrium Model of the Stability of an Armaments Race. *Proceedings of the Sixth Asilomar Conference on Circuits and Systems*, Pacific Grove, CA.

———— 1973. Some Applications of the Maximum Principle to the Problem of an Armaments Race. *Modeling and Simulation* 4:140–144.

———— 1974. Uncertainty and the Stability of the Armaments Race. *Annals of Economic and Social Measurement* 3:279–292.

———— 1985. Conflict, War, and Redistribution. *American Political Science Review* 79:943–957.

———— 1987a. Deterrence May Require Mixed Strategies. In *Challenges to Deterrence in the 1990's*, ed. S. Cimbala. New York: Praeger.

———— 1987b. Arms Races and the Outbreak of War: Application of Principal–Agent Relationships and Asymmetric Information. In *Peace, Defense and Economic Analysis*, eds. C. Schmidt and F. Blackaby. London: Macmillan.

BRODIE, B., ed. 1946. *The Absolute Weapon*. New York: Harcourt Brace.

———— 1959. *Strategy in the Missile Age*. Princeton, NJ: Princeton University Press.

BRODY, R. A. 1966. Cognition and Behavior: A Model of International Relations. In *Experience, Structure and Adaptability*, ed. O. J. Harvey. New York: Springer.

———— 1984. International Crises: A Rallying Point for the President? *Public Opinion* 6:41–43, 46.

BRODY, R. A., and B. PAGE. 1975. The Impact of Events on Presidential Popularity: The Johnson and Nixon Administrations. In *Perspectives on the Presidency*, ed. Aaron Wildavsky. Boston: Little, Brown.

BRODY, R. A., and C. R. SHAPIRO. 1987. Policy Failure and Public Support: Reykjavik, Iran, and Public Assessments of President Reagan. Presented at the annual meeting of the American Political Science Association, Chicago, September.

BRUNT, P. A. 1963. Introduction to Thucydides' *History of the Peloponnesian War*, trans. B. Jowett. New York: Twayne.

BRYEN, S. 1980. The War That Was. *Public Opinion* 3:10–11, 58.

BUENO DE MESQUITA, B. 1975. Measuring Systemic Polarity. *Journal of Conflict Resolution* 19:187–216.

———— 1978. Systemic Polarization and the Occurrence and Duration of War. *Journal of Conflict Resolution* 22:241–267.

———— 1980. Theories of International Conflict: An Analysis and an Appraisal. In *Handbook of Political Conflict*, ed. T. R. Gurr, pp. 361–398. New York: Free Press.

———— 1981. *The War Trap*. New Haven, CT: Yale University Press.

———— 1982. Conflict Forecasting Project: Iran and Soviet Union Analysis. Report to the Defense Advance Research Projects Agency, Washington, DC.

———— 1983. The Costs of War: A Rational Expectations Approach. *American Political Science Review* 77:347–357.

———— 1984. Forecasting Policy Decisions: An Expected Utility Approach to Post-Khomeini Iran. *PS* 27:226–236.

———— 1985. The War Trap Revisited. *American Political Science Review* 80:1113–1130.

BUENO DE MESQUITA, B., and D. LALMAN. 1986. Reason and War. *American Political Science Review* 80:1113–1150.

———— 1987. Empirical Support for Systemic and Dyadic Explanations of International Conflict. Mimeograph. Stanford, CA: Hoover Institution.

———— 1988. Arms Races and the Opportunity for Peace. *Synthese* 76:263–283.

BUENO DE MESQUITA, B., D. NEWMAN, and A. RABUSHKA. 1985. *Forecasting Political Events:*

The Future of Hong Kong. New Haven, CT: Yale University Press.

BUENO DE MESQUITA, B., and W. RIKER. 1982. Assessing the Merits of Selective Nuclear Proliferation. *Journal of Conflict Resolution* 26:283–306.

BUENO DE MESQUITA, B., and J. D. SINGER. 1973. Alliances, Capabilities, and War: A Review and Synthesis. *Political Science Annual* 4:273–280.

BULKELEY, R. 1983. Vegetius Vindicatus?: Giving an Old Hypothesis a Fair Break. *Current Research on Peace and Violence* 4:233–257.

BURNS, A. 1959. A Graphical Approach to Some Problems of the Arms Race. *Journal of Conflict Resolution* 3:326–342.

BURROWES, R., and B. SPECTOR. 1973. The Strength and Direction of Relationships between Domestic and External Conflict and Cooperation: Syria, 1961–1967. In *Conflict Behavior and Linkage Politics*, ed. H. Wilkenfeld. New York: McKay.

CALLEO, D. P. 1982. *The Imperious Economy.* Cambridge, MA: Harvard University Press.

CAMPBELL, D. T. 1958. Common Fate, Similarity, and Other Indices of the Status of Aggregates of Persons as Social Entities. *Behavioral Science* 3:14–25.

CANTRIL, H. 1967. *The Human Dimension: Experiences in Policy Research.* New Brunswick, NJ: Rutgers University Press.

CARNEIRO, R. L. 1970. A Theory of the Origin of the States. *Science* 169:733–738.

CARR, E. H. 1945. *Nationalism and After.* New York: Macmillan.

CASPARY, W. 1967. Richardson's Model of Arms Races: Description, Critique, and an Alternative Model. *International Studies Quarterly* 11:63–88.

——— 1970. The "Mood Theory": A Study of Public Opinion and Foreign Policy. *American Political Science Review* 64:536–547.

CHAFFEE, S. H. 1975. The Diffusion of Political Information. In *Political Communication: Issues and Strategies for Research*, ed. S. H. Chaffee. Beverly Hills, CA: Sage.

CHASE-DUNN, C. K. 1981. Interstate System and Capitalist World Economy: One Logic or Two? *International Studies Quarterly* 25:19–42.

CHASE-DUNN, C. K., and J. SOKOLOVSKY. 1983. Interstate Systems, World-Empires and the Capitalist World-Economy: A Response to Thompson. *International Studies Quarterly* 27:357–367.

CHATTERJI, S. D. 1963. Some Elementary Characterizations of the Poisson Distribution. *American Mathematical Monthly* 70:958–964.

CHENERY, H. 1975. *Redistribution with Growth.* London: Oxford University Press.

CHITTICK, W. O. 1970. *State Department, Press, and Pressure Groups: A New Role Analysis.* New York: Wiley.

CHOUCRI, N., with the collaboration of R. C. NORTH. 1972. In Search of Peace Systems: Scandinavia and the Netherlands, 1870–1970. In *Peace, War, and Numbers*, ed. B. Russett. San Francisco: Sage.

CHOUCRI, N. 1974. *Population Dynamics and International Violence: Propositions, Insights, and Evidence.* Lexington, MA: Lexington Books.

——— 1984. Perspectives on Population and Conflict. In *Multidisciplinary Perspectives on Population and Conflict*, ed. N. Choucri. Syracuse, NY: Syracuse University Press.

——— 1987. International Relations and International Migration: Theoretical Gaps and the Empirical Domain. Unpublished monograph, Department of Political Science, Massachusetts Institute of Technology, Cambridge, MA.

CHOUCRI, N., and M. BOUSFIELD. 1978. Alternative Futures: An Exercise in Forecasting. In *Forecasting in International Relations: Theory, Methods, Problems, Prospects*, pp. 308–326, eds. N. Choucri and T. W. Robinson. San Francisco: W. H. Freeman.

CHOUCRI, N., and R. C. NORTH. 1972. Dynamics of International Conflict: Some Policy Implications of Population, Resources and Technology. In *Theory and Policy in*

International Relations, eds. R. Tanter and R. H. Ullman. Princeton, NJ: Princeton University Press.

—— 1975. *Nations in Conflict: National Growth and International Violence*. San Francisco: W. H. Freeman.

—— 1986. Lateral Pressure and International Conflict: The Case of Japan. Paper presented at the annual meeting of the American Political Science Association, Washington, DC, September.

—— 1989. *Conflict and Contention: A Century of Growth and Expansion in Japan* (forthcoming).

CHOUCRI, N., and T. W. ROBINSON, eds. 1978. *Forecasting in International Relations*. San Francisco: W. H. Freeman.

CHOUCRI, N., and D. S. ROSS. 1981. *International Energy Futures: Petroleum Prices, Power and Payments*. Cambridge, MA: MIT Press.

CLAUDE, I. L., JR. 1962. *Power and International Relations*. New York: Random House.

COHEN, B. C. 1973. *The Public's Impact on Foreign Policy*. Boston: Little, Brown.

COLEMAN, J. S. 1964. *Introduction to Mathematical Sociology*. Glencoe, IL: Free Press.

CONVERSE, P. 1964. The Nature of Belief Systems in Mass Publics. In *Ideology and Discontent*, ed. D. Apter. New York: Free Press.

COSER, L. A. 1956. *The Function of Social Conflict*. New York: Free Press.

—— 1968. Conflict: Social Aspects. *International Encyclopedia of the Social Sciences* 31:232–236.

COTTON, T. Y. C. 1986. War and American Democracy: Voting Trends in the Last Five American Wars. *Journal of Conflict Resolution* 30:616–635.

CRAIG, G. A., and GEORGE, A. L. 1983. *Force and Statecraft: Diplomatic Problems of Our Time*. New York: Oxford University Press.

CREASY, E. 1851. *The Fifteen Decisive Battles of the World: From Marathon to Waterloo*. New York: Harper.

CUSACK, T. R., and M. D. WARD. 1981. Military Spending in the United States, Soviet Union, and the People's Republic of China. *Journal of Conflict Resolution* 25:429–469.

CYERT, R., and J. G. MARCH. 1963. *A Behavioral Theory of the Firm*. Englewood Cliffs, NJ: Prentice Hall.

DAHL, R. A. 1957. The Concept of Power. *Behavioral Science* 2:201–215.

DAHRENDORF, R. 1964. *Class and Class Conflict in Industrial Society*. Stanford, CA: Stanford University Press.

DAVIES, J. C. 1962. Toward a Theory of Revolution. *American Sociological Review* 27:5–19.

DAVIS, W. W., G. DUNCAN, and R. SIVERSON. 1978. The Dynamics of Warfare, 1816–1965. *American Journal of Political Science* 22:722–792.

DE PRADT, D. DE F. 1800. *La Prusse et sa Neutralité*. London: G. Cowie.

DE VATTEL, E. 1870. *The Law of Nations, Vol. 3*. Philadelphia: T. and J. W. Johnson.

DeBOER, C. 1984. The Polls: The European Peace Movement and Development of Nuclear Missiles. *Public Opinion Quarterly* 49:119–132.

DENTON, F. H., and W. PHILLIPS. 1968. Some Patterns in the History of Violence. *Journal of Conflict Resolution* 12:182–195.

DESSLER, D. 1987. *Structural Origins of Major War*, Ph.D. dissertation, Johns Hopkins SAIS, Washington, D.C.

DESTLER, I., L. GELB, and A. LAKE. 1984. *Our Own Worst Enemy: The Unmaking of American Foreign Policy*. New York: Simon and Schuster.

DEUTSCH, K. W., and R. L. MERRITT. 1965. Effects of Events on National and International Images. In *International Behavior: A Social–Psychological Analysis*, ed. H. Kelman. New York: Holt, Rinehart and Winston.

DEUTSCH, K. W., and J. D. SINGER. 1964. Multipolar Power Systems and International Stability. *World Politics* 16:390–406.

DIEHL, P. 1983. Arms Races and Escalation: A Closer Look. *Journal of Peace Research* 20:205–212.

—— 1985a. Armaments without War: An Analysis of Some Underlying Effects. *Journal of Peace Research* 22:249–259.

—— 1985b. Arms Races to War: An Analysis of Some Underlying Effects. *Sociological Quarterly* 26:331–349.

DIEHL, P., and J. KINGSTON. 1987. Messenger or Message? Military Buildups and the Initiation of Conflict. *Journal of Politics* 49:789–799.

DORAN, C. F. 1971. *The Politics of Assimilation: Hegemony and Its Aftermath.* Baltimore: Johns Hopkins University Press.

—— 1973. A Theory of Bounded Deterrence. *Journal of Conflict Resolution* 17:243–269.

—— 1974. A Conceptual and Operational Comparison of Power-Based Theories of Conflict: Toward Synthesis via a General Theory of Conflict Dynamics. Paper presented at the annual meeting of the International Studies Association, St. Louis, March.

—— 1975. Hierarchic Regionalism from the Core State Perspective. In *The Analysis of Foreign Policy Outcomes*, ed. W. D. Chittick. Columbus, OH: Charles Merrill.

—— 1983a. Power Cycle Theory and the Contemporary State System. In *Contending Approaches to World Systems Analysis*, ed. W. R. Thompson, pp. 165–182. Beverly Hills, CA: Sage.

—— 1983b. War and Power Dynamics: Economic Underpinnings. *International Studies Quarterly* 27:419–441.

—— 1985. Power Cycle Theory and the Systems Stability. In *Rhythms in Politics and Economics*, eds. P. M. Johnson and W. R. Thompson, pp. 292–312. New York: Praeger.

—— 1989a. *Systems in Crisis: New Imperatives of High Politics at Century's End* (forthcoming).

—— 1989b. Systemic Disequilibrium, Foreign Policy Role, and the Power Cycle: Challenges for Research Design. *Journal of Conflict Resolution* (forthcoming).

—— 1989c. Yardsticks and Metersticks for Power in International Relations: Implications for the Analysis of Systems Structure and Massive War. In *Power in World Politics*, eds. R. Stoll and M. D. Ward. Boulder, CO: Lynne Rienner (forthcoming).

DORAN, C. F., K. Q. HILL, and K. R. MLADENKA. 1979. Threat, Status Disequilibrium, and National Power. *British Journal of International Studies* 5:37–58.

DORAN, C. F., K. Q. HILL, K. R. MLADENKA, and K. WAKATA. 1974. Perceptions of National Power and Threat: Japan, Finland and the United States. *International Journal of Group Tensions* 4:431–454.

DORAN, C. F. and W. PARSONS. 1980. War and the Cycle of Relative Power. *American Political Science Review* 74:947–965.

DOYLE, M. 1986. Liberalism and World Politics. *American Political Science Review* 80:1151–1169.

EAST, M. A. 1971. Stratification in the International System. In *The Analysis of International Politics*, ed. J. N. Rosenau et al., pp. 219–319. New York: Free Press.

ECKHARDT, W., and T. F. LENTZ. 1967. Factors of War/Peace Attitudes. *Peace Research Reviews* 1:1–114.

EICHENBERG, R. 1989. Strategy and Consensus: Public Support for Military Policy in Industrial Democracies. In *National Security and Arms Control: A Reference Guide to National Policy Making*, eds. E. Kolodziej and P. Morgan. Westport, CT: Greenwood.

ELLSBERG, D. 1969. The Crude Analysis of Strategic Choices. In *Approaches to Measurement in International Relations: A Non-Evangelical Survey*, ed. J. Mueller. New York: Appleton-Century-Crofts.

ERIKSON, R. S. 1978. Constituency Opinion and Congressional Behavior: A Reexamination of the Miller Stokes Representation Data. *Public Opinion Quarterly* 42:510–535.

ERSKINE, H. G. 1970. The Polls: Is War a Mistake? *Public Opinion Quarterly* 34:134–150.

EYESTONE, R. 1977. Contagion, Diffusion and Innovation. *American Political Science Review* 71:441–447.

FAGEN, R. R. 1960. Some Assessments and Uses of Public Opinion in Diplomacy. *Public Opinion Quarterly* 24:448–457.

FAN, D. P. 1988. *Predictions of Public Opinion from the Mass Media: Computer Content Analysis and Mathematical Modeling.* Westport, CT: Greenwood.

FELLER, W. 1968. *An Introduction to Probability Theory and Its Applications*, Vol. I, 3rd Ed. New York: Wiley.

FEREJOHN, J., and M. FIORINA. 1974. The Paradox of Not Voting: A Decision Theoretic Analysis. *American Political Science Review* LXVIII:525–536.

FERRIS, W. 1973. The Power Capabilities of Nation-States. Lexington, MA: Lexington Books.

FINLEY, M. I. 1972. Introduction to Thucydides' *History of the Peloponnesian War*, trans. R. Warner. Baltimore: Penguin Books.

FISCHER, F. 1967. *Germany's Aims in the First World War.* New York: W. W. Norton.

——— 1975. *War of Illusions.* New York: W. W. Norton.

FISCHER, G. W., and J. P. CRECINE. 1980. Defense Budgets, Fiscal Policy, Domestic Spending and Arms Races. Paper presented at the annual meeting of the American Political Science Association.

FISCHOFF, B. 1982. For Those Condemned to Study the Past: Heuristics and Biases in Hindsight. In *Judgement under Uncertainty: Heuristics and Biases*, eds. D. Kahneman, P. Slovic, and A. Tversky, pp. 335–354. Cambridge: Cambridge University Press.

FISHER, H. A. L. 1935. *A History of Europe: Volume II. From the Beginning of the Eighteenth Century to 1935.* First published by Eyre & Spottiswoode, reprint by William Collins, Glasgow.

FORRESTER, J. W. 1979. Innovation and the Economic Long Wave. *Management Review* 68:16–24.

FREE, L., and W. WATTS. 1980. Internationalism Comes of Age . . . Again. *Public Opinion* 3:46–52.

FREEMAN, C., J. CLARK, and L. SOETE. 1982. *Unemployment and Technical Innovation.* London: Frances Pinter.

FREY, B. S. 1983. The Economic Model of Behavior: Shortcomings and Fruitful Development. Zurich: University of Zurich, Institute for Empirical Research in Economics.

FRIEDRICH, C. J. 1938. *Foreign Policy in the Making.* New York: W. W. Norton.

GALTUNG, J. 1964. A Structural Theory of Aggression. *Journal of Peace Research* 1:95–119.

——— 1967. Social Position, Party Identification, and Foreign Policy Orientation: A Norwegian Case Study. In *Domestic Sources of Foreign Policy*, ed. J. N. Rosenau. New York: Free Press.

GAMSON, W., and A. MODIGLIANI. 1966. Knowledge and Foreign Policy Options: Some Models for Consideration. *Public Opinion Quarterly* 30:187–199.

GEORGE, A. L. 1982. Case Studies and Theory Development. Paper presented to the Second Annual Symposium on Information Processing in Organizations, Carnegie-Mellon University, Pittsburgh, October 15–16.

GEORGE, A. L., and R. SMOKE. 1974. *Deterrence in American Foreign Policy.* New York: Columbia University Press.

GERGEN, D. R. 1980. The Hardening Mood towards Foreign Policy. *Public Opinion* 3:187–199.

GILLESPIE, J., and D. ZINNES. 1975. Progressions in Mathematical Models of International Conflict. *Synthese* 31:289.

—— eds. 1976. *Mathematical Systems in International Relations.* New York: Praeger.

GILLESPIE, J., D. ZINNES, and G. TAHIM. 1976. Deterrence as a Second Strike Capability: An Optimal Control Model and Differential Game Model. In *Mathematical Systems in International Relations,* eds. J. Gillespie and D. Zinnes. New York: Praeger.

GILPIN, R. 1975. *U.S. Power and the Multinational Corporation.* New York: Basic Books.

—— 1981. *War and Change in World Politics.* New York: Cambridge University Press.

—— 1986. The Theory of Hegemonic War. Paper delivered at the Conference on the Origins and Prevention of Major War, Durham, NH, October.

—— 1987. *The Political Economy of International Relations.* Princeton, NJ: Princeton University Press.

GOCHMAN, C. S., and Z. MAOZ. 1984. Militarized Interstate Disputes, 1816–1976. *Journal of Conflict Resolution* 28:585–616.

GOLDMAN, K., S. BERGLAND, and G. SJOSTEDT. 1986. *Democracy and Foreign Policy: The Case of Sweden.* Aldershot, U.K.: Gower.

GOLDSTEIN, J. 1985. Kondratieff Waves as War Cycles. *International Studies Quarterly* 29:411–444.

—— 1986. Long Cycles in War and Economic Growth. Ph.D. thesis, Department of Political Science, Massachusetts Institute of Technology, Cambridge, MA.

GORDON, M. R. 1974. Domestic Conflict and the Origins of the First World War: The British and German Cases. *Journal of Modern History* 46:191–226.

GRAHAM, T. W. 1986. *Public Attitudes toward Active Defense: ABM and Star Wars, 1945–1985.* Cambridge, MA: MIT Center for International Studies.

—— 1987. *American Public Opinion, War, Peace, Foreign Policy, and Nuclear Weapons: An Indexed Bibliography.* New Haven, CT: Yale University International Security and Arms Control Program.

—— 1988. The Pattern and Importance of Knowledge in the Nuclear Age. *Journal of Conflict Resolution* 32:319–334.

—— 1989a. American Public Opinion, NATO, Extended Deterrence, and Use of Nuclear Weapons: Future Fission. CSIA Occasional Paper No. 4. Lanham, MD: University Press of America.

—— 1989b. *The Politics of Failure: Strategic Nuclear Arms Control, Public Opinion, and Domestic Politics in the United States, 1945–1985.* Ph.D dissertation, Massachusetts Institute of Technology, Cambridge, MA.

GRAY, C. 1971. The Arms Race Phenomenon. *World Politics* 24:39–79.

—— 1976. *The Soviet–American Arms Race.* Lexington, MA: Lexington Books.

—— 1979. Nuclear Strategy: A Case for a Theory of Victory. *International Security* 4:54–88.

GUETZKOW, H. 1950. Long Range Research in International Relations. *American Perspective* 4:421–440.

GULICK, E. V. 1955. *Europe's Classical Balance of Power.* New York: W. W. Norton.

GURR, T. R. 1970. *Why Men Rebel.* Princeton, NJ: Princeton University Press.

GURR, T. R., and R. DUVALL. 1973. Civil Conflict in the 1960s: A Reciprocal Theoretical System with Parameter Estimates. *Comparative Political Studies* 6:135–170.

HAAS, E. B. 1953. The Balance of Power: Prescription, Concept, or Propaganda. *World Politics* 5:422–477.

—— 1971. The Balance of Power: Prescription, Concept or Propaganda? In *Power, Action and Interaction,* ed. G. H. Quester. Boston: Little, Brown.

—— 1982. Words Can Hurt You; Or Who Said What to Whom about Regimes. *International Organization* 36:207–243.

HAAS, E. B., and A. S. WHITING. 1956. *Dynamics of International Relations.* New York: McGraw-Hill.

HAAS, M. 1968. Social Change and National Aggressiveness, 1900–1960. In *Quantitative International Politics*, ed. J. D. Singer. New York: Free Press.

—— 1970. International Subsystems: Stability and Polarity. *American Political Science Review*. 64:98–123.

—— 1974. *International Conflict*. Indianapolis, IN: Bobbs-Merrill.

HAGAN, J. D. 1986. Domestic Political Conflict, Issue Areas, and Some Dimensions of Foreign Policy Behavior other than Conflict. *International Interactions* 12:291–313.

HAHN, H. 1970. Correlates of Public Sentiments about War: Local Referenda on the Vietnam Issue. *American Political Science Review* 64:1186–1198.

HALPERIN, M. H. 1974. *Bureaucratic Politics and Foreign Policy*. Washington, DC: Brookings.

HAMILTON, R. F. 1968. A Research Note on the Mass Support for 'Tough' Military Initiatives. *American Sociological Review* 33:439–445.

HARBERGER, A., ed. 1960. *The Demand for Durable Goods*. Chicago: University of Chicago Press.

HARDIN, R., J. MEARSHEIMER, G. DWORKIN, and R. GOODIN. 1985. *Nuclear Deterrence: Ethics and Strategy*. Chicago: University of Chicago Press.

HASTINGS, E. H., and P. K. HASTINGS, eds. 1987. *Index to International Public Opinion, 1985–86*. Westport, CT: Greenwood.

HASTINGS, M., and S. JENKINS. 1983. *The Battle for the Falklands*. New York: W. H. Norton.

HAYES, C. F. 1932. *A Political and Cultural History of Modern Europe*, Vol. I. New York: Macmillan.

HAYES, P. 1975. *Mathematical Methods in the Social and Managerial Sciences*. New York: Wiley.

HAZELWOOD, L. 1973. Externalizing Systemic Stress: International Conflict as Adaptive Behavior. In *Conflict Behavior and Linkage Politics*, ed. J. Wildenfeld. New York: McKay.

—— 1975. Diversion Mechanisms and Encapsulation Processes; the Domestic Conflict–Foreign Conflict Hypothesis Reconsidered. In *Sage International Yearbook of Foreign Policy Studies*, Vol. 3, pp. 213–243, ed. P. J. McGowan. Beverly Hills, CA: Sage.

HEREK, G. M., I. L. JANIS, and P. HUTH. 1987. Decision Making during International Crises. *Journal of Conflict Resolution* 31:203–226.

HERODOTUS. 1954. *Histories of Herodotus*. London: Penguin Books.

HERSHEY, J. C., and P. SCHOEMAKER. 1980. Risk Taking and Problem Context in the Domain of Losses: An Expected Utility Analysis. *Journal of Risk and Insurance* 47:111–132.

HINCKLEY, R. H. 1988. Public Attitudes toward Key Foreign Policy Events. *Journal of Conflict Resolution* 32:295–318.

HIRSCHMAN, A. O. 1969. *National Power and the Structure of Foreign Trade*. Berkeley, CA: University of California Press.

HOFFMANN, S. 1960. *Contemporary Theory in International Relations*. Englewood Cliffs, NJ: Prentice-Hall.

—— 1965. *The State of War*. New York: Praeger.

—— ed. 1978. *Primacy or World Order*. New York: McGraw-Hill.

HOLLIST, W. L. 1977a. Alternative Explanations of Competitive Arms Processes: Tests on Four Pairs of Nations. *American Journal of Political Science* 21:503–528.

—— 1977b. An Analysis of Arms Processes in the United States and the Soviet Union. *International Studies Quarterly* 21:503–528.

HOLSTI, K. J. 1970. National Role Conception in the Study of Foreign Policy. *International Studies Quarterly* 14:233–309.

—— 1985. The Necrologists of International Relations. *Canadian Journal of Political Science* 18:675–695.

HOLSTI, O. R. 1972. *Crisis, Escalation, War*. Montreal: McGill-Queens University Press.

—— ed. 1980. *Change in the International System*. Boulder, CO: Westview Press.

—— 1986. Public Opinion and Containment. In *Containment: Concept and Policy*, eds. T. L. Deibel and J. Lewis Gaddis. Washington, DC: National Defense University Press.

HOLSTI, O. R., P. T. HOPMANN, and J. D. SULLIVAN. 1973. *Unity and Disintegration in International Alliances*. New York: Wiley (Interscience).

HOLSTI, O. R., and J. N. ROSENAU. 1984. *American Leadership in World Affairs*. Boston: Allen & Unwin.

—— 1986. Consensus Lost, Consensus Regained? Foreign Policy Beliefs of American Leaders, 1976–1980. *International Studies Quarterly* 30:375–409.

—— 1988. Domestic and Foreign Policy Belief Systems among American Leaders. *Journal of Conflict Resolution* 32:248–294.

HOMANS, G. C. 1961. *Social Behavior: Its Elementary Forms*. New York: Harcourt, Brace and World.

HOPKINS, T. K., and I. WALLERSTEIN. 1979. Cyclical Rhythms and Secular Trends of the Capitalist World Economy: Some Premises, Hypotheses, and Questions. *Review* 2:483–500.

HÖTZSCH, O. 1909. Catherine II. In *The Cambridge Modern History*, Vol. 6, eds. A. W. Ward, G. W. Prothero, and S. Leathes. London: Cambridge University Press.

HOUWELING, H., and J. G. SICCAMA. 1981. The Arms Race–War Relationship: Why Serious Disputes Matter. *Arms Control* 2:157–197.

—— 1983. Time–Space Interaction in Warfare: Some Theoretical and Empirical Aspects of the Epidemiology of Collective Violence, 1816–1980. Paper presented at the European Consortium for Political Research, Freiburg, Federal Republic of Germany.

—— 1988. Power Transition as a Cause of War. *Journal of Conflict Resolution* 32:87–102.

HUGHES, B. 1978. *The Domestic Context of American Foreign Policy*. New York: Freeman.

HUNT, M. H. 1987. *Ideology and U.S. Foreign Policy*. New Haven, CT: Yale University Press.

HUNTINGTON, S. P. 1958. Arms Races: Prerequisites and Results. *Public Policy* 18:41–46.

—— 1971. Arms Races: Prerequisites and Results. In *Power, Action and Interaction*, ed. G. H. Quester. Boston: Little, Brown.

—— 1982. *The Strategic Imperative*. Cambridge, MA: Ballinger.

—— 1986. Playing to Win. *The National Interest* 2:8–16.

HUSSEIN, S. 1987. Modeling War and Peace. *American Political Science Review* 81:221–227.

HUTH, P., and B. RUSSETT. 1984. What Makes Deterrence Work?: Cases from 1900 to 1980. *World Politics* 36:496–526.

IGGERS, G. G. 1984. *New Directions in European Historiography*, rev. ed. Middletown, CT: Wesleyan University Press.

INTERNATIONAL INSTITUTE FOR STRATEGIC STUDIES. 1984. *The Military Balance*. London: IISS.

INTRILIGATOR, M. D. 1964. Some Simple Models of Arms Races. *General Systems* 9:143–164.

—— 1967. *Strategy in a Missile War: Targets and Rates of Fire*. Los Angeles: Security Studies Project, University of California, Los Angeles.

—— 1968. The Debate over Missile Strategy: Targets and Rates of Fire. *Orbis* 11:1138–1159.

—— 1971. *Mathematical Optimalization and Economic Theory*. Englewood Cliffs, NJ: Prentice-Hall.

—— 1975. Strategic Considerations in the Richardson Model of Arms Races. *Journal of Political Economy* 83:339–353.

—— 1982. Research on Conflict Theory: Analytic Approaches and Areas of Application. *Journal of Conflict Resolution* 26:307–327.

—— 1985. Arms Races and Instability. Paper presented at the annual meeting of the American Political Science Association, New Orleans, September.

——— 1986. Arms Races and Instability. *Journal of Strategic Studies* 9:113–131.
INTRILIGATOR, M. D., and D. L. BRITO. 1976a. Strategy, Arms Races, and Arms Control. In *Mathematical Systems in International Relations*, eds. J. Gillespie and D. Zinnes. New York: Praeger.
——— 1976b. Formal Models of Arms Races. *Journal of Peace Science* 2:77–88.
——— 1981. Nuclear Proliferation and the Probability of War. *Public Choice* 37:247–260.
——— 1984. Can Arms Races Lead to the Outbreak of War? *Journal of Conflict Resolution* 28:63–84.
——— 1985a. Heuristic Decision Rules, the Dynamics of an Arms Race, and War Initiation. In *Dynamic Models of International Conflict*, eds. U. Luterbacher and M. D. Ward, Boulder, CO: Lynne Rienner.
——— 1985b. Non-Armageddon Solutions to the Arms Race. *Arms Control* 6:41–57.
——— 1985c. Arms Races and Instability. Paper presented at the annual meeting of the American Political Science Association, New Orleans.
——— 1986a. Arms Races and Instability. *Journal of Strategic Studies* 9:113–131.
——— 1986b. Mayer's Alternative to the I–B Model. *Journal of Conflict Resolution* 30:29–31.
——— 1987. The Stability of Mutual Deterrence. In *Exploring the Stability of Deterrence*, ed. J. Kugler and F. Zagare. Boulder, CO: Lynne Rienner.
ISARD, W., and C. ANDERSON. 1985. Arms Race Models: A Survey and Synthesis. *Conflict Management and Peace Science* 8:27–98.
IUSI-SCARBOROUGH, G., and B. BUENO DE MESQUITA. 1988. Threat and Alignment Behavior. *International Interactions* LIV:85–93.
IYENGAR, S., and D. R. KINDER. 1986. More than Meets the Eye: TV News, Priming, and Public Evaluations of the President. In *Public Communications and Behavior*, ed. G. Comstock. Orlando, FL: Academic Press.
JACOB, P. E. 1940. Influences of World Events on U.S. Neutrality Opinion. *Public Opinion Quarterly* 4:48–65.
JACOBSON, H. K. 1985. *The Determination of the United States Military Force Posture: Political Processes and Policy Changes*. Washington, DC: The Woodrow Wilson Center, International Security Program.
JAMES, P. 1987. Externalization of Conflict: Testing a Crisis-Based Model. *Canadian Journal of Political Science* 20:2.
——— 1988. *Crisis and War*. Montreal and Kingston: McGill-Queens University Press.
JANTSCH, E. 1980. *The Self-Organizing Universe: Scientific and Human Implications of the Emerging Paradigm of Evolution*. New York: Pergamon Press.
JERVIS, R. 1976. *Perception and Misperception in International Politics*. Princeton, NJ: Princeton University Press.
——— 1979a. *The Illogic of American Nuclear Strategy*. Ithaca, NY: Cornell University Press.
——— 1979b. Deterrence Theory Revisited. *World Politics* 31:289–324.
——— 1984. *The Illogic of American Nuclear Strategy*. Ithaca, NY: Cornell University Press.
JERVIS, R., R. N. LEBOW, and J. STEIN. 1985. *Psychology and Deterrence*. Baltimore: Johns Hopkins University Press.
JOB, B. L. 1973. Alliance Formation in the International System: The Application of the Poisson Model. Paper presented at the annual meeting of the International Studies Association, New York, March.
JOB, B. L., and C. W. OSTROM. 1986. Opportunity and Choice: The U.S. and the Political Use of Force. Paper presented at the annual meeting of the American Political Science Association, Washington, DC, August.
JOHNSON, N. L., and S. KOTZ. 1977. *Urn Models and their Application: An Approach to Modern Discrete Probability Theory*. New York: Wiley.

JOHNSON, P. M., and W. R. THOMPSON, eds. 1985. *Rhythms in Politics and Economics*. New York: Praeger.

JOLL, J. 1984. *The Origins of the First World War*. New York: Longmans.

JUDAY, T. 1985. From Defeat to Victory: The Pattern of Russian/Soviet Participation in Three Global Wars. Paper delivered at the annual meeting of the Pacific Northwest Political Science Association, Vancouver, Canada, October.

JUTIKKALA, E. 1962. *A History of Finland*, trans. P. Sjoblom. New York: Praeger.

KAGAN, D. 1969. *The Outbreak of the Peloponnesian War*. Ithaca, NY: Cornell University Press.

KAHNEMAN, D., P. SLOVIC, and A. TVERSKY, eds. 1982. *Judgement under Uncertainty: Heuristics and Biases*. Cambridge: Cambridge University Press.

KAHNEMAN, D., and A. TVERSKY. 1979. Prospect Theory: An Analysis of Decisions under Risk. *Econometrica* 47:263–291.

KAISER, D. E. 1983. Germany and the Origins of the First World War. *Journal of Modern History* 55:442–474.

KAPLAN, M. 1957. *System and Process in International Politics*. New York: Wiley.

——— 1958. The Calculus of Nuclear Deterrence. *World Politics* 11:20–43.

KATZ, E., and P. F. LAZARSFELD. 1955. *Personal Influence*. New York: Free Press.

KECSKEMETI, P. 1961. *The Unexpected Revolution: Social Forces in the Hungarian Uprising*. Stanford, CA: Stanford University Press.

KEGLEY, C. W., and G. A. RAYMOND. 1987. The Long Cycle of Global War and Alliance Norms. Paper delivered at the annual meeting of the International Studies Association, Washington, D.C.

KEGLEY, C. W., N. R. RICHARDSON, and G. RICHTER. 1978. Conflict at Home and Abroad: An Empirical Extension. *Journal of Politics* 40:742–752.

KEHR, E. 1970. *Der Primat der Innenpolitik*. Berlin: de Gruyter.

KELLEY, H. H. 1972. Attribution in Social Interaction. In *Attribution: Perceiving the Causes of Behavior*, eds. E. E. Jones *et al.* Morristown, NJ: General Learning Press.

KENNAN, G. F. 1951. *American Diplomacy, 1900–1950*. Chicago: University of Chicago Press.

——— 1979. *The Decline of Bismarck's European Order: Franco-Russian Relations, 1875–1890*. Princeton, NJ: Princeton University Press.

——— 1984. *The Fateful Alliance: France, Russia, and the Coming of the First World War*. New York: Pantheon.

KENNEDY, P. 1988. *The Rise and Fall of the Great Powers: Economic Change and Military Conflict from 1500 to 2000*. New York: Random House.

KENT, G. 1963. *On the Interaction of Opposing Forces under Possible Arms Agreements*. Cambridge, MA: Harvard University, Center for International Affairs.

KEOHANE, R. O. 1980. The Theory of Hegemonic Stability and Changes in International Economic Regimes, 1967–1977. In *Change in the International System*, eds. O. Holsti, R. Siverson, and A. George. Boulder, CO: Westview Press.

——— 1984. *After Hegemony: Cooperation and Discord in the World Political Economy*. Princeton, NJ: Princeton University Press.

——— ed. 1986. *Neorealism and Its Critics*. New York: Columbia University Press.

KEOHANE, R. O., and J. S. NYE. 1977. *Power and Interdependence: World Politics in Transition*. Boston: Little, Brown.

KERNELL, S. 1978. Explaining Presidential Popularity. *American Political Science Review* 72:506–522.

KINDELBERGER, C. P. 1981. Dominance and Leadership in the International Economy. *International Studies Quarterly* 25:242–254.

KISSINGER, H. 1957. *A World Restored: Metternich, Castlereagh and the Problems of Peace, 1812–1822*. Boston: Houghton.

——— 1964. *A World Restored*. Boston: Houghton Mifflin.

———— 1979. *The White House Years.* Boston: Little, Brown.

KLUCKHOLN, C. 1960. *Mirror for Man.* Greenwich, CT: Fawcett Books.

KNORR, K. 1956. *The War Potential of Nations.* Princeton, NJ: Princeton University Press.

———— 1975. *The Power of Nations.* New York: Basic Books.

KOHUT, A. 1988. What Americans Want. *Foreign Policy* 70:150–165.

KONDRATIEFF, N. D. 1984 (from the Russian version of 1928). *The Long Wave Cycle.* New York: Richardson and Snyder.

KRAMER, B. M., S. M. KALICK, and M. MILBURN. 1983. Attitudes towards Nuclear Weapons and Nuclear War. *Journal of Social Issues* 39:7–24.

KRAMER, G. 1971. Short-Term Fluctuations in Voting Behavior. *American Political Science Review* 65:131–143.

KRASNER, S. D. 1976. State Power and the Structure of International Trade. *World Politics* 28:317–343.

———— 1985. *Structural Conflict: The Third World against Global Liberalism.* Berkeley, CA: University of California Press.

KREPS, D., and R. WILSON. 1982a. Reputation and Imperfect Information. *Journal of Economic Theory* 27:253–279.

———— 1982b. Sequential Equilibria. *Econometrica* 50:863–894.

KRIESBERG, L., and R. KLEIN. 1980. Changes in Public Support for U.S. Military Spending. *Journal of Conflict Resolution* 24:79–111.

KUGLER, J. 1984. Terror without Deterrence: Reassessing the Role of Nuclear Weapons. *Journal of Conflict Resolution* 28:470–506.

———— 1987. Anticipation Political Instability with Measures of Political Capacity. Paper presented at the annual meeting of the American Political Science Association, Chicago, September.

KUGLER, J., and W. DOMKE. 1987. Comparing the Strength of Nations. *Comparative Political Studies* 19:39–69.

KUGLER, J., and A. F. K. ORGANSKI. 1989. The End of Hegemony? *International Interactions* 15:113–128.

KUGLER, J., and F. ZAGARE, eds. 1987a. *Exploring the Stability of Deterrence.* Boulder, CO: Lynne Rienner.

———— 1987b. The Longterm Stability of Deterrence, mimeograph. Available from the authors.

KUPPERMAN, R., and H. SMITH. 1972. Strategies of Mutual Deterrence. *Science* 176:18–23.

———— 1976. Deterrent Stability and Strategic Warfare. eds. In *Mathematical Systems in International Relations*, eds. J. Gillespie and D. Zinnes. New York: Praeger.

KUSNITZ, L. 1984. *Public Opinion and Foreign Policy: America's China Policy, 1949–1979.* Westport, CT: Greenwood.

KUZNETS, S. 1955. *Modern Economic Growth: Rate, Structure and Spread.* New Haven, CT: Yale University Press.

LAKATOS, I. 1978. *The Methodology of Scientific Research Programs, Vol. 1.* London: Cambridge University Press.

LALMAN, D. 1988. Conflict Resolution and Peace. *American Journal of Political Science* (forthcoming).

LAMBELET, J.-C. 1971. A Dynamic Model of the Arms Race in the Middle East, 1953–1965. *General Systems* 16:145–167.

———— 1974. The Anglo-German Dreadnought Race, 1905–1914. *Peace Science Society (International) Papers* 22:1–46.

———— 1975. Do Arms Races Lead to War? *Journal of Peace Research* 12:123–128.

———— 1976. A Complementary Analysis of the Anglo-German Dreadnought Race, 1905–1916. *Peace Science Society (International) Papers* 26:49–66.

———— 1985. Arms Races as Good Things? In *Dynamic Models of International Conflict*, eds.

U. Luterbacher and M. D. Ward. Boulder, CO: Lynne Rienner.

LAMBELET, J.-C., U. LUTERBACHER, and P. ALLAN. 1979. Dynamics of Arms Races: Mutual Stimulation vs. Self-Stimulation. *Journal of Peace Science* 4:49–66.

LANGER, W. L. 1969. The Origin of the Russo-Japanese war. In *Explorations in Crises*, ed. W. L. Langer. Cambridge, MA: Harvard University/Belknap Press.

LAQUEUR, W. 1968. Revolution. *International Encyclopedia of the Social Sciences* 13:501–507.

LEBOW, R. N. 1981. *Between Peace and War*. Baltimore: Johns Hopkins University Press.

LEE, J. R. 1970. Rally 'Round the Flag: Foreign Policy Events and Presidential Popularity. *Presidential Studies Quarterly* 7:252–255.

LEIDY, M. P., and R. W. STAIGER. 1985. Economic Issues and Methodology in Arms Race Analysis. *Journal of Conflict Resolution* 29:503–530.

LEIGH, M. 1976. *Mobilizing Consent: Public Opinion and American Foreign Policy, 1937–1947*. Westport, CT: Greenwood.

LENG, R. J. 1983. When Will They Ever Learn? Coercive Bargaining in Recurrent Crises. *Journal of Conflict Resolution* 27:379–420.

LENG, R. J., and J. D. SINGER. 1988. Militarized Interstate Crises: The BCOW Typology and Its Applications. *International Studies Quarterly* 32:155–174.

LENIN, V. I. 1935. The War and Russian Social-Democracy. In *Selected Works*, ed. J. Fineberg. New York: International Publishers.

———— 1939. *Imperialism*. New York: International Publishers.

LEVY, J. S. 1981. Alliance Formation and War Behavior: An Analysis of the Great Powers, 1495–1975. *Journal of Conflict Resolution* 25:581–613.

———— 1982. The Contagion of Great Power War Behavior, 1495–1975. *American Journal of Political Science* 26:562–584.

———— 1983a. World System Analysis: A Great Power Framework. In *Contending Approaches to World Systems Analysis*, ed. W. Thompson. Beverly Hills, CA: Sage.

———— 1983b. *War in the Modern Great Power System, 1495–1975*. Lexington, KY: University Press of Kentucky.

———— 1983c. Misperception and the Causes of War. *World Politics* 36:76–99.

———— 1984. The Offensive/Defensive Balance of Military Technology: A Theoretical and Historical Analysis. *International Studies Quarterly* 28:219–238.

———— 1985. Polarity of the System and International Stability: An Empirical Analysis. In *Polarity and War: The Changing Structure of International Conflict*, ed. A. N. Sabrosky. Boulder, CO: Westview Press.

———— 1987. Declining Power and the Preventive Motivation for War. *World Politics* 40:82–107.

———— 1988a. Domestic Politics and War. *Journal of Interdisciplinary History* 18:653–673.

———— 1988b. When Do Deterrent Threats Work? *British Journal of Political Science* 18:485–512.

———— 1988c. The Role of Crisis Mismanagement in the Outbreak of World War I. Paper presented at the annual meeting of the American Political Science Association, Washington, DC, September.

———— 1989. The Causes of War: A Review of Theories and Evidence. In *Behavior, Society, and Nuclear War, Vol. I*, eds. P. E. Tetlock, J. L. Husbands, R. Jervis, P. C. Stern, and C. Tilly. New York: Oxford University Press.

LEVY, J. S., and R. COLLIS. 1985. Power Cycle Theory and the Preventative Motivation: A Preliminary Empirical Investigation. Paper presented at the annual meeting of the American Political Science Association, New Orleans.

LEWITTER, L. R. 1965. The Partitions of Poland. *The New Cambridge Modern History, Vol. 8*, ed. A. Goodwin. Cambridge: Cambridge University Press.

Li, R., and W. R. Thompson. 1975. The 'Coup Contagion' Hypothesis. *Journal of Conflict Resolution* 19:63–88.

Liossatos, P. 1980. Modeling the Nuclear Arms Race: A Search for Stability. *Journal of Peace Science* 4:169–185.

Liska, G. 1956. *International Equilibrium.* Cambridge, MA: Harvard University Press.

——— 1957. *International Equilibrium.* Cambridge: Cambridge University Press.

——— 1962. *Nations In Alliance.* Baltimore: Johns Hopkins University Press.

——— 1967. *Imperial America: The International Politics of Primacy.* Baltimore: Johns Hopkins University Press.

Lowi, T. J. 1985. *The Personal President.* Ithaca, NY: Cornell University Press.

Lucas, R. E. B. 1981. International Migration: Economic Causes, Consequences, Evaluation and Policies. Rockefeller Conference Paper on International Migration, June 1979. Reprinted in *Global Trends in Migration: Theory and Research on International Population Movements,* eds. M. M. Kritz, C. B. Keeley, and S. M. Tomasi. Staten Island, NY: Center for Migration Studies.

Lunch, W. L., and P. Sperlich. 1979. American Public Opinion and the War in Vietnam. *Western Political Quarterly* 32:21–44.

Luterbacher, U. 1975. Arms Race Models: Where Do We Stand? *European Journal of Political Research* 3:199–217.

Luterbacher, U., and M. D. Ward, eds. 1985. *Dynamic Models of International Conflict.* Boulder, CO: Lynne Rienner Publishers.

McGuire, M. C. 1977. A Quantitative Study of the Strategic Arms Race in the Missile Age. *Review of Economics and Statistics* 59:328–339.

Mack, A. 1975. Numbers Are Not Enough; A Critique of Internal/External Conflict Behavior Research. *Comparative Politics* 7:597–618.

McKeown, T. J. 1983. Hegemonic Stability Theory and 19th Century Tariff Levels in Europe. *International Organization* 37:73–91.

McKeown, T., and P. Anderson. 1985. A Bounded Rationality Model of War Initiation. Paper presented at the annual meeting of the American Political Science Association.

McNamara, R. 1984. The Military Role of Nuclear Weapons: Perceptions and Misperceptions. CISA Working Paper No. 45, Los Angeles, Center for International and Strategic Affairs.

McNeill, W. H. 1982. *The Pursuit of Power: Technology, Armed Force and Society Since A.D. 1000.* Chicago: University of Chicago Press.

Majeski, S. 1986a. Mutual and Unilateral Cooperation in Arms Race Settings. *International Interactions* 12:343–361.

——— 1986b. Technological Innovation and Cooperation in Arms Races. *International Studies Quarterly* 30:175–191.

Majeski, S., and D. Jones. 1981. Arms Race Modeling: Causality Analysis and Model Specification. *Journal of Conflict Resolution* 25:259–288.

Mandel, E. 1980. *Long Waves of Capitalist Development.* Cambridge: Cambridge University Press.

Mandelbaum, M., and W. Schneider. 1979. The New Internationalism: Public Opinion and American Foreign Policy. In *Eagle Entangled: U.S. Foreign Policy in a Complex World,* eds. K. Oye, D. Rothchild, and R. Lieber. New York: Longmans.

Maoz, Z. 1983. Resolve, Capabilities, and the Outcomes of Interstate Disputes, 1816–1976. *Journal of Conflict Resolution* 27:195–229.

March, J. G. 1981. Decisions in Organizations and Theories of Choice. In *Perspectives on Organization Design and Behavior,* eds. A. H. Van de Wen and W. F. Joyce. New York: Wiley.

Marttila and Kiley. 1987. *Americans Talk Security: A Survey of American Voters, Attitudes concerning National Security Issues*, No. 1. Boston: Marttila & Kiley Inc.

MAY, R. M. 1973. *Stability and Complexity in Model Ecosystems*. Princeton, NJ: Princeton University Press.

MAYER, A. J. 1967. Domestic Causes and Purposes of War in Europe, 1870–1956. In *The Responsibility of Power*, eds. L. Krieger and F. Stern. New York: Doubleday.

———— 1969. Internal Causes and Purposes of War in Europe, 1870–1956. *Journal of Modern History* 41:291–303.

———— 1977. Industrial Crises and War Since 1870. In *Revolutionary Situations in Europe, 1917–1922*, ed. C. L. Bertrand. Montreal: Interuniversity Centre for European Studies.

MAYER, T. 1986. Arms Races and War Initiation: Some Alternatives to the Intriligator–Brito Model. *Journal of Conflict Resolution* 30:3–28.

MAYNARD SMITH, J. 1968. *Models in Ecology*. Cambridge: Cambridge University Press.

———— 1974. The Theory of Games and the Evolution of Animal Behavior. *Journal of Theoretical Biology* 47:209–221.

MEARSHEIMER, J. J. 1983. *Conventional Deterrence*. Ithaca, NY: Cornell University Press.

MIDLARSKY, M. I. 1969. Status Inconsistency and the Onset of International Warfare. Ph.D. dissertation, Northwestern University, Evanston, IL. Reprinted in M. I. Midlarsky. 1975. *On War: Political Violence in the International System*. New York: Free Press.

———— 1970. Mathematical Models of Instability and a Theory of Diffusion. *International Studies Quarterly* 14:60–84.

———— 1978. Analyzing Diffusion and Contagion Effects: The Urban Disorders of the 1960s. *American Political Science Review* 72:996–1008.

———— 1981. Equilibria in the Nineteenth-Century Balance-of-Power System. *American Journal of Political Science* 25:270–296.

———— 1982. Scarcity and Inequality: Prologue to the Onset of Mass Revolution. *Journal of Conflict Resolution* 26:3–38.

———— 1983. Absence of Memory in the Nineteenth-Century Alliance System: Perspectives from Queuing Theory and Bivariate Probability Distributions. *American Journal of Political Science* 27:762–784.

———— 1984a. Political Stability of Two-Party and Multiparty Systems: Probabilistic Bases for the Comparison of Party Systems. *American Political Science Review* 78:929–951.

———— 1984b. Preventing Systemic War. *Journal of Conflict Resolution* 28:563–584.

———— 1986a. A Hierarchical Equilibrium Theory of Systemic War. *International Studies Quarterly* 30:77–105.

———— 1986b. The Balance of Power, Hierarchical Equilibrium, and Superpower Conflict: International Structure as an Information System. Presented at the annual meeting of the American Political Science Association, Washington, DC, August.

———— 1986c. *The Disintegration of Political Systems: War and Revolution in Comparative Perspective*. Columbia, SC: University of South Carolina Press.

———— 1988a. *The Onset of World War*. Boston: Unwin Hyman.

———— 1988b. Rulers and the Ruled: Patterned Inequality and the Onset of Mass Political Violence. *American Political Science Review* 82:491–509.

MIDLARSKY, M. I. and K. ROBERTS. 1985. Class, State, and Revolution in Central America: Nicaragua and El Salvador Compared. *Journal of Conflict Resolution* 29:163–193.

MILLER, J. G. 1976. *Living Systems*. New York: McGraw-Hill.

MILLER, N. R. 1977. Pluralism and Social Choice. *American Political Science Review* 77:734–747.

MILLER, W. 1964. Majority Rule and the Representative System of Government. In *Cleavages, Idealogies, and Party Systems*, eds. E. Allardt and T. Littunen. Helsinki: Transactions of the Westermarck Society.

MILLER, W., and D. STOKES. 1966. Constituency Influence in Congress. In *Elections and the Political Order*, eds. A. Campbell, P. Converse, W. Miller, and D. Stokes. New York: Wiley.

MINAMI, R. 1986. *Economic Development of Japan: A Quantitative Study*, trans. R. Thompson and R. Minami. New York: St. Martin's.

MINTZ, A. 1988. A Comparison of Israel and the United States. *Comparative Political Studies* 21, no. 3 (October): 368–81.

MITCHELL, C. E. 1966. GRIT and Gradualism—25 Years On. *International Interactions* 13:73–86.

MITCHELL, C. R., and M. NICHOLSON. 1983. Rational Models and the Ending of Wars. *Journal of Conflict Resolution* 27:495–520.

MODELSKI, G. 1978. The Long Cycle of Global Politics and the Nation-State. *Comparative Studies in Society and History* 20:214–235.

——— 1981. Long Cycles, Kondratieffs, and Alternating Innovations: Implications for U.S. Foreign Policy. In *The Political Economy of Foreign Policy Behavior*, eds. C. W. Kegley, Jr., and P. J. McGowan. Beverly Hills, CA: Sage.

——— 1982. Long Cycles and the Strategy of United States International Political Economy. In *America in a Changing World Political Economy*, eds. W. Avery and D. P. Rapkin. New York: Longmans.

——— 1983. Long Cycles of World Leadership. In *Contending Approaches to World Systems Analysis*, ed. W. R. Thompson. Beverly Hills, CA: Sage.

——— 1984. Global Wars and World Leadership Selection. Paper delivered at the Second World Peace Science Congress, Rotterdam, the Netherlands, June.

——— 1986. Long Cycles, Macrodecisions, and Global Wars. Paper delivered at the Conference on the Origins and Prevention of Major Wars, Durham, NH, October.

——— 1987a. A Global Politics Scenario for the Year 2016. In *Exploring Long Cycles*, ed. G. Modelski. Boulder, CO: Lynne Rienner.

——— 1987b. Is World Politics a Learning Process? Paper delivered at the annual meeting of the American Political Science Association, Chicago, September.

——— 1987c. *Long Cycles in World Politics*. Seattle: University of Washington Press.

MODELSKI, G., and S. MODELSKI, eds. 1988. *Documenting Global Leadership*. Seattle: University of Washington Press.

MODELSKI, G., and P. MORGAN. 1985. Understanding Global War. *Journal of Conflict Resolution* 29:473–502.

MODELSKI, G., and W. R. THOMPSON. 1987. Testing Cobweb Models of the Long Cycle. In *Exploring Long Cycles*, ed. G. Modelski. Boulder, CO: Lynne Rienner.

——— 1988. *Seapower and Global Politics, 1494–1993*. Seattle: University of Washington Press.

MODIGLIANI, A. 1972. Hawks and Doves: Isolationism and Political Distrust. *American Political Science Review* 66:960–978.

MOLL, K., and G. LUEBBERT. 1980. Arms Race and Military Expenditure Models. *Journal of Conflict Resolution* 24:153–185.

MOMMSEN, W. J. 1973. Domestic Factors in German Foreign Policy Before 1914. *Central European History* 6:3–43.

MOORE, G. H. 1986. *Business Cycles, Inflation, and Forecasting*, 2nd ed. Cambridge, MA: Ballinger.

MORGAN, P. 1977. *Deterrence*. Beverly Hills, CA: Sage.

MORGENTHAU, H. J. 1948. *Politics among Nations*. New York: Knopf.

——— 1973. *Politics among Nations: The Struggle for Power and Peace*, 5th Ed. New York: Knopf.

MORROW, J. 1984. A Twist of Truth: A Reexamination of the Effects of Arms Races on the Occurrence of War. Paper presented at the annual meeting of the American Political Science Association, Washington, DC, September.

——— 1985. A Continuous Outcome Expected Utility Theory of War. *Journal of Conflict Resolution* 29:473–502.

——— 1987. A Limited Information Model of Crisis Bargaining. Paper presented at the annual meeting of the International Studies Association.

MOST, B. A., P. SCHRODT, R. SIVERSON, and H. STARR. 1987. Border and Alliance Effects in the Diffusion of Major Power Conflict, 1815–1965. Paper presented at the International Studies Association annual meeting, Washington, D.C.

MOST, B. A., and R. M. SIVERSON. 1988. Arms and Alliances, 1870–1913: An Exploration in Empirical Comparative Foreign Policy. In *New Directions in the Comparative Study of Foreign Policy*, eds. C. Hermann, C. Kegley, and J. Rosenau. New York: Allen & Unwin (forthcoming).

MOST, B. A., and H. STARR. 1975. The Consequences of War for War: A Design for the Study of Contagion/Diffusion Effects. Paper presented at the annual meeting of the Peace Science Society (International), Midwest Section, Chicago.

——— 1976. Techniques for the Detection of Diffusion: Geopolitical Considerations in the Spread of War. Paper presented at the annual meeting of the International Studies Association, Toronto.

——— 1977. The Spread of War: An Empirical Critique of the Poisson/Modified Poisson Approach to the Study of Diffusion. Report No. F77–01. Bloomington, IN: Center for International Policy Studies, Indiana University.

——— 1980. Diffusion, Reinforcement, Geo-politics and the Spread of War. *American Political Science Review* 74:932–946.

——— 1981. Theoretical and Methodological Issues in the Study of Diffusion and Contagion: Examples from the Research on War. Paper presented at the annual meeting of the International Studies Association, Philadelphia, March.

——— 1982. Case Selection, Conceptualization and Basic Logic in the Study of War. *American Journal of Political Science* 26:834–856.

——— 1983. Conceptualizing 'War': Consequences for Theory and Research. *Journal of Conflict Resolution* 27:137–159.

——— 1984. International Relations Theory, Foreign Policy Substitutability, and 'Nice' Laws. *World Politics* 36:383–406.

——— 1985. Geopolitics and War: The Study of the Diffusion of International Conflict. Paper presented at the annual meeting of the Association of American Geographers, Detroit.

——— 1987. Polarity, Preponderance and Power Parity in the Generation of International Conflict. *International Interactions* 13:225–262.

——— 1989. Inquiry, Logic, and International Politics. Columbia, SC: University of South Carolina Press.

MOUL, W. 1987. A Catch to the War Trap. *International Interactions* 13:171–176.

MOYAL, J. E. 1949. The Distribution of Wars in Time. *Journal of Royal Statistical Society* 115:446–449.

MOYERS, B. D. 1968. One Thing We Learned. *Foreign Affairs* 46:657–664.

MUELLER, J. E. 1973. *War, Presidents, and Public Opinion*. New York: Wiley.

MULLINS, A. 1975. Manpower Data as a Measure of Arms Race Phenomena, mimeograph. Available from the author.

MUNTON, D. 1984. Public Opinion and the Media in Canada from Cold War to Detente to New Cold War. *International Journal* 39:171–213.

NAROLL, R. 1965. Galton's Problem: The Logic of Cross-Cultural Analysis. *Social Research* 32:428–451.

NEUMAN, W. R. 1986. *The Paradox of Mass Politics: Knowledge and Opinion in the American*

Electorate. Cambridge, MA: Harvard University Press.

NEUSTADT, R. 1960. *Presidential Power*. New York: Wiley.

NEWMAN, D. 1985. Security and Alliances: A Theoretical Study of Alliance Formation. Unpublished manuscript.

NINCIC, M. 1988. The United States, the Soviet Union, and the Politics of Opposites. *World Politics* 40:452–475.

NOELLE-NEUMANN, E. 1977. Turbulances in the Climate of Opinion: Methodological Applications of the Spiral of Silence Theory. *Public Opinion Quarterly* 41:143–158.

NORPOTH, H. 1987. Guns and Butter and Government Popularity in Britain. *American Political Science Review* 81:949–959.

NORTH, D., and R. P. THOMAS. 1974. *The Rise of the Western World: A New Economic History*. Cambridge: Cambridge University Press.

NORTH, R. C., and N. CHOUCRI. 1983. Economic and Political Factors in International Conflict and Integration. *International Studies Quarterly* 27:443–461.

NOTESTEIN, F. 1945. Population—the Long View. In *Food for the World*, ed. T. Schultz. Chicago: Chicago University Press.

O'LOUGHLIN, J. 1984. Geographic Models of International Conflicts. In *Political Geography: Recent Advances and Future Directions*, eds. P. J. Taylor and J. House. London: Croom Helm.

——— 1986. Spatial Models of International Conflicts: Extending Current Theories of War Behavior. *Annals of the Association of American Geographers* 76:63–80.

OLSON, M. 1982. *The Rise and Decline of Nations*. New Haven, CT: Yale University Press.

OPINION RESEARCH SERVICE. 1987. *American Public Opinion Cumulative Index, 1981–1985*. Louisville, KY: Opinion Research Service.

ORGANSKI, A. F. K. 1958; 1968. *World Politics*. New York: Knopf.

ORGANSKI, A. F. K., and J. KUGLER. 1980. *The War Ledger*. Chicago: University of Chicago Press.

——— 1986. Hegemony and War. Paper presented at the annual meeting of the International Studies Association, Anaheim, CA, March 26–29.

ORGANSKI, A. F. K., J. KUGLER, T. JOHNSON, and Y. COHEN. 1984. *Births, Deaths, and Taxes*. Chicago: Chicago University Press.

ORME, J. 1987. Deterrence Failures. *International Security* 11:96–124.

OSGOOD, C. E. 1962. *An Alternative to War or Surrender*. Urbana, IL: University of Illinois Press.

OSGOOD, R. E., and R. W. TUCKER. 1967. *Force, Order and Justice*. Baltimore: Johns Hopkins University Press.

OSTROM, C. W., and J. ALDRICH. 1978. The Relationship Between Size and Stability in the Major Power International System. *American Journal of Political Science* 22:743–771.

OSTROM, C. W., and B. L. JOB. 1986. The President and the Political Use of Force. *American Political Science Review* 80:554–566.

OSTROM, C. W., and R. MARRA. 1986. U.S. Defense Spending and the Soviet Estimate. *American Political Science Review* 80:819–842.

OSTROM, C. W., and D. SIMON. 1985. Promise and Performance: A Dynamic Model of Presidential Popularity. *American Political Science Review* 79:175–190.

OYE, K. A. 1983. International Systems Structure and American Foreign Policy. In eds. K. A. Oye, R. Lieber, and D. Rothchild, *Eagle Defiant: United States Foreign Policy in the 1980s*, pp. 3–32. Boston: Little, Brown.

OYE, K. A., R. J. LIEBER, and D. ROTHCHILD, eds. 1983. *Eagle Defiant: United States Foreign Policy in the 1980's*. Boston: Little, Brown.

PAGE, B. 1984. Presidents as Opinion Leaders: Some New Evidence. *Policy Studies Journal* 14:649–661.

PAGE, B., and R. Y. SHAPIRO. 1983. Effects of Public Opinion on Policy. *American Political Science Review* 77:175–190.

PAGE, B., R. Y. SHAPIRO, and G. R. DEMPSEY. 1987. What Moves Public Opinion? *American Political Science Review* 81:23–44.

PAGE, B., R. Y. SHAPIRO, P. GRONKE, and R. ROSENBERG. 1984. Constituency, Party and Representation in Congress. *Public Opinion Quarterly* 48:741–756.

PAGÈS, G. 1970. *The Thirty Years' War, 1618–1648*, trans. D. Maland and J. Hooper. New York: Harper.

PARK, K. H. 1986. Income Inequality and Political Violence. In *Inequality and Contemporary Revolutions*, ed. M. I. Midlarsky. Monograph Series in World Affairs, Vol. 22, Book 2. Denver, CO: Graduate School of International Studies, University of Denver.

PATCHEN, M. 1986. When Do Arms Buildups Lead to Deterrence and When to War? *Peace and Change* 11:25–46.

PEARSON, D. 1987. Financing Global Wars. Paper delivered at the annual meeting of the International Studies Association, Washington, DC.

PETERSEN, W. 1986. Deterrence and Compellence: A Critical Assessment of Conventional Wisdom. *International Studies Quarterly* 25:269–294.

PIPES, R. 1974. *Russia under the Old Regime*. New York: Scribner.

PITMAN, G. 1969. *Arms Races and Stable Deterrence*, Los Angeles: Security Studies Project, University of California, Los Angeles.

POLISENSKY, J. V. 1972. Social and Economic Change and the European-Wide War. In *The Thirty Years' War*, ed. T. K. Rabb. Lexington, MA: D. C. Heath.

——— 1978. *War and Society in Europe, 1618–1648*. Cambridge: Cambridge University Press.

POLLINS, B. M. 1985. Breaking Trade Dependency: A Global Simulation of Third World Proposals for Alternative Trade Regimes. *International Studies Quarterly* 29:287–312.

POLSBY, N. W. 1964. *Congress and the Presidency*. Englewood Cliffs, NJ: Prentice Hall.

POPPER, K. R. 1979. *Objective Knowledge: An Evolutionary Approach*. Oxford: Clarendon Press.

PRADOS, J. 1986. *The Soviet Estimate: U.S. Intelligence Analysis and Soviet Strategic Forces*. Princeton, NJ: Princeton University Press.

RAPOPORT, A. 1957. Lewis F. Richardson's Mathematical Theory of War. *Journal of Conflict Resolution* 1:249–304.

——— 1960. *Fights, Games, and Debates*. Ann Arbor, MI: University of Michigan Press.

RASLER, K. A., and W. R. THOMPSON. 1983. Global Wars, Public Debts, and the Long Cycle. *World Politics* 35:489–516.

——— 1985a. War Making and State Making: Governmental Expenditures, Tax Revenues, and Global Wars. *American Political Science Review* 79:491–507.

——— 1985b. Global War and Major Power Economic Growth. *American Journal of Political Science* 29:513–538.

——— 1989. *War and State Making: The Shaping of the Global Powers*. Boston: Unwin Hyman (forthcoming).

RATTINGER, H. 1976. From War to War. *Journal of Conflict Resolution* 20:502–531.

RAWLS, J. 1971. *A Theory of Justice*. Cambridge, MA: Harvard University Press.

RAY, J. L. 1987. *Global Politics*. Boston: Houghton Mifflin.

REILLY, J. E., ed. 1983. *American Public Opinion and U.S. Foreign Policy*. Chicago: Chicago Council on Foreign Relations.

RESEARCH WORKING GROUP. 1979. Cyclical Rhythms and Secular Trends of the Capitalist World-Economy: Some Premises, Hypotheses, and Questions. *Review* 2:483–500.

RICHARDSON, L. F. 1939. Generalized Foreign Politics. *British Journal of Psychology Monographs Supplement* 23.

——— 1951. Could an Arms Race End without Fighting? *Nature* 4274:567–569.

—— 1960a. *Arms and Insecurity*. Pittsburgh: Boxwood Press.

—— 1960b. *Statistics of Deadly Quarrels*. Pittsburgh: Boxwood Press.

RIGGS, R. E. 1960. Overselling the U.N. Charter—Fact and Myth. *International Organization* 14:277–290.

RIKER, W. H. 1962. *The Theory of Political Coalitions*. New Haven, CT: Yale University Press.

RIKER, W. H., and P. ORDESHOOK. 1973. *An Introduction to Positive Political Theory*. Englewood Cliffs, NJ: Prentice-Hall.

RITTER, G. 1968. *Frederick the Great: A Historical Profile*, trans. P. Paret. Berkeley, CA: University of California Press.

—— 1970. *The Sword and the Scepter: The Problems of Militarism in Germany*, Vol. 2. Coral Gables, FL: University of Miami Press.

ROSE, R. 1985. Can the President Steer the American Economy? *Journal of Public Policy* 5:267–280.

ROSECRANCE, R. 1963. *Action and Reaction in World Politics*. Boston: Little, Brown.

—— 1966. Bipolarity, Multipolarity, and the Future. *Journal of Conflict Resolution* 10:314–327.

—— 1973. *International Relations: Peace or War*. New York: McGraw-Hill.

—— 1986. *The Rise of the Trading State*. New York: Basic Books.

—— 1987. Long Cycle Theory and International Relations. *International Organization* 41:283–301.

ROSENAU, J. N. 1964. Internal War as an International Event. *International Aspects of Civil Strife*. Princeton, NJ: Princeton University Press.

—— 1969. *Linkage Politics*. New York: Free Press.

ROSS, M. H., and E. L. HOMER. 1976. Galton's Problem in Cross-National Research. *World Politics* 29:1–28.

ROUYER, A. 1987. Political Capacity and the Decline of Fertility in India. *American Political Science Review* 81:453–470.

RUMMEL, R. 1963. Dimensions of Conflict Behavior within and between Nations. *General Systems* 8:1–50.

RUPERT, M. E., and D. P. RAPKIN. 1985. The Erosion of U.S. Leadership Capabilities. In *Rhythms in Politics and Economics*, eds. P. M. Johnson and W. R. Thompson, pp. 155–180. New York: Praeger.

RUSSETT, B. 1963. The Calculus of Deterrence. *Journal of Conflict Resolution* 7:97–109.

—— 1967. *International Regions and the International System*. Chicago: Rand McNally.

—— 1968. Components of an Operational Theory of International Alliance Formation. *Journal of Conflict Resolution* 12:285–301.

—— 1970. International Behavior Research: Case Studies and Cumulation. In *Approaches to the Study of Political Science*, eds. M. Haas and H. S. Kariel. Scranton, PA: Chandler.

—— ed. 1972. *Peace, War, and Numbers*. Beverly Hills, CA: Sage.

—— 1974. The Revolt of the Masses: Public Opinion toward Military Expenditures. In *The New Civil–Military Relations*, eds. J. Lovell and P. Kronnenberg. New Brunswick, NJ: Transaction Books.

—— 1983a. Prosperity and Peace: Presidential Address. *International Studies Quarterly* 27:381–387.

—— 1983b. Theater Nuclear Forces: Public Opinion in Western Europe. *Political Science Quarterly* 98:179–276.

—— 1985. The Mysterious Case of Vanishing Hegemony. *International Organization* 39:207–231.

—— 1987. Economic Decline, Electoral Pressure, and the Initiation of International Conflict. New Haven, CT: Yale University Press.

—— 1989a. Economic Decline, Electoral Pressure, and the Initiation of Interstate Conflict. In *Prisoners of War? Nation-States in the Modern Era*, eds. C. Gochman and A. N. Sabrosky. Lexington, MA: D. C. Heath.

—— 1989b. Democracy, Public Opinion, and Nuclear Weapons. In *Behavior, Society, and Nuclear War, Vol. I*, eds. P. Tetlock, J. Husbands, R. Jervis, P. Stern, and C. Tilley. New York: Oxford University Press.

RUSSETT, B., and D. R. DeLUCA. 1981. 'Don't Tread on Me' Public Opinion and Foreign Policy in the Eighties. *Political Science Quarterly* 96:381–399.

—— 1983. Theater Nuclear Forces: Public Opinion in Western Europe. *Political Science Quarterly* 98:179–214.

RUSSETT, B., and E. C. HANSON. 1975. *Interest and Ideology: The Foreign Policy Beliefs of American Businessmen*. New York: Freeman.

RUSSETT, B., and H. STARR. 1981. *World Politics: The Menu for Choice*. San Francisco: W. H. Freeman.

—— 1985. *World Politics: The Menu for Choice*. New York: W. H. Freeman.

SAATY, T. 1968. *Mathematical Models of Arms Control and Disarmament*. New York: Wiley.

SABROSKY, A. N. 1980. Interstate Alliances: Their Reliability and the Expansion of War. In *The Correlates of War: II*, ed. J. D. Singer. New York: Free Press.

—— ed. 1985. *Polarity and War: The Changing Structure of International Conflict*. Boulder, CO: Westview Press.

SANDBERG, I. 1974. On the Mathematical Theory of Interactions in Social Groups. *IEEE Transactions* SMC–4:432–445.

SANDERS, D., H. WARD, and D. MARSH (with T. FLETCHER). 1987. Government Popularity and the Falklands War: A Reassessment. *British Journal of Political Science* 17:281–313.

SCHELLING, T. 1960. *The Strategy of Conflict*. Cambridge, MA: Harvard University Press.

—— 1966. *Arms and Influence*. New Haven, CT: Yale University Press.

SCHNEIDER, W. 1984. Public Opinion. In *The Making of America's Soviet Policy*, ed. J. Nye. New Haven, CT: Yale University Press.

—— 1987. Rambo and Reality: Having It Both Ways. In *Eagle Resurgent? The Reagan Era in American Foreign Policy*, eds. K. Oye, R. Lieber, and D. Rothchild. Boston: Little, Brown.

SCHRODT, P. A. 1985. Adaptive Precedent-Based Logic and Rational Choice: A Comparison of Two Approaches to the Modeling of International Behavior. In *Dynamic Models of International Conflict*, eds. U. Luterbacher and M. Ward. Boulder, CO: Lynne Rienner.

SCHUMPETER, J. A. 1939. *Business Cycles*. New York: McGraw-Hill.

—— 1951. *Imperialism and Social Classes*, trans. H. Norden. New York: Kelley.

SCOLNICK, J. M., JR. 1974. An Appraisal of Studies of the Linkages Between Domestic and International Conflict. *Comparative Political Studies* 6:485–509.

SEARS, D. O., R. LAU, T. TYLER, and H. ALLEN. 1980. Self-Interest vs. Symbolic Politics in Policy Attitudes and Presidential Voting. *American Political Science Review* 74:670–685.

SEMMEL, B. 1960. *Imperialism and Social Reform*. Cambridge, MA: Harvard University Press.

SHAKESPEARE, W. 1845. *King Henry IV*. London: Shakespeare Society.

SHAPIRO, R. Y., and B. PAGE. 1988. Foreign Policy and the Rational Public. *Journal of Conflict Resolution* 32:211–247.

SHEPSLE, K. 1972. The Strategy of Ambiguity: Uncertainty and Electoral Competition. *American Political Science Review* 17:555–568.

SHUMAN, J. B., and D. ROSENAU. 1972. *The Kondratieff Wave*. New York: World Publishing.

SILBERLING, N. J. 1943. *The Dynamics of Business*. New York: McGraw-Hill.

SIMAAN, M., and J. CRUZ. 1975. Formulation of Richardson's Model of Arms Race from a Differential Game Viewpoint. *Review of Economic Studies* 42:67–77.

—— 1976. Equilibrium Concepts for Arms Race Problems. In *Mathematical Systems in International Systems*, eds. J. Gillespie and D. Zinnes. New York: Praeger.

SIMMEL, G. 1898. The Persistence of Social Groups. *American Journal of Sociology* 4:662–698, 829–836.

——— 1956. *Conflict*, trans. K. H. Woldff. Glencoe, IL: Free Press.

SIMON, H. A., and C. P. BONINI. 1958. The Size Distribution of Business Firms. *American Economic Review* 48:607–617.

SINGER, J. D. 1958. Threat Perception and the Armament–Tension Dilemma. *Journal of Conflict Resolution* 2:90–105.

——— 1960. Threat Perception and the Armament–Tension Dilemma. In *Nuclear Weapons, Missiles, and Future War*, ed. A. McClelland. Chandler.

——— 1961. The Level-of-Analysis Problem in International Relations. *World Politics* 14:77–92.

——— 1969. The Global System and Its Subsystems: A Developmental View. In *Linkage Politics: Essays on the Convergence of National and International Systems*, ed. J. Rosenau. New York: Free Press.

——— 1970. The Outcome of Arms Races: A Policy Problem and a Research Approach. *Proceedings of the International Peace Research Association* 2:137–146.

——— 1980. Accounting for International War: The State of the Discipline. *Journal of Peace Research* 18:1–18.

SINGER, J. D., and S. BOUXSEIN. 1975. Structural Clarity and International War: Some Tentative Findings. In *Interdisciplinary Aspects of General System Theory*, ed. T. Murray. Washington, DC: General Systems Society.

SINGER, J. D., and T. CUSACK. 1981. Periodicity, Inexorability, and Steersmanship in International War. In *From National Development to Global Community*, eds. R. Merritt and B. Russett. London: Allen & Unwin.

SINGER, J. D., and M. SMALL. 1966a. The Composition and Status Ordering of the International System, 1815–1940. *World Politics* 18:236–282.

——— 1966b. Formal Alliances, 1815–1939: A Quantitative Description. *Journal of Peace Research* 3:1–32.

——— 1968. Alliance Aggregation and the Onset of War, 1815–1945. In *Quantitative International Politics*. New York: Free Press.

——— 1972. *The Wages of War, 1816–1965: A Statistical Handbook*. New York: Wiley.

SINGER, J. D., S. BREMER, and J. STUCKEY. 1972. Capability Distribution, Uncertainty, and Major Power War, 1820–1965. Beverly Hills, CA: Sage.

SIVARD, R. L. 1986. *World Military and Social Expenditures*. Washington, DC: World Priorities.

SIVERSON, R., and G. T. DUNCAN. 1976. Stochastic Models of International Alliance Initiation. In *Mathematical Models in International Relations*, ed. D. A. Zinnes and J. V. Gillespie. New York: Praeger.

SIVERSON, R., and J. KING. 1979. Alliances and the Expansion of War, 1815–1965. In *To Augur Well*, eds. J. D. Singer and M. Wallace. Beverly Hills, CA: Sage.

——— 1980. Attributes of National Alliance Membership and War Participation, 1815–1965. *American Journal of Political Science* 24:1–15.

SIVERSON, R., and M. SULLIVAN. 1983. The Distribution of Power and the Onset of War. *Journal of Conflict Resolution* 27:473–494.

SKOCPOL, T. 1979. *States and Social Revolutions*. Cambridge: Cambridge University Press.

SMALL, M., and J. D. SINGER. 1970. Patterns in International Warfare, 1816–1965. *Annals of the American Academy of Political and Social Science* 391:145–155.

——— 1973. Diplomatic Importance of States, 1816–1970: An Extension and Refinement of the Indicator. *World Politics* 25:577–599.

——— 1982. *Resort to Arms*. Beverly Hills, CA: Sage.

SMITH, C. J., JR. 1957. *Finland and the Russian Revolution: 1917–1922*. Athens, GA: University of Georgia Press.

SMITH, R. B. 1971. Disaffection, Delegitimation, and Consequences: Aggregate Trends for World War II, Korea, and Vietnam. In *Public Opinion and the Military Establishment*, ed. Charles C. Moskos. Beverly Hills, CA: Sage.

SMITH, T. C. 1980. Arms Race Instability and War. *Journal of Conflict Resolution* 24:253–284.

—— 1988. Curvature Change and the War Risk in Arming Patterns. *International Interactions* 14:201–228.

SMITH, T. W. 1985. The Polls: America's Most Important Problem, Part I: National and International. *Public Opinion Quarterly* 49:264–274.

SMOKE, R. 1977. *War: Controlling Escalation*. Cambridge, MA: Harvard University Press.

SNIDER, L. 1988. Political Strength, Economic Structure and the Debt Servicing Potential of Developing Countries. *Comparative Political Studies* 20:455–487.

SNYDER, G. H., and P. DIESING. 1977. *Conflict among Nations: Bargaining, Decisionmaking and System Structure in International Crises*. Princeton, NJ: Princeton University Press.

SNYDER, J. 1984. *The Ideology of the Offensive: Military Decision Making and the Disasters of 1914*. Ithaca, NY: Cornell University Press.

—— 1987. Myths of Empire: Domestic Structure and Strategic Ideology. Mimeograph, Columbia University, New York.

SOLZHENITSYN, A. 1974. *The Gulag Archipelago, 1918–1956*. New York: Harper and Row.

SOROKIN, P. A. 1937. *Social and Cultural Dynamics, Vol. III: Fluctuation of Social Relationships, War, and Revolution*. New York: American Book Company.

SPILERMAN, S. 1970. The Causes of Racial Disturbances: A Comparison of Alternative Explanations. *American Sociological Review* 35:627–649.

SPROUT, H., and M. SPROUT. 1969. Environmental Factors in the Study of International Politics. In *International Politics and Foreign Policy*, ed. J. N. Rosenau. New York: Free Press.

STARR, H. 1978. 'Opportunity' and 'Willingness' as Ordering Concepts in the Study of War. *International Interactions* 4:363–387.

STARR, H., and B. A. MOST. 1976. The Substance and Study of Borders in International Relations Research. *International Studies Quarterly* 20:581–620.

—— 1978. A Return Journey: Richardson, 'Frontiers,' and Wars in the 1946–1965 Era. *Journal of Conflict Resolution* 22:441–467.

—— 1983. Contagion and Border Effects on Contemporary African Conflict. *Comparative Political Studies* 16:92–117.

—— 1985. The Forms and Processes of War Diffusion: Research Update on Contagion in African Conflict. *Comparative Political Studies* 18:206–227.

STEELE, R. 1978. American Public Opinion and the War against Germany: The Issue of Negotiated Peace—1942. *Journal of American History* 65:704–723.

STEIN, A. A. 1976. Conflict and Cohesion. *Journal of Conflict Resolution* 20:143–172.

—— 1980. *The Nation at War*. Baltimore: Johns Hopkins University Press.

STEIN, A. A., and B. RUSSETT. 1980. Evaluating War: Outcomes and Consequences. In *Handbook of Political Conflict: Theory and Research*, ed. T. R. Gurr. New York: Free Press.

STEIN, J. G. 1985. Calculation, Miscalculation, and Conventional Deterrence I & II. In *Psychology and Deterrence*, eds. R. Jervis, R. N. Lebow, and J. Stein. Baltimore: Johns Hopkins University Press.

STIGLICZ, R. 1981. *Structural Clarity, Polarity, Power Concentration, and War*. Thesis, University of Minnesota, Minneapolis, MN.

STOCKHOLM INTERNATIONAL PEACE RESEARCH INSTITUTE. 1970. *SIPRI Yearbook of World Armaments and Disarmament 1968/69*. New York: Humanities Press.

STOHL, M. 1975. War and Domestic Political Violence: The Case of the United States 1890–1970. *Journal of Conflict Resolution* 19:379–416.

———— 1980. The Nexus of Civil and International Conflict. In *Handbook of Political Conflict*, chap. 7, ed. T. R. Gurr. New York: Free Press.

STOLL, R. J. 1984a. Bloc Concentration and Dispute Escalation among the Major Powers, 1830–1965. *Social Science Quarterly* 65:48–59.

———— 1984b. The Guns of November: Presidential Re-elections and the Use of Force. *Journal of Conflict Resolution* 19:379–416.

STOLL, R. J., and M. CHAMPION. 1985. Capability Concentration, Alliance Bonding, and Conflict among the Major Powers. In *Polarity and War: The Changing Structure of International Conflict*, ed. A. Sabrosky. Boulder, CO: Westview Press.

SYLVAN, D., and B. GLASSNER. 1985. *A Rationalist Methodology for the Social Sciences*. New York: Basil Blackwell.

TANTER, R. 1966. Dimensions of Conflict Behavior within and between Nations, 1958–1960. *Journal of Conflict Resolution* 10:41–64.

TAYLOR, A. J. P. 1954. The Struggle for Mastery in Europe, 1848–1918. London: Oxford University Press.

———— 1971. The Struggle for Mastery in Europe, 1848–1918. London: Oxford University Press.

TAYLOR, E. B. 1889. On a Method of Investigating the Development of Institutions Applied to the Laws of Marriage and Descent. *Journal of the Royal Anthropological Institute* 18:245–272.

THOMPSON, W. 1929. Population. *American Journal of Sociology* 34:959–975.

THOMPSON, W. R. 1983a. Succession Crises in the Global Political System: A Test of the Transition Model. In *Crises in the World-System*, ed. A. L. Bergesen. Beverly Hills, CA: Sage.

———— ed. 1983b. *Contending Approaches to World Systems Analysis*. Beverly Hills, CA: Sage.

———— 1983c. Uneven Economic Growth, Systemic Challenges, and Global Wars. *International Studies Quarterly* 27:341–355.

———— 1983d. Interstate Wars, Global Wars and the Cool Hand Luke Syndrome: A Reply to Chase-Dunn and Sokolovsky. *International Studies Quarterly* 27:369–374.

———— 1985. Polarity, the Long Cycle, and Global Power Warfare. Paper presented at the annual meeting of the American Political Science Association, New Orleans, LA.

———— 1986. Polarity, the Long Cycle, and Global Power Warfare. *Journal of Conflict Resolution* 30:587–615.

———— 1988. *On Global War: Historical–Structural Approaches to World Politics*. Columbia, SC: University of South Carolina Press.

THOMPSON, W. R., and K. A. RASLER. 1988. War and Systemic Capability Reconcentration. *Journal of Conflict Resolution* 32:61–86.

THOMPSON, W. R., and G. ZUK. 1982. War, Inflation, and the Kondratieff Long Wave. *Journal of Conflict Resolution* 26:621–644.

———— 1986. World Power and the Strategic Trap of Territorial Commitments. *International Studies Quarterly* 30:249–267.

THOMPSON, W. R., K. A. RASLER, and R. LI. 1980. Systemic Interaction Opportunities and War Behavior. *International Interactions* 7:57–85.

THOMSON, D. 1966. *Europe Since Napoleon*, 2nd ed. New York: Knopf.

THUCYDIDES. 1954. *History of the Peloponnesian War*, trans. R. Warner. Baltimore, MD: Penguin Books.

———— 1959. *History of the Peloponnesian War*, trans. T. Hobbes. Ann Arbor, MI: University of Michigan Press.

TILLY, C. 1975. Western State-Making and Theories of Political Transformation. In *The Formation of National States in Western Europe*, ed. C. Tilly. Princeton, NJ: Princeton University Press.

TOYNBEE, A. J. 1954. *A Study of History, Vol. 9*. London: Oxford University Press.

TROTSKY, L. 1923. The Curve of Capitalist Development. Reprinted in *Problems of Everyday Life*. New York: Monad Press.

TUFTE, E. R. 1978. *Political Control of the Economy*. Princeton, NJ: Princeton University Press.

TVERSKY, A., and D. KAHNEMAN. 1981. The Framing of Decisions and the Psychology of Choice. *Science* 211:453–458.

VASQUEZ, J. A. 1986. Capability, Types of War, Peace. *Western Political Quarterly* 38:313–327.

——— 1987. The Steps to War: Toward a Scientific Explanation of Correlates of War Findings. *World Politics* October, 108–145.

VÄRYNEN, R. 1983. Economic Cycles, Power Transitions, Political Management and War between the Major Powers. *International Studies Quarterly* 27:389–418.

——— 1987. *The Quest for Peace: Transcending Collective Violence and War among Societies, Cultures, and States*. London: Sage.

VERBA, S., R. BRODY, E. PARKER, N. NIE, N. POLSBY, P. EKMAN, and G. BLACK. 1967. Public Opinion and the War in Vietnam. *American Political Science Review* 61:313–333.

VINCENT, J. E. 1981. Internal and External Conflict: Some Previous Operational Problems and Some New Findings. *Journal of Politics* 43:128–142.

VON BULOW, B. 1931. *Memoirs of Prince von Bulow*. Boston: Little, Brown.

VON GENTZ, F. 1806. *Fragments on the Balance of Power*. London: Herries.

VON MARTENS, G. F. 1795. *Summary of the Law of Nations*. Philadelphia: Thomas Bradford.

WAGNER, R. H. 1982. The Theory of Games and the Problems of International Cooperation. *American Political Science Review* 26:3299–3358.

——— 1984. War and Expected-Utility Theory. *World Politics* 36:407–423.

WALLACE, M. D. 1971. Power, Status, and International War. *Journal of Peace Research* 1:23–35.

——— 1973a. Alliance Polarization, Cross-cutting, and International War, 1815–1964: A Measurement Procedure and Some Preliminary Evidence. *Journal of Conflict Resolution* 17:575–604.

——— 1973b. *War and Rank among Nations*. Lexington, MA: D. C. Heath.

——— 1979. Arms Races and Escalation: Some New Evidence. In *Explaining War: Selected Papers from the Correlates of War Project*, ed. J. D. Singer. Beverly Hills, CA: Sage.

——— 1981. Old Nails in New Coffins: The Para Bellum Hypothesis Revisited. *Journal of Peace Research* 18:91–96.

——— 1983. Armaments and Escalation: A Reply to Altfeld. *International Studies Quarterly* 27:233–235.

WALLACE, M. D., and J. D. SINGER. 1989. *A Structural History of the International System*. Columbia, SC: University of South Carolina Press (forthcoming).

WALLERSTEIN, I. 1974. *The Modern World System: Capitalist Agriculture and the Origins of the European Economy in the Sixteenth Century*. New York: Academic Press.

——— 1980. *The Modern World System: Mercantilism and the Consolidation of the European World Economy, 1600–1750*. New York: Academic Press.

——— 1984. *The Politics of the World-Economy*. Cambridge: Cambridge University Press.

——— 1986. Japan and the Future Trajectory of the World-System: Lessons from History? Unpublished paper, Fernand Braudel Center, State University of New York, Binghamton, NY.

WALTZ, K. N. 1959. *Man, the State and War*. New York: Columbia University Press.

——— 1964. The Stability of a Bi-polar World. *Daedalus* XCIII:881–909.

——— 1967. Electoral Punishment and Foreign Policy Crises. In *Domestic Sources of Foreign Policy*, ed. J. N. Rosenau. New York: Free Press.

——— 1975. Theory of International Relations. In *Handbook of Political Science: International Politics, Vol. 8*, eds. F. I. Greenstein and N. W. Polsby. Reading, PA: Addison-Wesley.

——— 1979. *Theory of International Politics*. Reading, PA: Addison-Wesley.

——— 1981. The Spread of Nuclear Weapons: More May Be Better. *Adelphi Paper Number 171*. The International Institute for Strategic Studies.

WARD, M. D. 1984a. Differential Paths to Parity: A Study of the Contemporary Arms Race. *American Political Science Review* 78:297–317.

——— 1984b. The Political Economy of Arms Races and International Tension. *Conflict Management and Peace Science* 7:1–23.

WARD, M. D., and A. M. KIRBY. 1986. Reexamining Spatial Models of International Conflicts. Boulder, CO: Working Paper Research Program on Political and Economic Change, University of Colorado.

WARD, M. D., and U. WIDMAIER. 1982. The Domestic–International Conflict Nexus: New Evidence and Old Hypotheses. *International Interactions* 9:75–101.

THE WASHINGTON POST. 1984. Khomeini Backs Bazaar on Control of Trade. August 30, A38.

WAYMAN, F. 1984. Bipolarity and War: The Role of Capability Concentration and Alliance Patterns among Major Powers, 1816–1965. *Journal of Peace Research* 21:61–78.

WEDGWOOD, C. V. 1972. The Futile and Meaningless War. In *The Thirty Years' War*, ed. T. K. Rabb. Lexington, MA: D. C. Heath.

WEEDE, E. 1978. U.S. Support for Foreign Governments, or Domestic Disorder and Imperial Intervention, 1958–1965. *Comparative Political Studies* 10:497–527.

——— 1980. Arms Races and Escalation: A Reply to Altfeld. *International Studies Quarterly* 27:233–235.

WEHLER, H. 1985. *The German Empire, 1871–1918*, trans. K. Traynor. Leamington Spa, U.K.: Berg Publishers.

WELSH, W. A. 1984. Inter-nation Interaction and Political Diffusion: Notes toward a Conceptual Framework. Paper presented at the annual meeting of the International Studies Association, Atlanta, March.

WESTERFIELD, H. B. 1955. *Foreign Policy and Party Politics: Pearl Harbor to Korea*. New Haven, CT: Yale University Press.

WHITE, J. A. 1964. *The Diplomacy of the Russo-Japanese War*. Princeton, NJ: Princeton University Press.

WILKENFELD, J. 1968. Domestic and Foreign Conflict Behavior of Nations. *Journal of Peace Research* 1:56–69.

——— 1972. Models for the Analysis of Foreign Conflict Behavior of States. In *Peace, War, and Numbers*, ed. B. M. Russett. Beverly Hills, CA: Sage.

——— ed. 1973. *Conflict Behavior and Linkage Politics*. New York: David McKay.

WILKINSON, D. 1980. *Deadly Quarrels*. Berkeley, CA: University of California Press.

WILLIAMS, N. 1969. *Chronology of the Expanding World, 1492 to 1762*. New York: David McKay.

WILLIAMS, R. M., JR. 1947. *The Reduction of Intergroup Tensions*, Paper No. 57. New York: Social Science Research Council.

WITTKOPF, E. 1986. On the Foreign Policy Beliefs of the American People: A Critique and Some Evidence. *International Studies Quarterly* 30:425–445.

——— 1987. Elites and Masses: Another Look at Attitudes toward America's Role. *International Studies Quarterly* 31:131–159.

WITTKOPF, E., and M. MAGGIOTTO. 1983. Elites and Masses: A Comparative Analysis of Attitudes toward America's World Role. *Journal of Politics* 45:307–333.

WITTMAN, D. 1979. How a War Ends: A Rational Model Approach. *Journal of Conflict Resolution* 23:743–763.

WOHLFORTH, W. C. 1987. The Perception of Power: Russia in the Pre-1914 Balance. *World Politics* 39:353–381.

WOHLSTETTER, A. 1974a. Is there a Strategic Arms Race? *Foreign Policy* 15:3–20.

―――― 1974b. Rivals but No Race. *Foreign Policy* 16:48–81.

WOLFSON, M. 1987. A Theorem on the Existence of Zones of Initiation and Deterrence in Intriligator–Brito Arms Race Models. *Public Choice* 54:291–292.

WRIGHT, Q. 1965. *A Study of War*, 2nd ed. Chicago: University of Chicago Press.

―――― 1942. *A Study of War*. Chicago: University of Chicago Press.

YAMAMOTO, Y., and S. A. BREMER. 1980. Wider Wars and Restless Nights; Major Power Intervention in Ongoing War. In *The Correlates of War: II*, ed. J. D. Singer. New York: Free Press.

YOUNG, A. 1792. *Travels during the Years 1787, 1788, 1789*. London: Bury St. Edmunds.

YOUNG, O. 1964a. The Impact of General Systems Theory. *General Systems* 9:254–293.

―――― 1964b. A Survey of General Systems Theory. *General Systems* 9:61–80.

ZAGARE, F. 1987. *The Dynamics of Deterrence*. Chicago: University of Chicago Press.

ZINNES, D. A. 1967. An Analytical Study of the Balance of Power Theories. *Journal of Peace Research* 4:270–288.

―――― 1976. *Contemporary Research in International Relations*. New York: Free Press.

ZINNES, D. A., and J. WILKENFELD. 1971. An Analysis of Foreign Conflict Behavior of Nations. In *Comparative Foreign Policy*, ed. W. F. Hanrieder. New York: David McKay.

ZINNES, D. A., R. C. NORTH, and H. E. KOCH, JR. 1961. Capability, Threat, and the Outbreak of War. In *International Politics and Foreign Policy*, ed. J. N. Rosenau. New York: Free Press.

ZIPF, G. K. 1949. *Human Behavior and the Principle of Least Effort*. Cambridge, MA: Addison-Wesley.

ZOLBERG, A. R. 1983. 'World' and 'System': A Mis-alliance. In *Contending Approaches to World Systems Analysis*, ed. W. R. Thompson, pp. 269–290. Beverly Hills, CA: Sage.

ZUK, G. 1985. National Growth and International Conflict: A Reevaluation of Choucri and North's Thesis. *The Journal of Politics* 47:269–281.

Index